GLOBAL HEALTH, HUMAN RIGHTS, AND THE CHALLENGE OF NEOLIBERAL POLICIES

Written by a respected authority on human rights and public health, this book delivers an in-depth review of the challenges of neoliberal models and policies for realizing the right to health. The author expertly explores the integration of social determinants into the right to health along with the methodologies and findings of social medicine and epidemiology. The author goes on to challenge the way health care is currently provided and makes the case that achieving equitable universal health coverage will require fundamental reforms of health systems and the integration of human rights norms.

AUDREY R. CHAPMAN currently holds the Healey Endowed Chair at the University of Connecticut School of Medicine and is affiliated with the UConn Human Rights Institute. She previously served as the Director of the AAAS Science and Human Rights Program and on expert committees appointed by the UN Office of the High Commissioner of Human Rights and the UNESCO human rights program.

GLOBAL HEALTH, HUMAN RIGHTS, AND THE CHALLENGE OF NEOLIBERAL POLICIES

AUDREY R. CHAPMAN

CAMBRIDGE
UNIVERSITY PRESS

CAMBRIDGE
UNIVERSITY PRESS

University Printing House, Cambridge CB2 8BS, United Kingdom

Cambridge University Press is part of the University of Cambridge.

It furthers the University's mission by disseminating knowledge in the pursuit of
education, learning, and research at the highest international levels of excellence.

www.cambridge.org
Information on this title: www.cambridge.org/9781107088122

First published 2016

A catalogue record for this publication is available from the British Library

Library of Congress Cataloguing in Publication data
Names: Chapman, Audrey R., author.
Title: Global health, human rights, and the challenge of neoliberal policies /
Audrey R. Chapman.
Description: Cambridge; New York : Cambridge University Press, 2016. |
Includes bibliographical references and index.
Identifiers: LCCN 2015043868 | ISBN 9781107088122 (hardback)
Subjects: | MESH: Global Health. | Human Rights. |
Delivery of Health Care. | Universal Coverage.
Classification: LCC RA441 | NLM WA 530.1 | DDC 362.1–dc23
LC record available at http://lccn.loc.gov/2015043868

ISBN 978-1-107-08812-2 Hardback

For Jack, Anja, Cooper, Tanner, and Kai

CONTENTS

ACKNOWLEDGMENTS

I have long been concerned with health and human rights issues, initially during the years when I served as the Director of the Science and Human Rights Program at the American Association for the Advancement of Science (AAAS) and then in my present position as a Professor of Community Medicine at the University of Connecticut School of Medicine. During this time I have had the good fortune of working with a number of leaders in the health and human rights field, including Paul Hunt, Alicia Ely Yamin, Leslie London, Eibe Reidel, Ted Schrecker, Lisa Forman, and Gillian MacNaughton, who deepened my understanding of the right to health. I also have had the benefit of involvement with the United Nations Committee on Economic, Social and Cultural Rights for more than a decade, membership in expert committees organized by the UN Office of the High Commissioner of Human Rights, and participation in UNESCO human rights initiatives.

This book could not have been completed without the assistance and contributions of a large number of people. I would like to thank colleagues and friends who provided insight, advice, and constructive criticism on draft chapters, particularly Professors Leslie London (University of Cape Town), Lance Minkler (University of Connecticut), Lisa Forman (University of Toronto), Everaldo Lamprea (Los Andes Law School, Bogatá), Carmel Williams (FXB Center for Health and Human Rights at Harvard University), and an anonymous reviewer for Cambridge University Press. Their suggestions significantly strengthened and improved the book.

I have been stimulated and enriched by participating in two networks at the University of Connecticut, the Economic and Social Rights Group and the Research Program on Global Health and Human Rights. I am appreciative of the insightful comments I received in response to presentations of sections of this book and their discussions of related issues.

I have also been fortunate to have research assistance for some sections of the book from Salil Benegal and Caitlin Perucchio.

I have had the benefit of several sources of funding during the time I worked on this book. Support from the Healey Memorial Chair in Medical Ethics and Humanities at the University of Connecticut School of Medicine provided considerable freedom to engage in the research. I am also appreciative of the willingness of the UConn School of Medicine to grant a sabbatical leave that enabled me to complete the book. Support for the research that provided the basis for several of the chapters was provided by two projects funded by the Canadian Institutes of Health Research (CIHR), one led by Ted Schrecker (then at the University of Ottawa) on the role of human rights in promoting realization of the social determinants of health and a second one led by Lisa Forman (University of Toronto) that focused on core health obligations. The Human Rights Institute at the University of Connecticut provided some funding for summer research assistants.

I also appreciate the assistance I received from my editors John Berger and Helen Francis at Cambridge University Press and my production manager Ramesh Karunakaran at Newgen Knowledge Works.

Above all, I have been privileged to have the support, understanding, encouragement, and patience of my husband Karim Ahmed during the years I worked on this book and our dog Jamie who provided companionship as I wrote.

The Right to Health as an Emergent Human Right

Several years ago I made a presentation at a faculty seminar at the Human Rights Institute of the University of Connecticut on the topic of the impact of globalization on the right to health. As I began, one member of the seminar group inquired, "Oh, is there such a thing as a right to health?" I was initially stunned. My questioner was a senior scholar in the human rights community who was well aware that a series of major international human rights instruments, most importantly Article 12 of the International Covenant on Economic, Social and Cultural Rights (1966), enumerate "the right of everyone to the enjoyment of the highest attainable standard of physical and mental health," which is often shorthanded as a right to health. Other international human rights instruments apply the requirements of the right to health to specific communities and groups. There are also health-related human rights provisions in regional human rights instruments and in many countries' constitutions. So from a legal perspective there was no question that a right to health existed.

As I reflected on the exchange, I realized that I was most likely being teased, especially since I was well known to be a passionate advocate of the right to health and to be someone who had done extensive work on aspects of the right, but it set me to thinking about the implications of the query. To what extent does legal enumeration in international and regional human rights instruments and constitutions accord the right to health a reality and substance? Legal positivists generally find the recognition of a right in a key legal document sufficient to affirm its validity, and many in the human rights community take this position. Currently nearly all countries have ratified or acceded to at least one of the international human rights instruments that have enumerated the right to health, thereby becoming legally bound to implement the rights and principles stipulated in them. Currently, some 160 countries have ratified the International Covenant on Economic, Social and Cultural Rights, among them the major western democracies with the exception of the United States. Moreover, an increasing number of nonstate actors, including humanitarian organizations and charitable funders, are now being guided by human rights norms as they seek to improve health access and outcomes (Gable 2007).

Nevertheless, I soon acknowledged that there are other important requirements if a human right is to have a reality and a substance, and the right to health does not fulfill all of them. That the vast majority of states have ratified or acceded to at least one of the major human rights instruments that enumerate a right to health does not mean they fulfill the requirements specified therein or even make a serious effort to do so. There is a vast disparity between rhetorical affirmations of various rights and their implementation. Although under international human rights law, ratification of human rights instruments imposes binding legal obligations, many states consider the requirements stipulated in the international human rights instruments that they have ratified, particularly those in the sphere of economic, social, and cultural rights, to be more in the nature of aspirational goals or perhaps even optional. While international human rights bodies have developed expansive interpretations of specific rights over time, including the right to health, many states have far more minimalist conceptions of what these rights entail. My experience in dealing with government officials in several developing countries also suggests that the policymakers with control over relevant subject areas covered by specific human rights instruments may not even be aware of the country's human rights commitments, let alone their policy requirements. Moreover, one influential country, the United States, has neither ratified the International Convention on Economic, Social and Cultural Rights nor acknowledged the legitimacy of human rights to health or health promotion.

The Right to Health as an Emergent Right

The right to health can be understood as an "emergent" human right. Richard Hiskes, who originated this terminology, employs the concept to justify the establishment of a new human right to a safe environment (2005). Unlike the right to health, the human right to a safe and/or healthy environment is not as yet enumerated in a major binding international human rights instrument. Hiskes argues that preservation of clean air, water, and soil for current and future generations requires the "muscular conception" of human rights (2009, 1–2), and therefore the right to safe environment should be recognized as a human right. Like other political and human rights theorists, most particularly Henry Shue (1980), Hiskes links the development of new human rights to the perception of serious or "standard threats" widely affecting members of a society that are acknowledged to require a collective response (2009, 43–47). Hiskes believes that new emergent risks that pose significant harms, particularly environmental pollution, degradation, and damage, similarly require a rights response (2009, Chapter Two).

So in what sense can the right to health be considered an emergent right? First, the articulation of health and health care as the subject of human rights and the inclusion of the right to health in major international and regional human rights instruments occurred relatively recently, especially in comparison with the civil and political rights that can trace their heritages back to the natural rights traditions in the seventeenth and eighteenth centuries. Second, the right to health initially attracted limited recognition but its standing and legitimacy has grown over time. Third, the interpretation of the right and the understanding of the related obligations have developed gradually. And fourth, implementation of the various dimensions of this complex right has been a slow process often dependent on a supportive environment, and in the last three decades the process has been challenged by the dominant neoliberal paradigm.

Although the term "emergent" suggests a unidirectional evolution toward a clearer conceptualization of the requirements of a specific human right and greater support, this is not necessarily the case. Emergent can also refer to ways a right confronts and adapts to major challenges and opportunities in its environment. This book argues that in contrast with the post–World War II environment in which the right to health was initially framed and incorporated in major international human rights instruments, the more recent international economic, political, and health landscape presents significant risks and challenges to the protection of health and the implementation of the right to health. These challenges include the diminishing support for the welfare state, the rise of neoliberal approaches to health policy prescribing privatization and commercialization of health institutions, the globalization of health and the economic order, and the influential role of transnational corporations in the pharmaceutical sector and the political and economic order. Additionally, new understandings of the importance of the social determinants of health call for refocusing elements of the right to health and a greater use of the findings of social medicine and social epidemiology.

The contemporary environment presents new opportunities as well. The widespread global commitment to achieving universal health coverage – at least in rhetoric – one of the key dimensions of the right to health, provides human rights advocates with an opening to identify what universality requires from a human rights perspective and to work with policymakers and other civil society groups toward its realization. However, whether the current economic and political landscape and its adverse impacts make universal health coverage a broadly feasible goal consistent with human right requirements is an important question.

If the goal of adopting a human rights approach is to influence policy development, as I believe it should be, it becomes even more important to understand the contemporary health landscape and policy environment. It does not make sense to advocate for the adoption of a right to health without contextualizing the requirements of doing so. Nor can a right to health be implemented without taking the challenges it confronts into account and developing a strategy for overcoming them.

Recognition of Health as the Subject Matter of a Human Right

Although health has long been valued both as an intrinsic good, valuable in and of itself, and as an instrumental good required for many of life's undertakings, the recognition of health as the subject matter of a human right is a relatively recent development. In the seventeenth century, the philosopher René Descartes wrote in his *Discours de la Méthode* "the preservation of health ... is without doubt the first good and the foundation of all other goods in this life" (Descartes 1637, 1953, 168 quoted in Anand 2004, 17). Health is widely perceived as essential to human flourishing because it enables a person to pursue the various goals and projects in life that she or he has reason to value (Anand 2004, 17–18). Norman Daniels's well-known interpretation attributes the special moral importance of health to its contribution to the range of exercisable or effective opportunities open to each person. Or to put the matter another way, meeting health needs allows people to choose among the life plans they can pursue given their talents and skills (Daniels 2008, 21). In another widely cited account, Martha Nussbaum identifies good health, including reproductive health, as one of the essential human capabilities necessary for leading lives that are fully human. She argues that the structure of social and political institutions should be chosen, at least in part, with a view to their ability to promote health at a minimum threshold level of capability for all members of society (Nussbaum 2000, 75–78). Summarizing why governments should take health more seriously, Richard Horton, the Editor-in-Chief of *The Lancet*, a leading medical journal, states that "Health policies matter because they underlie the fundamental commitments of governments to the dignity of their people. Health matters because when politicians intervene in health policy they are intervening not with our health, but with the futures we all value and long for" (2013, 980).

Health services and health systems are also considered to have ethical import for their role in protecting fair equality of opportunity (Daniels 2008, 57) and to be important social goods for their roles in the prevention of death and disability, the relief of pain and suffering, and the restoration of functioning. Beyond these tangible benefits, the association of health care with meaningful and memorable aspects of personal life – birth, illness, and death – adds a symbolic dimension. Because all human beings are vulnerable to disease and death and many health problems are beyond their control and therefore undeserved, health care also has special interpersonal significance through expressing and nurturing bonds of empathy and compassion (President's Commission for the Study of Ethical Problems in Medicine and Biomedical Research 1983, 11–12). It has also been noted that concepts of health care are embedded in the moral visions and commitments of a society. Or to put it another way, "a society's commitment to health care reflects some of its most basic attitudes about what it is to be a member of the human family" (President's Commission for the Study of Ethical Problems in Medicine and Biomedical Research 1983, 17).

Given the ethical import of health and health care, the health system should be viewed as central to the fabric of social and civic life. A variety of ethicists and human rights scholars characterize health systems as a core social institution, akin in many respects to the key roles of the judicial system in a democratic political system, and not simply a delivery point for biomedical interventions (Freedman et al. 2005, 19–20; Backman and Hunt 2008, 82; Yamin and Norheim 2014, 299). The characteristics and capabilities of health systems communicate and embody the values and norms of a society both through the interpersonal relationships and in the very structure of the health system. People's interaction with the health system defines in central ways their experience of the state and their place in the broader society (Freedman 2005, 21).

In the past sixty years, health status and access to health care have become the subject of a special kind of ethical claim: they have been recognized as the subject matter of human rights. Human rights differ from other types of ethical claims in several important ways. A distinctive value of human rights, which differentiates it from other moral discourses, is that rights confer specific claims or entitlements on right holders and give the right holder the grounds to press these claims if enjoyment of the right is threatened or denied (Freeman 2002, 61). In the case of a human right, these claims are considered to be universal, that is, vested in all persons in every society by virtue of their shared humanity. Respect for human dignity is the grounding of the human rights paradigm. Because rights are considered to be universal, characteristics such as nationality, race, sex, and economic and social position become irrelevant. Indeed nondiscrimination on any of these grounds constitutes a fundamental human rights principle. Designating something as a human right accords it a special normative status: while not absolute or exceptionless, a human right is considered to take priority over other moral, legal, and political claims (Nickel 1987, 3). In contrast with other types of ethical standards, human rights incorporate a stronger standard of accountability. A right is socially guaranteed and as such necessitates correlative duties – for individuals to respect them and for governments to take positive measures to protect and uphold the obligations they encompass (Nickel 1987, 3). A human rights approach also seeks to promote active agency by rights holders, particularly by those individuals and groups vulnerable to human rights violations, and to develop an active civil society shaping, prioritizing, and overseeing implementation (London 2008).

This book refers to health and human rights in two different ways. The first is a right to health that confers a legal entitlement. The second is human rights-based approaches to health, often shortened to rights-based approaches to health. A human rights-based approach has been defined as "a conceptual framework that is normatively based on international human rights standards and operationally directed to promoting and protecting human rights" (Backman 2012, 20). As such it is a potentially relevant standard for all countries that claim to respect international human rights standards. Human rights-based approaches offer a set of norms or principles, many derived from the Universal Declaration of Human Rights (United Nations 1948), relevant to the framing, implementation, and evaluation of health policies. In contrast, a right to health, or more precisely to the enjoyment of the highest attainable standard of physical and mental health, refers to specific entitlements, requirements, and obligations enumerated in a specific human rights instrument, such as the International Covenant on Economic, Social and Cultural Rights (ICESCR or the Covenant).

According to Amartya Sen, to frame a moral claim as a human right implies that it is of special importance and it is subject to social influence (2004). From the above discussion, it is clear that health and health care are widely considered to be of special importance, and many would add of special moral importance. Additionally, the fields of social epidemiology, social medicine, and medical sociology have shown that health and the opportunities to lead healthy lives are significantly influenced by what is termed the social determinants of health, the conditions in which people grow, live, work, and age (Commission on the Social Determinants of Health 2008). Or to state this in another way, "people's health or clinical 'health outcomes' and their antecedent capabilities to be healthy are significantly socially produced (i.e., nurture, protected, restored, neglected or thwarted) by a range of political, economic, legal, cultural and religious institutions and processes operating locally, nationally and globally" (Venkatapuram 2011, 3). I would add a third set of conditions for something to become the subject matter of a human right, the shared belief that the subject matter is a high priority social good to be collectively promoted and protected.

For the right to health these preconditions were not met until after World War II and in some countries more recently, and in still others, including the United States, not at all. Historically the health of populations and the availability of health care were not considered to be a major governmental responsibility, with the exception perhaps of measures taken to improve sanitation (Toebes 1999, 8). While health was valued as an important and beneficial asset, it was assumed to be in the private rather than the public or social domain. Until the nineteenth century little was understood about the cause of disease or of effective prevention and treatment measures. Before the development of scientifically grounded medical practice, much of health care could be provided by lay people rather than by professionals. Over the centuries, families, private charities, and religious organizations cared for the sick and dying, usually without any assistance from the public sector (President's Commission for the Study of Ethical Problems in Medicine and Biomedical Research 1983, 12–13).

Greater governmental involvement in health policy initially dated to the second half of the nineteenth century. The initiation of national welfare and health policies is usually associated with the reforms of Otto von Bismarck, the German chancellor from 1862 to 1890, who enacted a sickness insurance program together with retirement and disability benefits and a workers' compensation program. This development was originally motivated by the goals of achieving a more productive labor force, fostering a healthier general populace, and ameliorating social unrest, not investing individuals with social welfare benefits. By the end of the century many countries in Europe had some form of health insurance although most of them were not as comprehensive in form as Bismarck's program (Callahan and Wasunna 2006, 88).

Health or health care became the explicit subject matter of a human right following World War II. Like other social and economic rights, the framing of a right to health or health care reflected an expanded sense of government responsibility for the welfare of its citizens consistent with the emergence of the modern welfare state. The deprivations of the great depression, the devastation of World War II, and the atrocities of the Holocaust served as catalysts for this to occur.

The social safety net and welfare policies introduced after World War II also reflected new expectations as to what people should expect from the state. Changed relationships among members of the society and their relationship with their government are captured in the notion of social citizenship. Social citizenship "connotes a relationship of members of society to each other through the state that recognizes a positive obligation of the state to ensure the conditions exist for the realization of the shared dignity of all human beings" (Cameron 2007, 163). Others have associated this transformation in social relationships with the concept of solidarity, a kind of communal or communitarian moral premise. According to Daniel Callahan and Angela Wassuna, the principle of solidarity "encompasses the mutual responsibility of citizens for the health care of each other, equitable access to care, and it assumes that, in the face of illness and the threat of death, we are bound together by common needs that require a community response" (2006, 90). Callahan and Wasunna also claim that the concept of solidarity and not a commitment to human rights underlies support for universal health care, at least in Europe (2006, 90). However, it is more likely that solidarity is complementary with and strengthens a human rights approach.

The development of social and economic rights required a new understanding of human rights. In the traditional liberal approach to civil and political rights enumerated in documents like the United States Bill of Rights, rights are conceptualized primarily as restrictions on the state's power and as such confer a negative duty on the state not to act in ways that infringe an individual's rights. In contrast, social and economic rights, such as the rights newly identified in the Universal Declaration of Human Rights (United Nations 1948), entail positive obligations for the state to fulfill with resource and distributive consequences (Flood and Gross 2014b, 451–452). Health and health care as the content of a human rights entitlement are among the rights enumerated in the Universal Declaration. Article 25 stipulates that "everyone has a right to a standard of living adequate for the health and well being of himself and of his family, including food, clothing, housing, and medical care and necessary social services ..."

The 1966 International Covenant on Economic, Social, and Cultural Rights constitutes the first enumeration of the right to health in an international human rights instrument legally binding on the countries that ratify the document and thereby become a state party to it. Article 12 mandates that the steps to be taken to achieve full realization of this right shall include those necessary for "(a) provision for the reduction of the stillbirth rate and infant mortality and for the healthy development of the child; (b) the improvement of all aspects of environmental and industrial hygiene; (c) the prevention, treatment, and control of epidemic, endemic, occupational and other diseases; and (d) the creation of condition which would assure medical services and medical attention to all in the event of sickness" (1966, Article 12 (2)).

Subsequently, other international human rights instruments, regional human rights conventions, and national constitutions have also enumerated the right to health. The International Convention on the Elimination of All Forms of Racial Discrimination (1965), the Convention on the Elimination of All Forms of Discrimination Against Women (1979), and the Convention on the Rights of the Child (1989) all have provisions relating to the right to health. Various regional human rights instruments also enshrine this right including the European Social Charter (1961), the African Charter on Human and Peoples' Rights (1986), and the Additional Protocol to the American Convention on Human Rights in the Area of Economic, Social and Cultural Rights (1988).

In addition, constitutions of many countries have relevant provisions. One survey found that two-thirds of national constitutions currently do so (Kinney and Clark 2004), but not necessarily in the form of an explicit legal entitlement. Some constitutions have a provision addressing health or health care as a programmatic statement, for example, as a directive for state policy. The establishment of a constitutional right to health appears primarily in newer constitutions of emerging democracies. In contrast, countries with stronger public health systems providing a wider range of health entitlements are often older established democracies in which the health care system developed in the context of a welfare state without explicit reference to health rights (Flood and Gross 2014a, 5)

Status of the Right to Health

The status of the right to health has in large part reflected the manner in which social and economic rights are viewed. Economic and social rights have confronted a struggle for acceptance on the same basis as civil and political rights, especially in the Anglo-American countries. Importantly, the stature and visibility of the right to health have improved over time.

The watershed decision to incorporate social and economic rights in the Universal Declaration of Human Rights was not without controversy, but studies of the drafting history of these provisions show there was considerable support for doing so (Morsink 1999; Whelan 2010). It is true that the text approaches social and economic rights differently from the civil and political rights enumerated in the Universal Declaration. Economic and social rights are accorded to everyone as a member of society, and not on an individual basis as the civil and political rights enumerated are, and unlike civil and political rights, social and economic rights are conditioned on the organization and resources of each state, as augmented by international cooperation (Article 22). Johannes Morsink, the author of a study of the drafting history of the Universal Declaration, contends that this phrasing reflects efforts by the drafters to call special attention to social and economic rights because they were so new and not because they considered them to be less important than the older civil and political rights (Morsink 1999, 334).

However, after the cold war began, the reservations of representatives of the United States government and, to somewhat lesser extent, European governments increased. In post–cold war international forums, U.S. officials frequently denigrated the standing of social and economic rights because of their perceived association with socialism and the Soviet bloc. This interpretation of the origins of economic and social rights has been disputed by some scholars who trace them back to President Franklin Roosevelt's Four Freedom's speech in 1941 (Whelan 2010, 25–26). This may be historically correct, but when economic and social rights were championed by the Soviet bloc it stimulated U.S. opposition.

Despite the human rights community's rhetoric of the indivisibility, interdependence, and interrelatedness of all human rights, economic and social rights have often been considered to be inferior to civil and political rights. A categorization of three generations of human rights put forward by Karel Vasak in 1977 to explain differences in the historical development and bases of various types of human rights was widely adopted, but not for the purposes Vasek intended. The language of generations, originally meant to reflect the historical development of the rights, became translated into status differences. First generation civil and political rights came to be considered more significant and to be more important. Until recently, even the United Nations human rights apparatus invested less attention and fewer resources on social and economic rights as did the major inter-national human rights organizations like Amnesty International.

Conservative and libertarian thinkers have been among the most consistent opponents and detractors of economic and social rights. Conservative and libertarian objections reflect their opposition to the activist state required to promote economic and social rights and to the imposition of taxes to raise the resources necessary to achieve the reali-zation of these rights. Taxation to secure the resources required for the implementation of economic and social rights is considered to be an unjust interference with the liberty of the individual (Tobin 2012, 60–61). The recent resurgence of libertarian views and the neoliberal advocacy of limited government and privatization of social services represent a chal-lenge to the right to health. The impact of neoliberal policies will be dis-cussed at greater length in Chapter Three.

The lesser status accorded to economic and social rights has also reflected claims that economic and social rights are not true human rights. Maurice Cranston, who formulated the most widely cited version of the philosophical argument against economic and social rights, argued that traditional civil and political rights to life, liberty, and property are "universal, paramount, categorical moral rights" but that economic and social rights cannot logically be considered to be universal human rights. He went on to warn that the attempt to do so could potentially under-mine the whole enterprise of protected human rights (1973, 54). Aryeh Neier, the former Executive Director of Human Rights Watch and then the President of the Open Society Institute, holds similar views (2006).

The distinction between "negative" rights that require only forbearance on the part of others and "positive" rights that require others to provide goods and services if they are to be implemented underlies Cranston's and many other critics' arguments (Donnelly 1989, 33). However, this line of reasoning has been widely discounted. It is now generally accepted that all human rights have both negative and positive dimensions (Donnelly 1989, 31) and all give rise to three types of government obligations: the duties to respect, protect, and fulfill the rights (Yamin 2008, 8). Moreover, it is acknowledged that the implementation of civil and political rights also involves the investment of resources.

The "progressive realization principle" constitutes another factor affect-ing the status and implementation of economic, social, and cultural rights. It is often assumed that civil and political rights are immediately and fully binding. Whether this is a feasible standard or accurately reflects the real-ity of the experience of most states is another matter. In contrast, major human rights documents qualify the obligation to implement economic, social, and cultural rights making it gradual and conditional on the availability of resources and capacity of the particular state. Article 2 (1) of the International Covenant on Economic and Social Rights (ICESCR) specifies that each state party "take steps, individually and through international assistance and cooperation, especially economic and technical, to the maximum of available resources with a view to achieving progressively the full realization of the rights recognized in the present Covenant by all appropriate means" (1966). By so doing, the ICESCR and other instruments with similar language concede that full and immediate realization of the right to health will generally not be achievable in a short period of time, particularly in poor countries. The progressive realization benchmark also implies that valid expectations and concomitant obligations of state parties are not uniform or universal, but instead they are relative to levels of development and available resources. Some analysts believe that such a relative standard, particularly in the absence of specific guidelines for the steps to be taken toward implementation, diminishes the status of economic and social rights as human rights. Others are more aware that all human rights, including civil and political rights, have imperfect implementation and under positive circumstances all types of rights progress toward improved realization.

An additional critique sometimes leveled against economic and social rights is that because they are complex and expensive to implement it may not be feasible to achieve their realization in all countries and for all people. This criticism generally ignores the conditional obligations to implement the rights subject to the availability of resources in the international human rights instruments (International Covenant on Economic, Social and Cultural Rights, article 2.1). Moreover, as Amartya Sen argues, this criticism does not invalidate social and economic rights as rights: "The understanding that some rights are not fully realized, and may not even be fully realizable under present circumstances, does not, in itself, entail anything like the conclusion that these are, therefore, not rights at all. Rather, that understanding suggests the need to work towards changing the prevailing circumstances to make the unrealized rights realizable, and ultimately, realized" (2004, 348). He also points out that if the feasibility of guaranteeing complete and comprehensive fulfillment now were made into a necessary condition for the cogency of every right, it would also disqualify many political rights (2004, 348).

Importantly, the manner in which economic and social rights are viewed has changed significantly in the past fifteen years both in the international community and within many countries. The greater intellectual development of the content of these rights, including the right to health, has contributed to the process of the rights being taken more seriously. Although they are not official United Nations documents, the 1986 Limburg Principles on the Implementation of Economic, Social and Cultural Rights (The Limburg Principles 1987) and the 1997 Maastricht Guidelines on Violations of Economic, Social and Cultural Rights (Van Boven et al. 1998), developed by groups of international experts, helped provide frameworks for thinking about these rights. Various international human rights treaty bodies, particularly the UN Committee on Economic, Social and Cultural Rights, which oversees implementation of the ICESCR, have now drafted interpretations of the major social and economic rights, including the right to health.

Increased attention and greater resources have been invested in these rights within the United Nations human rights apparatus. During her tenure as the United Nations High Commissioner for Human Rights (1997–2002) Mary Robinson sought to elevate the status of economic and social rights. In 2002, the UN Commission on Human Rights (now the Human Rights Council) appointed its first Special Rapporteur to investigate and report on the implementation of the right to health.

Human rights obligations related to health are increasingly serving as a source of inspiration, a focal point, and an organizing strategy for civil society activists. As Paul Hunt, the first Special Rapporteur on the right to physical and mental health, noted in one of his reports, "As never before, civil society – especially in low-and-middle-income countries – is engaging with health and human rights" (2007, para 15). In addition, major international human rights NGOs like Amnesty International, Human Rights Watch, and the International Commission of Jurists, International Human Rights League, International Service for Human Rights, and others are devoting more attention to health and human rights issues as are some national medical associations and public health organizations, such as the British Medical Association and the American Public Health Association. A group of human rights NGOs consisting primarily of health professionals, such as Physicians for Human Rights and the International Federation of Health and Human Rights Organizations, have come on the scene. Médecins San Frontières, Partners in Health, Doctors for Global Health, and other humanitarian organizations of health professionals are increasingly using human rights as an advocacy tool and are giving more attention to health and human rights. The People's Health Movement, a global organization with national chapters that seek to promote social transformation and the right to health, has launched a global Right to Health and Healthcare Campaign. Nevertheless, civil society's recognition of health issues as human rights issues remains limited (Hunt 2007, paras 13–17).

Another development, which both reflects and advances the growing stature of the right to health, is the increasing judicialization of claims based on health and human rights standards. For many human rights advocates, particularly those with a legal background, the willingness of judicial bodies to accept jurisdiction over cases relating to the failure of a government to implement a specific human right entitlement constitutes a major source of legitimacy. The number of health-related rights cases has grown most exponentially in Latin America, but the increase seems to be part of a global trend. Litigation has played an important role in efforts to uphold health and human rights entitlements particularly in relationship to access to antiretroviral treatment for HIV/AIDS, the protection of prisoners' right to health care services, access to affordable generic drugs, struggles over reproductive rights, and efforts to secure underlying preconditions of health, such as water, food, and the right to live in a healthy environment (Gloppen and Roseman 2011, 2). However, the justiciability of the right to health continues to remain a contested issue in many jurisdictions. Also analysts disagree about whether the courts can serve as an effective accountability mechanism for health rights. Specifically assessments differ on whether litigation can advance equity and justice for health or more frequently just provides benefits to individual claimants, predominantly from the middle and upper classes, seeking access to curative treatments (Yamin and Gloppen 2011; Tobin 2012, 193; Yamin 2013, 514).

Also noteworthy, the ICESCR now has an optional protocol similar to those of other major international human rights instruments. A draft Optional Protocol to the International Covenant on Economic, Social and Cultural Rights was adopted by the UN General Assembly in 2008 and received a sufficient number of ratifications to enter into force on May 5, 2013. The Optional Protocol enables the CESCR to review complaints relevant to its mandate from individuals and groups who have exhausted all domestic remedies in the countries that have ratified the Protocol. It also has an inquiry mechanism that permits the Committee to investigate, report on, and issue recommendations related to grave or systematic violations of the ICESCR (United Nations 2008).

The greater visibility and status of rights-based approaches to health also comes from the role human rights has played in the global HIV/AIDS crisis. HIV/AIDS constitutes one of the most important global health issues. The number of people living with HIV worldwide rose to 34 million in 2013, in part because more people are getting access to life-sustaining antiretroviral treatments and thereby surviving (McNeil, Jr. 2015,1). Concern with HIV/AIDS played an important role in motivating pioneering work in the 1990s by Jonathan Mann, the first coordinator of WHO's global AIDS program, on the relationship between health and human rights (Hunt 2007, paras 7 and 8). Writing in the 1994 inaugural issue of the journal *Health and Human Rights*, which was to become an important vehicle for conveying cutting-edge research and reflection in the field, Mann and a series of coauthors identified three types of important linkages between health and rights: (1) the impact (positive and negative) of health policies, programs, and practices on human rights; (2) the understanding that human rights violations have health impacts; and (3) the fundamental linkages between the promotion and protection of health and human rights (Mann et al. 1994). During his too brief life, Mann focused on these three linkages in the context of the HIV/AIDS epidemic and thereby gave health and human rights greater visibility. Human rights approaches have played an important role in addressing the HIV/AIDS crisis in helping to define global and national policies, changing attitudes, and advocating for additional resources. Human rights approaches have been used to design, develop, and implement HIV policies and programs (Gruskin and Ahmed 2012, 191–193).

Progress in the Understanding of the Obligations the Right to Health Entails

Enumeration of the right to health, whether in a human rights instrument or the constitution of a state, is usually framed in broad-brush strokes. These documents rarely specify what commitment to a right to health entails in terms of the specific entitlements it provides to rights holders, the requirements it imposes on health systems, and the concomitant obligations on states, who are the primary duty holders of human rights. Therefore, implementation requires conceptualization and operationalization of the right. This has been slow in coming for the right to health. Until 2000, there was no authoritative interpretation of the right to health that set forth what the right entailed. The absence of an authoritative interpretation also inhibited the monitoring of and accountability for the right.

In 2000, after several years of discussion, the Committee on Economic, Social and Cultural Rights, the United Nations human rights treaty monitoring body for the International Covenant on Economic, Social and

Cultural Rights (ICESCR), adopted an expansive interpretation of the right to health in the form of a general comment that is widely considered the most authoritative interpretation of the right. By providing an international standard, the Committee's General Comment No. 14 on the Right to the Highest Attainable Standard of Health has led to wider agreement on the major elements of the right to health. Although general comments (also sometimes termed general recommendations) by UN human rights monitoring bodies do not have the same legal standing as the provisions of international human rights instruments, this general comment has been widely influential.

The appointment of a Special Rapporteur for the right to health within the UN human rights system in 2002 has also contributed to the process of gaining greater clarity about the requirements of the right. Paul Hunt, the first such Special Rapporteur, who served between 2002 and 2008, played an important role in elaborating and operationalizing the normative content of the right to health, building upon the provisions of General Comment 14, which as a member of the Committee he had helped to draft. His reports cover and provide greater depth on a number of important topics including right to health indicators (2003), sexual and reproductive rights (2004), mental disabilities (2005), reduction of maternal mortality (2006), the prioritization of health interventions and the role of water and sanitation (2007) in the right to health, and the role of health systems (2008). His successor, Anand Grover, continued this process contributing reports on development and the right to health (2011a), occupational health, especially of vulnerable populations (2011b), access to medicines in the context of Trade Related Aspects of Intellectual Property Rights (2009), and health care financing in the context of the right to health (2012). Both special rapporteurs also conducted missions to a number of countries to evaluate their implementation of the right and the issues it raised. In addition, Hunt undertook missions to the World Trade Organization, the World Bank, and the International Monetary Fund as well as to the pharmaceutical company Glaxo Smith Kline and used the latter mission as input into the development of human rights guidelines for pharmaceutical companies in relation to access to medicines (2008).

So how far has the right to health progressed as an emergent right? A recent analysis of the status and the understanding of the right to health by John Harrington and Maria Stuttaford suggests that "In the last decade, the human right to health has moved to the centre of political debate and social policy across the globe" (2010, 1). They observe that "Civil society organizations have put the right at the heart of campaigns for health justice at national and global levels. It features prominently in the output of the United Nations (UN) and regional human rights bodies, as well as national courts and legislatures: national constitutions increasingly include explicit recognition of the right to health" (2010, 1). They go on to note that scholars now labor to develop its normative content and to contextualize its application; that the right to health is playing a central and prominent role in shaping the development of health policy and the delivery of health services; and that an understanding as to the meaning and implementation of the right to health has been developed and accepted (2010, 1). As a result of "this remarkable transformation" (2010, 2), they conclude that we have moved beyond the period of defensiveness to an acceptance of the right.

But I think this is an overly optimistic assessment of how far we have progressed, and so do several other scholars. In 2013, Alicia Ely Yamin evaluated progress as follows: "Over the last fifteen – and especially the last ten – years, there has been a proliferation of rights-based approaches to health (RBAs) and of interpretive work regarding those RBAs. We have a much better – albeit still imperfect and contested – understanding of the scope of the right to health as well as the role that social determinants and health systems play in people's ability to effectively enjoy the right" (2013, 516). I think Yamin is much closer to the mark. Chapter Two will provide an overview of the current interpretation of the right to health and its gaps.

Challenges to Implementing the Right to Health

The purpose of a human right is to frame public policies and private behaviors so as to protect and promote the human dignity and welfare of all members and groups within society, particularly those who are vulnerable and poor, and to effectively implement them. Legal recognition and identification of the obligations a right entails are steps toward this goal. Importantly though, realization requires a human right to be operationalized and implemented. All human rights confront challenges on an ongoing basis related to their acceptance, translation into appropriate institutions and policies, implementation, and accountability. One set of challenges derives from the complex requirements of human rights. Human rights are demanding standards requiring support from their prospective beneficiaries/rights holders and imposing extensive obligations on the states responsible for their realization. This is particularly so in the case of the right to health, one of the most demanding of rights in terms of its scope, requirements, institutional prerequisites, financing, and goals. Alicia Ely Yamin has described health as perhaps the most radical of subjects for human rights in part because a rights-based approach to health challenges our assumptions about justice, society, and humanness itself (2008, 1–2).

Implementation of rights-based approaches to health also faces more difficulties than many other rights because of the specialized nature of the subject matter as well as its dependence upon health professionals for implementation. Human rights advocates often lack a detailed understanding of how the health system functions and how human rights standards can and should shape health services. Conversely, the health professionals who dominate the health sector in both public and private institutions and run key international health organizations, as well as ministries of health across the globe, frequently lack familiarity with international human rights law (Backman 2012, 24). Paul Hunt commented that most of the health professionals he met had not even heard of the right to health, and if they had, they usually had no idea of what it means, either conceptually or operationally (2007, paras 41–43).

A second set of challenges can come from the political, social, and economic environment in which the rights are to be implemented. In that regard, it is relevant to note that the contemporary economic, social, and cultural context differs significantly from the postwar conditions and political cultures that underpinned the initial framing of economic and social rights and offers many more challenges to the implementation of a rights-based approach to health. Although in the postwar period many countries were grappling with the terrible devastation of World War II and certainly were not as affluent as they are today, there was support for human rights values and a welfare state model in which the government plays a key role in the protection and promotion of the economic and social well-being of its citizens. Many governments in industrialized economic systems aspired to develop comprehensive welfare programs, including the provision of health services. Whether these goals reflected an explicit commitment to human rights or instead were inspired by concepts of solidarity and/or social citizenship as claimed by some (Callahan and Wasunna 2006, 9, 110–111), the ideals and principles were supportive of human rights values and requirements.

In contrast, major changes in the world during the past thirty-five years present significant challenges to the realization of social and economic rights. Ironically, as the right to health has evolved and become more widely recognized as an appropriate normative foundation and ethical requirement for health policy development, there has been a global paradigm shift engendered by the increasing hegemony of market-based approaches that make rights-based approaches far more difficult to implement. Neoliberalism, the economic and political philosophy underlying this paradigm, contends that markets are the appropriate basis for organizing all areas of economic and social life, regardless of the deleterious effects on human welfare and human dignity. In contrast with a human rights approach, which vests fundamental responsibility for realizing health-related human rights obligations in the state and thereby requires a strong and effective state apparatus, neoliberalism promotes political policies minimizing the role of the state. It advocates transferring the provision of health and other social services to the private sector on a for-profit basis. Neoliberal policies also envision health to be an economic commodity rather than the social good conceptualized by human rights law.

Today private providers play a major role in the health sector of both developed and developing countries. Private health provision does not change the responsibilities of the state to implement its health rights obligations, but it significantly complicates the process of doing so. In many cases, privatization has also led to increased out-of-pocket payments for health services that poor households cannot afford. Privatization also discourages investments in the public health sector and encourages disproportionate investment in secondary and tertiary care sectors at the expense of primary care (Grover 2012, paras 2 and 3).

Health costs have risen sharply during the past thirty years making it more difficult for people to afford necessary health care and governments to finance comprehensive health services. Financial constraints are prompting many governments to cut back on health entitlements, to reduce the population groups who are eligible, and to increase co-pays and fees for covered services. High costs of health care combined with the absence of comprehensive social insurance coverage have created financial barriers that prevent millions of persons from seeking and receiving needed health care. The cost of health care has been most problematic for low-income people, but even many of those in the middle class have problems covering health costs. Many low- and middle-income countries suffer from poor population health services coverage, high out-of-pocket expenditures, and entrapment in vicious cycles of ill health and poverty (Schnell-Adlung 2013, 44). It is estimated that health care costs push some 100 million people into poverty each year (Bennet et al. 2010).

The underfunding of public health institutions has taken a major toll on the strength and the effectiveness of health systems in many countries, which are so central to achieving a rights-based approach to health and more broadly of providing access to good quality health services. WHO

laments that in too many countries health systems "are on the point of collapse, or are accessible only to particular groups of the population" (WHO
2007, 1). WHO links unacceptably low-health outcomes in much of the
developing world and the persistence of deep inequities in health status
in all countries to failing or inadequate health systems (WHO 2007, 1).
It even seems questionable whether many governments, particularly in
poor and middle-income states, have the institutional and infrastructure
capabilities and medical and health staff needed to meet the requirements
imposed by the right to health.

Like other human rights instruments, the International Covenant
on Economic, Social and Cultural Rights (ICESCR) takes for granted a
Westphalian international order built on the sovereignty of nation-states
and the ability of governments to determine and implement their public
policies. However, the acceleration of globalization in the fifty years since
the ICESCR was adopted has qualified the exercise of sovereignty, particularly for small and many middle-income states. Globalization, a process characterized by the growing interdependence of the world's people,
involving the integration of economies, culture, technologies, and governance, has limited the policy options of states and affected implementation
of the right to health. While globalization is not a new phenomenon, the
rapidity and degree to which states are being drawn into a global economy,
polity, and culture is a new development. Also new, the hegemony of the
market economy and free trade constitute the central characteristics of
contemporary globalization (Howard-Hassmann 2010, 7). In a globalized
system many states, particularly poor ones, have significant constraints on
both their ability and their freedom to implement human rights obligations, or, to describe the situation in another way, global market integration is shrinking the ability of all governments to make decisions about
health without taking into consideration such factors as economic competitiveness, credit worthiness, debt payments to external creditors, and
complying with trade agreements conditions, even when these are contrary to a human rights paradigm and impose health-negative effects
(O'Connell 2007). The growing strength and roles of international institutions, particularly international financial institutions like the World Bank,
the International Monetary Fund, and the World Trade Organization,
and the neoliberal policies they advocate have also restricted the ability of
some states to meet their human rights obligations.

Some two billion people, one-third of the world's population, most of
whom live in low- and middle-income countries, still lack access to the
medicines necessary for their health care. It is estimated that improving

access to essential medicines could save some ten million lives each year. Providing meaningful incentives for the development of new medications for the world's poor could reduce the disease burden even further (Grover 2011b). However, the dominant role of private corporations in health research and in the pharmaceutical sector skews the development of medications to those that can make the greatest profit rather than those that can address the medical needs of the largest number of people. Global research and investments in health focus on diseases relevant to high-income countries. Too few investments are targeted toward the medicines and vaccines needed by poor- and middle-income countries. The escalating prices of pharmaceuticals also play a major role in decreasing access to needed medicines.

In turn, the trends noted above significantly complicate the goal of achieving universal health coverage, a goal that an increasing number of countries aspire to attain. The World Health Assembly has defined universal coverage "as access to key promotive, preventive, curative and rehabilitative health interventions for all at an affordable cost, thereby achieving equity in access" (World Health Assembly 2005). While a wide variety of states have taken steps to improve access to health services and provide improved financial protection, many of them are encountering serious obstacles (Sangiorgio 2013). The current economic and political environments and health landscapes are not conducive to having necessary inputs in place. Additionally, in response to financial constraints and changes in policy priorities, many of the states that have at least nominally already achieved universal coverage, such as countries in Europe, are cutting back both on entitlements and eligibility for coverage.

Overview of the Book

Chapter Two, Evaluating Current Interpretations of the Right to Health, delineates the normative and conceptual foundations of the right to health and evaluates its adequacy. The analysis identifies the settled and unsettled issues in the understanding of the right and gaps in its interpretation of the right to health. A central goal will be to assess the extent to which the current interpretation of the right offers guidelines for informing health policy from a human rights perspective.

Chapter Three, The Right to Health in an Era of Market Dominance, focuses on the implications of the increasing hegemony of a market paradigm for the right to health. The chapter assesses the challenges neoliberalism poses on normative, policy, and societal levels for a human rights-based approach to health. It also considers the effects of health care commercialization for health systems, that is, the provision of health services through market relationships to those able and willing to pay for them. Additionally, the chapter discusses the factors contributing to the escalating costs of health services and its consequences for the affordability of and access to health care.

Chapter Four, Private Sector Provision, Health, and Human Rights, uses a human rights lens through which to evaluate private sector health services provision and the privatization or transfer of health services and/ or insurance from the public to the private sector. It identifies factors that encourage privatization of health services. It explores the extent and ways in which privatization of health services potentially is and is not compatible with human rights commitments. It also discusses international human rights law provisions relevant to privatization of health services and whether there is a specific right to private medical services. In addition, it identifies ways to potentially mitigate the impact of private health provision on the right to health.

Chapter Five on Globalization, Health, and Human Rights addresses the impact of globalization and global institutions on the health sector and its human rights implications. After a brief discussion of the economic consequences of globalization, the chapter considers the impact of globalization on health status, health systems, and the availability of health personnel in poor countries. This is followed by a section reviewing how globalization has affected the social determinants of health. The chapter then explores the impact of transnational actors on the right to health including the World Health Organization (WHO), corporations, the World Bank, the World Trade Organization (WTO) and its International Agreement on Trade-Related Aspects of Intellectual Property Rights (TRIPS), and international aid donors. The final section of the chapter reviews human rights responses and assesses their potential effectiveness.

Chapter Six, Access to Medicine, focuses on the topic of access to medicines as a fundamental component of realizing the right to health. It addresses constraints and obstacles to providing more equitable access to medicines, including the role of intellectual property law and specifically, the World Trade Organization's Agreement on Trade-Related Aspects of Intellectual Property (TRIPS) and TRIPS Plus agreements, the implications of the rising cost of medicines, and the lack of human rights accountability of the private corporations that dominate drug development and marketing. The chapter also reviews how human rights-based advocacy and mobilization have responded to these constraints and in some cases been successful in lowering prices and improving access to drugs. Additionally, the chapter proposes human rights-based policy approaches to improving access to medicines.

Chapter Seven, The Social Determinants of Health, Health Equity, and Human Rights, focuses on the importance of incorporating a more explicit commitment to equity and the social determinants of health into the right to health paradigm. With inequalities in both rich and poor countries on a steep upward trajectory in a neoliberal economy, a human rights approach requires an explicit agenda to promote equity. The chapter discusses how both income differences and the extent of societal inequalities affect health outcomes. The chapter also evaluates differences in a human rights approach to the underlying determinants of health and the orientation of the World Health Organization's Commission on the Social Determinants of Health to the social determinants of health. To make a human rights approach more amenable to incorporating an equity agenda and the social determinants for health will require methodological and conceptual changes as well as a reorientation of priorities. The chapter proposes and explains these requirements.

Chapter Eight, Achieving Universal Health Coverage, builds on the discussions in the previous chapters to evaluate potential human rights contributions to efforts to realizing universal health coverage and the obstacles posed by the trends discussed in the previous chapters. Universality is a fundamental characteristic of a human rights approach. Yet there has been little attention to identifying the specifics of what universal coverage based on the right to health requires. Importantly, not all potential paths to a universal health system are consistent with human rights criteria. Chapter Eight considers the extent to which a human rights approach can illuminate the conceptual framework, the scope of coverage, establishment of priorities, the types of funding mechanisms, the allocation of resources, and the appropriate steps to achieving universal health coverage.

References

Additional Protocol to the American Convention on Human Rights in the Area of Economic, Social and Cultural Rights (1988) (not yet in force), www.oas.org/juridico/english/treaties/a-52.html

African Charter on Human and Peoples' Rights, OAU Doc. CAB/LEG/67/3Rev.5, entered into force October 21, 1986.

Anand, Sudhir. (2004) "The Concern for Equity in Health," in Sudhir Anand, Fabienne Peter, and Amartya Sen, eds., *Public Health, Ethics, and Equity*, Oxford and New York: Oxford University Press, pp. 5–15.

Backman, Gunilla. (2012) "Introduction," in Gunilla Backman, ed., *The Right to Health: Theory and Practice*, Lund: Studentlitteratur, pp. 23–30.

Bennett, Sara, Ozawa, Sachiko, and Rao, Krishna D. (2010) "Which Path to Universal Health Coverage? Perspectives on the World Health Report 2010," *PLoS Medicine* 7 (11), www.plosmedicine.org, e10001001. Doi:10.1371/journal.pmed.1001001.

Callahan, Daniel and Wasunna, Angela A. (2006) *Medicine and the Market: Equity v. Choice*, Baltimore, MD: The Johns Hopkins University Press.

Cameron, Barbara (2007) "Accounting for Rights and Money in the Canadian Social Union," in Margot Young, Susan B. Boyd, Gwen Brodsky, and Shelagh Day, eds., *Poverty: Rights, Social Citizenship, Legal Activism*, Vancouver: UBC Press, pp. 162–180.

CESCR (Committee on Economic, Social and Cultural Rights) (1990) General Comment 3: The Nature of States Parties Obligations (Art. 2, para.1 of the Covenant), contained in E/1991/23.

(1994) General Comment No. 5: Persons with Disabilities, U.N. Doc. E/1995/22.

(2000) General Comment 14: The Right to the Highest Attainable Standard of Health, U.N. Doc. E.C.12.2000.4.EN.

Commission on Social Determinants of Health (2008) *Closing the Gap in a Generation: Health Equity through Action on the Social Determinants of Health*. Geneva: World Health Organization.

Convention on the Elimination of All Forms of Discrimination Against Women (1979) G.A. Res. 34/180, 34 U.N. GAOR Supp. (No. 46) at 193, U.N. Doc. 34/36.

Convention on the Rights of the Child (1989) G.A. Res. 44/25, 44 U.N. GAOR Supp. (No. 49) at 165, U.N. Doc. A/44/736.

Cranston, Maurice (1973) *What Are Human Rights?* London: Bodley Head.

Daniels, Norman (2008) *Meeting Health Needs Fairly*, Cambridge and New York: Cambridge University Press.

Donnelly, Jack (1989) *Universal Human Rights in Theory & Practice*, Ithaca, NY and London: Cornell University Press, 1989.

European Social Charter (1961) 529 U.N.T.S. 221 (entered into force 1953).

Flood, Colleen M. and Gross, Aeyal (2014a) "Introduction: Marrying Human Rights and Health Care Systems: Contexts for a Power to Improve Access and Equity," in Colleeen M. Flood and Aeyal Gross, eds., *The Right to Health at the Public/Private Divide: A Global Comparative Study*, New York: Cambridge University Press, pp. 1–18.

(2014b) "Conclusion: Contexts for the Promise and Peril of the Right to Health," in Colleeen M. Flood and Aeyal Gross, eds., *The Right to Health at the Public/*

Private Divide: A Global Comparative Study, New York: Cambridge University Press, pp. 451–480.

Freedman, Lynn P. (2005) "Achieving the MDGs: Health Systems as Core Social Institutions," *Development* 48 (1): 19–24.

Freedman, Lynn P., Waldman, Ronald J., de Pinho, Helen, Wirth, Meg E. et al. (2005) *Who's Got the Power: Transforming Health Systems for Women and Children*, London and Sterling, Virginia: Earthscan for the Millennium Project.

Freeman, Michael (2002) *Human Rights: An Interdisciplinary Approach*, Polity Press: Cambridge, UK and Blackwell Publishers, Inc.: Malden, MA.

Gable, Lance (2007) "The Proliferation of Human Rights in Global Health Governance," *Journal of Law, Medicine & Ethics* 35: 536–539.

Gloppen, Siri and Roseman, Mindy Jane (2011) "Introduction: Can Litigation Bring Justice to Health?" in Alicia Ely Yamin and Siri Gloppen, eds., *Litigating Health Rights: Can Courts Bring More Justice to Health?* Cambridge: Harvard University Press, pp. 1–16.

Grover, Anand (2009) Report of the Special Rapporteur on the Right of Everyone to the Enjoyment of the Highest Attainable Standard of Physical and Mental Health, submitted to the Human Rights Council/Commission, UN Doc. A/HRC/11/12, focusing on access to medicines, Trade-Related Aspects of Intellectual Property Rights (TRIPS and free trade agreements).

(2011a) Report of the Special Rapporteur on the Right of Everyone to the Enjoyment of the Highest Attainable Standard of Physical and Mental Health, submitted to the United Nations Human Rights Council/Commission, UN Doc. A/HRC/17/25, focusing on development and the right to health.

(2011b) Report of the Special Rapporteur on the Right of Everyone to the Enjoyment of the Highest Attainable Standard of Physical and Mental Health, submitted to the Human Rights Council/Commission, UN Doc. A/HRC/20/25, focusing on occupational health, especially of vulnerable populations.

(2012) Report of the Special Rapporteur on the Right of Everyone to the Enjoyment of the Highest Attainable Standard of Physical and Mental Health, submitted to the United Nations General Assembly, UN Doc. A/67/302, focusing on health financing in the context of the right to health.

Gruskin, Sofia and Ahmed, Shahira (2012) "HIV and AIDS," in Gunilla Backman, ed., *The Right to Health: Theory and Practice*, Lund: Studentlitteratur, pp. 191–224.

Harrington, John and Stuttaford, Maria (2010) "Introduction," in John Harrington and Maria Stuttaford, eds., *Global Health and Human Rights: Legal and Philosophical Perspectives*, London and New York: Routledge, pp. 1–11.

Hiskes, Richard P. (2005) "The Right to a Green Future: Human Rights, Environmentalism, and Intergenerational Justice," *Human Rights Quarterly* 27(4): 1346–1364.

(2009) *The Human Right to a Green Future: Environmental Rights and Intergenerational Justice*, Cambridge, England and New York: Cambridge University Press.

Horton, Richard (2013) "Offline: Why Governments Should Take Health More Seriously," *The Lancet* 381: 980.

Howard-Hassmann, Rhoda E. (2010) *Can Globalization Promote Human Rights?* Philadelphia: University of Pennsylvania Press.

Hunt, Paul (2003) Report of the Special Rapporteur on the Right of Everyone to the Enjoyment of the Highest Attainable Standard of Physical and Mental Health, submitted to the United Nations General Assembly, UN Doc. A/58/427, focusing on right to health indicators.

Hunt, Paul (2004) Report of the Special Rapporteur on the Right of Everyone to the Enjoyment of the Highest Attainable Standard of Physical and Mental Health, Paul Hunt, on His Mission to the World Trade Organization, Commission on Human rights, March 1, 2004, E/CN.4/2004/49/Add.1.

(2005) Report of the Special Rapporteur on the Right of Everyone to the Enjoyment of the Highest Attainable Standard of Physical Health, submitted to the Human Rights Council, UN Doc. E/CN.4/2005/51 focusing on persons with mental disabilities.

(2006) Report of the Special Rapporteur on the Right of Everyone to the Enjoyment of the Highest Attainable Standard of Physical Health, submitted to the Human Rights Council, UN Doc E/CN. 4/2006/48 providing a human rights based approach to right to health indicators.

(2007) Report of the Special Rapporteur on the Right of Everyone to the Enjoyment of the Highest Attainable Standard of Physical and Mental Health, submitted to the United Nations General Assembly, UN Doc A/62/150 providing preliminary observations on prioritizing health interventions in a way that is respectful of human rights and considering the underlying determinants of health.

(2008) Report of the Special Rapporteur on the Right of Everyone to the Enjoyment of the Highest Attainable Standard of Physical and Mental Health, submitted to the Human Rights Council, January 2008, U.N. Doc. A/HRC/7/11 focusing on the role of health systems in realizing the right to the highest attainable standard of health.

International Covenant on Economic, Social, and Cultural Rights (1966) G.A. Res. 2200 (XXI), 21 U.N. GAOR Supp. No. 16 at 49, U.N. Doc. A/6316.

International Convention on the Elimination of Racial Discrimination (1965) United Nations General Assembly Resolution 2106 (XX) of December 21, www.hrcr.org/docs/CERD/cerd.html.

Kinney, Eleanor D. and Clark, Brian Alexander (2004) "Provisions for Health and Health Care in the Constitutions of the Countries of the World," *Cornell International Law Journal* 37: 285–315.

London, Leslie (2008) "What Is a Human Rights-based Approach to Health and Does It Matter?" *Health and Human Rights* 10 (1): 65–80.

Mann, Jonathan, Gostin, Lawrence, Gruskin, Sofia, Brennan, Troyen, Lazzarini, Zita, and Fineberg, Harvey V. (1994) "Health and Human Rights," *Health and Human Rights* 1 (1): 6–23.

McNeil, Jr., Donald G. (2015) "H.I.V. Treatment Should Start at Diagnosis, U.S. Health Officials Say," *The New York Times*, May 28, A1.

Morsink, Johannes (1999) *The Universal Declaration of Human Rights: Origins, Drafting, and Intent*, Philadelphia: University of Pennsylvania Press.

Neier, Aryeh (2006) "Social and Economic Rights: A Critique," *Human Rights Brief*: 1–3.

Nickel, James W. (1987) *Making Sense of Human Rights: Philosophical Reflections on the Universal Declaration of Human Rights*, Berkeley, Los Angeles, and London: University of California Press.

Nussbaum, Martha C. (2000) *Women and Development: The Capabilities Approach*, Cambridge: Cambridge University Press.

O'Connell, Paul (2007) "On Reconciling Irreconcilables: Neoliberal Globalisation and Human Rights." *Human Rights Law Review* 3: 483–509.

President's Commission for the Study of Ethical Problems in Medicine and Biomedical Research (1983) *Securing Access to Health Care, Vol. One Report: The Ethical Implications of Differences in the Availability of Health Services*, Washington, DC.

Sangiorgio, Miriam (2013) "Towards Universal Health Coverage: Update from the 66th World Health Assembly," *Health Diplomacy Monitor* 4(4): 14–16.

Schnell-Adlung, Xenia (2013) "Health Protection: More than Financial Protection," in Alexander S. Preker, Marianne E. Lindner, Dov Chernichovsky, and Onno P. Schellekens, eds., *Scaling Up Affordable Health Insurance: Staying the Course*, Washington, DC: The World Bank, pp. 13–48.

Sen, Amartya (2004) "Elements of a Theory of Human Rights," *Philosophy and Public Affairs* 32 (4): 315–356.

Shue, Henry (1980) *Basic Rights: Subsistence, Affluence, and U.S. Foreign Policy*, Princeton: Princeton University Press.

Tobin, John (2012) *The Right to Health in International Law*, Oxford and New York: Oxford University Press.

Toebes, Brigit C. A. (1999) *The Right to Health as a Human Right in International Law,* Antwerp, Groningen and Oxford: Intersentia-Hart.

United Nations (1948) Universal Declaration of Human Rights, adopted and proclaimed by the United Nations General Assembly Resolution 217A (III) on 10 December.

(2008) Optional Protocol to the International Covenant on Economic, Social and Cultural Rights, adopted by United Nations General Assembly Resolution A.RES.63.117 on 10 December.

van Boven, Theo C., Flinterman, Cees, and Westendorp, Ingrid (1998) The Maastricht Guidelines on Violations of Economic, Social and Cultural Rights, Netherlands Institute of Human Rights, Utrecht.

Venkatapuram, Sridhar (2011) *Health Justice*, Cambridge, UK and Malden, MA: Polity Press.

Whelan, Daniel J. (2010) *Indivisible Human Rights: A History*, Philadelphia and Oxford: University of Pennsylvania Press.

World Health Assembly (2005) Sustainable Health Financing, Universal Coverage and Social Health Insurance, World Health Assembly Resolution 58.33, World Health Organization, www.who.int/health_financing/...wharesoluti.

World Health Organization (2007) Everybody's Business: Strengthening Health Systems to Improve Health Outcomes, who./int/healthsystems/strategy/everybodys_business.pdf.

Yamin, Alicia Ely (2008) "Will We Take Suffering Seriously? Reflections on What Applying a Human Rights Framework to Health Means and Why We Should Care," *Human and Human Rights Journal* 10 (1): 1–19.

(2013) "The Right to Health: Where Do We Stand and How Far Have We Come: Review of John Tobin, the Right to Health in International Law," *Human Rights Quarterly* 35 (2): 509–516.

Yamin, Alicia Ely and Gloppen, Siri, eds. (2011) *Litigating Health Rights: Can Courts Bring More Justice to Health?* Cambridge: Harvard University Press.

Yamin, Alicia Ely and Norheim Ole Frithjof (2014) "Taking Equality Seriously: Applying Human Rights Frameworks to Priority Setting in Health," *Human Rights Quarterly* 36 (2): 296–324.

2

Evaluating Interpretations of the Right to Health

The first chapter characterized the right to health as an emergent human right. It noted that the conception of the right and the understanding of the related obligations of states have evolved over time, but even now the conceptualization of the right is still incomplete. It also mentioned that the continuing lack of consensus about the foundations, scope, and obligations related to the right to health poses obstacles to the implementation of the right. This chapter offers a critical assessment of progress to date in providing a meaningful foundation for the implementation of the right and its application to pressing health issues, some of which were briefly identified in Chapter One and will be analyzed in greater depth in subsequent chapters.

General Comment No. 14 on the right to health (GC 14) (CESCR 2000), adopted by the UN Committee on Economic, Social and Cultural Rights (CESCR) in 2000, is generally understood to be the most authoritative interpretation of the right. CESCR has further refined its interpretation through its statements and review of state parties' reports. For purposes of full disclosure, I will note that I was one of the experts involved in discussions with members of the Committee preceding the drafting of GC 14, and I was also able to observe the drafting process. While I believe that the general comment is a significant contribution to interpreting the right to health, particularly in scoping out dimensions of the right and addressing issues current at the time it was adopted, I am also aware of its limitations. As a baseline document it had to set different kinds of priorities than a follow-up document would if written today. Moreover, even though GC 14 is considerably longer than any of CESCR's previous general comments had been up to that time, it was still constrained by space considerations that affected the number of topics it could address and the amount of detail it could provide. Also, quite understandably, the general comment reflected a late twentieth-century perspective. Health issues and the interpretation of the relationship between health and human rights have continued to evolve since then.

Other UN human rights treaty bodies, particularly the Committee on the Rights of the Child (CRC) and the Committee to Eliminate Discrimination Against Women (CEDAW), have also adopted interpretations of the right to health. CEDAW adopted a general recommendation on women and health the year before the CESCR's general comment (CEDAW 1999). CEDAW's general recommendation, which like a general comment provides an authoritative interpretation of a right or an aspect of a right, focuses on requirements for states to eliminate discrimination against women in their access to health care services throughout the life cycle, particularly in the areas of family planning, pregnancy, and during the postnatal period. The CRC has written two general comments on health-related topics: the first is on adolescent health (CRC 2003). A more recent general comment on the right of the child to the enjoyment of the highest attainable standard of health (CRC 2013) offers a comprehensive interpretation of the right to health from the perspective of promoting rights to child health. This latter general comment both reflects the approach taken in the earlier general comment of the CESCR and goes beyond it in a number of ways to address some structural issues. As noted in Chapter One, the Special Rapporteurs on the right to health, of which there have now been three, have also played an important role in translating and operationalizing the right.

This chapter can only begin to address the many topics related to the interpretation of the right to health. Subsequent chapters will continue the analysis in relationship to the issues on which they focus. The chapter will focus on GC 14 noting both its strengths and its limitations. It should be noted that technically GC 14 applies only to state parties, the 162 countries (as of June 2014) that have ratified or acceded to the International Covenant on Economic, Social and Cultural Rights. Nevertheless, both human rights advocates and judiciaries in other countries have also referred to the document. This chapter will shorthand references to obligations and refer to the obligations of states rather than state parties.

Expansion of the Scope of the Right to Health

One of the major issues underlying the conceptualization of the right to health is the extent to which the interpretation is constrained by the provisions of Article 12 in the ICESCR (1966), the first international human rights instrument to identify health as the subject of a binding human right. Specifically, is it permissible to expand the scope of the right and the corresponding obligations of states beyond this text? To what extent should developments in the understanding of the determinants of health and the relationship between health and human rights in the more than half century since the Covenant was drafted shape the interpretation?

Looked at with twenty-first century eyes, Article 12 has a limited scope and is quite outdated. The text recognizes "the right of everyone to the enjoyment of the highest attainable standard of physical and mental health." To that end, it identifies a number of steps to be taken by state parties to the Covenant (the term for states that have ratified a human rights treaty). The four steps it specifies are:

(a) The provision for the reduction of the stillbirth rate and infant mortality and for the healthy development of the child;
(b) The improvement of all aspects of environmental and industrial hygiene;
(c) The prevention, treatment, and control of epidemic, endemic, occupational, and other diseases; and
(d) The creation of conditions that would assure medical service and medical attention in the case of sickness to all (1966, Article 12.2).

General Comment 14 (CESCR 2000) expands the interpretation of the right to health well beyond the original provisions outlined in the ICESCR, which the general comment characterizes as illustrative, non-exhaustive examples of state parties' obligations related to the right to health (para 7). It justifies its widening the scope of its interpretation by referring to the dramatic changes in the world health situation since 1966 and the widening notion of health in the period since the Covenant was drafted: "More determinants of health are being taken into consideration, such as resource distribution and gender differences. A wider definition of health also takes into account such socially related concerns as violence and armed conflict" (para 10). It also mentions new obstacles for the realization of the right, such as the appearance of formerly unknown diseases, such as HIV/AIDS, and the greater prevalence of others, such as cancer, as well as the rapid growth of the world population (para 10).

Key expansions in the general comment include interpreting the right to health as an inclusive right extending not only to the availability of timely and appropriate health care, but also incorporating what it terms the underlying determinants of health, such as access to safe and potable water and adequate sanitation, an adequate supply of safe food, healthy occupational and environmental conditions, and access to health-related education and information, including on sexual and reproductive health (para 11). Significantly, the general comment updates the language and revises the conceptual underpinnings of Article 12 by emphasizing the need for a gender perspective and a comprehensive national strategy for eliminating discrimination against women (paras 20 and 21). In addition, the general comment emphasizes the participation of the population in all health-related decision-making at the community, national, and international levels (paras 37, 43.f, 54). The obligations of state parties to the ICESCR identified in the general comment are far more extensive than those listed in Article 12 and include the provision of maternal, child, and reproductive health services (para 14); the extension of the benefits of health services to all individuals; universal immunization against the principal infectious diseases; prevention, treatment, and control of endemic, occupational, and other diseases (paras 15 & 16); the provision of equal and timely access to basic preventive, curative, rehabilitative health services, and health education on the prevention and treatment of health problems (para 17). Additionally, the general comment addresses the special obligations of the state to provide for the satisfaction of the health needs of the most vulnerable and devotes separate paragraphs to several of these groups (paras 25–27 & 43a). GC 14 also has two other innovations: an extensive list of core obligations that are immediately realizable and not subject to the availability of resources (paras 43 and 44) and a section on violations with numerous potential examples (paras 46–52). There is also a more detailed itemization of international obligations (paras 38–42).

The Committee's expansion of the elements of the right seems warranted and a means to address the inadequacies of Article 12 of ICESCR and to update the interpretation. There have been many important developments in the understanding of health, health promotion, and health protection in the past half century. To mention but a few, social science research has underscored the importance of gender, social, economic, and racial factors in determining health needs and status. There is now far greater awareness than at the time the Covenant was drafted about the importance of incorporating a gender perspective. Research has shown that the health status of the individual and the community reflects a wide range of nonmedical determinants such as levels and models of development, the nature of the environment, education, income, social status, housing, and nutrition. Advances in epidemiological research have sensitized policymakers to the importance of public health interventions and preventive strategies of health promotion.

But some analysts have criticized the Committee's expansion of the conception of the right to health. And because general comments are "soft law," unlike the texts of human rights instruments, which establish binding obligations for the states that ratify them, some governments have rejected the extension of their obligations as specified in the general comment. John Tobin is among the critics of the expansion in the conception of the right to health because he does not believe the expanded interpretation has a basis either in the text of Article 12 or its drafting history. According to Tobin, "it is important to guard against an approach whereby the right to health is conceived of as a repository for everything that impacts upon the health of an individual" (2012, 132). He further claims that the inclusion of elements of other rights, such as provisions for access to food, clothing, and housing, which are components of the right to an adequate standard of living enumerated in the ICESCR, violates requirement of internal system coherence. Instead, he would have preferred recognition of the interdependence of the right to health with other rights (2012, 130), something that is mentioned in the text of the general comment (para 3). He has less concern with the expansive interpretation in the general comment on the health of the child adopted by the Committee on the Rights of the Child because the text of the Covenant on the Rights of the Child (1989) makes explicit reference to several underlying determinants of a child's health (Article 24) (Tobin 2012, 130).

I disagree with Tobin because I understand the role of a general comment differently than he does. He is an "originalist" believing it is necessary to hew closely to how the right to health was originally conceived more than a half century ago. I have a more dynamic and evolutionary view of human rights, and in particular of the right to health, as indicated by my characterization of it as an emergent human right. Moreover, as Tobin notes, within a few years of the ICESCR's adoption of new human rights instruments, such as the Convention on the Rights of the Child, the Convention on the Elimination of All Forms of Discrimination Against Women, and later the Convention on the Rights of Persons with Disabilities were adopted with novel or modified duties with respect to the right to health that were not envisioned in the drafting process for the ICESCR (2012, 59–60). New issues and responses to them have continued to arise since that time as well. Writing a general comment affords a human rights treaty monitoring body the opportunity – and I would add the obligation – to update and reinterpret a right to make it more consistent with contemporary understandings of the subject matter and requirements to fulfill the right. Given the limitations of Article 12, a right to health solely based on a narrow reading of its text would not have resulted in a meaningful right.

Foundations of the Right to Health

The foundations of and justification for the right to health have been a source of controversy. The Universal Declaration of Human Rights recognizes the inherent dignity and the equal and inalienable rights of all members of the human family (1948, Preamble) as the grounding for human rights, but it does not identify the manner in which human dignity translates into specific human rights. Similarly, the preamble of the International Covenant on Economic, Social and Cultural Rights (ICESCR) links the rights enumerated therein with human dignity: "Recognizing that these rights derive from the inherent dignity of the human person" (1966), but it does not indicate how or why health or any other of the rights in the Covenant arise from human dignity. General Comment 14 also fails to do so. Article 1 relates health to human dignity but in a manner that establishes human dignity more as a goal of the right. It states "every human being is entitled to the enjoyment of the highest attainable standard of health conducive to living a life in dignity" (CESCR 2000). The text does not go on to illuminate that statement or to explain how or why health is associated with human dignity or of special moral importance. Moreover, it is a tautology to identify human dignity both as the foundation and the objective of the right to health. The failure to provide a stronger conceptual foundation has disappointed some advocates of the right and been a source of criticism. It has also complicated efforts by some judiciaries to interpret the right to health (Yamin 2011, 358–359).

Although commitment to human dignity is a widely shared value, human dignity is elusive as to its precise meaning and requirements. The concept of human dignity is not clearly conceptualized in any of the international human rights instruments. For human rights theorists, human dignity refers to the intrinsic worth of all human beings and the obligation that all human beings be treated with appropriate respect, but work on human rights has not yet identified the contents of what doing so entails. Dignity's intrinsic meaning in human rights documents is often left to an intuitive understanding or an assumed shared understanding. However, societies, groups, and communities hold a diversity of worldviews, social and religious values, and cultural understandings that inform and shape their interpretations of human dignity. The same could be said of their approach to health and the links between human dignity and health "Beyond the narrowest questions of excruciating pain, though, in the realm of health, the conditions necessary for a life of dignity do not constitute an absolute and universal idea but rather are necessarily dependent on 'historical, cultural and even individual contexts'" (Yamin 2011 citing Bohrequez Monslave and Aguirre Roman 2009). Referencing human dignity without further explication implies a level of social or ethical consensus that simply does not exist (Caulfield and Chapman 2005; Chapman 2011).

A number of commentators on the right to health, primarily philosophers who are generally sympathetic to human rights, have raised issues about the formulation and interpretation of the right to health. Norman Daniels acknowledges that a rights-based approach has several great strengths: it establishes specific governmental accountabilities for promoting population health; it addresses a broad range of environmental, legal, cultural, and social determinants of health; it emphasizes the importance of setting specific goals and targets for achieving the rights that bear on health and also monitors and evaluates progress toward these goals; it insists on good governance; and it stresses the need for transparency and participation in efforts to secure the right (2008, 313–314). Nevertheless, he believes the absence of a proper philosophical foundation, the lack of a theory of justice, and the failure to address priority setting make the right to health less meaningful (2008, 314–315). Others have raised similar issues. Jennifer Ruger also discusses the problem of a lack of a systematic philosophical grounding for the right to health (2010, 119). According to Sridhar Venkatapuram, the grounding of human rights in legal instruments rather than in some general ethical theory leaves health rights unable to show how the idea of rights can be coherent in the context of limited resources (2011, 182–183). Upendra Baxi's concern relates to the lack of a proper theory of justice or justice language in the right to health and more generally in the UN human rights system (2010).

It might be possible to develop a more systematic philosophical foundation and greater theoretical rigor for the right to health. Jennifer Ruger, for example, envisions the possibility of using capability theory for this purpose (2010). But how important is it to do so or to have a more rigorous philosophical conception of the right to health for it to be meaningful and effective as a human right? John Tobin, who comes from a legal rather than philosophical background, rejects the need for a comprehensive theory to ground the right to health. Using a term first coined by Cass Sunstein, he characterizes the international legal instruments which recognize the right to health as examples of "incompletely theorized agreements." The concept of incompletely theorized agreements describes a process by which a consensus is reached on an issue in circumstances where there is not agreement on the reasons or principles that justify the agreement (Tobin 2012, 49).

According to Tobin, the concept of incompletely theorized agreements is well-suited to capture the nature of international human rights instruments, which "must accommodate 'a moral universe that is diverse and pluralistic,' and allow for agreement between states without the need to adhere to a particular theory of general principles" (Tobin 2012, 49). He understands this process as enabling states to agree on the inclusion of the right to health and other rights within international treaties as a moral interest worthy of recognition without formal agreement on the principles or theory underlying the right. However, he acknowledges that these same differences among states have militated against the prospect of achieving detailed agreement as to the specific measures required for implementation of the right to health (Tobin 2012, 49–50).

Formulation of the Right

The formulation or wording of a right is fundamental to understanding its requirements. So what can be said about the "right of everyone to the enjoyment of the highest attainable standard of physical and mental health?" Notably, drafters of the ICESCR's provision on the right to health chose not to adopt the broad and encompassing World Health Organization (WHO) definition of health. The preamble to the WHO Constitution conceptualizes health as "a state of complete physical, mental and social well-being and not merely the absence of disease or infirmity" (World Health Organization 1958, 11). Some critics argue that the WHO approach mistakenly implies that good health is an end rather than a limited means to a fruitful and meaningful life (Boyle 1977; Callahan 1990). As such, it is a problematic grounding for a human right because it would entail a duty to guarantee complete physical, mental, and social well-being for all of its citizens. This is simply an impossible goal. GC 14 follows the more limited phrasing in the ICESCR, but the CRC's general comment on the right of the child to the enjoyment of the highest attainable standard of health appears to favor the WHO definition of health (CRC 2013, para 4).

While the "highest attainable standard of health" is more delimited than a "state of complete physical, mental, and social well-being," it still leaves many questions unanswered. First, like the other rights recognized in the ICESCR, the subject of the right, health, is never conceptualized or defined. Second, to whose health does it refer? Is it the highest attainable standard of an individual or a community standard; and if the latter, is it an average across a group or national community or a basic minimum applicable to the entire population? The general comment states that "the notion of the highest attainable standard takes into account both the indi-vidual's biological and socioeconomic preconditions and a State's available resources" (para 9), which implies that it differs for each person in a soci-ety as well as across societies. While that is an accurate statement, it hardly offers a manageable norm. Third, who determines the content and scope of the "highest attainable standard of health"? Conceptions of health in a particular society reflect cultural, social, political, and economic circum-stances, and perceptions of what is normal or habitual. The emergence of a women's health movement during the past forty years, which identified deep-rooted and multifaceted gender inequality in access to health ser-vices and thereby changed expectations of women's health needs, offers but one example. Moreover, groups within a society may differ signifi-cantly on their expectations for health. Fourth, how is the "highest attain-able level of health" to be evaluated and measured? This constitutes a very complicated undertaking, especially if monitoring is conducted on a disaggregated basis so as to be able to determine the status of vulnerable groups as a human rights approach requires. And if realizing the highest attainable level is resource dependent, as Article 2.1 of the ICESCR indi-cates it is, how should the pool of available resources be determined? These issues are not clarified in General Comment No. 14 or elsewhere by the Committee or other human rights bodies.

Although the right to health is sometimes interpreted as a right to health care, clearly the conceptualization in Article 12 and GC 14 is broader. Article 12 represents a hybrid incorporating the approaches to health offered by the disciplines of medicine and public health. Medicine focuses primarily on the health status of the individual, generally in the context of physical, and to a lesser extent mental, illness and disability. In contrast, public health is concerned with protecting the health of popu-lations and ensuring the conditions in which people can be healthy, and most public health improvements require collective efforts (Dawson 2011, 33). The two paradigms of medicine and public health give rise to concep-tions of health and related rights that in the case of the former tends to emphasize access to health care and for the latter on health protection, the social determinants of health, and preventive health services. Article 12 integrates both approaches, but the phrasing of the text does not clearly articulate the hybrid nature of the right, nor how the two very different approaches are to be integrated. Neither does General Comment No. 14 call sufficient attention to the public health dimensions of the right.

While the general comment does not offer a definition of health, it does state that the right to health is not to be understood as a right to be healthy (para 8), which of course no state can ensure, but as a right to a variety of facilities, goods, services, and conditions necessary for the realization of the highest attainable standard of health (para 9). According to its text, the right to health contains both freedoms and entitlements. The freedoms it identifies are the right to control one's health and body, including sexual and reproductive freedom, and the right to be free from interference such as from torture, nonconsensual medical treatment, and experimentation. The entitlements initially listed relate to the right to a system of health protection, which provides equality of opportunity for people to enjoy the highest attainable level of health (para 8).

As mentioned, one of the most important innovations in the general comment is the interpretation of the right to health as an inclusive right incorporating the underlying determinants of health as well as access to a variety of facilities, goods, services, and conditions necessary for its realization. The underlying determinants that are identified are access to safe and potable water and adequate sanitation, an adequate supply of safe food, healthy occupational and environmental conditions, and access to health-related education and information, including on sexual and reproductive health (para 11). However, the general comment is unspecific as to the precise requirements for any of these underlying determinants. For example, how much water and at what cost, if any, should the entitlement to safe and potable water entail; how should adequate sanitation be understood; what constitutes an adequate supply of safe food, and adequate housing? Underscoring the importance of the underlying determinants, the general comment also includes the provision of many of them in its list of core obligations that are not subject to the availability of resources (paras 43 and 44). The Committee's expanded conception of the right to health hearkens back to the 1978 Alma-Ata conference (Alma-Ata Declaration 1978). Chapter Seven will have a more extended discussion of the underlying determinants and the importance of the social determinants of health to a rights-based approach.

Progressive Realization and the Availability of Resources

Article 12, as well as GC 14, needs to be interpreted in the context of Article 2.1 of the ICESCR. This article articulates what is sometimes referred to as the progressive realization principle. It specifies that each state party, which are the countries that have ratified or acceded to the Covenant, "take steps, individually and through international assistance and cooperation, especially economic and technical, to the maximum of available resources" (1966). By doing so the text qualifies the fundamental obligation to implement the rights enumerated in the instrument making it conditional on the availability of resources. This wording is very different than the framework of the International Covenant on Civil and Political Rights, which has no similar provision. On the other, it expands the pool of potential resources by including various forms of international assistance. The progressive realization clause, which the Covenant and other human rights instruments with economic and social rights provisions also incorporate, reflects acceptance of the reality that full and immediate realization of enumerated economic and social rights, including the right to health, will generally not be achievable in a short period of time, particularly in poor countries. That these countries will also need to progressively implement civil and political rights is an issue that has not been adequately addressed.

The progressive realization benchmark implies that valid expectations and concomitant obligations of state parties are not uniform or universal, but instead they are relative to levels of development and available resources. The dilemma is how to assess what the phrases "to take steps" and "to the maximum of its available resources" entail in specific circumstances. No human rights body has framed a methodology to do so. Evaluation of the implementation of the progressive realization norm also requires guidelines, as yet not formulated, to assess whether states are moving expeditiously and effectively toward the goal of the full realization of specific rights as well as specificity about the allotted time period for doing so.

Under international law, primary responsibility for implementing human rights rests primarily with national governments, who are responsible to their own citizens and residents. However, the obligation to offer "international assistance and co-operation" noted in Article 2.1 extends duties beyond a state's own borders. By doing so it indicates that states, particularly those with greater financial and technical resources, have human rights responsibilities to other countries. The formulation of Article 2.1 also underscores the importance of international financial aid and technical assistance as a component of the total pool of resources available to poor states for implementing the rights in the Covenant.

Although the general comment acknowledges the constraints imposed on the realization of the right to health by the limits of available resources, it emphasizes that progressive realization over a period of time should not be interpreted as depriving state parties' obligations of all meaningful content (para 31). It also notes the obligation of state parties to take

steps that are "deliberate, concrete, and targeted towards the full realization of the right" (para 30) so as "to move as expeditiously and effectively
as possible towards the full realization of Article 12" (para 31). However,
the general comment does not specify what those steps should be. Nor
does it indicate how progress is to be evaluated. Importantly, the general
comment also reminds state parties that there is a strong presumption
that retrogressive measures taken in relation to the right to health are not
permissible (para 32).

In 2007, anticipating an optional protocol to ICESCR coming into force
that would permit the Committee to receive and consider communications alleging violations of economic, social, and cultural rights from individuals and groups, the Committee adopted a statement clarifying how it
would evaluate the obligation "to take steps to the maximum of available
resources." The statement reiterates that the availability of resources does
not alter the immediacy of an obligation, nor can resource constraints
alone justify inaction. According to CESCR, when confronted with inadequate resources, a state party still has an obligation to ensure the widest possible enjoyment of economic, social, and cultural rights possible.
Moreover, it must protect the most disadvantaged and marginalized members or groups by adopting relatively low-cost targeted programs (CESCR
2007, para 4).

The statement indicates that in considering a communication concerning an alleged failure of a state party to take steps to the maximum of available resources, the Committee would examine the following:

(a) the extent to which the measures taken were deliberate, concrete,
     and targeted toward the fulfillment of economic, social, and cultural
     rights;
(b) whether the state party exercised its discretion in a nondiscrimina-
     tory and nonarbitrary manner;
(c) whether the state party's decision (not) to allocate available resources
     is in accordance with international human rights standards;
(d) where several policy options are available, whether the state party
     adopts the option that least restricts Covenant rights;
(e) the time frame in which the steps were taken;
(f) whether the states had taken into account the precarious situation of
     disadvantaged and marginalized individuals or groups, whether they
     were nondiscriminatory, and whether they prioritized grave situa-
     tions or situations or risk (CESCR 2007, para 8).

The statement also notes that in judging whether a state party has taken reasonable steps to the maximum of its available resources to achieve progressively the realization of the provisions of the Covenant, the Committee would place great importance on whether there was transparent and participative decision-making processes at the national level (CESCR 2007, para 11).

The text goes on to say that in the event a state party uses resource constraints as an explanation for any retrogressive steps taken, the Committee would evaluate the situation using such objective criteria as:

(a) the country's level of development;
(b) the severity of the alleged breach, in particular whether the situation concerned the enjoyment of the minimum core content of the Covenant;
(c) the country's current economic situation, in particular whether the country was undergoing a period of economic recession;
(d) the existence of other serious claims on the State party's limited resources; for example, resulting from a recent natural disaster or from recent internal or international armed conflict;
(e) whether the State party had sought to identify low-cost options; and
(f) whether the State party had sought cooperation and assistance or rejected offers of resources from the international community for the purposes of implementing the provisions of the Covenant without sufficient reason (CESCR 2007, para 10).

So how far does this statement go in making the standard to take steps to the maximum of available resources sufficiently specific and meaningful so as to illumine obligations and enable the state, nongovernmental organizations, and UN bodies to monitor performance? Certainly it offers a beginning, but that is about all. The criteria focus primarily on the process followed and not on the action taken. The Committee still has not offered parameters to compute the pool of available resources either for health or for all economic, social, and cultural rights. Neither has the Committee or any other international human rights body specified the range of resources countries should be expected to invest in health expressed either as a percentage of the overall budget or as a per capita figure. Nor has the Committee offered a benchmark of the approximate level of improvement in fulfilling any of its obligations any state should be expected to achieve in four or five years at its next reporting cycle. At best the criteria seem to offer more of a way to judge intent rather than performance.

Obligations

The norms identified in international human rights law give rise to obligations to implement specific requirements through the adoption of appropriate laws and policies. These requirements entail both negative obligations for the state to refrain from certain behavior and positive obligations to undertake measures to provide for the realization of specific human rights. The ICESCR considers legislative measures as being particularly appropriate for giving effect to economic, social, and cultural rights (Grover 2009, para 27). Recommended legislative initiatives to accomplish goals are mentioned in several paragraphs of GC 14 (CESCR 2000, paras 35, 36, 56). There are also procedural requirements prescribed by international human rights standards including respecting due process in decision making, establishing mechanisms for participation of the relevant stakeholders, ensuring access to information and transparency, instituting accountability mechanisms, and providing remedies for violations (Grover 2009, para 33).

Like other human rights, the right to health imposes three types or levels of obligations on state parties: to respect, protect, and fulfill components of the right. According to General Comment 14, the obligation to respect requires state parties to refrain from interfering directly or indirectly with a guaranteed right. To put it another way, states are under an obligation to refrain from interfering with the enjoyment of the right to health by denying or limiting access to services or facilities, blocking equal treatment for all people, or enforcing discriminatory practices. For example, a government is required to respect the right to health by abstaining from enforcing discriminatory practices that would deny or limit equal access for all persons to curative and palliative health services, including prisoners or detainees, minorities, asylum seekers, and illegal immigrants. Additional obligations to respect include desisting from limiting access to contraceptives and other means of maintaining sexual and reproductive health, from censoring, withholding or intentionally misrepresenting health information, and from preventing people's participation in health-related matters. GC 14 also directs states to refrain from unlawfully polluting air, water, and soil, as for example, through industrial water from state-owned facilities, and from limiting access to health services as a punitive measure (para 34).

The duty to protect is the state's obligation not to allow other entities to deprive its people of a guaranteed right. For example, a government has a responsibility to prevent other actors within its jurisdiction, including corporations, from infringing the right to health, as for example by failing to enforce laws to prevent the pollution of water, air, and soil by extractive and manufacturing industries. According to GC 14, the obligation to protect requires the state to adopt legislation or to take other measures ensuring equal access to health care and health-related services provided by third parties; to ensure that privatization of the health sector does not constitute a threat to the availability, accessibility, acceptability, and quality of health facilities, goods, and services; to control the marketing of medical equipment and medicines by third parties; and to ensure that medical professionals meet appropriate standards of education and ethical codes of practice. These latter requirements are particularly important in an era in which the provision of health services is increasingly privatized in many states. Additionally, states are obliged to ensure that harmful social or traditional practices do not interfere with access to pre and postnatal care and family planning and to prevent third parties from coercing women to undergo traditional practices, such as female genital mutilation (para 35).

The duty to fulfill requires the state to work actively to implement the requirements of a right and to that end to establish laws, institutions, and policies, make the necessary investments, and adopt a national health policy with a detailed plan for realizing the right to health. One example given in the general comment is the need to establish an appropriate infrastructure providing widespread access to health services (para 36). Other obligations to fulfill identified in the general comment include the provision of maternal, child, and reproductive health services (para 14); the improvement of all aspects of environmental and industrial hygiene through the prevention and reduction of the population's exposure to harmful substances and the assurance of hygienic working conditions (para 15); the extension of the benefits of health services to all individuals; universal immunization against the principal infectious diseases; prevention, treatment, and control of endemic, occupational, and other diseases (paras 15 & 16); the provision of equal and timely access to basic preventive, curative, and rehabilitative health services; and health education on the prevention and treatment of health problems (para 17).

Health of Women and Reproductive Health

An appropriate conceptualization of the right to health requires updating the language and compensating for the lack of attention to the health of women and to sexual and reproductive health in Article 12. Like many other documents written before the women's movement rose to prominence, the ICESCR purports to be gender neutral but is prone to generating universal standards from a male perspective and ignoring differences between women and men. Drafters of the Covenant, mostly men, failed to take women's health needs into account in very fundamental ways. Article 12 does not refer to women's health or mention sexual or reproductive health. Given that sexual and reproductive ill health gives rise to nearly 20 percent of the global burden of ill health for women and 14 percent for men (Hunt 2004: para 11), this is an important omission. Although one of the four steps Article 12.2 specifies reducing the stillbirth rate (International Covenant on Economic, Social and Cultural Rights 1966, 12.2 (a)), it does not link efforts to do so with providing better health services for women before or during pregnancy. Article 12 is conspicuously silent about lowering maternal morbidity and mortality, estimated worldwide to be 526,300 in 2000 and about 343,000 in 2008 (Hogan et al. 2010).

CEDAW, adopted in 1989, has several provisions dealing with health obligations. Its Article 12.1 directs that "States Parties shall take all appropriate measures to eliminate discrimination against women in the field to health care in order to ensure, on a basis of equality of men and women, access to health care services, including those related to family planning." It goes on to mandate that state parties ensure women have appropriate services in connection with pregnancy, confinement, and the postnatal period, granting free services when necessary (Convention to Eliminate All Forms of Discrimination Against Women 1979, 12.2).

Two landmark international conferences further expanded the understanding of reproductive rights. Agreements formulated at these meetings, however, do not have the status of binding international law. The Programme of Action of the 1994 International Conference on Population and Development in Cairo calls for a wide range of measures to promote the empowerment and autonomy of women. This document explicitly recognizes women's reproductive rights and, to that end, mandates provision of comprehensive and factual information and a full range of reproductive health care services, including family planning, that are accessible, affordable, acceptable, and convenient to all users (Programme of Action 1994, chapters IV and VII). One of its fundamental principles is worded as follows:

> Everyone has the right to the enjoyment of the highest attainable standard of physical and mental health. States should take all appropriate measures to ensure on a basis of equality of men and women, universal health care services, including those related to reproductive health care, which includes family planning and sexual health. Reproductive health-care programmes should provide the widest range of services without any form of

coercion. All couples and individuals have the basic right to decide freely and responsibly the number and spacing of their children and to have the information, education and means to do so (Programme of Action 1994, chapter II, Principle 8).

The Fourth World Conference on Women, held in Beijing in 1995, also emphasized "women's right to the enjoyment of the highest standard of health must be secured through the whole life cycle in equality with men" and noted that women are affected by many of the same health conditions as men, but experience them differently (Report of the Fourth World Conference on Women 1995, para 92). Building on the WHO formulation of health, it defines reproductive health as "a State of complete physical, mental and social well-being and not merely the absence of disease or infirmity, in all matters related to the reproductive system and its function and process" (Report of the Fourth World Conference on Women 1995, para 94). It notes that reproductive health implies that people are able to have a satisfying and safe sex life and to do so both women and men have the right to have access to safe, effective, affordable, and acceptable methods of family planning of their choice to regulate their fertility which are not against the law and for women to have appropriate health care services that will enable them to go safely through pregnancy and childbirth (Report of the Fourth World Conference on Women 1995, para 94).

CEDAW's 1999 General Recommendation: Women and Health covers many of these same concerns as well as addressing other issues. For example, it affirms that access to health care, including reproductive health, is a basic right (para 1). It mentions biological factors that differ for women in comparison with men (para 12a) but reminds states there are also societal factors that are determinative of the differing health status of women and men (para 5). It states that measures to eliminate discrimination require a health care system to have services to prevent, detect, and treat illnesses specific to women (para 11). It directs state parties to implement a comprehensive national strategy to promote women's health throughout their lifespan aimed at both prevention and treatment of diseases and conditions affecting women, as well as responding to violence against women (para 29). To enable CEDAW to evaluate whether measures to eliminate discrimination against women in the field of health care are appropriate, it asks state parties to report with reliable data disaggregated by sex on the incidence and severity of diseases and conditions hazardous to women's health and nutrition and on the availability and cost effectiveness of preventive and curative measures (para 9).

GC 14 builds on these developments. Reproductive rights are mentioned at several points, including as one of the obligations of comparable priority linked to core obligations (CESCR 2000, para 44 (a)). Like CEDAW's general recommendation, the text of the CESCR's general comment emphasizes the need for a gender perspective in health-related policies, planning, programs, and research that recognizes the important role of both biological and sociocultural factors in influencing the health of women and men (2000, par 21). Further, it identifies the need for disaggregating health and socioeconomic data according to sex in order to identify and remedy inequalities in health (para 20). The general comment also calls for the development of a comprehensive national strategy for eliminating discrimination against women that incorporates interventions aimed at the prevention and treatment of diseases affecting women, as well as policies to provide access to a full range of affordable and high quality health care, including sexual and reproductive health. According to the text, a major goal should be reducing women's health risks, particularly lowering rates of maternal mortality and protecting women from domestic violence. It also notes the importance of removing the barriers interfering with women's access to health services, education, and information, including with regard to sexual and reproductive health. In addition, it mentions the need to shield women from the impact of harmful traditional cultural practices and norms that deny them their full reproductive rights (paras 20 & 21).

To address the full range of women's reproductive rights, it is also necessary to deal with the issue of abortion, something the international human rights community has been reluctant to do. Combatting the scourge of unsafe abortions is part of the challenge of achieving the right to universal reproductive health care. Unsafe abortions kill some 68,000 women each year making it a right to life and right to health issue of major proportions (Hunt 2004, para 30). Paul Hunt proposes that women with unwanted pregnancies should at least be offered reliable information and compassionate counseling, including information on where and when pregnancies may be terminated legally. He advocates that where abortions are legal, they must be safe. He also states that in all cases women should have access to quality services for the management of complications arising from abortions. Additionally, he recommends that punitive provisions be removed against women who undergo abortions (2004, para 30).

The Protocol to the African Charter on Human and Peoples' Rights on the Rights of Women (2003), which was primarily drafted as a civil society initiative, includes a groundbreaking provision addressing the need to make abortion legal. Article 14.2 (c) of the Protocol provides that states parties shall take all appropriate measure to "protect the reproductive rights of women by authorizing medical abortion in cases of sexual assault, rape, incest, and where continued pregnancy endangers the mental and physical health of the mother or the life of the mother or the foetus." While an important step forward, the Protocol has not succeeded in promoting country and municipal-level initiatives to translate a legal right into meaningful access to services. Also, to date, the inscription of abortion as a legal right has done little to promote and protect women's reproductive agency (Ngwena 2010, 864).

Right to Health of Vulnerable Communities

One of the hallmarks of a human rights approach is a commitment to protecting the rights of vulnerable and disadvantaged individuals and groups. Recognition of the need to protect the rights and interests of the vulnerable and disadvantaged has been a recurrent theme in the work of the CESCR and finds expression in GC 14. Many of the general comments the Committee has adopted to interpret provisions of the ICESCR and statements it has issued identify the vulnerability of specific disadvantaged groups in relation to the topic being addressed and call for action to protect and promote their rights. In addition, the Committee's review of state parties' performance frequently raises questions about the adequacy of protections for these groups (Chapman and Carbonetti 2011). In General Comment 5, on persons with disabilities, the CESCR states that governments must take positive action to ensure that structural disadvantages are eliminated and appropriate preferential treatment is given to people with disabilities in order to achieve the objective of full participation and equal standing in society (CESCR 1994, para 9). Presumably this principle would apply to other vulnerable groups as well. Similarly, the Committee's general comment on nondiscrimination explains that eliminating substantive discrimination may require the state party to adopt special measure to attenuate or suppress conditions that perpetuate discrimination. According to the Committee, such measures are legitimate as long as they represent reasonable, objective, and proportional means to redress de facto discrimination and are discontinued if and when substantive equality has been achieved (2009, paras 8–9).

GC 14 identifies the special obligations of the state to provide for the satisfaction of the health needs of those individuals and groups whose poverty, disabilities, or background make them vulnerable. Following the identification of a set of obligations relating to the health of women, there are paragraphs addressing duties to children and adolescents (para 22), older persons (para 25), persons with disabilities (para 26), and indigenous peoples (para 27). The Committee observes that several of these groups have the right to specific measures to improve their access to health services and care. However, except in the case of health services for women and indigenous people, none of these sections sets out what kinds of measures should be adopted. The general comment also reiterates that even in times of severe resource constraints vulnerable members of society must be protected by the adoption of low-cost targeted programs (para 18).

Paul Hunt's reports as Special Rapporteur address a series of issues related to vulnerable communities. His 2004 report discusses the profound disparities between the health of indigenous and nonindigenous populations (para 55), and calls for urgent and concerted efforts at local, national, and international levels toward reversing these trends (para 56). He also identifies some of the requirements to begin to do so (para 58). Hunt's 2005 report includes a section on the much neglected topic of mental disability issues covering intellectual disability, consent to treatment, and the right to community integration (paras 76–90). He points out that persons with all sorts of mental disabilities, intellectual or psychiatric, are vulnerable to human rights abuses because of their varying ability to protect their own interests without assistance (para 79). Also persons, in particular children, with intellectual disabilities are vulnerable to a range of health complications associated with their conditions (para 80). Adding to the body of work on right to health issues of vulnerable and special needs groups, Anand Grover, the second special rapporteur on the right to health, wrote a thematic study on the realization of the right to health of older persons (Grover 2011).

The 2006 Convention on the Rights of Persons with Disabilities explicitly recognizes the right of members of this community to enjoy the highest attainable standard of health without discrimination on the basis of their disabilities (art. 19). Its provisions include the need of states to provide persons with disabilities with the same range, quality, and standard of free or affordable health care as provided for other persons (art. 19 a) and for them to provide health services specifically needed by persons with disabilities because of their conditions (art. 19 b). It also prohibits discrimination against persons with disabilities in the issuance of health insurance (art. 19 3).

Evaluative Criteria

The criteria that General Comment 14 articulates to evaluate whether obligations related to the right to health are being realized constitutes one of its most helpful and widely cited contributions. It sets forth four criteria: availability, accessibility, acceptability, and quality (para 12). Availability refers to the extent to which the facilities, goods, and services required for the fulfillment of a specific right are available in sufficient quantity for the population within the state. Accessibility has four dimensions: (1) non-discrimination, whether the facilities, goods, and services are accessible to all without discrimination on any of the prohibited grounds; (2) physical accessibility, the extent to which the facilities, goods, and services are within safe physical reach for all sections of the population, especially vulnerable and marginalized groups; (3) economic accessibility, whether the goods, services, and facilities related to the rights are affordable for all, including socially disadvantaged groups; and (4) information accessibility, whether the population has the right to seek, receive, and impart information relevant to the right. Acceptability is a measure of whether the facilities, good, and services are culturally appropriate and respectful of ethical standards. Quality entails whether the facilities, goods, and services are scientifically appropriate and of good quality.

However, neither the general comment nor subsequent work by the CESCR has operationalized the application of these criteria. This failure complicates applying the criteria to evaluate specific health systems and the impact of particular policies.

Nondiscrimination and Equal Treatment

Like other human rights, one important dimension of the right to health is conforming to the standard of nondiscrimination. The prohibition against discrimination is an obligation of immediate effect, that is, not subject to progressive realization. Nondiscrimination imposes both negative and positive obligations on states. The negative duty requires that states not engage in discrimination, that is, make de jure or de facto distinctions that have the intention or the effect of restricting rights to health on the basis of the forbidden grounds (i.e., race, sex, ethnicity, color, language, religion, national or social origin, political opinion, property, or other status) outlined in international human rights law. Conversely, the positive duty obliges states to eradicate existing discriminatory laws and practices (Grover 2009, para 18).

GC 14 observes that the Covenant proscribes any discrimination in access to health care and underlying determinants of health on all of the grounds identified in the Covenant and others added subsequently – race, color, sex, language, religion, political or other opinion, national or social origin, property, birth, physical or mental disability, health status (including HIV/AIDS), sexual orientation, and civil, political, social, or other status, because doing so would nullify or impair the equal enjoyment of the right to health (para 18) and equal treatment. The general comment also notes that many measures designed to eliminate health-related discrimination can be pursued with minimum resource implications through legislation or the dissemination of information.

The discussion of equality of access to health care and health services in GC 14 articulates the responsibility of states to provide for those who do not have sufficient means through offering them health insurance and health care facilities (para 19). GC 14 also observes that inappropriate health resource allocation can lead to discrimination that may not be overt and provides the example of states' disproportionate investments in curative health services that are often accessible only to a small, privileged fraction of the population (para 19). Unfortunately the disproportionate investment in expensive tertiary care rather than primary and preventive health care characterizes many countries across varying levels of development.

Core Obligations

To compensate for the limitations of the progressive realization standard, GC 14 stipulates that state parties have an immediate obligation to fulfill some obligations, one of which is to ensure nondiscrimination and another to satisfy a "minimum core content" of each economic, social, and cultural right (Committee on Economic, Social and Cultural Rights 1990, para 10). The minimum core content has been identified with the nature or essence of a right, that is, the essential elements without which it loses its substantive significance as a human right. It has also been described as a "floor" below which conditions should not be permitted to fall. Many human rights activists have reservations about an emphasis on core obligations because of the risk that the "floor" will become a "ceiling." The concern is that the identification of a minimum core content will reveal to state parties how little they have to do in order to be in compliance with their obligations, and that states will choose to do that minimum and nothing more (Chapman and Russell 2002, Introduction). It is worth noting, however, that if states actually did fulfill their core obligations, it would often represent significant progress.

In 1990, when the Committee first dealt with the concept of a minimum core obligation in General Comment No. 3 it emphasized the connection between the minimum core obligation and the minimum essential levels of a right. It also put forward a quite delimited and modest sense of what the minimum core obligations would be. According to that text, "The Committee is of the view that a minimum core obligations to ensure the satisfaction of, at the very least, the minimum essential levels of each of the rights is incumbent upon every State party. Thus, for example, a State party in which any significant number of individuals is deprived of basic foodstuffs, essential primary health care, basic shelter and housing, or the most basic forms of education is, prima facie, failing to discharge its obligations under the Covenant" (CESCR 1990, para 10).

One implication of the minimum state obligations approach outlined in General Comment No. 3 is that all states, regardless of the resources available, are required to fulfill these obligations. In the general comment, the Committee affirms that even in highly straitened circumstances a state has irreducible obligations that it is assumed to be able to meet. However, the general comment also acknowledges that any assessment as to whether a state has discharged its minimum core obligation must take its resource constraints into account (CESCR 1990, para 10). The Committee tries to paper over this seeming inconsistency with the observation that a state may still claim that it cannot meet even those most minimum obligations. If it does, however, the burden of proof will shift to the state to justify its claim. It also emphasizes that even where the available resources are demonstrably inadequate, the state party still must strive to ensure the widest enjoyment of the rights feasible under the circumstances and must seek to protect vulnerable members of society by the adoption of relatively low-cost targeted programs (CESCR 1990, paras 10 and 11).

General Comment No. 3 does not provide a methodology for determining minimum state obligations. Its guidance is limited to providing a handful of examples, one of which is primary health care, which is also the only health-related core obligation mentioned. As the Committee has drafted general comments on individual rights in the Covenant, it has identified the minimum core content of a number of these. In doing so, it has expanded the obligations qualifying as minimum or core state obligations.

The section on core obligations in General Comment No. 14 has an expansive list that goes considerably beyond the example of essential primary health care given in General Comment No. 3. Ironically, primary health care, which many analysts would likely identify as a central right to a health care obligation, is not listed in GC 14 despite being cited in General Comment No. 3 and the Alma-Ata Declaration (1978). A note at the end of GC 14 claims that forms of primary, secondary, and tertiary health care frequently overlap and often interact making it difficult to identify criteria for assessing which levels of health care states must provide in relation to the normative understanding of Article 12 (CESCR 2000, endnote 9). While it is correct that the term primary care can encompass different health service requirements, some narrow and others, as in the Alma-Ata Declaration, much broader, the Committee could have defined the requirements it had in mind. Other human rights bodies have highlighted the importance of primary care. Article 24 of the Convention on the Rights of the Child (1989) specifies that state parties provide necessary medical assistance and health care to all children with an emphasis on the development of primary health care (1989, Article 24.2 (b)). Similarly, the CRC's general comment on the child's enjoyment of the highest attainable standard of health directs states to prioritize universal access for children to primary health-care services provided as close as possible to where children and their families live (CRC 2013, para 36).

Instead, General Comment 14 offers an extensive list of other core obligations related to the right to health. Furthermore, in contrast with General Comment No. 3's willingness to acknowledge the potential impact of resource constraints, GC 14 insists that "a state party cannot, under any circumstances whatsoever, justify its non-compliance with the core obligations ... which are non-derogable" (CESCR 2000, para 47). The core obligations identified include the following:

(1) ensure the right of access to health facilities, goods and services on a nondiscriminatory basis, especially for vulnerable or marginalized groups;
(2) ensure for everyone access to the minimum essential food which is sufficient, nutritionally adequate and safe, to ensure their freedom from hunger;
(3) ensure access to basic shelter, housing and sanitation, and an adequate supply of safe and potable water;
(4) provide essential drugs as defined by the World Health Organization's Program on Essential Drugs;

(5) ensure equitable distribution of all health facilities, goods, and services;

(6) adopt and implement a national public health strategy and plan of action, on the basis of epidemiological evidence, addressing the health concerns of the whole population and giving special attention to vulnerable or marginalized groups, that is devised, and periodically reviewed, on the basis of a participatory and transparent process with mechanisms, such as indicators and benchmarks, by which progress can be closely monitored (para 43).

In addition to this list, the next paragraph of the general comment identifies another set of "obligations of comparable priority." Although the general comment is not clear as to the meaning of this label, having observed the drafting process, it is my impression that the Committee meant for this second list to have the same status and requirements as the preceding paragraph. The following is the list of the obligation of comparable priority:

(1) to ensure reproductive, maternal (prenatal and postnatal), and child health care;

(2) to provide immunization against the community's major infectious diseases;

(3) to take measures to prevent, treat, and control epidemic and endemic diseases;

(4) to provide education and access to information concerning the main health problems in the community, including methods of preventing and controlling them;

(5) to provide appropriate training for health personnel, including education on health and human rights (para 44).

Taken together the lists of core obligations and obligation of comparable priority impose quite a comprehensive mandate of obligations to fulfill and would require a level of investment of resources well beyond the capacity of poor countries and even many middle-income countries to provide. The general comment calls on other countries to provide international assistance to enable developing countries to fulfill their core as well as other right to health obligations, but the core obligations defined in the general comment would require a level of ongoing assistance to a large number of countries, which is unrealistic. Implementing these core obligations would also necessitate having an activist, committed government, with a carefully honed set of public policies related to the right to health, a capacity to implement a wide-ranging set of health services, and an ability and willingness to invest substantial levels of resources. Many governments in the current neoliberal era would be adverse to these requirements. Some of the core obligations, for example, to adopt and implement a national public health strategy and plan of action through a participatory process, are primarily matters of policy, but even the formulation of such a national plan would require detailed epidemiological evidence on a disaggregated basis that many countries are likely to lack. Other dimensions of core obligations would be even more complex and expensive to implement, especially given the mandate to cover the entire population so as to ensure equitable distribution of all health facilities, goods, and services (43e); to provide essential drugs (34d); to ensure access to basic shelter, housing and sanitation, and an adequate supply of safe and potable water (43c); to provide immunization against the major infectious diseases occurring in the community (44b); and to take measure to prevent, treat, and control epidemic and endemic diseases (44c).

One reason that the Committee may have erred on the side of developing an expansive list of core minimum obligations was the confusion of the drafting group between two approaches: the minimum core content of the right and minimum state obligations. Minimum core content, which identifies the essential elements of a right, is primarily a conceptual notion. It does not necessarily presume that all dimensions of the minimum core content will be translated into immediate obligations. As I discovered in a project in which a group of international human rights experts identified what they believed the minimum core content should be of the right they focused on, experts are likely to offer a quite expansive conception, too expansive to translate into a reasonable set of obligations that all states should be expected to implement regardless of available resources (Chapman and Russell 2002). In contrast, minimum core state obligations refer to what a state must do immediately to be in compliance with a right. I believe that the drafters of the Covenant erred by translating a broadly framed minimum core content into core obligations.

Understandably several interpreters have been critical of the Committee's expansive view of minimum core obligations. As John Tobin comments, "the vision of the minimum core obligations of states under the right to health, as advanced by the ESC Committee, is disassociated from the capacity of states to realize this vision. It simply does not offer a principled, practical, or coherent rationale which is sufficiently sensitive to the context in which the right to health must be operationalized" (2012, 240). Lisa Forman, who is more sympathetic to the concept of core obligations, observes "The suggestion that a country where many lack adequate healthcare, running water, food or shelter is a prima facie violator of social rights sounds like nothing more than an admonishment to the country not to be poor" (2010, 68). Other interpreters have questioned the extent to which the list meets the actual health needs of all countries and warrants prioritization in all contexts (Pillay 2002, 61, 66–68).

Despite the limitations noted above, the concept of minimum core obligations can potentially make an important contribution. To do so, however, the criteria used to determine the selection of the core obligations would need to be made clearer and be based on principles that could be widely affirmed. The list would also need to be pared down to a more narrowly framed set of priorities that were practicable and warranted prioritization across different types of national contexts.

Collective Dimensions of the Right to Health

With the exception of a few rights, such as the rights to self-determination, development, peace, and a clean environment, human rights have traditionally been regarded as individual rights. It is therefore not surprising that many human rights theorists and advocates contend that only individuals can be rights holders. Jack Donnelly's claim that economic, social, and cultural rights, as well as civil and political rights, are the rights of individuals and only of individuals is typical of this line of interpretation. "If human rights are the rights that one has simply as a human being, then only human beings have human rights: if one is not a human being, then by definition one can not have a human right" (Donnelly 1989, 20). Donnelly acknowledges that individual persons may hold human rights both as separate individuals and as members of a community, as in the case of cultural rights, but he also maintains that such rights are held by individual members of the group and are not rights of groups as groups (Donnelly 1989, 19–31, 143–160). Like other human rights, the right to health is frequently portrayed solely or primarily as an individual right.

However, the Universal Declaration of Human Rights tempered the individualism characteristic of classical theories of natural rights. It conceives of persons as members of families and communities and not as isolated individuals who must be given incentives for entering into civil society (Nickel 1987, 9). Significantly, the phrasing of Article 22, an umbrella article that introduces the social and economic rights enumerated in the Declaration, links economic and social rights with membership in society: "Everyone, as a member of society, has the right to social security and is entitled to the realization ... of the economic, social and cultural rights indispensable for his dignity and the development of his personality." Additionally, the Universal Declaration recognizes the importance of the role of the community to human development in assigning individuals corresponding duties to the community. In the only statement about duties in the Universal Declaration, the text asserts that "Everyone has duties to the community in which alone the free and full development of his personality is possible" (Article 29).

Like other human rights, particularly social, economic, and cultural rights, the right to health has strong social and collective dimensions. Indeed, as Richard Hiskes notes, "to call rights 'human' is to recognize their ineluctably social character" (2009, 29). He points out that human identity is defined within human relationships that then produce rights as requirements of moral agency and dignity to make these relationships possible (2009, 29).

There are five reasons that it is important to acknowledge the collective dimensions of the right to health. Firstly, the conception of the right to health in Article 12 of the ICESCR has important public health components linking the health of the individual to the community. While medicine focuses on the health status of the individual, public health is concerned with protecting the health of populations and ensuring the conditions in which people can be healthy. Relatedly, the infrastructure of the health system, the variety of facilities, goods, services, and conditions GC 14 describes as central to the realization of the right (para 9), are usually delivered to communities and groups and not individuals. Furthermore, when a right to health is interpreted and operationalized solely as an individual entitlement to a specific health benefit, it may undermine or even contradict public health efforts to promote health benefits for collectives and to build people-centered health systems (London et al. 2014).

Secondly, the underlying dimensions of health identified as an intrinsic dimension of the right to health (para 11) are social and not individual factors. The provision of the underlying determinants of health, more broadly referred to as the social determinants of health, requires holistic societal level initiatives to improve daily living conditions – the circumstances in which people are born, grow, live, work, and age – and to tackle the inequitable distribution of power, money, and resources, which serve as the structural drivers of those conditions of daily life. The World Health Organization's Commission on the Social Determinants of Health links initiatives to improve access to the social determinants of health with a movement to overcome global social injustice (2008). Chapter Seven addresses the requirements of incorporating the social determinants of health in a right to health approach.

Thirdly, a human rights approach has a special concern with vulnerable groups and communities and improving the enjoyment of rights by members of these groups and not just addressing the human rights status of individuals. For example, GC 14 incorporates a section labeled "special topics of broad application" which describes the obligations related to a series of vulnerable groups: women (paras 20 and 21), children and adolescents (paras 2–24), older persons (para 25), persons with disabilities (para 26), and indigenous peoples (para 27). In the paragraph on indigenous communities, the Committee notes that "in indigenous communities, the health of the individual is often linked to the health of the society as a whole and has a collective dimension" (CESCR 2000, para 27). The same could be said more generally about the health of the individual and the society. When monitoring state party performance, the Committee focuses on the status of these vulnerable groups.

Fourthly, with the advent of the increasing use of litigation to achieve access to health services the failure to recognize that human rights are vested collectively in the society as well as individually in persons may encourage outcomes that benefit individuals at the expense of the society. Studies of litigation in Latin America, particularly in Argentina, Brazil, and Colombia, show the health rights cases in these countries frequently consist of individual efforts to obtain access to expensive medical treatments not in the basic package of health entitlements that are bought by members of the middle class. Litigants are generally successful in obtaining coverage for expensive low-priority services, and as a result, take resources that could be more equitably invested in preventive services that would be able to improve the health status of the poor and disadvantaged members of society. If this trend continues, the misplaced resource allocation could increase inequities, counter to the principles underlying the right to health (Yamin 2011, 350–353). It is also likely to exacerbate health-related inequalities. Conversely, where civil society adopts principles of solidarity, framed as the mutual responsibility of citizens for dealing with the health needs of each other through community-based responses, rights-based approaches are more likely to address rather than to aggravate health inequalities (London et al. 2014).

Fifthly, focusing on the collective dimensions of the right to health and group rights can be helpful to efforts to achieve meaningful empowerment of people from disadvantaged communities. Empowerment of disadvantaged groups requires providing opportunities for such groups to frame their own rights-related agenda and advocate for change. Disadvantaged communities need to have the means to shape perceptions of their own interests as input to the policymaking agenda. To do so entails their overcoming both internalized and external forms of domination (Yamin 2009, 5, 13–14). Case studies from South Africa show how recognizing the collective nature of the right to health can strengthen the collective agency of the most vulnerable and facilitate the building of pro-poor people-centered health systems (London et al. 2014).

Perhaps the Committee's most significant reflection on the collective dimensions of health comes in the penultimate note in GC 14. It states the following: "Regardless of whether groups as such can seek remedies as distinct holders of rights, States parties are bound by both the collective and individual dimensions of article 12." It goes on to say, "Collective rights are critical in the field of health; modern public health policy relies heavily on prevention and promotion which are approaches directed primarily to groups" (CESCR 2000, note 30). It is too bad that this statement is buried in an endnote at the end of the document.

The failure of General Comment 14 and more broadly the health and human rights community to devote sufficient attention to the significant public health dimensions of the right to health has led Benjamin Meier and Larisa Morsi to reinterpret the obligations related to the right to health from a collective perspective. Their work is premised on a belief that the right to health advanced in the ICESCR is a limited, atomized right that focuses on individual access to health care at the expense of collective health promotion and disease prevention (Meier and Mori 2005, 117). They comment, "Securing population health is not merely the health of many individual persons, but a collective 'public' good that is greater than the sum of its constituent part" (2005, 124). They argue that a society-based collective right to public health that complements the individual human right to health is particularly a necessary precondition for fulfilling health rights in an age of globalization. This is because globalization has created new underlying determinants of health unaccounted for by a limited individual right to health (2005, 104). Conversely, a human rights framework offers unparalleled opportunity to combat the injurious effects of globalization (2005, 125).

While I am sympathetic to their stress on the importance of the public health dimensions of the right to health, I think that the right to health is and has been more than a limited, atomized right. Moreover, it would be problematic and ultimately unsuccessful to try to carve out a separate right to public health. Instead, it would be preferable to strengthen the public health dimensions within the right to health and rights-based approaches to health.

Violations

As noted in the next section of this chapter, monitoring is central to efforts to establish accountability for implementing human rights. Economic, social, and cultural rights present a particular challenge because of the difficulty in interpreting and translating progressive realization into an operational standard. Monitoring progressive realization requires access to good quality disaggregated data collected in a uniform way at periodic intervals so as to be able to assess trends. Few countries have such data available, and those whose governments do may be reluctant to share the information with human rights monitors. Moreover, human rights monitoring bodies, including the major UN committees, usually lack the statistical capacity to work with such data, especially if it were to be submitted in a disaggregated manner.

In 1996 at a time when few economic, social, and cultural rights had as yet been adequately conceptualized and monitoring was at a very preliminary stage, I proposed a new approach to monitoring economic, social, and cultural rights that would focus on identifying serious problems or violations of the rights rather than seek to assess progressive realization (Chapman 1996). The 1986 Limburg Principles on the Implementation of the International Covenant on Economic, Social and Cultural Rights, formulated by a group of distinguished experts in international law, defined a violation as a failure by a state party to comply with an obligation contained in this instrument (1987). It recognized that these failures might be acts of either commission or omission. The Limburg Principles were quite specific in identifying seven circumstances in which a state party would be in violation of the Covenant. As of 1996, however, these provisions had received very little attention.

My 1996 article explained in some detail that a "violations approach" could provide a more feasible and appropriate methodology both for monitors on the ground and for reviewers evaluating the compliance of individual countries with international standards. One major advantage is that the monitoring of violations does not depend on access to extensive and comparable good quality statistical data. The article pointed out that despite the considerable inadequacies, superficiality, and lack of good quality statistical data in state parties' reports, the CESCR had been able to identify some violations of economic, social, and cultural rights. The Committee's statement to the World Conference on Human Rights provided an eloquent testimony to the importance of addressing what were termed "massive and direct denials of economic, social and cultural rights" (CESCR 1993, para 5).

On the tenth anniversary of the Limburg Principles, another group of experts (including myself) convened in Maastricht to discuss violations of economic, social, and cultural rights. Building on the Limburg Principles, the Maastricht Guidelines affirm that "As in the case of civil and political rights, the failure by a State Party to comply with a treaty obligation concerning economic, social and cultural rights is, under international law, a violation of that treaty" (Maastricht 1997, para 5). The Maastricht Guidelines define the nature of violations of economic, social, and cultural rights in relation to the three types of obligations on states: the obligations to respect, protect, and fulfill. According to the Maastricht Guidelines, the failure to implement any or all of these three categories of obligations constitutes a violation of these rights. To determine whether an action or omission amounts to a violation of a right, the Maastricht Guidelines distinguish between the inability and unwillingness of a state to comply with its treaty obligations. Nevertheless, the Guidelines place the burden on the state of proving that it is unable to carry out its obligations (para 13). Like the Limburg Principles, the Maastricht Guidelines indicate that a violation can occur through acts of commission or acts of omission by states and provides examples of both (para 13).

GC 14 includes a section on violations that closely follows the Maastricht Guidelines. It confirms that it is just as possible to violate economic and social rights as it is civil and political rights. It reiterates the Maastricht Guidelines caution that in determining which actions or omissions amount to a violation of the right to health, it is necessary to distinguish between inability and unwillingness of the state party to comply with its obligations. Nevertheless, if resource constraints render the state unable to comply with its obligations, it has the burden of justifying that it has put forward every effort to use all the available resources at its disposal. Also a state party cannot, under any circumstances, justify noncompliance with the core obligations set out in the general comment (para 47). The general comment observes that violations of the right to health can occur through the direct action of states or other entities insufficiently regulated by states (para 48).

Just as the general comment puts forward three categories of government obligations to respect, protect, and fulfill human rights, it has the same three categories of violations. Lists are provided of examples of the types of violations the Committee has encountered (paras 50–52). For example, violations of the obligation to respect through state actions, policies, or laws that contravene the right to health include denial of access to health facilities, goods, and services to particular individuals and groups as a result of de jure or de facto discrimination; deliberate withholding or misrepresentation of information vital to health protection or treatment; and the failure of the state to take its legal obligations into account when entering into bilateral or multilateral agreements (para 50). Examples of violations of the obligation to protect referred to in the general comment relate to the failure of the state to take necessary measures to safeguard persons within their jurisdiction from infringements of the right to health by third parties. Some examples noted are the failure to regulate the activities of individuals, groups, or corporations; the failure to protect consumers and workers from practices and products detrimental to health; and the failure to protect women against violence or to discourage the continued observance of harmful medical or cultural practices (para 51). Violations of the obligation to fulfill occur through the failure of the state to take necessary steps to ensure realization of the right to health. Examples identified include the failure to adopt or implement a national health policy designed to ensure the right to health for everyone; insufficient expenditure or the misallocation of public resources, which results in the nonenjoyment of the right to health by individuals or groups; the failure to monitor the realization of the right to health at the national level; and the failure to adopt a gender-sensitive approach to health (para 52).

The violations approach has been little used even by the CESCR. Some advocates have been concerned that adoption of a violations approach would weaken the call for eventual full implementation of economic and social rights by concentrating on the most flagrant abuses. However, the violations approach was not meant to replace the ultimate goal of full implementation of the rights in the Covenant, but rather, to provide a simple and effective monitoring method. A related objection has focused on the concern that calling governments to account for violations might be a risky strategy for nongovernmental organizations (NGOs) in some countries who would become vulnerable to reprisals. Also official international and regional human right bodies seem reluctant to use the language of violations. For example, when conducting evaluations of state parties' performance the CESCR seems far more comfortable in pointing out areas that need improvement without labeling the inadequacy, even when serious, as rising to the status of a violation.

A violations approach may, however, become better accepted in the future. Litigation over failures to implement health entitlements has become more common in many countries, particularly in Latin America. In addition, the Committee will be amassing a database of state parties' inadequacies and failures through hearing cases referred through its optional protocol mechanism.

Monitoring and Accountability

Accountability is a central feature of human rights. "Without accountability, a State can use progressive realization and the scarcity of resources as an excuse to do virtually nothing – or to respond to whichever interest group has the loudest voice" (Hunt and Leader 2010, 44). GC 14 calls for each state to develop a national health strategy and plan of action based on the principles of accountability, transparency, and independence of the judiciary (para 55). It recommends that states should consider establishing national mechanisms for monitoring the implementation of national health strategies and plans of action with provisions on the targets to be achieved and the time frame for their achievement (para 56).

Monitoring human rights standards is central to the development of a meaningful international human rights system. Otherwise, countries that ratify specific human rights instruments cannot assess their own performance in promoting effective realization of the enumerated rights. Further, without effective monitoring, states cannot be held accountable for implementation of, or be made liable for violations of, these rights. Monitoring state compliance is a complex and exacting process. Effective monitoring requires the systematic collection and analysis of appropriate data, preferably on a disaggregated basis, so as to be able to assess differences among groups in the population. The determination of which data are relevant depends on translating the abstract legal norms in which the various human rights instruments are framed into operational standards. To accomplish this task, specific rights need to be adequately conceptualized and then relevant measurement standards developed, often in the form of indicators.

The general comment contemplates monitoring through the identification of appropriate right-to-health indicators and national benchmarks of the targets to be achieved (para 58). Although many of the experts and civil society members working with the Committee during the drafting process advocated that the Committee identify at least a preliminary set of indicators, members of the Committee resisted doing so.

Development of a widely accepted set of indicators on the right to health and their use has been a slow process. Paul Hunt, the first Special Rapporteur on the right to health, developed a conceptual framework for a health rights approach to indicators based on three categories: structural, process, and outcome indicators. Structural indicators address whether or not key structures and mechanisms necessary for the implementation of the right to health are in place, such as the ratification of relevant international human rights treaties and the adoption of national laws and policies that expressly promote and protect the right to health. Process indicators measure the success of programs, activities, and interventions meant to implement the right to health, and outcome indicators assess the impact of programs, activities, and interventions on health status and related issues (2003).

Hunt's most ambitious project on indicators was to work with a team of researchers to identify a set of right to health indicators and then attempt to use them to assess the health systems of 194 countries from a human rights perspective (Backman et al. 2008). One of the findings of the project was the absence of appropriate available data for this monitoring, especially in the international domain. This is because the health information systems in many countries are seriously deficient, and the collection of disaggregated data necessary for human rights monitoring remains an enormous challenge for many countries (Backman et al. 2008, 2078–2079). Rectifying this situation presents something of a chicken-and-egg dilemma as to what should come first – the improvement of the infrastructure to collect statistical data on which basis to develop indicators or the formulation of the indicators to provide direction as to which kinds of data are necessary. In either case there will be a need to improve data infrastructures in order to establish accessible, transparent, and effective systems for monitoring and accountability of health systems for implementing the right to health.

Priority Setting

The right to health is very broad in scope, demanding of resources, and complex to implement. The progressive realization standard recognizes the need to move toward full realization of all dimensions of the right gradually over an indefinite period of time. Although they were meant to do so, the core obligations identified in General Comment No. 14 do not provide a sufficiently focused and feasible set of priorities for immediate implementation. Finite budgets for health give rise to difficult policy choices, especially in a neoliberal era in which all social spending is ideologically constrained. Under these circumstances, the determination of a methodology for priority setting from a human rights perspective becomes very important. As noted earlier, some critics have identified the absence of priority setting mechanisms as one of the weaknesses of a right to health approach (Daniels 2008, 314–315; Venkatapuram 2011, 182–183).

Unfortunately, despite the need, there has been resistance to priority setting amongst some of those working on health and human rights issues. Paul Hunt observes in one of his reports that some in the human rights community respond to the prioritization problem by arguing that all policy makers need to do is allocate more resources to health (2007, para 16). While it is true that many countries spend far less than the minimum expenditure per capita that is needed (but not yet defined as a specific human rights obligation), Hunt points out that even when more resources are available, it is unlikely that they will support all health needs or all components of the right to health (2007, para 17). Hunt notes one of the most difficult questions he was asked on country missions is: "Given a finite budget, how can the Minister of Health prioritize health interventions in a manner that is consistent with the Government's national and international human rights obligations" (2007, para 12)? He also mentions that priority-setting raises profound human rights issues, especially because in practice prioritization has often privileged the health needs of wealthy, urban populations over the entitlements of the rural poor and marginalized the entitlements of disadvantaged groups (2007, para 15).

Hunt offers some preliminary observations as to how the human rights community might proceed with priority setting. Many of the elements he proposes are procedural in nature. He notes priority setting from a human rights perspective will demand close collaboration between human rights specialists and health specialists, including epidemiologists and health economists (2007, para 19). He cautions that it will be difficult, if not impossible, for a health authority to apply the right to health to the issue of prioritization without also integrating human rights throughout its responsibilities (2007, para 21). Because the right to health includes entitlements to the underlying determinants of health, right to health priority setting will require priority setting across a range of sectors, and not just the health sector (2007, para 22). He underscores that priority setting must take place within the framework of a comprehensive national health strategy that spells out how the state will progressively implement the various elements of the right to health (2007, para 24). He emphasizes that human rights priority setting requires the active and informed participation of all stakeholders (2007, para 25) and must give particular regard to improving the situation of the disadvantaged, particularly those living in poverty (para 26). In addition, the process of prioritization should not compromise implementation of the core obligations arising from the right to health (2007, para 28).

A more recent examination of applying human rights frameworks to priority setting in health concludes that specific priority setting decisions cannot all be derived from transcendent human rights principles. Like Hunt and like the procedurally oriented "accountability for reasonableness" framework developed by Daniels and Sabin (1997) for health policy priority setting, the authors, Alicia Ely Yamin and Ole Frithjof Norheim, propose that what human rights requires is a process of meaningful democratic deliberation. However, they also acknowledge that there are challenges to implementing rights-based priority setting in view of its emphasis on equality, meaningful participation, and accountability that require society to grapple with overcoming failures of deliberation and accountability in the health system (Yamin and Norheim 2014).

Concluding Reflections

As this chapter shows, the health and human rights community has made considerable progress in giving the right to health a meaningful content, depth, and richness that go well beyond the narrow and inadequate framing of Article 12 of the ICESCR. Nevertheless, there is still a need for considerable additional work if the right is to be translated into meaningful policies and to be effectively monitored. Each of the sections of this chapter has noted advances and limitations in the understanding of the right and alluded to some of the difficulties in translating its norms.

Many components of the right to health are still confined to broad-brush strokes that require further conceptualization and translation into operational standards. To mention but a few, the very definition of the right is unclear as to what it means and requires. The four criteria of availability, accessibility, acceptability, and quality are too abstract to be applied effectively as evaluative standards. The obligation to ensure equitable distribution of all health facilities, goods, and services needs explanation as to what equitable distribution requires. Similarly, there is a need to specify what the right of access to health facilities, goods, and services on a nondiscriminatory basis actually entails, especially for vulnerable groups. Does it, for example, involve underwriting the costs of health services for all those who otherwise could not afford them, and if so, up to what level? The subject of minimum core obligations should be reconsidered and reframed in a more coherent and manageable manner. The health and human rights community has not reached consensus on approving the indicators that have been proposed for monitoring or a process for priority setting.

There are also central dimensions of the right to health and a rights-based approach to health that have been neglected. Given the importance of health systems for fulfilling the right to health, it is disappointing that there is so little work on the human rights requirements of health systems, specifically which health facilities, goods, and services are essential from a human rights perspective. In view of the link between available resources and expectations about realizing the right, another priority is determining the minimum level of resources states should be expected to invest in the health sector expressed either as a per capita figure or as a percentage of the budget. The whole area of budget analysis as a tool for monitoring the implementation of human rights obligations needs to be further developed. Hopefully the discussion of the role of budget analysis in Anand Grover's 2009 Special Rapporteur's report will generate some interest (Grover 2009). While accountability is one of the most important components of a human rights approach, it is also one of the least understood (Hunt 2008, para 65). There is very little work on the central elements of human rights accountability vis-à-vis the health system and how it should be realized and monitored.

Each of the subsequent chapters of this study will continue this assessment of progress and limitations in the development of the right. The chapters will note the extent to which the current framing of the right provides a basis to address the challenges of neoliberalism and commercialization of health, globalization, private health provision, incorporating the social determinants of health, access to essential medicines, and shaping approaches to universal health coverage.

References

Alma-Ata Declaration (1978) Report of the International Conference on Primary Health Care, Alma-Ata, 6-12 September 1978, in World Health Organization, "Health for All" Series, No. 1, Geneva: WHO.

Backman, Gunilla, Hunt, Paul, Khosla, Rajat, Jaramillo-Strouss, Camila, et al. (2008) "Health Systems and the Right to Health: An Assessment of 194 Countries," The Lancet 372 (December 13): 2047–2085.

Baxi, Upendra (2010) "The Place of the Human Right to Health and Contemporary Approaches to Global Justice: Some Impertinent Interrogations," in John

Harrington and Maria Stuttaford, eds., *Global Health and Human Rights: Legal and Philosophical Perspectives*, London and New York: Routledge, pp. 12–27.

Bohrequez Monslave, V. and Aguirre Roman, J. (2009) "Tensions of Human Dignity: Conceptualization and Application to International Human Rights Law," *Sur: International Journal on Human Rights* 11 (6): 39–59.

Boyle, Joseph M., Jr. (1977) "The Concept of Health and the Right to Health," *Social Thought* 3: 5–17.

Callahan, Daniel (1990) *What Kind of Life: A Challenging Exploration of the Goals of Medicine*, New York: Touchstone Books.

Caulfield, Timothy and Chapman, Audrey R. (2005) "Human Dignity as a Criterion for Science Policy," *PLOS Medicine*, 2 (8) (August): 0101–0103.

CESCR (Committee on Economic, Social and Cultural Rights) (1990) General Comment 3: The nature of States Parties Obligations (Art. 2, para.1 of the Covenant), contained in E/1991/23.

(1993) Report on the Seventh Session, Annex III.

(1994) General Comment No. 5: Persons with Disabilities, U.N. Doc. E/1995/22.

(2000) General Comment 14: The Right to the Highest Attainable Standard of Health, U.N. Doc. E.C.12.2000.4.EN.

(2007) Statement by the Committee: An evaluation of the obligation to take steps to the "maximum available resources" under an optional protocol to the Covenant, U.N. Doc. E/C.12/2007/1.

(2009) General Comment No. 20: Non-Discrimination in Economic, Social and Cultural Rights (art. 2, para. 2), U.N. Doc. E/C./GCC/20.

Chapman, Audrey R. (1996) "A 'Violations Approach' for Monitoring the International Covenant on Economic, Social, and Cultural Rights," *Human Rights Quarterly* 18 (3): 23–66.

(2011) "Human Dignity, Bioethics, and Human Rights," *Amsterdam Law Forum*, 3 (1): 3–12.

Chapman, Audrey R. and Carbonetti, Benjamin (2011) "Human Rights Protections for Vulnerable and Disadvantaged Groups: The Contributions of the UN Committee on Economic, Social and Cultural Rights," *Human Rights Quarterly* 33 (3): 682–732.

Chapman, Audrey R. and Russell, Sage, eds. (2002) *Core Obligations: Building a Framework for Economic, Social and Cultural Rights*, Antwerp, Oxford, and New York: Intersentia.

Commission on Social Determinants of Health (2008) *Closing the Gap in a Generation: Health Equity through Action on the Social Determinants of Health*. Geneva: World Health Organization.

Committee on the Elimination of Discrimination against Women (1999) General Recommendation No. 24, article 12: Women and Health, U.N. Doc. CEDAW/C/1999/1/WG.11.WP.2/Rev.1.

Committee on the Rights of the Child (2003) General Comment No. 4, Adolescent Health and Development in the Context of the Convention on the Rights of the Child, U.N. Doc. CRC/GC/2003/4.

Committee on the Rights of the Child (CRC) (2013) General comment No. 15 on the Right of the Child to the Enjoyment of the Highest Attainable Standard of Health (art. 24), CRC/C/GC/15.

Convention on the Elimination of all Forms of Discrimination Against Women (1979) G. A. Res. 34/180, 34 U.N. GAOR Supp. (No. 46) at 193, U.N. Doc. 34/36.

Convention on the Rights of Persons with Disabilities (2006) U.N. Doc. A/AC.265/2006/L.7 and Corr. 1.

Convention on the Rights of the Child (1989) G.A. Res. 44/25, 44 U.N. GAOR Supp. (No. 49) at 165, U.N. Doc. A/44/736.

Daniels, Norman (2008) *Meeting Health Needs Fairly*, Cambridge and New York: Cambridge University Press.

Daniels, Norman and Sabin, James (1997) "Limits to Health Care, Fair Procedures, Democratic Deliberation, and the Legitimacy Problem for Insurers," *Philosophy and Public Affairs* 26: 325–327.

Dawson, Angus (2011) "Resetting the Parameters: Public Health as the Foundation of Public Health Ethics," in Angus Dawson, ed., *Public Health Ethics: Key Concepts and Issues in Policy and Practice*, Cambridge: Cambridge University Press, pp. 1–19.

Donnelly, Jack (1989) *Universal Human Rights in Theory & Practice*, Ithaca, New York, and London: Cornell University Press.

Forman, Lisa (2010) "What Future for the Minimum Core? Contextualising the Implications of South Africa Socioeconomic Rights Jurisprudence for the International Human Right to Health," in John Harrington and Maria Stuttaford, eds., *Global Health and Human Rights: Legal and Philosophical Perspectives*, Routledge: London and New York: pp. 62–80.

General Comment No. 15: The Right to Water, U.N. Doc. E/C.12/2002/11.

Grover, Anand (2009) Report of the Special Rapporteur for the Special Rapporteur on the Right of Everyone to the Enjoyment of the Highest Attainable Standard of Physical and Mental Health, submitted to the Economic and Social Council, U.N. Doc. E/2009/90.

(2011) Thematic Study on the Realization of the Right to Health of Older Persons by the Special Rapporteur on the Right of Everyone to the Enjoyment of the Highest Attainable Standard of Physical and Mental Health, Human rights Council, Eighteenth session, U.N. Doc. A/HRC/18/37.

Hiskes, Richard P. (2009) *The Human Right to a Green Future: Environmental Rights and Intergenerational Justice*, Cambridge and New York: Cambridge University Press.

Hogan, Margaret C., Foreman, Kyle J., Naghavi, Mohsen, Ahn, Stephanie, Y., et al. (2010) "Maternal Mortality for 181 Countries, 1980–2008: A Systematic

Analysis of Progress towards Millennium Development Goal 5," *The Lancet* 375: 1609–23.

Hunt, Paul (2003) Report of the Special Rapporteur on the Right of Everyone to the Enjoyment of the Highest Attainable Standard of Physical and Mental Health, submitted to the United Nations General Assembly, U.N. Doc. A/58/427, focusing on right to health indicators.

(2004) Report of the Special Rapporteur on the Right of Everyone to the Enjoyment of the Highest Attainable Standard of Physical and Mental Health, Paul Hunt, on His Mission to the World Trade Organization, Commission on Human rights, March 1, 2004, E/CN.4/2004/49/Add.1.

(2005) Report of the Special Rapporteur on the Right of Everyone to the Enjoyment of the Highest Attainable Standard of Physical Health, submitted to the Human Rights Council, U.N. Doc. E/CN.4/2005/51 focusing on persons with mental disabilities.

(2006) Report of the Special Rapporteur on the Right of Everyone to the Enjoyment of the Highest Attainable Standard of Physical Health, submitted to the Human Rights Council, U.N. Doc. E/CN. 4/2006/48 providing a human rights based approach to right to health indicators.

(2007) Report of the Special Rapporteur on the Right of Everyone to the Enjoyment of the Highest Attainable Standard of Physical and Mental Health, submitted to the United Nations General Assembly, U.N. Doc. A/62/150 providing preliminary observations on prioritizing health interventions in a way that is respectful of human rights and considering the underlying determinants of health.

(2008) Report of the Special Rapporteur on the Right of Everyone to the Enjoyment of the Highest Attainable Standard of Physical and Mental Health, submitted to the Human Rights Council, January 31, 2008, U.N. Doc. A/HRC/7/11 focusing on the role of health systems in realizing the right to the highest attainable standard of health.

Hunt, Paul and Leader, Sheldon (2010) "Developing and Applying the Right to the Highest Attainable Standard of Health: The Role of the UN Special Rapporteur (2002–2008)," in John Harrington and Maria Stuttaford, eds., *Global Health and Human Rights: Legal and Philosophical Perspectives*, New York: Routledge, pp. 28–61.

International Covenant on Civil and Political Rights (1966) G.A. Resolution 2200 A (XXI), 21 U.N. GAOR, Supp. (No. 16) at 52, U.N. Doc. A/6316.

International Covenant on Economic, Social, and Cultural Rights (1966) G.A. Res. 2200 (XXI), 21 U.N. GAOR Supp. No. 16 at 49, U.N. Doc. A/6316.

London, Leslie, Himongo, Chuman, Fick, Nicole, and Stuttaford, Maria (2014) "Social Solidarity and the Right to Health: Essential Elements for People-centered Health Systems," *Health Policy and Planning*, 30 (7): 938–945.

Meier, Benjamin Mason and Mori, Larisa M. (2005) "The Highest Attainable Standard: Advancing a Collective Human Right to Public Health," *Columbia Human Rights Law Review* 37 (1): 101–147.

Ngwena, Charles G. (2010) "Inscribing Abortion as a Human Right: Significance of the Protocol on the Rights of Women in Africa," *Human Rights Quarterly* 32 (4): 783–864.

Nickel, James (1987) *Making Sense of Human Rights: Philosophical Reflections on the Universal Declaration of Human Rights,* Berkeley, Los Angeles, and London: University of California Press.

Pillay, Karrisha (2002) "South Africa's Commitment to Health Rights in the Spotlight: Do We Meet the International Standard?" in Sage Russell and Danie Brand, eds., *Exploring the Core Content of Economic and Social Rights: South African and International Perspectives,* Pretoria: Protea Book House, pp. 61–70.

Programme of Action of the International Conference on Population and Development (1994) Report of the International Conference on Population and Development, U.N. Doc.A/CONF.171.13.

Protocol to the African Charter on Human and Peoples' Rights and on the Rights of Women in Africa (2003) adopted in the 2nd Ordinary Session of the Assembly of the African Union, AHG/Res. 240 (XXXI), entered into force 25 November 2005.

Report on Indicators for Promoting and Monitoring the Implementation of Human Rights (2008) Twentieth meeting of chairpersons of the human rights treaty bodies, Geneva, 26–27 June, U.N. Doc. HRI/MC/2008/3.

Ruger, Jennifer Prah (2010) *Health and Social Justice,* Oxford and New York: Oxford University Press.

The Limburg Principles on the Implementation of the International Covenant on Economic, Social and Cultural Rights (1987) *Human Rights Quarterly* 9: 121–135.

The Maastricht Guidelines on Violations of Economic, Social and Cultural Rights (1997) formulated in Maastricht from 22–26 January 1997 by a group of more than thirty experts convened by the International Commission of Jurists, the Urban Morgan Institute of Human Rights, and the Centre for Human Rights of the Faculty of Law of Maastricht University. The Maastricht Guidelines are reprinted in *Economic, Social and Cultural Rights: A Compilation of Essential Documents* 1997, Geneva: International Commission of Jurists, pp. 81–91.

The Report of the Fourth World Conference on Women (1995) U.N. Doc. A/CONF.177/20.

Tobin, John (2012) *The Right to Health in International Law,* Oxford and New York: Oxford University Press.

United Nations (1948) Universal Declaration of Human Rights, adopted and proclaimed by the United Nations General Assembly Resolution 217A (III) on December 10.

(2010) Treaty Collection, Chapter IV, Human Rights, 18 April, http://treaties.un.org/Pages/Treaties.aspx?id+48=subsid+A&lang+en.

Venkatapuram, Sridhar (2011) *Health Justice*, Cambridge, UK: Polity Press.

World Health Organization (1958) "The Preamble to the Constitution," in *The First Ten Years of the World Health Organization*, Geneva: WHO.

Yamin, Alicia Ely (2009) "Suffering and Powerlessness: The Significance of Promoting Participation in Rights-based Approaches to Health," *Health and Human Rights Journal* 11 (1): 5–22.

(2011) "Power, Suffering, and Courts: Reflections on Promoting Health Rights through Judicialization," in Alicia Ely Yamin and Siri Gloppen, eds., *Litigating Health Rights: Can Courts Bring More Justice to Health?* Cambridge, MA: Harvard University Press, pp. 333–372.

Yamin, Alicia Ely and Norheim, Ole Frithjof (2014) "Taking Equality Seriously: Applying Human Rights Frameworks to Priority Setting in Health," *Human Rights Quarterly* 36: 296–324.

3

Health and Human Rights in the Neoliberal Era

Efforts to realize human rights can be challenged or supported by the social, political, and economic environment in which they are being implemented. The Introduction briefly identified some of the factors that make the current health landscape problematic for implementation of a rights-based approach. This is the first of several chapters that further elaborates on this issue. Chapter Three focuses on the challenges and constraints imposed by the ideological orientation and economic and political policies associated with neoliberalism, the dominant economic and political paradigm promoted by international financial institutions and shaping public policies both at the global level and in many countries and for the past three decades. Later chapters explore the implications of privatization and globalization for the right to health and the difficulties of assuring access to essential medicines when dependent on a commercially oriented pharmaceutical sector.

As the Introduction noted, the contemporary economic, cultural, and policy context for the implementation of a rights-based approach to health differs significantly from the postwar conditions and political cultures in which the modern human rights system evolved and the right to health was framed. Although many countries were grappling with the devastation of the war and the demands of reconstruction in the early years after World War II, there was considerable support in most high-income countries for a welfare state model in which the government assumes major responsibility for the economic and social welfare of its citizens and for human rights values. These developments were often undergirded by a concept of social citizenship that had emerged during the war years, particularly in Europe, the notion that all members of society have a right to certain social services and programs such as health care, education, old age pensions, and unemployment insurance (Teeple 2000, 45). Key to this idea of social citizenship was a commitment to a universal standard of entitlement: the premise that social rights are granted on the basis of membership in a society and not market performance or a person's place and productivity in the workplace (Callahan and Wasunna 2006, 89). The policies and programs instituted to achieve these goals in the countries where they were embraced differed in time and circumstance, and the nature and scope of the health entitlements provided varied, but in many countries populations came to expect and governments sought to provide expanded health benefits. Whether these goals and the resultant reforms reflected an explicit commitment to human rights norms or instead were inspired by concepts of solidarity and/or social citizenship resulting from the war experience, as claimed by some (Callahan and Wasunna 2006, 9, 110–111), the principles and policies adopted were generally consistent with a human rights approach.

Most of the governments that held power in the industrialized democratic countries after the war also shared an acceptance of the responsibility of the state to promote economic growth and widely distribute the benefits of an expanding economy. While their economies were based on free markets and private property, many countries established expansive welfare programs and implemented strong state regulation of the economy. In these regimes, sometimes referred to as "welfare capitalism," the market was no longer considered to be self-regulating, but was aligned with social priorities by means of state action. Fiscal and monetary policies, usually labeled as "Keynesian," were widely implemented to regulate the economy and to dampen the impact of business cycles. Many states also imposed a regulatory environment that placed a web of economic, social, and political constraints around market processes and corporate activities that sometimes restrained but in other instances set economic and industrial strategy. Another element of the postwar policies in many countries was initiatives to accord labor and the middle class a larger share of the economic pie and thereby to reduce the economic benefits that went to the privileged classes. These policies were able to deliver high rates of economic growth and promote mass consumption in advanced capitalist countries until the early 1970s (Harvey 2005, 10–11, 15).

In contrast, neoliberalism, the economic and political paradigm that has been shaping public policies at the international level and in many countries for the past thirty years, displaces protecting human rights and improving human welfare as a central policy goal in favor of promoting the hegemony of markets as the most appropriate basis for organizing economic and social life, including health systems. The "market" refers to a mode of exchange in which the needs of society are satisfied through the buying and selling of goods and services. The market can also be conceptualized as the social allocation of goods and services by means of a price mechanism (Teeple 2000, 85). The principle of distribution governing the marketplace is very different than a human rights approach. It is "to each according to the amount she values the good, which frequently translates into to each according to the amount she is willing to pay for the good" (Kaveny 1999, 216). In contrast, human rights are guided by assessments of what is needed to protect human dignity, particularly of vulnerable individuals and groups, and the policies and services essential to promote well-being.

It should be noted that neoliberalism differs from the liberal regimes that some human rights theorists identified as a prerequisite for support of human rights. According to Rhoda Howard and Jack Donnelly, the autonomy and equality central to human rights are manifestations of the central liberal commitment to the equality worth and dignity of each person. They also claim that the standard list of human rights in the Universal Declaration of Human Rights can easily be derived from the liberal conception of the individual and the state. Although they acknowledge that market distribution tends to be grossly unequal, they argue that the principle of equal concern and respect does imply respect for a floor of basic economic welfare preventing degrading inequalities. They distinguish their model of liberalism from what they term the propertied libertarian liberalism of the minimal or night watchman state, which would protect property rights while rejecting all other economic and social rights (Howard and Donnelly 1986, 1989, 66–75).

Other human rights theorists have taken issue with Howard and Donnelly's views. Neil Mitchell argues that Howard and Donnelly have not defined liberalism appropriately. Instead he asserts that they have merely stipulated a set of values and labeled them liberalism. He particularly challenges their claim that there is a basis for economic and social rights protections in liberalism (Mitchell et al. 1987).

Perhaps most importantly for the discussion here, contemporary neoliberalism has little resemblance to the liberal regime Howard and Donnelly characterize. Instead neoliberalism, or as it is sometimes referred to, "supercapitalism," (Reich 2008) has features of the libertarian liberalism of the minimal night watchman state they reject. It is relevant here to note the distinction Daniel Callahan and Angela Wasunna make between two approaches to the incorporation of market mechanisms in health systems. The first are those that aim for major structural changes in health systems, such as privatizing major institutions, sharply reducing the government's role, and introducing competition into as many parts of the system as possible. In contrast, the second introduces market mechanisms selectively seeking to use them to introduce greater efficiency without changing the underlying health care system (2006, 37). Contemporary neoliberalism advocates the former approach, adopting market mechanisms aiming for major changes in the way the health system functions and its underlying values.

To put it another way, neoliberalism values market exchange as "an ethic in itself, capable of acting as a guide to all human action, and, substituting for all previously held ethical beliefs" (Harvey 2005, 3). Proponents of the free market argue it is the source of capitalism's purported political liberties and economic opportunity and claim that it is the most neutral or nonpolitical manner to providing for the needs of society (Teeple 2000, 85). To advance its drive toward small government, the unfettered rule of the market, and preferential policies and benefits for those with economic resources, neoliberal advocates seek the reduction or elimination of the social responsibilities of the state and the transfer of the management or ownership of state-run social service institutions to private enterprise.

Neoliberal advocates justify the imposition of market approaches into the health field on several grounds. They argue that the private sector is more efficient and cost-effective and hence can deliver health services more effectively (O'Connell 2007). Efficiency is linked with the introduction of competition and giving patients greater choice (Lister 2013, 32). For many market proponents, liberty and a wide scope of choice are dominant values (Callahan and Wasunna 2006, 13). Neoliberals also tend to discount the deleterious effects of market-based approaches for human welfare, access to essential social services, equity, or human dignity.

Neoliberal reforms and the ideology underlying them have been much criticized by the small group of human rights analysts and scholars who have addressed the impact of neoliberalism on the right to health and human rights values. Paul O'Connell argues, for example, that the neoliberal model is inimical, both in theory and practice, to the protection of human rights. According to O'Connell, the conditions for the violation of human rights are structurally embedded in the neoliberal program (2007, 483, 508). There is particular concern among human rights advocates with the implications of treating essential health services as just another commodity subject to the ability of those who need treatment to pay for it. Others point out that when access to health care is dependent on income, it explicitly legitimates inequalities and the exclusion of the poor (Freedman 2005, 22; Yamin and Norheim 2014, 302).

This chapter explores the impact of neoliberal policies and their implications for a human rights-based approach to health. It begins with a brief discussion of the welfare state model and its displacement by the neoliberal paradigm. Following a presentation of key elements of neoliberalism, it considers the ways in which neoliberalism conflicts with a human rights framework. It then explores the impact of neoliberal policies on economic and social systems. The remainder of the chapter documents the manner in which neoliberal policies impact the health sector and how these developments affect implementation of the right to health. Specifically, the chapter considers the deleterious impacts of the commodification and commercialization of health care, the results of imposing cost recovery requirements for health services, and reasons why market models are inappropriate in health systems.

The Welfare State

The welfare state refers to a concept of government in which the state plays a key role in the protection and promotion of the economic and social well-being of its citizens. It is based on the principles of equality of opportunity, equitable distribution of wealth, and public responsibility for those who are unable to otherwise avail themselves of the minimal requirements for a good life. It usually includes at least some public provision of basic health services, education, and housing, in some cases at low cost or without charge. Most welfare states rely on redistributionist or progressive taxation to fund the benefits and services provided (*Britannica Online Encyclopedia* 2012).

The often-cited work by Gösta Esping-Anderson (1990) identifies three typologies or ideal types of welfare states. The first is the social democratic state based on the principle of universalism, granting access to benefits and services based on citizenship. The second type is the Christian democratic welfare states based on the principle of subsidiarity and the dominance of social insurance schemes to provide benefits that retain social stratification. His third type is the liberal regime characterized by market dominance and private provision, which limits state intervention to ameliorating poverty and providing for basic needs, the latter primarily on a means-tested basis. In the third category social stratification continues to be high. Some subsequent work has confirmed his typology. Some researchers have used the three ideal types to classify specific countries. One 2011 publication, for example, identified Sweden, Norway, and Denmark as pure social democratic cases; Austria, France, and Germany as pure Christian democratic welfare states, and the United States as the only truly liberal welfare state. Various other countries were categorized as hybrids (Ferragina and Seeleib-Kaiser 2011).

Modern health welfare benefits originated with the welfare programs Chancellor Otto von Bismarck established in Prussia in the middle of the nineteenth century. The Bismarckian tradition relied on private sickness funds, organized regionally, and with the exception of their nationalization during the Nazi period, jointly managed by employers and employees (Attenstetter 2003, 38). Many other European countries also had some form of health insurance by the end of the nineteenth century, but few of them were as comprehensive as the German sickness funds (Callahan and Wasunna 2006, 88–89). To provide a few examples, Norway adopted the beginnings of a system of health insurance in the second half of the nineteenth century (Johnsen. 2006, 2–23). Japan also had some type of public or social health insurance covering groups in the population for some types of health service prior to the World War II (Tatara and Okamoko 2009).

Various proposals for more extensive health and welfare reforms were made in the prewar period and during World War II. In the United States, Franklin Roosevelt, who ascended to the presidency during the depths of the great depression, responded to the economic crisis by establishing the New Deal program consisting of social security benefits, heavier taxes on the wealthy, new controls on banks, and a major work relief program for the unemployed. In 1941, he made his "Four Freedoms" speech in which he envisioned a world founded on four essential freedoms, the third of which was freedom from want (Roosevelt 1941). In his 1944 State of the Union address, Roosevelt proposed the idea of a second bill of rights to complement the civil and political rights in the U.S. constitution, which would include the right to a useful and remunerative job; the right to earn enough to provide adequate food and clothing and recreation; the right of every family to a decent home; the right to a good education; the right to adequate protection from the economic fears of old age, sickness, accident, and unemployment; and importantly the right to adequate medical care and the opportunity to achieve and enjoy good health (Whelan 2010, 25). Moreover, Roosevelt argued the state had an obligation to protect and promote what we now term economic and social rights by providing the institutional support necessary for their realization (Whelan 2010, 31). Political opposition, led by the American Medical Association and medical profession, to Roosevelt and his successor President Harry Truman's proposals for universal health care undermined efforts to institute a right to health or health care in the United States, but these principles were to influence the drafting of the Universal Declaration of Human Rights and the International Covenant on Economic, Social and Cultural Rights (Whelan 2010, 30–31) and find expression in the welfare state reforms adopted by many states.

Most other comprehensive health reform initiatives dated from the postwar period. In Britain the Beveridge Report and a white paper were published during the war, setting forth the founding principles of what was to become the National Health Service: funding through a single payer financed by general taxation, comprehensive benefits from the point of use, and universal rights and eligibility for care. Following the war, the Labor government established the National Health Service in 1948 (Boyle 2011). Other countries adopted universal health care more gradually. In the case of Canada, for example, beginning in 1946 publicly funded health care was introduced on a piecemeal basis by various provincial governments. In 1957, the federal government agreed to fund 50 percent of the costs of the provincial health care, and legislation in 1966 set up a framework for each province to institute a universal health care plan (Canadian Museum of Civilization n.d.). The Swedish health care reforms came even later; the current Swedish universal health care system was instituted in 1970s and early 1980s (Anell et al. 2012, 21). In the case of a few states, for example Sweden, the health reforms to establish universal health care were based on explicit human rights principles or commitments (Anell et al. 2012, 21), but in the majority of cases they were not. Instead universal health care was conceptualized as a welfare state provision.

The Decline of the Welfare State and the Rise of Neoliberal Approaches

The late 1970s have been viewed both as the high-water mark and as the beginning of the decline for the postwar political consensus that brought welfarist policies to most Western European states and some other industrialized countries. By the mid 1970s most industrialized countries – with the notable exception of the United States – had established some form of public provision to finance or provided universal or near-universal healthcare. In September 1978 the World Health Organization's World Health Assembly, comprised of delegates from 134 countries, overwhelmingly endorsed the Alma Ata Declaration and its objective of ensuring "Health for All" by the year 2000. But the goals of the Alma Ata Declaration as well as the underlying welfarist consensus were soon to be challenged by political and economic developments (Lister 2013, 1–3).

In the course of the 1970s the great postwar economic boom fizzled out. A 1973/74 oil price shock following an Arab-Israeli war led to a major recession, falling living standards, and inflation in many parts of the world. In the wake of these developments, many developing countries were unable to finance debt servicing of earlier loans from private and public lending institutions. When the government of Mexico announced it would default on its loans, the International Monetary Fund (IMF) and World Bank agreed to provide needed capital to Mexico and other developing countries to prevent default, but the international financial institutions conditioned these bailouts on recipient countries adopting strict adjustments in their economic policies designed to improve the ability of the countries to repay their loans. These policies required drastic reductions in public expenditure, increases in tax revenue, trade liberalization, privatization of state-owned companies, currency devaluation, trade liberalization, and deregulation of the economy. Poor- and middle-income countries requiring the loans then and in subsequent years had no choice but to agree to implement these macroeconomic structural adjustment policies (Rowden 2009, 65–68). According to Alicia Ely Yamin, health was the domain most affected by the imposition of these neoliberal policies (2011, 340). The economic problems in poor- and middle-income countries had a counterpart in a prolonged deep recession in the industrialized countries marked by "stagflation," high unemployment, low growth, and high inflation rates.

Business circles and conservative political groups and writers opposed to the welfare state had long argued about the unaffordability of welfare entitlements and attacked what they termed "big government" as an infringement on individual freedoms (Teeple 2000, 46–49). The economic downturn seemed to provide credence to these arguments, and the political pendulum swung in favor of those advocating policies that sought to reestablish conditions for capital accumulation and restore the power of market oriented economic elites. The Conservative Party's coming into office in Britain in 1979 with Margaret Thatcher as Prime Minister and Ronald Regan's election the following year as the U.S. President coincided with and reinforced the beginnings of a paradigm shift based on the wholesale introduction of market-based approaches into public policies (Lister 2013, 40–41). Both Thatcher and Reagan attacked the welfare state claiming that government was ineffective and the private sector was inherently more efficient and more responsive as a provider of services. Thatcher undertook an initially unpopular campaign to privatize government-owned enterprises. Constrained by popular opposition from dismantling the National Health Service (NHS), her government created a market within the NHS so that some parts of the organization became providers selling services to the others (Fisher 2007). Similarly, Ronald Reagan came into office on a platform to cut taxes and reduce the size of the federal government, but he was unable to dismantle the publicly funded Medicare and Medicaid health entitlements. The institution of market-based initiatives made a great political leap in the 1980s and 1990s as more countries adopted market-based policies either voluntarily or under pressure from international financial institutions.

The dissolution of the Soviet Union in 1991 following Michail Gorbachev's unsuccessful efforts to liberalize the stagnant Soviet economy was another development encouraging the adoption of market-based policies. The Soviet failure tarnished the reputation of command economies and likely reduced the attraction of other state-centered socialist approaches as well (Callahan and Wasunna 2006, 35). As countries formerly under Soviet domination regained their independence, they turned uncritically to market-based solutions. This series of events removed a political and ideological counterweight to resurgent unregulated capitalism.

The adoption of neoliberal policies and paradigms has been uneven (Evans and Sewell 2013). The United States under Reagan and Britain under Thatcher were the epicenter of the rise of neoliberalism, and U.S. policies have been key to its continued prominence. In contrast, continental European countries have adopted market reforms but also retained many of their protective social welfare policies and institutions. In key Latin American states, such as Brazil, the combination of democratic pressures and nationalist economic traditions also shaped a hybrid set of policies that melded an increased openness to global markets with a continued economic role for the state and in recent years the increasing provision of health entitlements.

Some countries have followed other economic approaches. China's rapid rate of economic growth resulted from policies that combined elements of market logic with the continued central role of the state and party in the formulation of economic strategy. The high rates of economic growth of the so-called "Asian tigers," South Korea, Taiwan, Singapore, and Hong Kong, were guided by statist developmental strategies and not neoliberal policies, and these countries also made gradually increasing public investments in welfare spending.

Conceptualizing Neoliberalism

The package of political and economic policies advocating the roll-back of the welfare state and the substitution of market-based approaches in its place has come to be known as "neoliberalism." Neoliberalism, also referred to as market fundamentalism, neoliberal globalization, and New Right policies, presumes that markets are the most appropriate basis for organizing economic and social life, including health systems, and places a heavy burden of proof on those who propose alternative social relationships (Harvey 2005; Somers 2008). Neoliberal thought maintains that human well-being can best be advanced within an institutional framework characterized by free markets, a minimal state, free trade, the absence of economic regulation, and strong individual property rights. In social sectors where markets did not exist, such as health care, education, water, and social security, neoliberal proponents advocated their creation. The central value in neoliberalism is promoting greater choice – although in reality neoliberal policies generally produce greater choice only for those with economic resources.

Neoliberalism is founded on the philosophy of classical liberalism articulated in the writings of Adam Smith and hearkens back to its concepts of laissez-faire and the appropriate role of government (O'Connell 2007). Like Adam Smith, it posits the existence of a self-regulating market governing economic and social affairs. It represents a return to "the non-redistributive laissez-faire liberalism of the seventeenth and eighteenth centuries, which held that the main function of government is to make the country safe and the environment predictable for the participants in a market economy" (Jaggar 2002, 425).

Neoliberalism has the following major elements (Martinez and Garcia 2000; Teeple 2000; Harvey 2005; O'Connell 2007; Rowden 2009):

- Neoliberal doctrine advocates for the dominance of market approaches. It puts forward the view that markets are the most appropriate basis for organizing economic and social life, including health systems, and discounts the deleterious effects of market-based approaches for human dignity and welfare, access to essential social services, and equity. It supports these policies with the claim that market-based approaches will be more efficient and cost-effective and therefore ultimately benefit everyone.
- A central tenet of neoliberalism is that capital and private enterprise should be freed from any restrictions imposed by the government/the

state regardless of the social and economic consequences. Neoliberal thought advocates for deregulation, including the elimination of regulations protecting labor and financial markets, health, and the environment.

- Neoliberalism promotes trade liberalization to eliminate trade barriers and to facilitate the flow of capital and goods across national borders. It advocates permitting foreign investment in all sectors of the economy even if doing so results in the displacement of domestic economic actors.
- Neoliberal doctrine seeks to reduce the role of the state/government, including the diminishment or even elimination of its social responsibilities. It reconceptualizes the role of the state from serving public provision to promoting and supporting the private sector. In the process the institutional capacity of the state to deliver public sector services has been severely undermined.
- Neoliberal policies support financialization, the proliferation of financial markets and their penetration into almost every area of economic and social life. Financialization has been associated with the expansion of speculative assets at the expense of mobilizing and allocating investment for genuine economic activity. This process, and a defining characteristic of neoliberalism itself, has been to redistribute income to a class of rentiers (persons or entities receiving income from property or securities) (Fine and Hall 2012, 45, 47, 48).
- Neoliberal ideology advocates for privatizing infrastructure, utilities, and social services through selling them to private investors or transferring their management to the private sector. Privatization and deregulation are viewed as the way to eliminate bureaucratic red tape, increase efficiency and productivity, improve quality, and reduce costs (Harvey 2005, 64). In countries where neoliberal prescriptions have been widely implemented in the health sector, it has led to the partial or full commercialization of health services increasing their cost and restricting their availability to those able to pay for them.
- Another goal of neoliberalism is to cut public expenditures for social services like health and education, including reducing welfare programs and the safety net for the poor. Although the claim is often made that generous entitlements are unaffordable, neoliberal advocates favor reductions in social expenditures as a policy objective even when extra spending is not necessary. For example, nearly half of U.S. states, twenty-four as of June 2014, refused to expand Medicaid even though the federal government would have covered 90 to 100 percent of the

costs under the Affordable Care Act (The Henry J. Kaiser Family Foundation 2014).

- Neoliberalism seeks to secure private and corporate property rights and increase the benefits going to the wealthy through favorable public policies and, if necessary, active state intervention. While neoliberalism argues that the government should not interfere in the operation of the market, it is supportive of the use of the power of the government to protect capital and private property, even if necessary through highly coercive policies (Schrecker 2011, 54). As North American legal scholar Cass Sunstein has commented, "Those who denounce state intervention are the ones who most frequently and successfully invoke it. The cry of laissez faire mainly goes up from those who, if really 'left alone' would instantly lose their wealth-absorbing power" (quoted in Yamin 2008, 9). While social welfare has fallen under neoliberalism, corporate welfare has risen.

All of these policies have had a significant detrimental impact on economic and social rights.

Normative Dissonance of Neoliberal and Human Rights Approaches

Many human rights theorists and advocates perceive neoliberal ideologies as fundamentally incompatible with the human rights regime, and this is a view I share. Paul O'Connell argues that neoliberalism and human rights are conflicting paradigms. He views neoliberalism as inimical, both in theory and practice, to the protection of human rights. He warns that "advocates for human rights, be they grassroots campaigners, academics or members of the global human rights officialdom, must take a strong stance against prevailing orthodoxies of neoliberalism in order to genuinely advance and entrench a culture of human rights protection" (2007). Margaret Somers goes further. She warns that the neoliberal paradigm, particularly neoliberal globalization, challenges not only the existence of particular economic and social entitlements but also the extent to which a "right-to-have rights" is recognized (2008).

The orientation and principles of neoliberalism contravene the human rights ethos in many ways. In contrast with neoliberalism's placing the unfettered market at the center of its thinking and values, human rights are grounded on the recognition of the inherent dignity and worth of the human person and the commitment to the protection and promotion of human welfare. The human rights paradigm treats access to health and essential inputs such as water, sanitation, and adequate nutrition as entitlements and public goods, and not as commodities as in the neoliberal economic model. While neoliberal policies tend to benefit the most economically advantaged, human rights confer priority on the fulfillment of the needs of the most disadvantaged and vulnerable, the very groups neoliberal economic policies tend to harm the most. The fulfillment of economic and social rights depends on the existence of an effective and activist state, something that is anathema to neoliberalism (Chapman 2009, 100).

Some human rights advocates point out that market-based priority setting for essential services is incompatible with a rights framework (Yamin and Norheim 2014, 304). Market-based approaches make access to health dependent on the ability to pay, and not on human need. By doing so, market-based approaches implicitly accept that some members of society are likely to be excluded by financial barriers from needed health care. However, the extent to which a rights framework precludes intrusion of price mechanisms into the allocation of health care remains contested. A recent article distinguishes between essential and nonessential services in the potential permissibility of some market-based rationing. However, as the authors also acknowledge, it is sometimes difficult to draw a line between essential and nonessential health needs (Yamin and Norheim 2014, 304).

Yet another source of incompatibility is that neoliberal approaches rest on an excessively individualistic conception of society in which individuals are isolated from their social context. Some neoliberals would go so far as to claim that society is only a random collection of individuals, each pursuing his or her own self-interest. Although human rights seek to protect and promote the rights of individuals, modern conceptions of human rights also acknowledge that the individual functions as an intrinsic part of a community with mutual responsibilities and obligations for one another (Meier and Morsi 2005; Hiskes 2009; London et al. 2014). This is particularly the case as regards the right to health. As Alicia Yamin reflects, "Progressively realizing the highest attainable standard of health for diverse individuals and groups necessarily involves constantly evolving claims about what we owe each other and how to arrange social institutions to best provide it" (Yamin 2008, 9). For this and other reasons Chapter Two characterizes the right to health as having a strong community or social dimension as well as conferring an individual entitlement.

Relatedly, neoliberalism eliminates or excludes the concept of the public good and notions of social citizenship and social responsibility and replaces it with individual responsibility for health care, education, and social security. By shifting responsibility for social provision away from the state and toward individuals and households it legitimizes the reduced role of the state and the reduction or elimination of even limited entitlements.

Neoliberal thought does not deny the existence of rights, but it tends to have a narrow conception of the purview of human rights. Neoliberal thinkers tend to acknowledge a limited set of political and civil rights, particularly those that support the freedom of individual action and the right to own and dispose of property. This narrow liberal or libertarian conception of rights rests on a misleading distinction between so-called "negative" rights that are assumed to require only freedom from state interference and "positive" rights that are thought to imply affirmative entitlements to state intervention and therefore the expenditure of money (Yamin 2008, 8). In recent years, international law has recognized that all categories of human rights – civil and political and economic and social rights – require both forbearance on the part of the state and affirmative action and expenditures. Moreover, all human rights impose the same three types of correlative duties: to respect, protect, and fulfill the rights (Shue 1980, 35–64; Yamin 2008, 8).

An important reason that the neoliberal outlook cannot countenance social and economic rights, such as health care, as being legitimate human rights or genuine entitlements is that in the marketplace no one has a claim on the resources from society necessary to provide adequate food, education, housing, and health care. Recognition of social and economic rights also implies limits on the ways in which markets operate and the extent to which they permeate relationships (Schrecker 2011, 157). Additionally, implementation of social and economic rights requires using the power of the state to redistribute wealth and resources, another anathema to neoliberalism (Yamin 2008, 9).

A human rights approach rests on a conception of health and heath care as social or public goods of special moral importance that are designed to benefit whole populations. In contrast, neoliberalism tends to promote a view of health care as a commodity whose cost, price, availability, and distribution, like other consumer goods, should be left to the marketplace. As Edmund Pellegrino reflects (1999), commodification makes health care into a consumer commodity little different than television sets and pantyhose. It transforms the transactions between health care provider and patients into a commercial relationship. Moreover, if health care is a commodity, there is no room for the nonplayer, the person who can't "buy-in" – the poor, uninsured, and the uninsurable. Instead the special needs of the disabled, infirmed, aged, and chronically ill become the occasion for higher premiums or exclusion from enrolment. For these reasons, according to Pellegrino, health and medical care cannot and should not fit the conceptual model of commodities: "They center too much on universal human needs which are much more fundamental to human flourishing than any commodity per se. They depend on highly intimate personal interrelationships to be effective. They are not objects fashioned and owned by health professionals, nor are they consumed by patients like other commodities" (Pellegrino 1999, 251). Although Pellegrino does not adopt human rights terminology, he argues that a good society is one that provides those goods that are most closely linked to being human, and for Pellegrino heath care is one of the first of these goods (Pellegrino 1999, 259).

Economic and Social Impact of Neoliberalism

Economic Record of Neoliberalism

Despite the widespread adoption of neoliberal policies predicated on their supposed potential to promote economic growth, the actual economic record of neoliberalism is less than stellar. As one critic points out, "neoliberal public policies have been remarkably unsuccessful at achieving that they claim to be their aim: economic efficiency and social well-being" (Navarro 2007, 51). Others characterize neoliberalism to be more successful as a means of shifting the balance of political and economic power and funneling profits into the financial sector than to serve as an instrument for reinvigorating capitalist growth (Evans and Sewell 2013, 50). Neoliberal policies have given rise to a series of severe economic cycles and crises, the most severe of which was the Great Recession. The relatively slow growth of the industrialized economies, capped by the deep economic crisis beginning in 2007, has further tarnished the reputation of neoliberal policies but without identifying alternative economic models. While neoliberal policies have generally failed to stimulate sustainable economic growth and improve the well-being of the population, they have restored class power to ruling elites, as in the United States and to some extent Britain, and created conditions favorable to capitalist class formation, as in China, India, Russia, and elsewhere (Harvey 2005, 156).

Neoliberalism and the Growth of Inequality

Under neoliberalism economic inequalities have grown more marked both within and between countries as a consequence of the dynamics of capital accumulation under advanced capitalism and the neoliberal economic and political policies adopted. This is understandable because markets, when unregulated, tend to lead to higher levels of inequality. Neoliberal policies further amplify this tendency by shaping the operation of the market in ways that advantage the economic elite at the expense of the rest of the society (Reich 2008, 2011; Stiglitz 2013). Inequality has spiked in both developed and developing countries around the world. In some OECD countries inequality started to increase in the late 1970s and early 1980s, and then from the late 1980s the increase in income inequality became more widespread, affecting even countries traditionally with low inequality, such as Denmark, Sweden, and other Nordic countries. Currently in OECD countries the average income of the richest 10 percent of the population is nine times that of the poorest 10 percent, but the ratio varies widely from country to country: it reaches 10 to 1 in Italy, Japan, Korea, and the UK; around 14 to 1 in Israel, Turkey, and the United States, and 27 to 1 in Chile and Mexico (OECD 2011, 22–23).

The United States, the greatest adopter and foremost proponent of neoliberal policies, has the highest level of inequality among the advanced industrial countries, and its level of inequality is increasing (Stiglitz 2013, 27). Nobel economist Joseph Stiglitz describes trends in the United States as follows: "the rich are getting richer, the richest of the rich are getting still richer, the poor are becoming poorer and more numerous, and the middle class is being hollowed out" (2013, 9). Data from 2012 indicate that the top 1 percent control nearly 20 percent of U.S. income, significantly up from about 8 percent in the 1970s, and the richest 20 percent of Americans hold more than 50 percent of the nation's income. In contrast, the middle 20 percent receive only about 14 percent, and the poorest segment got only 3 percent. These figures approximate levels of inequality seen in the late nineteenth century's Gilded Age (Chin and Culotta 2014, 820). Particularly disturbing from a human rights perspective, given the special concern with protecting the vulnerable and the link between poverty and poor health status (Braveman and Gruskin 2003), the median household net worth fell absolutely as well, losing one-third of its value between 2003 and 2013 (Bernasek 2014, 6). These trends indicate that the riches accruing at the top have come at the expense of those down below (Stiglitz 2013, 8).

Longitudinal surveys and cross-sectional data have documented the extraordinarily high levels of inequality in poor- and middle-income economies as well, and there is concern that growing inequality in developing countries like China, India, South Africa, and Indonesia may inhibit future growth (Ravallion 2014, 853–854). The Gini coefficient, an estimate of levels of inequality ranging from a low of 0 to a high of 1.0, has risen to about 0.40 in the United States. It is currently estimated to be even higher in some other countries: 0.52 in China, 0.55 in India, and 0.70 in South Africa, the latter one of the highest in the world (Hvistendahl 2014, 833–844). In China the richest 10 percent now makes 13 times as much as the poorest 10 percent (Hvistendahl 2014, 832). The rise of inequality in South Africa with the worsening economic position of the Black majority has occurred primarily as a consequence of the neoliberal policies adopted after the end of the apartheid system despite a progressive constitution entrenching economic and social rights, including the right to health. Trends, however, are different in several Latin American countries: the historically large gulf between income classes has narrowed somewhat in thirteen of the seventeen Latin American countries since 2000, primarily as a result of government policies and investment in education and social welfare programs adopted by progressive political leaders (Hvistendahl 2014, 834–835).

In his landmark book, *Capital in the Twenty-First Century*, Thomas Piketty analyzes a huge database of income, inheritance, and national wealth data from two centuries compiled for more than twenty countries to document historical trends in income distribution (2014). His analysis of these data shows that modern capitalism has an inherent tendency to concentrate wealth at the top of society. The main driver of inequality is the tendency of returns on capital to exceed the rate of economic growth over the long term. As a result, families who own capital tend to acquire more and more wealth, and the entrepreneur becomes more and more dominant over those who own nothing but their labor (Piketty 2014, 571).

Piketty describes inequality in the developed economies, particularly the United States, as having reached an extreme point approaching "terrifying" disparities that are potentially threatening to democratic societies and to the values of social justice on which they are based (2014, 571). "Modern economic growth and the diffusion of knowledge have made it possible to avoid the Marxist apocalypse but have not modified the deep structures of capital and inequality – or in any case not as much as one might have imagined in the optimistic decades following World War II" (2014, 1). He cautions that "[W]hen the rate of return on capital exceeds the rate of growth of output and income, as it did in the nineteenth century and seems quite likely to do again in the twenty-first, capitalism automatically generates arbitrary and unsustainable inequalities that radically undermine the meritocratic values on which democratic societies are based" (2014, 1).

However, Piketty is not an economic determinist in regard to inequalities of wealth and income. He underscores that the history of the distribution of wealth has always been deeply political and cannot be reduced to purely economic mechanisms (2014, 20). "The history of inequality is shaped by the way economic, social and political actors view what is just and what is not, as well as by the relative power of those actors and the collective choices that result" (Piketty 2014, 20). In an essay written with Emmanuel Saez, he summarizes his view as follows: "Inequality does not follow a deterministic process ... There are powerful forces pushing alternately in the direction of rising or shrinking inequality. Which one dominates depends on the institutions and policies that societies choose to adopt" (2014, 842).

His historical analysis lends credence to the view that inequality does not necessarily follow a deterministic or unilinear process. During the first half of the twentieth century income inequality declined in Europe and the United States as a result of the physical destruction of the two world wars, the Great Depression, and the regulatory and fiscal policies adopted to deal with these developments (2014, 146–150). Then in the years following World War II, many nations adopted policies to distribute wealth in a relatively equitable manner through devoting increasing shares of the national income to social spending or what Piketty terms the evolution of the social state. A concurrent rise in industrial productivity and a population boom boosted economies and benefited the middle class (2014, 475–477). This period of more equitable development, which roughly coincides with the heyday of the Welfare State, ended in the 1980s with the movement into a period of low growth and the adoption of neoliberal economic and political policies.

For Piketty there is no simple solution to the increase in inequality. Historically decreases in inequality have occurred during periods with a high rate of economic and population growth as in Europe during the three decades following World War II. He anticipates that today only China and perhaps some other emerging economies will be able to sustain the growth rates of 4 to 5 percent that are necessary. He predicts growth rates in developed economies will not exceed 1.00 to 1.15 percent in the long run, regardless of the economic policies adopted (2014, 572).

Nevertheless Piketty believes there are ways in which democracy can gain control over capitalism and ensure the general interest takes precedence over private interest while preserving the economic openness on which growth depends. He foresees that one of the most important issues in coming years will be the development of new forms of property and democratic control of capital. In particular, he advocates for the availability of economic information and financial transparency as key to democratic governance and participation (2014, 569). His key proposal is the institution of a progressive annual tax on capital, with rates ranging between 1 and 5 to 10 percent depending on the amount of capital held by individuals to contain the unlimited growth of global inequality of wealth. He also acknowledges the challenges in doing so: it would require a high level of international cooperation and in Europe greater regional political integration, both of which would be difficult to achieve (2014, 572–573).

Joseph Stiglitz's critique of the level of inequality in the United States and its detrimental impacts in his book *The Price of Inequality* (2012, 2013) complements Piketty's analysis. Like Piketty, Stiglitz rejects the inevitability of the increase in inequality and instead sees it as a product of political and economic policies that have favored the economic elite at the expense of the rest of the society. According to Stiglitz, wealth holders' financial resources translate into political inequality and political inequality gives rise to policies that increase economic inequality. In a political system like that of the United States, which is overrun by money, wealth holders are able to design the rules of the game enabling them to retain high after-tax rates of resources relative to economic growth. He documents how neoliberal economic and political policies adopted during the past thirty years have curtailed welfare programs for the poor while increasing corporate welfare. In the process, the gross inequities have reduced the median incomes of the poor and middle class and depressed the living standards for the majority in our society.

Health Implications of Inequality

Economic inequality, particularly the kind of extreme levels that exist today, has significant health implications. The relevance of work on the social determinants of health to the right to health will be developed at greater length in Chapter Eight, but briefly, research has shown that income constitutes one of the most important social determinants of health (Braveman and Gruskin 2003, 81). The WHO Commission on the

Social Determinants of Health cites data from countries at a wide range of economic levels that show a correlation between the place of people on the social gradient, the societal social and economic ladder, and their health outcomes and life expectancy: according to the Commission on the Social Determinants of Health, the poor health of the poorest of the poor and health inequities within and across societies are caused by the unequal distribution of income, goods, and services and of the consequent chance of leading a flourishing life (Commission on the Social Determinants of Health 2008, 30–32). As an example, America's poor have a life expectancy that is almost 10 percent lower than those at the top of the socioeconomic ladder (Stiglitz 2013, 17).

Moreover, there is increasing evidence that economic and social inequality, and not just absolute deprivation, is bad for health. Or to put the matter another way, research has shown that more equal societies tend to have better health (Subramanian and Kawachi 2004; Wilkinson 2005; Wilkinson and Pickett 2006; Wilkinson and Pickett 2009). In their book *The Spirit Level: Why Greater Equality Makes Societies Stronger*, Richard Wilkinson and Kate Pickett document that more unequal societies are associated with lower life expectancy, higher rates of infant mortality, higher rates of depression, greater obesity, a higher incidence of mental illness, greater levels of drug and alcohol addiction, and other poor health indicators (2009, 19, 81). While the benefits of greater equality in a society extend to everyone, they tend to be greatest among the poor (Wilkinson and Pickett 2009).

Economic inequality also affects the quality of social life and has implications for human rights. Chapter Seven focuses on the social determinants of health and will develop this theme. Briefly, more egalitarian societies tend to have greater social trust and ability to cooperate, and their members are less likely to discriminate against vulnerable groups. Conversely, people living in more unequal societies have lower levels of the social capital necessary to sustain commitment to human rights. People feel greater hostility, are less likely to be involved in community life, and they are much less likely to trust one another (Wilkinson 2005, 25). Richard Wilkinson associates the higher levels of violence common in more unequal societies to the way that low social status assaults peoples' sense of dignity and self-worth and the inclination of people who feel disrespected to respond violently to save face. He contrasts this behavior with the more affiliative and cooperative social strategies appropriate to friendship and social alliances that are more likely to flourish between equals.

Support for a human rights approach, particularly for social and economic rights, also depends on the existence of a sense of social solidarity and community across a society that is conducive to a redistribution of resources. Extreme levels of inequality, such as being experienced in the United States, lead to an economic and social divide that militates against the development of social solidarity linkages across income levels. It also contributes to the unwillingness of those at the top to contribute their fair share to the funding of the public goods necessary to the functioning of the society. As Stiglitz comments, America's economic divide has grown so large it is hard for those in the top 1 percent to imagine what life is like at the bottom of the economic ladder, and increasingly in the middle as well (2013, 11). He suggests that the real solution to the inequality crisis lies in focusing on community rather than on the self-interest, which is the mantra of neoliberalism, both community as a means to prosperity and as a goal in its own right (2013, xxi). The dilemma is how to change this frame of reference.

Impact of Neoliberal Policies on Health Systems

Commercialization and Privatization of Health Services

Maureen Mackintosh and Meri Koivusalo conceptualize the commercialization of health services as encompassing several interrelated processes: (1) the provision of health care services through market relationships to those able to pay for them; (2) investment in and provision of those services and of inputs to them for cash income or profit; and (3) health care finance through individual payment and private insurance (2005, 3). Commercialization overlaps with, but also differs from, the privatization of health services and financing, which entail the ownership and/or management by nongovernmental entities. This chapter addresses issues related to commercialization while the next focuses on the impact of privatization on the right to health. Because commercialization and privatization are often interrelated processes, it may be somewhat artificial to analyze them sequentially. While commercial behavior is more common in privatized health services and financing, commercialization has also been introduced into publicly owned bodies (UNRISD 2007, 1). Commercialization can apply to select health services or market relationships can permeate the health system more broadly, as it has in the case of the United States.

The United States, with its commercialized fee-for-service medical system, has the most thoroughly market-driven medical system and provides a caution for other countries. In 1980, Arnold Relman, then the editor of *The New England Journal of Medicine*, a leading medical journal, wrote a landmark article in which he sounded a warning that the American health system was becoming a medical-industrial complex driven by financial incentives rather than an ethic of care (1980). According to Relman, health care, driven by profit, had become a competitive business; advertising and marketing of pharmaceuticals and health services were common; and costs were rising relentlessly (1980). Subsequent developments further entrenched commercial practices. For-profit insurance plans that scarcely existed a few decades ago are now dominant (Relman 2010); health care providers are even more frequently influenced by economic incentives and many are very entrepreneurially oriented (Relman 2010); the pharmaceutical industry spends more on marketing and administration than on research and development and uses its immense wealth and power to co-opt Congress into passing favorable laws and regulators (the U.S. Food and Drug Administration) to adopt less stringent standards (Angell 2004); and fields of medicine, like psychiatry, have been seriously distorted by economic considerations (Whitaker 2010). In the process, health care has become a commodity; commercialization has led to overutilization of health services (Brownlee 2007); and escalating medical costs have subverted the finances of individual patients and the U.S. economy (Relman 2010). Currently, the United States spends about twice as much per capita as other advanced industrialized countries on health care but still provides inadequate health care, and, alone among the advanced industrialized states, its health system has not achieved universality of health coverage.

Commercialization has also been a factor in health systems elsewhere. There have been sustained and continuing attempts to apply market reforms to health systems in many developing countries, frequently stimulated by the policies of the World Bank and other aid agencies.

OECD countries have implemented market-based approaches on a more piecemeal basis. Two European countries within OECD, the UK (primarily England) and Portugal, have had more of a commitment to market-style reforms in their health systems, often despite their cost, political unpopularity, and the lack of evidence that they delivered the anticipated benefits (Lister 2013, 35). The UK has corporatized hospitals and introduced competition and quasi-markets into publicly funded health services (Lister 2013, 44). In recent years Sweden has also adopted fairly comprehensive profit-driven health sector reforms both at the primary care level and selectively at the tertiary level (Dahlgren 2012, 1).

Health care costs have been growing rapidly during the past several decades. One estimate is that since 1970 total real per capita health spending has increased fourfold in advanced economies while spending as a share of GDP has increased from 6 to 12 percent. Rising income, the aging of populations, technological advancements, and health policies have been identified as drivers of growth in health spending (Gupta et al. 2012, 5). The rising cost of several of these factors, particularly advances in technology and pharmaceuticals, are intertwined with the commercialization of these sectors.

Commercialization of health care has significant implications for the affordability of health care, which is a major human rights concern. Commercialization provides incentives to raise prices for medical services and inputs, often with no relationship to their actual costs, but instead to estimates of what the market will bear. Market approaches also promote a more expensive curative medicine model focused on treatment rather than a public health oriented preventive approach. In commercialized health systems the practice of medicine has often become compromised as physicians, particularly those who are specialists, face pressures to behave more like entrepreneurs rather than as healers. At least in the United States, there is a considerable tendency to unnecessarily medicalize conditions, to overdiagnose (Welch et al. 2011) and to overtreat patients (Brownlee 2007). Hoped-for-profits to benefit their shareholders and their executives drive commercially based companies operating in the health sector (Lister 2013, 10–11).

That there is a rough correlation between the degree of reliance on market-driven solutions and the cost of health care can be seen in the per capita costs of health care in the United States, the most commercialized health care system, as compared with other developed countries. The U.S. health care system is the most expensive in the world, with a per capita health expenditure in 2011 of $8,508 as compared with $3,800 in Australia, $4522 in Canada, $4,118 in France, $4,495 in Germany, and $3,405 in the UK (Thomson et al. 2013, 5). Yet, despite investing almost twice as much per capita as other developed countries, the United States underperforms these countries on key dimensions of health system performance including quality, access, efficiency, equity, and healthy lives. A recent Commonwealth Fund report, a foundation specializing in health research, ranked the United States last overall among the eleven developed nations studied on its combination of performance indicators, as it had in a series of previous studies (Davis et al. 2014).

An item-for-item comparison for some procedures and medications can also show just how much more everything costs due to U.S.

commercialization of health care, contributing to the high price of health care and incurring $2.7 trillion in medical expenses. According to 2012 data compiled by the International Federation of Health Plans, the average price of an angiogram in the United States is $914 compared with $35 in Canada. Colonoscopies, the most expensive screening test that healthy Americans routinely undergo, can cost $6,000 to $9,000 in the United States – although health insurance companies usually negotiate down the cost significantly thus lowering the U.S. average to $1,185 (without the added fees for sedation by an anesthesiologist, a practice common in the United States but not other countries), while the price in Switzerland is less than half as much. Americans, on average, pay about four times as much for a hip replacement than Europeans. A hip replacement, with an average cost of $40,364 in the United States, is a fraction of the cost, $7,731, in Spain. An MRI scan, which averages at $1,121 in the United States, is only $319 in the Netherlands. The cost of hospital stays in this country is more than triple the cost in European countries although it is not any longer in length (Rosenthal 2013).

Institutional Corruption of the Pharmaceutical Industry

Much has been written about how the extensive financial links between the pharmaceutical, medical device, and medical supply industries and medical researchers and practitioners engender serious conflicts of interest that may unduly influence professional judgments and threaten the integrity of scientific investigations, the objectivity of medical education, and the quality of patient care. This problem has been particularly well documented in the United States, but it also exists in other industrialized societies with strong pharmaceutical industries, such as France, Germany, and Japan (Rodwin 2011). A 2009 U.S. Institute of Medicine Study (IOM) cited survey data to show the breadth and diversity of these relationships between industry and physicians, researchers, and educators in academic and community settings. It found, for example, that gifts from drug companies to physicians are ubiquitous; visits to physicians' offices by drug and medical device company representatives and the provision of drug samples are widespread; many faculty members receive research support from industry; faculty members and community-based physicians provide scientific, marketing, and other consulting services to companies, and some serve on company boards or as directors, or participate in industry speakers' bureaus as well; and commercial sources provide about half of the total funding for continuing medical education programs (Lo and Field 2009, S-2). The IOM study also documented some of the disturbing consequences of these ties including physicians and researchers failing to disclose substantial payments from drug companies as required by their universities, relevant government agencies, and/or medical journals; illegal payments or gifts to physicians made by medical device and pharmaceutical companies; companies and academic investigators suppressing negative results from industry-sponsored clinical trials or delaying publication; academic researchers agreeing to put their name on manuscripts after the data were collected and analyzed and drafts were written by individuals paid by industry; and professional societies and other groups that develop clinical practice guidelines choosing not to disclose their industry funding and their concomitant conflicts of interest (Lo and Field 2009, S-2).

On a structural level, the distortions and misrepresentations of the pharmaceutical corporations have resulted in what has been termed "institutional corruption." This term has been used to refer to the misalignment of the private profit-maximizing objectives of the pharmaceutical sector with public health needs, particularly in the United States (Gagnon 2013). Institutional corruption has occurred at three levels. First, through intense lobbying and large political contributions the pharmaceutical industry has been able to influence the U.S. Congress to pass legislation that has compromised the regulatory role and mission of the Food and Drug Administration (FDA). Second, primarily as a result of industry pressure, Congress has underfunded FDA enforcement capacities and instead turned to industry-paid user fees since 1992. With its lack of resources and dependence on pharmaceutical funding, the FDA has enacted industry-friendly rules that allow companies to design their own clinical trials in ways that minimize detection and reporting of harms while maximizing evidence of benefit. As a result of this regulatory capture, FDA approves drugs with few therapeutic advantages, fails to ensure sufficient testing for serious risks, and inadequately safeguards the public from harmful side effects. Because FDA criteria for approval provide little or no information to clinicians on how to prescribe new drugs, physicians are reliant on the information provided by pharmaceutical corporations, which often contains misleading claims. Third, the rampant conflict of interest described above in the relationship between physicians and industry has commercialized the role of physicians, undermining the capacity of physicians to function as independent, trusted advisers to patients (Light et al. 2013).

Cost Recovery and Imposition of Fees

Realization of the right to health is predicated on the affordability of health care services both for the state to meet its rights-based obligations and for its individuals to be able to fund their needed health care without an undue financial burden. Accessibility, identified in General Comment No. 14 as one of the essential elements of a right to health, includes economic accessibility (affordability). According to the general comment, health facilities, goods, and services must be affordable to all, and payment for health care services, as well as services related to the underlying determinants of health, has to be based on the principle of equity, so as to ensure that these services, whether privately or publicly provided, are affordable for all, including socially disadvantaged groups (CESCR 2000, para 12 (b) iii). Achieving these goals is difficult in a market-driven health system.

When the World Bank adopted a policy in the mid-1980s making the imposition of fees and cost recovery mechanisms for health care a condition of eligibility for loans, the fundamental rationale was that user fees would improve efficiency and provide needed resources for the health system (Rowden 2013, 176–177). It was also claimed that cost-sharing would dampen demand by discouraging unnecessary use of health services (Lister 2013, 154). However, cost-sharing measures in poor countries also deter sick patients from seeking needed care (Callahan and Wasunna 2006, 212). Moreover, evidence suggests that cost-sharing fees are not an effective mechanism for cost containment (Callahan and Wasunna 2006, 214). Nor has cost-sharing generated meaningful resources for health care (Lister 2013, 153–158).

During the 1980s and 1990s deep loan-mandated health budget cuts, introduction of user fees, and privatization greatly transformed the health systems of dozens of developing countries (Rowden 2013, 175). By 1998 about 40 percent of the World Banks' health, nutrition, and population projects, nearly 75 percent of which were in Africa, required the introduction or increased application of user fees. These fees could be quite substantial. Regardless of their resources, poor people were expected to pay for their own drugs and medical inputs, even at public facilities. Sometimes public hospitals also imposed a separate charge for consultations and services, especially for surgeries. Private health providers expected full payment for consultations at the point of service.

Cost-sharing measures have obvious equity implications. The burden of cost sharing falls heaviest on households with low incomes because price is more of a deterrent to use when it consumes a greater percentage of a household's funds. Patient charges are more likely to reduce access to health services for vulnerable groups: the poor, the elderly, the young, and the chronically sick. In turn, reduction in utilization or delays in seeking treatment are likely to lower their health status (Callahan and Wassuna 2006, 212). A variety of household surveys have shown that user fees and other cost-recovery mechanisms decrease access to health care for the poor (Katz 2005; UNICEF 2008; Oxfam International 2009). A 2004 DfID (UK Department for International Development) report, for example, documents that user fees are often associated with reduced use of services, especially by the poor and vulnerable in low-income countries; there is also a higher failure for them to complete treatments and delays in seeking treatment. Out-of-pocket payments to providers to finance health systems prevent millions of people around the world from seeking care and result in financial catastrophe and impoverishment for many of those who do obtain care. Surveys in eighty-nine countries covering 89 percent of the world's population indicate that 150 million people suffer financial catastrophe annually from payment for health services (Xu et al. 2006).

Today there is a shift in the international consensus away from the imposition of user fees in poor countries and a greater commitment, at least in theory, for using public financing mechanisms to promote universal health coverage. Numbers of high profile studies and prominent groups have recommended the removal of user fees to promote progress toward universal health coverage, particularly in poor countries. Even the World Bank has moved away from its earlier ideologically driven approach to requiring user fees for eligibility for loans and financing for projects (Rowden 2013, 178). Studies in countries that have eliminated user fees indicate that doing so increases use of services: in African countries the increases have ranged from 17 percent in Madagascar to 84 percent in Uganda (Lister 2013, 158). However, not all countries that imposed user fees in the 1990s in response to World Bank pressure have decreased or removed user fees. A 2006 survey of thirty-two African countries found twenty-seven still imposing fees (Lister and Labonté 2009, 190). Moreover, before fees can be removed without leading to a falling quality of care, levels of public funding available for health care must be increased, and at least as of 2005 many countries in Africa, which cancelled the fees public health clinics had imposed, had not provided the resources needed to compensate for the loss of income (Gilson and McIntyre 2005).

User fees are also imposed in most industrialized countries in the form of co-payments or co-insurance charges for health services. In the wake of the recession that began in 2007, many developed countries with publicly funded health care or social insurance systems increased these charges. As another cost saving measure, health packages often exclude coverage of some medical services and inputs, most often dental services, glasses, and pharmaceuticals. Many industrialized countries seek to reduce the regressive effects of cost sharing through annual caps on the out-of-pocket maximum to be paid for medical care. Some others reduce the level of coinsurance charged once patients have reached a specific threshold. A number of European countries exempt some categories of vulnerable patients from cost sharing – for example children, low-income, chronically ill, and the disabled (Callahan and Wasunna 2006, 214; Thomson et al. 2012, 6).

A recent survey of health care system financing and coverage in fourteen developed countries conducted by The Commonwealth Fund indicates that out-of-pocket health care spending per capita (presumably for office consultations) ranged from $338 in the UK and $464 in Japan at the lower end of the spectrum to $987 in the United States and $1455 in Switzerland at the higher end. Hospital spending per capita went from $1298 in Canada and $1304 in Germany to $2030 in Switzerland and $2730 in the United States. For those countries where data were available for annual spending on pharmaceuticals the per capita figures ranged from Denmark ($300) and Norway ($388) at the lower end of the spectrum and Canada ($752) and the United States ($995) at the higher end (Thomson et al. 2013). These charges can be a burden for some patients.

A 2010 survey indicated that some adults in these countries had to forego medical care because of their inability to afford user fees or the full cost of the services in the past year. The percentages were relatively low in some countries (5 percent in the UK, 6 percent in the Netherlands, 10 percent in Sweden and Switzerland) but still higher than would have been anticipated for countries that are considered to have universal health coverage. The figure for the United States was particularly troublingly: 37 percent of the respondents reported they had gone without recommended care, did not see a doctor when they were ill, or failed to fill prescriptions because of cost considerations (Thomson et al. 2014, 8).

Pressures for Reductions in Health Expenditures

One of neoliberalism's central claims is that generous health entitlements are not economically viable and sustainable. Neoliberal advocates have long advocated for cutbacks in social expenditures in countries at both ends of the economic spectrum, those that are affluent as well as those that are poor. Neoliberal health care reforms begun during the 1980s led to massive cuts in public health expenditures shrinking per capita spending in the poorest thirty-seven countries by half. The 1991 reforms in India squeezed still further the already significantly underfunded public health system. There was also a significant decline in health spending in most African countries even though they already had a low funding base. By the turn of the millennium health care in most low- and middle-income countries was characterized by a crumbling public health system with inadequate infrastructure, increased penetration of the private sector to fill the vacuum created by the retreat of public services, and a consequent rise in catastrophic out-of-pocket expenditures to pay for health care from the private sector (Sengupta 2013, 5).

The global financial crisis that began in 2007 also resulted in drastic reductions in health spending in some countries, sometimes because of actual or anticipated financial constraints and sometimes because the recession provided a justification for the imposition of austerity measures. Some countries have faced reductions in tax revenues, but the decision to respond to this problem by disproportionately cutting social welfare spending instead of reducing or postponing investment in other sectors, as for example, corporate subsidies or defense spending, has often been ideologically motivated. Several countries slashed social spending while continuing to subsidize the same banks whose irresponsible policies caused the financial crisis. Moreover, some revenue shortfalls have been artificially created through ideologically driven tax cuts. For example, the state of Kansas used reductions in its tax revenues to justify draconian across the board cuts in health spending and other government services. However, the state's declining revenues resulted from income tax cuts, among the largest ever enacted by a state in the United States, which largely benefitted the wealthy (The New York Times Editorial Staff 2014).

A WHO study of health policy responses to the Great Recession in Europe indicates that many countries adopted austerity policies that resulted in cuts in their national health budgets, sometimes up to 20 percent (Bulgaria, Croatia, Estonia, Hungary, Iceland, Ireland, Italy, Greece, Latvia, Romania, Portugal, and Spain). Some countries reduced the state's contribution rate either across the board or for specific population groups, and several increased employer/employee contribution rates either across the board or for specific population groups (Mladovsky et al. 2012, 15). Many European countries also responded by removing some types of services from the public medical benefits package and instituting or increasing user charges for health services. Some of these increases in patient co-payments have been quite substantial (Saltman and Cahn 2013). In Spain, Portugal, Greece, and Ireland, reductions in government funding for their national health services of more than 20 percent mandated by the conditionality in the bailout packages provided by the International Monetary Fund, the European Central Bank, and the European Commission to stabilize their banking sectors led to the unraveling of universal health care systems (Legido-Quigley et al. 2013). Both the economic crisis and the decisions of some governments to restrict access to health care, close facilities, lay off doctors and health workers, and/or increase the cost of health services have had deleterious health effects in Europe. Researchers have documented outbreaks of infectious diseases, increased rates of HIV transmission, higher incidence of mental disorders, increases in the number of suicides, and lower levels of reported satisfactory health status. The demise of universal health care in Spain and Greece has been particularly devastating. Greece's austerity measures and the structural reforms adopted have led to significant reductions in health access including for child health services, mental health services at a time in which mental health problems have increased, and prenatal services for pregnant women, the latter leading to a substantial rise in the stillbirth rate (21 percent increase between 2008 and 2011) (Karanikolos et al. 2013; Kentikelenis et al. 2014).

A human rights paradigm requires that countries take special precautions to protect vulnerable and disadvantaged groups in periods of economic downturn if economic adjustments require cut backs in benefits (Chapman and Carbonetti 2011, 694), but this has not happened in most of the countries reducing their health spending. To the contrary, vulnerable groups, such as immigrants and the unemployed, have frequently suffered the greatest impact. For example, Spain no longer provides any of the estimated 873,000 undocumented workers in the country with non-emergency care (Legido-Quigley et al. 2013). Also, the structure of benefits in countries with social insurance schemes like Greece has meant that the long-term unemployed have lost their coverage (Karanikolos et al. 2013). The situation in Greece has also eliminated right to health guarantees for children (Kentikelenis 2014, 750).

Some analysts argue that the Great Recession augers an era of prolonged low economic growth with long-term implications for financing health entitlements. Richard Saltman and Zachary Cahn, for example, propose that the current low rates of economic growth in European countries may reflect long-term structural changes requiring the streamlining of their health systems. They link the slowdown in European growth with the impact of globalization and longer term structural forces that have shifted economic growth and wealth production from developed countries, particularly in Europe, to countries in East Asia (Saltman and Cahn 2013). However, the assessment of the unaffordability of health entitlements often fails to take into account economic alternatives to reduce budget deficits and other approaches to stabilizing health spending: ending or significantly reducing tax subsidies for corporations and the wealthy segments of the population would increase tax revenues so as to have greater resources for social welfare expenditures; introducing caps or making them more rigorous on the costs of medical services and inputs, particularly the level of profits and costs of pharmaceuticals, would make health care more affordable; moving to different payment approaches such as substituting capitation payments for fee-for-payment reimbursement schemes would also reduce health care costs. Here the example of Iceland is relevant. Like Spain, Ireland, and Portugal, Iceland had a severe banking crisis, but its government and population rejected the terms of a proposed IMF financial rescue package, which required significant reductions in spending for social services. Instead the government allowed its banks to collapse and increased its investment in social protection and measures to get people back to work. Iceland also retained its restrictive policies on alcohol and cigarettes, again contrary to the advice of the IMF. As a result, Iceland did not suffer the kind of adverse health effects of other countries. Moreover, unlike other European countries imposing austerity policies that cut social welfare benefits, its economy has gradually recovered (Karanikolos et al. 2013, 1329).

The Failure of Markets in Health Care

The rationale for adopting market-based approaches is that market mechanisms can impose greater efficiency and thereby lower the cost, but many health analysts and some economists believe that market approaches are not appropriate for health care. According to economist Robert Evans, "There is in health care no 'private, competitive market' of the form described in the economics textbooks, anywhere in the world. There never has been, and inherent characteristics of health and health care make it impossible that there ever could be" (1998, 9). Even a number of World Bank studies acknowledge that market mechanisms in the financing of health care "will not ensure either equity or economic efficiency because of the characteristics of the health care market on both the supply and demand side, which suggest the presence of market failure conditions" (summed up by Dunlop and Martins and quoted in Lister 2013, 28).

Some of the reasons for market failure in health care on the supply side are:

- There are too few providers to allow competitive pressures to drive down prices;
- There is insufficient standardization of quality, and
- There is unequal knowledge on the part of both patients and providers (Lister 2013, 28).

Demand side limitations include the following:

- Dependence on the professional expertise of doctors and of nursing staff opens up the possibility of supplier-induced demand or of patients failing to receive adequate care;
- The prevalence in advanced economies of "third party" payment systems (public or private insurance or tax-funded systems) reduces the incentives for the doctor and patient to minimize the cost of care;
- The uneven and uncertain demand for health care, which raises the need for risk-pooling;
- The reluctance of patients suffering pain or life-threatening illness to choose not to have treatment as compared with a customer for other, more optional, goods and service;
- The potential for exclusion of patients likely to be more costly, such as those with chronic conditions or from low-income groups, through "cherry-picking" by insurance companies (Lister 2013, 37).

Market advocates assume that patients will be well informed and make careful and rational decisions based on cost/benefit analysis. However, studies done in the United States indicate that information about an essential feature of market transactions – costs – is typically not disclosed to patients until long after treatment. Patients are not informed about either the total cost or the out-of-pocket costs. Often the provider – the physician – does not know this information. It is often difficult to know these costs in advance because different payers, both private insurers and government payers, often negotiate separate rates for the same procedure. In order to inform the patient or the provider it would be necessary to know the exact requirements of the patients' plans in terms of co-payments, deductibles, out-of-pocket maximums and the specifics of other types of coinsurance, as well as how much of those co-insurance requirements the particular patient has already met. Typically, only those without insurance coverage are charged the full price listed on the charge master. Yet another complication is that many treatments involve charges for multiple procedures at multiple points in time, administered by multiple practitioners, each of which may bill separately, and sometimes involving separate facility charges (Hall 2014, 44).

Weakening of Health Systems

As Paul Hunt, the first Special Rapporteur on the right to health noted, a strong and effective health system is fundamental to a healthy and equitable society as well as to the realization of the right to health (2008). However, too few countries currently have what could be characterized as a strong and effective health system. A 2007 publication of WHO laments that in too many countries health systems "are on the point of collapse, or are accessible only to particular groups of the population" (p. 1). A recent characterization of the crisis for health care mentions "fragmented, disintegrated systems, riven by competition and conflicting interests" (Lister 2013, 15). Health systems in many industrialized countries bear the scars of cutbacks in response to decisions to reduce health spending, while in the case of poor and some middle-income countries, years of low financing of health systems, partly as a result of the pressures to privatize and commercialize health services imposed by international financial institutions and partly due to the crushing debt burden on many poor countries, have significantly weakened public health institutions. Ineffective and failing health systems have significant and enduring consequences for their populations. WHO links unacceptably low-health outcomes across much of the developing world and the persistence of deep inequities in health status in all countries to failing or inadequate health systems (WHO 2007, 1).

Health reforms utilizing a market-based approach have contributed to this serious deficiency in a variety of ways. Many details of these reforms have already been noted. To review some of the most important, the constraints on public funding of health have weakened the public health system and forced the population even in poor countries to rely on private health providers they cannot afford. A shift from the conception of health as a social good to an emphasis on the individual management of risk has encouraged neglect of the public health dimensions of the health system that benefit the whole population and are so crucial to the prevention of disease and disability. It has also sometimes resulted in the neglect of the social determinants of disease. Opening the health sector to trade and competition has split purchasers and providers and increased segmentation and fragmentation of the health system (Commission on the Social Determinants of Health 2008, 95–96).

Contrary to the core obligation "to ensure equitable distribution of all health facilities, goods and services" (CESCR 2000, para 43 (e)), health care is inequitably distributed around the world. The situation is most prevalent in low- and middle-income countries, but it exists in many high-income countries as well. Patients in lower socioeconomic strata, those living in poor neighborhoods, and those residing in rural areas are less likely to receive equitable access to health facilities, goods, and services (Commission on the Social Determinants of Health 2008, 94). The commercialization of health care in some cases shapes and in others aggravates the inequitable distribution of health facilities, goods, and services because commercially oriented providers locate their practices and services in potentially profitable locations. This encourages investment in urban and suburban areas in which higher income populations live and aggravates the underservicing of populations in poor and rural areas.

The requirement in some countries undergoing market-oriented reforms in health care that public providers should generate enough financial resources to cover the cost of their services has also been an aggravating factor in the maldistribution of facilities, and it is likely to grow worse in the future. Because the possibilities of generating enough resources are better in profitable than nonprofitable areas, many public health centers in rural and low-income areas experience greater financial problems than for-profit facilities in more affluent areas. Also public facilities are likely to treat more patients with complex and severe health problems than for-profit providers who may be reluctant to do so, especially in health systems where they receive capitation fees. Public health centers in one province in Sweden where the need for services was far greater than the resources generated became unprofitable and were then forced to close down (Dahlgren 2012, 8). Similarly, the National Health Service in Britain recently declared three hospitals in London to be effectively bankrupt and put them under a special administrator as a preliminary to privatizing them (Royce 2014).

The experience of Sweden provides an example of the impact of profit-driven health sector reforms in contributing to the inequitable distribution of health facilities. Sweden is one of the countries in which neoliberal reforms have had the greatest impact on the health sector. A law adopted in 2006 gives all private for-profit providers, including those providing primary health care services, the right to decide where their tax financed services are to be located. The law has resulted in increased geographic inequities in the supply of tax financed health services. Although the law stimulated an expansion of primary health services, 88 percent of these new health services were located in areas with an already very good or good general service level. More than half were located in the three biggest cities where there was, particularly in the better-off areas, a relative oversupply of health centers and family doctors. Only one of the 168 new centers was situated in an area with a low general service and none in rural and sparsely populated areas. Also within the major cities high-income areas have been favored at the expense of low-income areas. This distribution resulted in five public health centers closing and no new public health centers were established. The failure to open new public health centers reflects the requirement in the law that country councils are forced to finance new private for-profit providers before they can establish public health centers in underserved areas, and there were no funds remaining to make an investment in public health centers (Dahlgren 2012, 1–5). Göran Dahlgren observes that "Tax payers living in 'unprofitable' areas are thus in many counties paying taxes for securing the profit for private providers in profitable areas" (2012, 3).

Göran Dahlgren asks "Should tax financed health services be forced to close where they are most needed in order to follow the rules of the market?" (2012, 8). Neoliberal advocates would answer yes. After all, they have designed health reforms with this in mind. But doing so fundamentally contravenes a human rights approach.

Concluding Reflections

As Chapter Four will discuss, international human rights law does not prescribe the type of economic systems required for the fulfillment of human rights obligations enumerated in the International Covenant on Economic, Social and Cultural Rights (ICESCR). Neither of the two general comments that discuss this issue, General Comment No. 3 (1990) and General Comment No. 14 (2000), stipulate how health care services should be delivered or paid for as long as the health care provision is consistent with human rights obligations. Clearly, however, not all methods of delivery and finance are equally conducive to the realization of the right to health. This chapter underscores the various ways in which market-oriented approaches are inimical to a human rights approach to health. Neoliberalism, which favors imposing market-oriented approaches to restructure health system, comprises a major challenge to the right to health. Both the values neoliberalism espouses and the policies it advocates constitute an impediment to the goal of securing better health for all.

Health systems can embed and reinforce inequality within the health sector and more broadly in the society or they can constitute a mechanism for combating poverty and inequality (Mackintosh 2006, 393). The increasing commercialization of health care since the 1970s, which has formed part of the broader pattern of adopting market-based approaches, has profoundly reshaped the public policy capabilities of health systems and their role in addressing inequality. Or to put the matter another way, commercialization is fundamentally detrimental to improving health equity. The analysis in this chapter concurs with Daniel Callahan and Angela Wasunna's assessment that "The principal, and well-recognized, danger of market practices is that they will increase health inequities, giving those with economic resources an advantage over those without" (2006, 257).

Many analysts do not dispute the tendency of the market to increase health inequities, but their rejoinder is that the market is more efficient. But the so-called choice between equity and efficiency, between welfare-oriented and market-oriented approaches, is a false dichotomy. Market-oriented approaches do not improve choices for the majority of people in many countries who cannot afford higher-end health care alternatives and sometimes are even priced out of all forms of commercialized health care. Moreover, contrary to neoliberal claims that market approaches are more efficient, international experience has demonstrated that greater reliance on the market to deliver health care is associated with high cost, inefficiency, inequity, and public dissatisfaction (Evans 1998, 8).

Importantly, there is also a correlation between lower levels of commercialization of health expenditure and better health outcomes. Or to put the finding another way, commercialization of expenditure is significantly associated with worse health outcomes. Spending more of a country's total income on private health care is not associated with better health life expectancy or lower child mortality (Mackintosh and Koivusalo 2005, 14). Conversely, countries that spend more of their GDP on health through public expenditure or social insurance tend to have significantly better health outcomes. Health outcomes in more affluent countries are positively associated with both higher incomes and more public and social health expenditure relative to GDP (Mackintosh and Koivusalo 2005, 15).

Nevertheless the process toward greater commercialization and privatization of health provision has effectively been unidirectional, with no obvious means by which the policies can be reversed, even when proven ineffective (Lister 2013, 9). In part, this reflects the difficulty of doing so, such as substituting public provision in seriously weakened health systems. Continuing ideological preferences and commitments also play a role. Important economic actors, as for example, the OECD, continue to promote market-based reforms despite their inability to provide significant evidence that existing reforms have delivered any improvements in efficiency or reductions in cost (Lister 2013, 9). But perhaps most significantly, important and powerful economic interests, such as large-scale multinational corporations, privatized health institutions, and pharmaceutical manufacturers, which draw large profits from health care expenditures, have vested interests in retaining the current approach.

References

Anell, Anders, Glenngård, Anna H., and Merkur, Sherry (2012) "Sweden," *Health Systems in Transition* 5: full issue.

Angell, Marcia (2004) *The Truth About the Drug Companies*, New York: Random House.

Attenstetter, Christa (2003) "Insights from Health Care in Germany," *American Journal of Public Health* 93 (1): 38–44.

Bernasek, Anna (2014) "The Typical Household Now Worth a Third Less," *The New York Times*, July 27, BU 6.

Boyle, Sean (2011) "United Kingdom (England)," *Health Systems in Transition* 13 (1), full issue.

Braveman, Paula and Gruskin, Sofia (2003) "Poverty, Equity, Human Rights and Health," *Bulletin of the World Health Organization* 81: 539–545.

Britannica Online Encyclopedia (2012) www.britannica.com/EBchecked/topic/639266/welfare-state.

Brownlee, Shannon (2007) *Overtreated: Why Too Much Medicine Is Making Us Sicker and Poorer*, New York, Berlin, and London: Bloomsbury.

Callahan, Daniel and Wasunna, Angela A. (2006) *Medicine and the Market: Equity v. Choice,* Baltimore: The Johns Hopkins University Press.

Canadian Museum of Civilization (n.d.) "Making Medicare: The History of Health Care in Canada: 1914–2007," www.civilization.ca/cmc/exhibiions/history/medicare/medicole.shtml.

CESCR (Committee on Economic, Social and Cultural Rights) (1990) General Comment No. 3, The Nature of States parties' Obligations, U.N. Doc. E/1991/23, annex III at 86 (1990), reprinted in Compilation of General Comments and General Recommendations Adopted by Human Rights Treaty Bodies, U.N. Doc. HRI/GEN/1, Rev. 6 at 14 (2003).

(2000) "General Comment 14: The Right to the Highest Attainable Standard of Health," U.N. Doc. E.C.12.2000.4.EN.

Chapman, Audrey (2009) "Globalization, Human Rights, and the Social Determinants of Health," *Bioethics* 23 (2): 97–111.

Chapman, Audrey R. and Carbonetti, Benjamin (2011) "Human Rights Protections for Vulnerable and Disadvantaged Groups: The Contributions of the UN Committee on Economic, Social and Cultural Rights," *Human Rights Quarterly* 33 (3): 682–732.

Chin, Gilbert and Culotta, Elizabeth (2014) "The Science of Inequality: What the Numbers Tell Us," *Science* 344 (6186): 819–821.

Commission on the Social Determinants of Health (2008) *Closing the Gap in a Generation: Health Equity Through Action on the Social Determinants of Health,* Geneva: World Health Organization.

Dahlgren, Göran (2012) "Profit Driven Health Sector Reforms: Experiences from Sweden," background paper for the 15th Turkish National Public Health Congress, October 2–6.

Davis, Karen, Stemikis, Kristof, Schoen, Cathy and Squires, David (2014) *Mirror, Mirror on the Wall: How the Performance of the U.S. Health Care System Compares Internationally, 2014 Update,* www.commonwealthfund.org/publications/fund-reports/2014/jun/mirror-mirror.

Esping-Andersen, Gösta (1990) *The Three World of Welfare Capitalism,* Cambridge and Princeton: Polity Press and Princeton University Press.

Evans, Peter B. and Swewll, William H., Jr. (2013) "Neoliberalism: Policy Regimes, International Regimes, and Social Effects," in Peter A. Hall and Michèle Lamont, eds., *Social Resilience in the Neoliberal Era,* New York: Cambridge University Press, pp. 35–68.

Evans, Robert G. (1998) Going for the Gold: The Redistributive Agenda Behind Market-Based Health Care Reform, Nuffield Occasional Papers, Health Economics Series Paper No. 3, www.nuffieldtrust.org.uk/>Publications.

Ferragina, Emanuele and Seeleib-Kaiser, Martin (2011) "Welfare: Past, Present, Futures," *Policy & Politics* 39 (4): 583–611.

Fine, Ben and Hall, David (2012) "Terrains of Neoliberalism: Constraints and Opportunities for Alternative Models of Service Delivery," in David McDonald and Greg Ruiters, eds., *Alternatives to Privatization: Public Options for Essential Services in the Global South,* London: Routledge; Pretoria: HSRC, pp. 45–70.

Fisher, Peter (2007) "The NHS from Thatcher to Blair," International Association of Health Policy, www.healthp.org/node/71.

Freedman, Lynn P., Waldman, Ronald J. de Pinho, Helen, Wirth, Meg E. et al. (2005) *Who's Got the Power: Transforming Health Systems for Women and Children,* London and sterling, Virginia: Earthscan for the Millennium Project.

Gagnon, Marc-André (2013) "Corruption of Pharmaceutical Markets: Addressing the Misalignment of Financial Incentives and Public Health," *Journal of Law, Medicine & Ethics* 39 (3): 571–580.

Gilson, Lucy and McIntyre, Di (2005) "Removing User Fees for Primary Care in Africa," *British Medical Journal* 331 (7519): 762–765, doi: 10.1136/bmj.331.7519.762.

Gupta, Sanjeev, Clements, Benedit, and Coady, David (2012) "The Challenge of Health Care Reform in Advanced and Emerging Economies," in Benedit Clements, David Coady, and Sanjeev Gupta, eds., *The Economics of Public Health Care Reform in Advanced and Emerging Economies*, Washington, DC: International Monetary Fund, pp. 3–22.

Hall, Alicia (2014) "Financial Side Effects: Why Patients Should Be Informed of Costs," *Hastings Center Report* 44 (3): 41–47.

Harvey, David (2005) *Neoliberalism: A Brief History*, Oxford: Oxford University Press.

Hiskes, Richard P. (2009) *The Human Right to a Green Future: Environmental Rights and Intergenerational Justice*, Cambridge and New York: Cambridge University Press.

Howard, Rhoda E. and Donnelly, Jack (1986) "Human Dignity, Human Rights, and Liberal Regimes," *American Political Science Review* 80: 801–817.

    (1989) "Human Dignity, Human Rights, and Political Regimes," in Jack Donnelly, ed., *Universal Human Rights in Theory & Practice*, Ithaca and London: Cornell University Press, pp. 66–74.

Hunt, Paul (2008) "Report of the Special Rapporteur on the right of everyone to the enjoyment of the highest attainable standard of physical and mental health, submitted to the Human Rights Council, 31 January 2008," U.N. Doc. A/HRC/7/11, focusing on the role of health systems in realizing the right to the highest attainable standard of health.

Hvistendahl, Mara (2014) "While Emerging Economies Boom, Equality Goes Bust," *Science* 344 (6186): 832–835.

Jaggar, Alison M. (2002) "Vulnerable Women and Neo-liberal Globalization: Debt Burdens Undermine Women's Health in the Global South," *Theoretical Medicine* 23: 425–440.

Karanikolos, Marina, Mladovsky, Philipa, Cylus, Jonathan, Thomson, Sarah, et al. (2013) "Financial Crisis, Austerity, and Health in Europe," *The Lancet* 381: 1323–1331.

Katz, Alison (2005) "The Sachs Report: Investing in Health for Economic Development – or Increasing the Size of the Crumbs from the Rich Man's Table?" *International Journal of Health Services* 1 (35): 171–188.

Kaveny, M. Cathleen (1999) "Commodifying the Polyvalent Good of Health Care," *Journal of Medicine and Philosophy*, 24 (3): 207–223.

Kentikelenis, Alexander, Karanikolos, Marina, Reeves, Aaron, McKee, Martin, et al. (2014) "Greece's Health Crisis: From Austerity to Denialism," *The Lancet* 383: 748–753.

Legido-Quigley, Helena, Urdaneta, Elena, Gonzalez, Alvaro, La Parra, Daniel, et al. (2013) "Erosion of Universal Health Coverage in Spain," *The Lancet* 382: 1977.

Light, Donald. W, Lexchin, Joel, Darrow, Jonathan J. (2013) "Institutional Corruption of Pharmaceuticals and the Myth of Safe and Effective Drugs," *Journal of Law, Medicine & Ethics* 41 (3); 590–600.

Lister, John (2013) *Health Policy Reform: Global Health versus Private Profit*, Farringdon and Oxfordshire, UK: Libri Publishing.

Lister, John and Ronald Labonté (2009) "Globalization and Health Systems Change," in Ronald Labonté, Ted Schrecker, Corinne Packer, and Vivien Runnels, eds., *Globalization and Health: Pathways, Evidence and Policy*, New York and London: Routledge, pp.181–212.

Lo, Bernard and Field, Marilyn J., eds. (2009) *Conflict of Interest in Medical Research, Education and Practice*, Washington, DC, National Academy of Sciences.

London, Leslie, Himongo, Chuman, Fick, Nicole, and Stuttaford, Maria (2014) "Social Solidarity and the Right to Health: Essential Elements for People-centered Health Systems," *Health Policy and Planning*, 30 (7): 938–945.

Mackintosh, Maureen (2006) "Commercialisation, Inequality and the Limits to Transition in Health Care: A Polyanyian Framework for Policy Analysis," *Journal of International Development* 18: 393–406.

Mackintosh, Maureen and Koivusalo, Meri (2005) "Health Systems and Commercialization: In Search of Good Sense," in Maureen Mackintosh and Meri Koisuvalo, eds., *Commercializatin of Health Care: Global Dynamics and Policy Responses*, Houndmills, Basingstoke, Hampshire, and New York: Palgrave Macmillan, pp. 1–21.

Martinez, Elizabeth and Garcia, Arnoldo (2000) "What is Neoliberalism?" National Network for Immigration Rights, www.globalexchange.org/references/econ101/neoliberalsimdefined.

Meier, Benjamin Mason and Mori, Larisa M. (2005) "The Highest Attainable Standard: Advancing a Collective Human Right to Public Health," *Columbia Human Rights Law Review* 37 (1): 101–147.

Mitchell, Neil, Howard, Rhoda E., and Donnelly, Jack (1987) "Liberalism, Human Rights, and Human Dignity: A Debate," *American Political Science Review* 81: 921–927.

Mladovsky, Philipa, Srivastava, Divya, Cylus, Jonathan, and Karanikolos, Marina (2012) "Health Policy Responses to the Financial Crisis in Europe," Policy Summary No. 5, WHO Regional Office for Europe and European Observatory on Health Systems and Policy.

Navarro, Vincente (2007) "Neoliberalism as a Class Ideology: Or, the Political Causes of the Growth of Inequalities," *International Journal of Health Services* 371 (1): 47–62.

O'Connell, Paul (2007) "On Reconciling Irreconcilables: Neoliberal Globalisation and Human Rights," *Human Rights Law Review* 7 (3): 483–509.

OECD (2011) *Divided We Stand: Why Inequality Keeps Rising*, www.oecd.org/els/social/inequality.

Pellegrino, Edmund D. (1999) "The Commodification of Medical and Health Care: The Moral Consequences of a Paradigm Shift from a Professional to a Market Ethic," *Journal of Medicine and Philosophy* 24 (3): 243–266.

Piketty, Thomas (2014) *Capital in the Twenty-First Century*, trans. Arthur Goldhammer, Cambridge and London: Harvard University Press.

Piketty, Thomas and Saez, Emmanuel (2014) "Equality in the Long Run," 344 (6186): 838–847.

Ravallion, Martin (2014) "Income Inequality in the Developing World," *Science* 344 (6186): 851–855.

Reich, Robert B. (2008) *Supercapitalism: The Transformation of Business, Democracy, and Everyday Life*, New York: Vintage Books.

    (2011) *Beyond Outrage: What Has Gone Wrong with Our Economy and Our Democracy, and How to Fix Them*, New York: Vintage Books.

Relman, Arnold (1980) "The New Medical-Industrial Complex," *The New England Journal of Medicine* 303: 963–972.

    (2010) "Health Care: The Disquieting Truth," *The New York Review of Books*, September 30, www.nybooks.com/articles/archives/2010/sep30/health-care-disquieting-truth?pagination=false.

Rodwin, Marc A. (2011) *Conflicts of Interest and the Future of Medicine: The United States, France and Japan*, New York: Oxford University Press.

Roosevelt, Franklin D. (1941) Four Freedoms Speech: Annual Message to Congress on the State of the Union, www.fdrlibrary.

Rosenthal, Elisabeth (2013) "The 2.7 Trillion Medical Bill: Colonoscopies Explain Why U.S. Leads the World in Health Expenditure," *The New York Times*, June 1, p. 1, www.nytimes.com/2013/...colonoscopies-explain...

Rowden, Rick (2009) *The Deadly Ideas of Neoliberalism: How the IMF Has Undermined Public Health and the Fight Against AIDS*, London and New York: Zed Books.

    (2013) "The Ghosts of User Fees Past," *Health and Human Rights Journal* 15 (1): 175–185.

Royce, Robert (2014) "Bankrupt Hospitals in England Turn to Private Sector," Managed Care, www.managedcaremag.com/content/bankrupt-hsopitals-england.

Saltman, Richard B. and Cahn, Zachary (2013) "Restructuring Health Systems for an Era of Prolonged Austerity: An Essay," *BMJ* 346:f3972 doi: 10.1136/bmj.f3972.

Schrecker, Ted (2011) "The Health Case for Economic and Social Rights Against the Global Marketplace," *Journal of Human Rights* 10 (2): 151–177.

Sengupta, Amit (2013) "Universal Health Coverage: Beyond Rhetoric, Municipal Services Project," Occasional Paper No. 20, Kingston, Ontario and Bellville, South Africa, www.municipalservicesproject.org.

Shue, Henry (1980) *Basic Rights: Subsistence, Affluence, and U.S. Foreign Policy*, Princeton: Princeton University Press.

Somers, Margaret R. (2008) *Genealogies of Citizenship: Market, Statelessness, and the Right to Have Rights*, Cambridge: Cambridge University Press.

Stiglitz, Joseph E. (2012, 2013) *The Price of Inequality: How Today's Divided Society Endangers Our Future*, New York: W.W. Norton.

Subramanian, S. V. and Kawachi, Ichiro (2004) "Income Inequality and Health: What Have We Learned So Far?" *Epidemiology Review* 26 (1): 78–91.

Tatara, Kozo and Okamoko, Etujo (2009) "Japan," *Health Systems in Transition* 11 (5): full issue.

Teeple, Gary (2000) *Globalization and the Decline of Social Reform: Into the Twentieth Century*, Aurora, ON: Garamond Press.

The Henry J. Kaiser Family Foundation (2014) "Status of State Action on the Medicaid Expansion Decision, 2014," www.kff.org/.

The New York Times Editorial Staff (2014) "Kansas' Ruinous Tax Cuts," *The New York Times*, July 14, p. A16.

Thomson, Sarah, Osborn, Robin, Squires, David, M., and Jun, Miraya (2014) *International Profiles of Health Care Systems, 2012*, New York, The Commonwealth Fund, www.commonwealtfund.org/~/media/Files/Publications/Fund Report.

UNICEF (2008) "Nationwide Needs Assessment or Emergency Obstetric and Newborn Services in Sierra Leone," Reproductive and Child Health Programme, Ministry of Health and Sanitation.

United Nations (1948) Universal Declaration of Human Rights, adopted December 10, 1948. United Nations General Assembly Res. 217 A (III). www.un.org/en/documents/udhr/.

UNRISD (United Nations Research Institute for Social Development) (2007) "Commercialization and Globalization of Health Care: Lessons from UNRISD Research," UNRISD Research and Policy Brief 7.

Welch, H. Gilbert, Schwartz, Lisa M., and Woloshin, Steven (2011) *Over-Diagnosed: Making People Sick in the Pursuit of Health*, Boston: Beacon Press.

Whelan, Daniel J. (2010) *Indivisible Human Rights: A History*, Philadelphia and Oxford: University of Pennsylvania Press.

Whitaker, Robert (2010) *Anatomy of an Epidemic: Magic Bullets, Psychiatric Drugs, and the Astonishing Rise of Mental Illness in America*, New York: Crown.

WHO CMH (2001) *Macroeconomics and Health: Investing in Health for Economic Development*, chaired by Jeffrey Sachs, Geneva: World Health Organization.

WHO (World Health Organization) (2007) *Everybody's Business: Strengthening Health Systems to Improve Health Outcome,* Geneva: WHO.

Wilkinson, Richard (2005) *The Impact of Inequality: How to Make Sick Societies Healthier,* New York and London: The New Press.

Wilkinson, Richard G. and Pickett, Kate E. (2006) "Income Inequality and Population Health: A Review and Explanation of the Evidence," *Social Science and Medicine* 62: 1768–1784.

Wilkinson, Richard and Pickett, Kate (2009a) *The Spirit Level: Why Equality Matters,* New York: Bloomsbury Press.

Wilkinson, Richard and Pickett, Kate (2009b) *The Spirit Level: Why Greater Equality Makes Societies Stronger More Equal Societies Almost Always Do Better,* New York, Berlin, and London: Bloomsbury Press.

World Bank (1993) *World Development Report 1993: Investing in Health,* New York: Oxford University Press.

(2004) *World Development Report: Making Services Work for Poor People,* Washington, DC: World Bank.

World Health Organization (2006) *The World Health Report 2006 – Working Together for Health,* Geneva: WHO, www.who.int/whr/2006/en/.

World Health Organization (WHO) (2007) *Everybody's Business: Strengthening Health Systems to Improve Health Outcome,* Geneva: WHO.

Xu, Ke, Evans, David B., Kadama, Patrick, Nabyonga, Juliet (2006) "Understanding the Impact of Eliminating User Fees: Utilization and Catastrophic Health Expenditures in Uganda," *Social Science & Medicine* 62: 866–876.

Yamin, Alicia Ely (2008) "Will We Take Suffering Seriously? Reflections on What Applying a Human Rights Framework to Health Means and Why We Should Care," *Health and Human Rights* 10 (1): 1–19.

(2011) "Power, Suffering, and Courts: Reflections on Promoting Health Rights Through Judicialization," in Alicia Ely Yamin and Siri Glopeen, eds., *Litigating Health Rights: Can Courts Bring More Justice to Health,* Cambridge: Harvard University Press, pp. 333–372.

Yamin, Alicia Ely and Norheim, Ole Frithjof (2014) "Taking Equality Seriously: Applying Human Rights Frameworks to Priority Setting in Health," *Human Rights Quarterly* 36 (2): 296–324.

4

Private Sector Provision, Health, and Human Rights

The obligations outlined in General Comment 14 of the Committee on Economic, Social and Cultural Rights (2000) assume that governments have the ability to shape health policy from a human rights perspective and to guide its implementation. However, in the contemporary health landscape services are increasingly delivered through private health sector institutions, and governments lack direct control over some or many components of the health system. If the history of health care in Europe and other parts of the industrialized world in the first seven or eight decades of the twentieth century can be depicted in terms of an ever-extending state involvement in health (Maarse 2006, 981), the trend in the past thirty-five years has been for their health systems to rely more on the private sector. As the World Health Organization (WHO) observes, "private provision is a substantial and growing sector that is capturing an increasing share of the health market across the world" (2010b, para 1). Today private health institutions and providers play a major role in the health sector of both developed and developing countries. Even the National Health Service in England, long an icon of state funded universal health care, has undergone major structural changes opening services up to competition with the private sector, ostensibly to improve efficiency (Holmes 2013). Increasing privatization has also affected the delivery of many other public utilities and services, including water, sanitation, social security, and education that have a bearing on the social determinants of health (De Feyter and Gómez Isa 2005).

Private provision of health services and health insurance does not change the role of the state as the ultimate guarantor of the realization of health rights obligations, but it makes implementing its responsibilities more difficult. Additionally, the goals and priorities of private health care institutions tend to differ significantly from those in the human rights paradigm. Fragmentation of the health system complicates oversight and the promotion of rights-based approaches to health. Segmentation of the health system in some countries, with a poorly functioning public sector catering primarily to the poor and better quality private health institutions catering to the more affluent, tends to undermine support for investing in improvement in institutions for the public provision and financing of health care and likely erodes commitment to the right to health as well. Fragmentation and segmentation also increase overall transaction costs, often at the expense of reducing total coverage (Levcovitz 2007), and in many cases, lead to higher prices and increased out-of-pocket costs. Working effectively with and through private sector providers also requires management skills and complex health information systems that many governments, particularly those in poor- and middle-income countries, often lack.

To date, the issues that private sector health provision raises for a human rights-based approach to health have received little systematic attention from the health and human rights community. International human rights law does not specify how health care services should be delivered or paid for as long as the health care provision is consistent with human rights obligations. Although some UN human rights committees have acknowledged that reliance on private health care may be problematic, they have generally not been inclined to address the topic in a systematic manner or offer guidance at the level of depth and complexity it requires. Nor is there much literature on the topic. The 2012 report of the second Special Rapporteur for the right to health on financing in the context of the right to health to date is notable because it is one of the few examinations of a component of privatization within the official UN human rights community.

This chapter uses a human rights lens to evaluate private sector health services provision and the privatization of health care and insurance. It explores the extent and ways in which privatization of health services potentially is and is not compatible with human rights commitments. It also considers ways that an expanding or dominant role for the private health sector can complicate efforts to promote and protect the right to health. Additionally, the chapter identifies factors and policies that can mitigate or exacerbate the impact of private health provision on the realization of the right to health.

Identifying issues that private sector health provision and insurance pose for a right to health does not imply that public health institutions necessarily conform to human rights requirements. Clearly, there is no automatic correlation between countries in which the public health sector predominates and those whose health systems have implemented a human rights approach. Government operated health systems have been criticized for a number of failings such as inefficiencies due to their hierarchical structures and bureaucratic systems and processes, some of which are justified (Marriott 2009, 16). It has also been claimed that in many poor countries the wealthy disproportionately benefit from public health spending (International Finance Corporation 2007, 8–9). Another criticism is that welfare schemes in less developed countries, including health benefits, have been biased toward the protection of white-collar, salaried, and some blue-collar workers, and not the poor (Rudra 2008, 13, 15).

The greater benefit that higher-income, urban populations receive from public health spending can be explained in part by the tendency of many of these countries to invest a disproportionate share of their health resources in expensive tertiary care teaching hospitals located in urban areas where relatively better-off (but not wealthy) and more politically influential urban populations are located. This is an obvious right-to-health failing that privatization is more likely to accelerate than to counter. Moreover, it should be noted that privatization also accelerates a disproportionate investment in secondary and tertiary care as well as frequently leading to an increased disparity in the availability of health facilities, goods, and services in urban areas as compared with rural areas (Grover 2012, para 3).

Private Health Sector Provision

Private sector actors and institutions play a variety of roles in health systems: delivering health care services, owning and/or managing health facilities, providing health insurance, conducting medical and health-related research, making health-related information technology available, and controlling the development and sale of pharmaceuticals. Private sector health delivery covers many different realities. It includes both for-profit and not-for-profit actors and institutions. It incorporates faith-based and nongovernment secular, nonprofit organizations as well as individual health care entrepreneurs and private for-profit firms and corporations (World Health Organization 2010b, para 1).

The relative size and functions of the private health sector differ significantly from country to country. Its composition and character often reflect political, historical, social, and economic factors. In some countries with well-developed public health systems, private health provision plays a relatively minor and supplementary role, but in others there are some types of ambulatory, hospital, and in-patient care. In developed countries private provision usually entails care by well-trained medical professionals in settings with sophisticated equipment whether in private practice settings, clinics, or hospitals (World Health Organization 2010b, paras 2–3).

In contrast, in many poor countries the private sector is diverse and fragmented. Recent investments in health in many of these countries have led to an explosion of unregulated private health services with high levels of individual out-of-pocket payments (USAID 2012, 5). In these countries the private health sector is likely to be dominated by informal for-profit and small-scale providers, many of whom who are unlicensed, unregulated, uninspected, and some of whom are untrained in modern medical practice, such as traditional healers, birth attendants, small drug shops, and stalls in markets (Mackintosh 2006, 396; Marriott 2009, 9). In low-income countries in sub-Saharan Africa and Asia small scale private provision dominates outpatient care while public provision tends to be the rule in hospital in-patient services.

Individual entrepreneurship is also prevalent in middle-income countries, but large private firms, including multinational corporations, are capturing a growing share of the market, particularly the high-income segment, and increasingly competing for contracts with public and social security systems. In Latin America and upper-middle-income countries elsewhere, there is increasing social segmentation. The affluent and those in formal employment have private insurance-based health care while there is lower quality and frequently resource-deprived public provision for the rest of the population (World Health Organization 2010b, paras 2–4).

The role of private providers and insurers may depend on the level of the health system. In some predominantly public health systems, primary care is publicly funded but mostly privately provided. This is the case in many European countries, Japan, Australia, and New Zealand. In contrast, hospitals remain mostly public in these countries (Mossialos and Wenzl 2015, 9).

Privatization of Health Systems

Technically privatization refers to the transfer of ownership of an institution or of a service from a public to a private actor or alternatively the removal of public authorities from the operation of an institution or service despite the state nominally retaining ownership (De Feyter and Gómez Isa 2005, 1). The term is also sometimes applied more generally to private provision of health services. Privatization can involve selling public health-care facilities and delivery organizations to private enterprises; contracting out publicly provided services to private enterprises; and/or government policies to encourage greater reliance on private healthcare insurance. These initiatives are often accompanied by the introduction or increase of out-of-pocket payment for health care services in the form of co-payments or deductibles (Buchanan 2009, 90). The process of privatization can be policy driven, which is the result of purposive government action, or it can be brought about by spontaneous or unorganized processes in society. It can occur through the government reducing the scope of public intervention or through contracting out or outsourcing. In contracting or outsourcing, the government contracts with private agents to accomplish specific health care responsibilities (Maarse 2006, 986–988).

Hans Maarse cautions against conceptualizing privatization as entailing a simple dichotomy between public and private because doing so ignores the gray area between them and also disregards the evolutionary character of privatization. Instead, he proposes applying the notion of a continuum ranging from precursors of privatization to moderate forms of privatization to radical forms of privatization (Maarse 2006, 988). Others point to the considerable overlap that can exist between the public and private sectors. Staff employed by the public health system may also practice privately either legally or by ignoring government regulations. Public hospitals may operate private wards or allow work for private gain on their premises, as when doctors admit private patients. When public services become heavily dependent on fee income, as in China, there may be little to distinguish them from private health enterprises (Mills et al. 2002). There is also a continuum of the type and degree of government control and the regulation imposed on private sector actors and institutions. In some health systems private providers operate independently with little regulation. At the other end of the spectrum, some governments contract with private providers for specific health services with their roles strictly regulated.

In some predominantly public health systems there is a purchaser-provider split between health financing and health provision whereby the government funds health services but contracts with private health providers, private insurance companies, and private health management organizations to provide services. The United Kingdom (UK) serves as an example of a formerly public health system that has increasingly adopted such a model. In the 1980s, Margaret Thatcher's administration began the process of applying private sector management principles to health care, and additional policy changes have increasingly opened up the provider side of the National Health Service to market forces. By 2000, even clinical services were opened to market competition. Under the Health and Social Care Act, which came into force in April 2013 despite widespread public opposition, private providers, now in the majority, and the remaining public providers compete for contracts on an equal footing. Private financing has also come to play a greater role through an increasing proportion of private insurance and more co-payments. During the process of these changes the National Health Service has become fragmented, and the dismantling of the geography-based architecture of the NHS has weakened the ability of the health system to perform health promotion and disease prevention functions (Global Health Watch 2014, 96–105).

Some public health systems underwrite the cost of private health providers. In recent years Sweden has introduced privatized health care, initially by introducing purchaser-provider systems with competitive bidding that increased the number of private for-profit providers of primary care services. The government also sold one major acute care hospital in Stockholm to a venture capital company. In the second phase of Sweden's reforms, all private for-profit providers of primary health services who met certain criteria were able to have their services tax financed (Dahlgren 2012, 1). In Brazil, most primary health care is provided by a network of public providers and facilities, while the tax-funded Sistema Unico de Saúde (SUS, the United Health System) purchases most secondary and tertiary care from the private sector (Global Health Watch 2014, 90).

The health system in Israel provides an additional example of the ways that the relationship between private and public sector actors can become quite complex. The universal national health insurance system in Israel operates through four private networks that insure members and also provide health services to them. Each has its own set of clinics and hospitals. The government funds and strictly regulates these quasi-private, quasi-public entities, including specifying what the basic health benefit package should contain and how much can be charged for co-payments for physician visits and pharmaceuticals (Rosen and Samuel 2009). Each of these sickness funds also offers supplementary insurance at an extra charge, and private insurance is also available (Gross 2014, 160).

Factors Encouraging the Privatization of Health Services

Hans Maarse identifies a series of factors accounting for increasing privatization of health services in European countries, many of which are relevant to other parts of the world as well. The first and most significant he mentions is the change in policy orientation and preferences wrought by the advent of neoliberal ideas in public policy, including in the health care sector (2006, 1003). Others have also written about the privatization euphoria of the 1980s and 1990s, which affected health care as well as other public services (McDonald and Ruiters 2012, 6). In developed countries, commercial actors and higher-income medical groups have usually been the primary groups promoting neoliberal health policies and they have typically been the chief beneficiaries. In contrast, international funding agencies have often served as the primary advocates in the case of middle- and lower-income countries (Gilson et al. 2011, 204). As noted in Chapter Three, neoliberalism favors a reduction of the role of the state in the provision of social services, a decrease in state budgets, deregulation, and the transfer of social services formerly provided by the state, including health care, to the private sector (Gómez Isa et al. 2005, 13). Proponents of neoliberal policies anticipate these policies will increase productivity and efficiency while improving the quality of health care. The introduction or extension of cost-sharing is seen as a way to enhance individual responsibility. Privatization is additionally viewed by advocates of neoliberal policies as a way to make health care more consumer-driven and to enhance consumer choice (Maarse 2006, 1003–1004). However, data that will be reviewed later in this chapter do not support claims that private sector providers have been more efficient, accountable, or medically effective than public sector providers. In fact, there is evidence of privatization resulting in the contrary trends.

If European health care policy making reflects the pull of neoliberal ideas, the encouragement or scaling up of private sector provision in many poor and middle-income countries has resulted from the push of neoliberal market solutions by the World Bank, the U.S. Agency for International Development, the Global Fund, other international health organizations, and the Gates Foundation, with increased privatization made a condition for receiving aid. Private sector proponents have argued that the failures of the public health sector call for a greater role for private health providers and insurers in poor- and low-income countries (International Finance Corporation 2007). However, critics of the admittedly poorly functioning public health sector in many of these countries often fail to acknowledge the impact of World Bank-mandated austerity and funding limits on publicly provided health services in undermining their viability. As a result of neoliberal health reforms, some undertaken voluntary and some initiated at the behest of international funders, the government share of health expenditures, already quite low, fell precipitously; health workers were laid off; the rural–urban divide increased, regional disparities in access to health care widened; and the public health systems in many countries deteriorated (Sengupta 2013).

Thus in many poor countries the deterioration, and in some cases the near collapse of public sector health facilities, have made privatization a default option. In the case of India, for example, the reliance on private health care, even by the poor, results primarily from the fact that after many years of very low public expenditure on health, one of the lowest public investments in health in the world, the country's public health facilities are very limited, of poor quality, and often poorly run (Dréze and Sen 2013, 148–150). Many communities lack facilities or have dysfunctional ones due to shortages of doctors and health workers and the failure to be provided with equipment and sufficient supplies of medicines (Sengupta 2013, 7). The result is that India has one of the most privatized health systems in the world: private health care accounts for 80 percent of outpatient and 60 percent of inpatient care (Sengupta 2013, 2–5).

The rationale for greater private provision in middle-income and poor countries promoted by the World Bank, the U.S. Agency for International Development, and other funders rests on five main arguments: (1) the private sector is already the majority provider in many poor countries and therefore should be at the center of scaling-up; (2) greater private provision can complement and take the strain off public health services; (3) private provision is more efficient, more effective, and of better quality; (4) private provision can reach the poorest members of the population; and (5) the private sector can improve accountability through competition (Marriott 2009, 10).

An Oxfam International briefing paper takes issue with these claims: (1) In terms of the prevalence of private providers, Oxfam points out that if shops are removed from the calculation and only clinics staffed by trained health workers are counted, the share of services provided by the private sector in poor countries falls dramatically (Marriott 2009, 11). (2) The argument that greater private health care provision can complement and relieve the government fails to take into account the reality that private sector provision of comprehensive health services to poor people is generally not profitable and therefore usually requires significant public subsidies. (3) On the issue of efficiency, the growth in private sector participation in health in many countries has been associated with high costs and low efficiency. Rising costs in market-based health care systems reflect inbuilt incentives to pursue the most profitable treatments rather than those dictated by medical need (Marriott 2009, 16). Moreover, genuine competition, which ostensibly could encourage lower prices (but certainly has not done so in the United States), is difficult to achieve in low- and middle-income countries with the paucity of options in health provision (Marriott 2009, 17–18). Additionally, the claim of the higher quality of private sector provision is not supported by research data (Smith et al. 2005, 9; Marriott 2009, 19). (4) Contemporary data and historical experience show that broader privatization and commercialization can dramatically increase inequality in both access and health outcomes (Marriott 2009, 22). To counter the argument that the private sector can reach the poor, Oxfam references data from forty-four middle- and low-income countries suggesting there is an inverse correlation between the level of private sector participation in primary health care and access to treatment (Marriott 2009, 22). (5) Finally, on the crucial issue of accountability in health provision, Oxfam finds little evidence to support the World Bank theory that private providers are more responsive to patients than public ones. It further cautions that when the private sector provides health services on behalf of the state, it can make it more difficult for citizens to hold their governments accountable (Marriott 2009, 24–25).

Maarse identifies budgetary strain as a second important factor pushing privatization forward. Public health systems in Europe and elsewhere are increasingly coming under economic pressure because of the rising costs of health care due to a variety of factors, including the higher cost of new drugs and technologies, the aging of the population along with the tendency for older persons to require more health care, and rising expectations about the use and quality of health care services. Public sector health care cost control initiatives encourage privatization through cost sharing and outsourcing. As health costs have escalated, many developed countries have imposed increasingly higher co-pays for covered services and reduced funding for the basic services basket. Israel provides an example where the ratio of public-to-private financing for health care, which was 75-to-25 in the 1980s, was 58-to-42 by 2011 affecting access to medical treatment and the affordability of prescribed drugs because of their cost (Gross 2014, 161–163). While the transfer from public to private provision often does not lower total health care spending, by transferring the cost it does reduce pressures on government budgets (Maarse 2006, 1004). In fact, the growth in private sector participation in health in many countries has been associated with higher costs and lower efficiency. This trend reflects the fact that private sector health institutions often have inbuilt incentives to overtreat and to pursue higher priced and more profitable treatments (Marriott 2009, 16).

To deal with economic constraints, made worse by the global economic recession beginning in 2007–2008, several European countries have made major structural changes in the health sector to reduce public responsibility for health service funding and/or delivery. To provide a few examples, since 2007 about 50 percent of all primary care services in Sweden have been shifted to private providers (Dahlgren 2008). In 2006, the Netherlands shifted its sickness funds to a regulated private market structure, with most individuals responsible for a substantially larger segment of the cost of the insurance (Saltman and Cahn 2013).

The situation in poor- and middle-income countries tends to be the converse of wealthier countries' efforts to offload services to the private sector so as to reduce governmental expenditures. Private sector provision of comprehensive health services to poor people is generally not profitable and therefore requires significant public subsidies to make the investment attractive. Recognizing this need, the International Finance Corporation, a subsidiary of the World Bank, advocates that both governments and donors earmark a higher proportion of public money and aid to fund private sector health entities – which then reduces the financial resources available for the public sector (World Bank 2011, 47–48). In some countries, Brazil for example, the expansion of the private health sector has been subsidized by the state at the expense of investments in public sector health institutions. This policy has compromised the ability of the underfunded public subsector to improve the quality of health services and to improve access to care (Paim et al. 2011, 1787).

Privatization may also be encouraged by consumer preference based on public failures or the perceived inadequacy of public health institutions. In some high-income countries, people choose private providers even when public health services are available at a lower cost because they believe they will gain access to a better quality of care or escape from long waiting lists (Maarse 2006, 1005). In some developing countries private sector providers are more geographically accessible and have a greater availability of staff and drugs. Reforms, such as the introduction of user charges in public facilities, have also driven people away from the public sector (Smith et al. 2005, 8–9).

Growing affluence also tends to increase the demand for private health care services outside the public sector along with the ability to pay for them. In health systems where affluent persons can opt out of the public health system by purchasing private insurance or paying for their own health care, their doing so risks the loss of political and economic support for public provision and the investment in good quality public health services. This then encourages the development of a two-tier health system with the affluent using better quality private health services. For that reason some health systems with a commitment to health equity and/or human rights, for example Canada and Israel, have prohibited the purchase of insurance to cover the same basket of services provided in the public system.

Private Health Sector Provision and International Human Rights Law

In principle, international human rights law is agnostic on the question as to how health care services should be delivered or paid for as long as the health care provision is consistent with human rights obligations. General Comment No. 3 of the UN Committee on Economic, Cultural and Social Rights (CESCR), adopted in 1990, states that the Committee is neutral on the type of economic systems required for the fulfillment of human rights obligations enumerated in the International Covenant on Economic, Social and Cultural Rights (ICESCR). To quote paragraph 8:

> The Committee notes that the undertaking "to take steps ... by all appropriate means ..." neither requires nor precludes any particular form of government or economic system ..., provided only that it is democratic and that all human rights are thereby respected. Thus in terms of political and economic systems the Covenant is neutral and its principles cannot accurately be described as being predicated exclusively upon the need for, or the desirability of a socialist or capitalist system, or a mixed, centrally planned, or laisser-faire economy ... (CESCR 1990, para 8).

The CESCR's General Comment No. 14, adopted ten years later, has a similar perspective:

> The most appropriate feasible measures to implement the right to health will vary from one State to another. Every State has a margin of discretion in assessing which measures are most suitable to meet its specific circumstances. The Covenant, however, clearly imposes a duty on each State to take whatever steps are necessary to ensure that everyone has access to health facilities, goods, and services so that they can enjoy, as soon as possible, the highest attainable standard of physical and mental health (CESCR 2000, para 53).

The General Comment directs that privately or publicly provided health care services must be affordable to all, including socially disadvantaged and poorer households (CESCR 2000, para 12 (b) iii). The general comment places the responsibility for overseeing the conduct of private sector providers on the state. It stipulates that state parties should take appropriate steps to ensure that members of the private business sector are aware of and consider the importance of the right to health in pursuing their activities (CESCR 2000, para 55). In addition, according to the text, the obligation to protect requires that the privatization of the health sector does not constitute a threat to the availability, accessibility, acceptability, and quality of health facilities (CESCR 2000, para 35).

The Committee on the Elimination of Discrimination Against Women's (CEDAW) General Recommendation on Health makes the important point that "States parties cannot absolve themselves of responsibility in these areas [women's ill-health] by delegating or transferring these powers to private sector agencies" (Committee to Eliminate All Forms of Discrimination Against Women 1999, para 17). In 2011 CEDAW applied this principle in a landmark case on maternal mortality, *Alyne da Silva Pimentel v. Brazil*. The case dealt with the preventable maternal death of a woman in childbirth in a private health care facility due to inadequate care. As a matter of international human rights law, the Committee found Brazil directly responsible for the failure to monitor private institutions when medical services were outsourced to such institutions (Cook 2013, 107). CEDAW's decision also determined that state parties are obligated to ensure that private health care facilities comply with national and international reproductive health care standards (Bueno de Mesquita and Kismödi 2012). The significance of the decision will depend in part on what kinds of measures Brazil takes to implement the ruling and whether other human rights treaty bodies and domestic courts follow this precedent.

Of the human rights treaty monitoring bodies, to date, the Committee on the Rights of the Child (CRC) has given the most attention to issues relating to private provision of health care. In 2002, the CRC devoted a day of general discussion to the theme of "The Private Sector as Service Provider and its Role in Implementing Child Rights." Paul Hunt, who was to become the first Special Rapporteur on the right to the highest attainable level of health, represented the Committee on Economic, Social and Cultural Right. His statement reiterated the position that international human rights law was neutral with regard to the privatization of service provision neither requiring nor precluding any particular form of government or economic system, provided they were democratic and observant of all human rights. He did add that the adoption of any national policy, including privatization, should be preceded by an independent, objective, and publicly available assessment of the impact on human rights requirements, especially on the right to health of the poor (Committee on the Rights of the Child 2002, paras 10–18). Hunt did not, however, identify the specifics of the criteria to apply.

Like other human rights treaty bodies, the CRC's 2013 general comment on the child's right to health reiterates the principle of state responsibility regardless of whether it delegates the provision of services to nonstate actors (CRC 2013a, para 75). The CRC also calls on all nonstate actors engaged in health promotion and services, especially those in the private sector, to act in compliance with provisions of the Convention on the Right of the Child (para 77). Further, the Committee states that private health insurance companies should not discriminate against pregnant women, children, or mothers on any prohibited grounds and should adopt measures ensuring that inability to pay for health insurance does not restrict access to health services (para 82).

In 2013, the CRC also adopted a second general comment on state obligations regarding the impact of the business sector on children's rights that reiterates some of the central points in its general comment on the child's right to health. CRC's General Comment No. 16 identifies three overall responsibilities of states in relationship to business activities: to ensure that the activities and operations of business enterprises do not adversely impact on children's rights (para 5.a); to create an enabling and supportive environment for business enterprises to respect children's rights (para 5.b); and to ensure access to effective remedy for children whose right have been infringed by a business enterprise (para 5.c). The CRC's general comment acknowledges that there is no international legally binding instrument on the business sector's responsibilities vis-à-vis human rights. Nevertheless, it maintains that businesses must meet responsibilities regarding children's rights, and reminds states of their obligation to ensure they do so (para 8).

Not many human rights practitioners or theorists have addressed the issues that private provision and financing of health services present, and there is a difference in views among those that do. Many human rights analysts who are critical of privatization focus primarily on issues related to commercialization and neoliberal health policies, issues that were discussed in Chapter Three, rather than privatization per se (Pellegrino 1999; O'Connell 2010). Moreover, not all human rights interpreters believe that privatization is necessarily in conflict with the realization of the right to health.

M. Gregg Bloche (2005) contends that privatization in itself is no more or no less likely to fail in fulfilling human rights obligations than is public financing and provision of health services. His position is that both private and public systems can be designed to respect, protect, and fulfill human rights and both are equally susceptible of not doing so. He claims that private provision of medical care has little effect in practice on legal accountability for violations of international human rights law (221–224). Bloche acknowledges that privatization is risky in societies where social cohesion is low, where there is disregard for the rule of law, and where there is a general state failure – the situation besetting many poor countries – but he counters that in such states it is equally unlikely that public actors will fulfill their human rights responsibilities (217). According to Bloche, the debate about the comparative human rights compliance of private and public systems is a distraction from the task of ensuring that health care systems, whatever their character, abide by human rights obligations. He argues that the failure to commit sufficient resources to achieve human rights law's health aims is not the fault of privatization: "It is a matter of moral indifference of epic scale, given the millions of lives per year that the modest investment in health programs would save" (Bloche 2005, 228). While he is correct that the failure to invest sufficient resources in the health system is a major failing of many governments, privatization often contributes to the failure to realize right to health objectives.

Brigid Toebes (2006) takes another approach. Aware of the potential hazards of privatization for the realization of the right to health, she proposes conducting a human rights impact analysis to assess the consistency of specific privatization proposals and laws with the requirements of the right to health. Toebes examined privatization of health insurance in the Netherlands using the criteria outlined in General Comment 14: availability, accessibility, acceptability, and quality (CESCR 2000, para 12). The aim of her analysis was to determine the kinds of checks and balances governments must create when they privatize health systems in order to ensure compliance with the international human rights obligation for the right to health (Toebes 2006, 112). However, the privatization of health insurance in the Netherlands was too recent for her to have the data to assess the impact of privatization. Also, while the Committee's four criteria provide a starting point, the Committee has not sufficiently operationalized how they should be translated into a human rights assessment or monitoring program.

Toebes' approach of evaluating the empirical reality of the impact of privatization and/or commercialization on the right to health in a specific country context is very important, and not only because it provides a middle path between two contending perspectives on the role of the private sector in health systems. The role of private health providers and insurers differs very considerably across health systems as does their interface with the government. It is necessary to evaluate both in the context of specific health care systems to be able to assess the potential impact on a human rights approach.

A Right to Private Health Care?

Aeyal Gross raises the question as to whether there is a human right to private health care, and if so, what the implications of this entitlement are in a publicly funded health system (2013). The increasing privatization of health care makes the question of a right to private health care an important issue, albeit with different implications depending on the type of health system. Gross's concern is that using rights discourse to articulate claims to private health care or private insurance in a publicly supported health system may reinforce rather than challenge privatization and do so in ways that exacerbate inequality. He discusses landmark litigations in Canada and Israel, two universal publicly funded health systems.

In the Canadian case, *Chaoulli v. Quebec* (2005), the Canadian Supreme Court struck down a law prohibiting private health insurance for medically necessary hospital and physician services covered by Canada's Medicare health system that had been instituted to preserve equality of access, considered to be a core and defining feature of the system. The ruling was justified on the basis of what was portrayed as long and unacceptable waiting times in the public health care system. However, as Gross points out, if this was the concern, the ruling should have focused on attempting to reduce waiting times in order to improve access for all. Instead, it improves access to services just for those with sufficient income to be able to afford purchasing private insurance (2013, 139–140). The good news is that *Chaoulli* has not led to the development of a two-tier health system, as some human rights advocates feared it would, because the government responded to the decision by investing increased funds in the public system to reduce waiting times (Yamin and Norheim 2014, 302–303).

In the Israeli case, Kiryati (HJC 4253/02, 2009), the petitioners tried to claim a right to private health services that would allow patients to choose their doctor, specifically surgeons, within public hospitals by making an additional out-of-pocket payment. The High Court of Justice rejected the petition. Its judgment noted that approving this arrangement would open the door to the possibility of a wide array of health services becoming available through additional payments over and above the health tax that all residents pay to fund Israel's national health insurance scheme. According to the decision, doing so would separate those with the means to be able to afford special services, such as paying to choose a doctor, from others insured under the National Health Insurance Law and would thereby violate the fundamental principles of the public health care system in Israel: justice, equality, and mutual assistance (Gross 2013, 141).

So is there a human right to private health care? It depends in part on the context of the nature of the entitlement to health care and the type of health system in a specific country. There would certainly be such a right in health systems with a legal commitment to a universal health entitlement where the public health system had delegated some or all of the delivery of health care to private providers, as in the case of Brazil. Moreover, the decision in the CEDAW case, *Alyne da Silva Pimentel v. Brazil*, as well as the implications of the CESCR's prescription that privatization not affect the availability and accessibility of health care (2000, para 12.b (iii)) underscore that in a privatized health system with legal entitlements to health care the government has the responsibility to ensure that appropriate health services are available in the private sector.

The situation is quite different in public health systems with universal entitlements where some residents seek government-supported health benefits above and beyond those that are universally available. Here it would be problematical to recognize rights to supplementary private health care because of the implications for equity and the affordability to the government. In several Latin American countries, particularly Brazil, Costa Rica, and Columbia, patients are turning to the courts in large numbers to claim rights to medication and treatments that are not necessarily part of the package provided by the public health system. In 2008, Colombian courts heard more than 140,000 such health rights cases, and the Constitutional Court responded in a landmark judgment by ordering a radical restructuring of the health system (Yamin et al. 2011, 112–117). Most of these suits for access to supplementary health benefits in Colombia are won by litigants because of the judiciary's expansive concept of health rights. While the number of cases is higher in Latin America than elsewhere, this "epidemic" of health litigation appears to be part of a global trend. It is noteworthy that most of those who use the courts to secure these additional benefits are not the poor but instead members of the middle and lower-middle classes. This judicialization of health often has deleterious consequences by imposing extra health costs for expensive treatments and undermining the rational allocation of health funds. Given that the health budget is limited, these extra health benefits to individuals divert resources from health programs designed to serve the population as a whole (Gloppen and Roseman 2011; Ferraz 2011).

The proverbial "sticky wicket" is those situations in which the public health system does not appear to be able to provide basic health entitlements within a reasonable period of time, as was claimed in *Chaoulli v. Quebec* (2005). The question that Chaouilli raised is what constitutes a reasonable period of time. There are no clear-cut and widely applicable guidelines in the health community. Nor does a human rights perspective seem to have any specific wisdom on this thorny topic.

Impact of Privatization on the Right to Health

Privatized health care affects both the values on which effective realization of health rights depend and the institutional capacity of the government to implement a right to health approach. The following are the ways in which privatization has a potential detrimental impact.

The degree to which private health provision inhibits the realization of the right to health depends on a number of factors that will be discussed later in the chapter.

Solidarity

Support for a human rights approach to health may depend on, or at least be strengthened by, a strong sense of societal solidarity or social citizenship. By segmenting the population according to their ability to afford different types of health care, extensive private sector health care provision can give rise to societal divisions and thereby weaken the bonds on which societal solidarity depends. Solidarity is both a moral concept and a public value. The notion of solidarity is associated with mutual respect, support for the weak and needy, shared responsibility, and commitment to the common good. Solidarity supports the principle that all members of society, including and particularly those in need, have access to health care, regardless of their ability to pay. "Solidarity is not a woolly notion about the common good. It has a specific meaning that a health care system is organized and managed on the basis of universal access, without risk selection, not based on income related premiums, and lacks significant differences in the benefit package" (den Exeter 2010, 224). Solidarity has been counterposed with the self-centered individualism associated with the cultural habits, societal norms, and liberal values characteristic of the United States (Barr 2007, 20–36). According to one of the few studies of solidarity as it shapes attitudes toward health care in Europe, the basic understanding is that everyone who is able to do so will make a fair financial contribution to a collectively organized insurance system that guarantees equal access to health and social care for all members of society (Meulen et al. 2001, 1). In some countries, solidarity underpins a commitment to a uniform standard of health care for all members of the society regardless of their economic status.

Surveys conducted over a decade ago showed overwhelming popular support in a variety of European countries for the then current universal health care systems with a broad range of benefits. Similarly, they revealed little evidence for self-interest-oriented motives affecting the preference for solidarity health care arrangements (Gevers et al. 2001). They did, however, point to signs that the aging of the population and the concomitant increased demands for care services were beginning to strain the sense of solidarity between generations in some countries. Younger age groups appeared to be growing more reluctant to underwrite the higher costs for the financing of health care and social care provisions for the elderly (Meulen et al. 2001, 3).

There is concern on the part of some analysts that the increasing use of market forces in the health sector will weaken the sense of solidarity across income groups and the willingness to subsidize the health care of persons from lower-income groups and persons with chronic diseases, and survey data from the Netherlands suggest this is occurring. Government policies instituting cost controls and promoting a greater role for individual responsibility for health in the Netherlands, which reflect neoliberal policy priorities, may also result in a declining commitment to solidarity. In addition, the emphasis on individual responsibility makes more room for supplementary private health insurance arrangements for the benefit of the well-off over and above the basic health insurance required of or provided to all persons. Studies of the Dutch population point to decreasing levels of public support for "unlimited" solidarity and for "irresponsible" forms of health behavior. Also a larger portion of the Dutch population now believes it would be too costly to grant everyone the right to all possible medical treatments (Meulen and Maarse 2008). Some analysts anticipate these developments will encourage the development of a two-tier system of health care with fuller coverage and benefits for those who can afford to pay extra for them (Meulen et al. 2001, 4). If this occurs, adequate protection of the weak, the sick, and the unemployed could be seen as a matter of choice dependent on negotiations between unequally endowed groups (Arts and Verburg 2001, 26). Some authors have therefore questioned whether the existing European public health care systems will be sustainable if commitments to solidarity decline (Arts and Verburg 2001, 16). It will be important to monitor the effects of privatization in Europe.

Assuming that the right to health and other economic and social rights require some commitment to social solidarity, if only through an implicit social contract, an important question is how privatization and commercialization will impact countries that do not have the benefit of Europe's historical traditions of social solidarity. Many low- and middle-income countries can be considered fragile societies with deep ethnic, language, economic, and sometimes racial divisions. Will privatization and commercialization of key social services retard the development of political trust and social solidarity? Conversely, can a strong policy commitment to universal health care with financial cross-subsidization and uniform benefits promote the emergence of a sense of social solidarity based on an implicit social contract among the members of the country and between them and the government? There is a need for further and continuing research on these issues.

Obligation to Protect

Privatization expands the human rights obligation for the state to regulate third-party actors, especially private health providers and insurers, so as to protect the human rights of all persons. By so doing, it often requires the state to assume different and more complex roles. A United Nations Department of Economic and Social Affairs paper on "Privatisation of Public Sector Activities" describes the role of government in the context of privatization as shifting from producing and delivering services to enabling and regulating them. The paper points out that these roles require different skills:

> Governments need to be able to analyse market condition, set policy frameworks, draw up, negotiate and enforce contracts, regulate monopolies; coordinate, finance and support producers: enable community self-provision; and provide consumers with information on their options and remedies (quoted in De Feyter and Gómez Isa 2005, 2).

But just as governments are privatizing more health care services and thereby needing to assume a greater vigilance over the private sector, the neoliberal policies promoting privatization have also resulted in cutbacks on the size and capacity of the public sector making it more difficult to do so. The smaller, weaker, and less resourced governments fashioned by neo-liberalism are less able to implement human rights obligations to protect their members from abuses by third-party institutions and actors or to effectively regulate private sector health institutions. They are also likely to be less inclined to do so.

Accountability

Accountability, a fundamental human rights requirement, is also more difficult to achieve in a privatized or mixed health system. In theory the government is responsible for assuring that the private sector operates in a manner consistent with human rights principles, but in reality it is often difficult for the government to do so. In many cases when the health reforms based on privatization of health insurance or delivery were introduced, such as in Colombia, governments lacked legislation to guide the behavior of private agents and institutions and to supervise, monitor, and regulate private health insurance companies, privately managed care organizations, or other private providers so as to ensure access to quality services and protect consumers. In such situations, it is not surprising that significant numbers of violations occurred (Homedes and Ugalde 2005, 92).

Also in many countries the private health sector consists of a very large number of actors and institutions. Unless there is a comprehensive registration or licensure system and an effective health information system, which often does not exist in middle- and low-income countries, governments may not even have an accurate sense of the number and location of the private sector health institutions, what kinds of health services are being provided by specific actors, and the quality of these services, let alone who they are serving and how much they are charging.

GC 14 identifies the need to adopt and implement a national strategy and plan of action to achieve the right to health as a core obligation. It specifies that the plan should be based on human rights principles, accord particular attention to vulnerable and marginalized groups so as to ensure that all sectors of the population may enjoy the right to health, and enable individuals and groups to participate in the decision-making process (CESCR 2000, para 43.f). However, it is difficult to envision how this could take place in a mixed or highly privatized health system, or how this kind of planning could effectively direct the operations of private actors.

Citizens frequently encounter problems with holding their governments or private health institutions accountable for the provision of health care entitlements in a mixed or privatized health system. This can be a serious problem because privately managed health plans often have incentives to deny approval for covered services and medications so as to reduce expenses and increase profits. Individuals may also have difficulties securing reimbursements for authorized health services and medications because of a lack of institutional capacity within the health system or because the managers intentionally delay doing so. Furthermore, unlike providers, consumers of health care lack economic clout and rarely are organized. Short of a mass movement calling for structural health reform it may be difficult to bring about changes. Often there are no accessible and affordable mechanisms for redress of infringements of health entitlements by private sector providers. Litigation is often not an option because it is too expensive or too complex. Even a simplified litigation process that does not require formal representation by legal counsel to claim entitlements from a privately managed health system may have problems with delays and the implementation of decisions.

Colombia offers an example of the difficulties in securing health entitlements in a privately managed health system. In 1993, neoliberal reforms in Colombia established a managed-care health system operated by private insurance companies coupled with the government setting the capitation rate and the content of the benefits packages (Yamin et al. 2011, 109). Since the capitation rate the government paid for each enrolled individual member was fixed, private insurance companies could only increase earnings through cost-containment strategies, primarily by denying requests for services and medications. The situation was compounded by the failure of the Ministry of Health and the Superintendance of Health, the governmental regulatory agency charged with oversight, to discipline health insurance companies and providers that systematically refused to deliver pharmaceuticals and medical procedures included in the basket of guaranteed health services (Lamprea 2014, 140–141). In response, many thousands of Colombians sought legal remedies through filing informal and expedited *tutela* injunctions. But even when successful, as the majority of litigants in Colombia eventually were, there were harmful consequences from the delays, including prolongation of suffering, medical complications of health status, permanent disability and death (Abadia and Oviedo 2009), and the expenditure of time and energy to pursue the litigation.

Moreover, the very large number of Colombians seeking remedies – nearly 800,000 cases were filed between 1999 and 2009 – overwhelmed the legal system. Much of this litigation involved services and treatments that the claimants were entitled to under obligatory insurance plans. The situation finally resulted in the Constitutional Court calling for structural reforms of the health system (Yamin et al. 2011, 117). Also, in a country with major economic inequalities and political divisions, data indicate that cases were brought at higher rates in wealthier departments than in poorer departments, aggravating disparities in access to health benefits (Yamin et al. 2011, 114–116).

Access and Equity

According to Anand Grover, "the global trend toward privatization in health systems poses significant risks to the equitable availability and accessibility of health facilities, goods and services, especially for the poor and other vulnerable or marginalized groups" (2012, para 3). Data from many sources provide evidence that broad privatization and commercialization can dramatically increase inequality in both access and health outcomes (Marriott 2009, 22). These trends are not new. An analysis by two development economists, Nancy Birdsall and John Nellis of the Center for Global Development (Washington, DC), done more than a decade ago, concluded that many privatization programs have worsened the distribution of assets and income, at least in the short run (Birdsall and Nellis 2003).

Studies of the impact of neoliberal reforms in Latin American countries document that ten and twenty years after their implementation countries are spending more resources on health care, but there is increased inequity, less efficiency, and higher dissatisfaction without improving quality of care (Homedes and Ulgalde 2005, 92). A multicountry study concluded that the expansion of private insurance in a number of Latin American countries did not succeed in improving access to health services for vulnerable groups. Instead it often generated additional co-payments and raised costs, which then worsened access to needed services (Waitzkin et al. 2007). Research in Colombia documents the extent to which public health programs there have deteriorated while privatization increased health expenditures and failed to improve efficiency and equity. The increase in public expense predominantly benefited the wealthy while the poor continue to have difficulties in accessing services because of high co-payments (Homedes and Ugalde 2005).

A study of privatization of health services in fifteen sub-Saharan countries in Africa showed similar trends. Only two in ten persons were able to afford private providers. Another three in ten utilized the poorly functioning public facilities, but five in ten persons were priced out of access to all health care (Marriott 2009).

Similar trends have also been documented after the implementation of neoliberal health reforms in high-income economies. A study of the neoliberal health reforms in Sweden found that economic access to primary care services has been reduced for low-income patients (Dahlgren 2012). Government subsidies for private providers were also resulting in public funds being transferred from people living in low-income areas to people living in high-income areas, even though the health needs of people in low-income areas were greater (Dahlgren 2008).

Comparisons of Private and Public Health Systems and Institutions

There is very little rigorous research comparing private and public health systems and institutions in part because it is difficult to conduct a systematic comparison of private and public sector health institutions. In some health systems, there is a division of labor between the private and public health sectors with some functions or levels of the health system predominantly privatized and others remaining in the public sector. It is also not uncommon for the private and public health sectors to service different types of populations further complicating the analysis. Also private health institutions rarely collect or, if they do, share the necessary data to undertake an analysis of the factors relevant to human rights concerns.

Research conducted some fifteen years ago in OECD countries other than the United States (because the United States was considered an outlier in terms of the level of private finance and delivery) concluded the following: First, reforms that increase the role for the private sector in financing health care increase health expenditures. Conversely, high shares of public finance do better at cost containment. Second, systems that rely heavily on private finance for health care tend to be less progressive and equitable than those that use public finance. Relatedly, allowing richer individuals to opt out of contributions to public insurance is likely to decrease the progressivity of a given finance system as well as their support for the public system. Third, high levels of private finance do not appear to be associated with later lower growth of public finance. Fourth, there is little evidence on the impact of private finance on improvements of the efficiency of the public sector (Propper and Green 1999).

Another group of researchers conducted a systematic analysis of peer reviewed studies comparing the performance of private and public health care institutions in low- and middle-income countries (Basu et al. 2012). The research, which drew on eight search databases, identified 102 articles meeting their study criteria, fifty-nine of which were research studies and thirteen meta-analyses, with the remainder case study reviews. As might be expected, findings varied considerably across countries studied. Nevertheless, the researchers who conducted the analysis concluded, "Our review indicates that current data do not support claims that the private sector has been more efficient, accountable, or medically effective than the public sector" (Basu et al. 2012, 11). Efficiency tended to be lower in the private than the public sector, attributable in part to perverse incentive for unnecessary testing and treatment. The issue as to whether more patients accessed care in the private or public sectors depended on whether unlicensed and uncertified providers, such as drug shop owners, were excluded from the analysis. If so, the public sector predominated. The findings found a need for quality improvements in both sectors. Providers in the private sector more frequently violated medical standards of practice and had poorer patient outcomes, but private service providers also demonstrated greater hospitality to patients and timeliness. Public sector medical services experienced more limited availability of equipment, medications, and trained health workers. Significantly financial barriers to care, such as the user fees, were reported for both the private and public sectors. There was also evidence for "competitive dynamics," sometimes referred to as an "infrastructure inequality trap" characterized by public funds and personnel being redirected to private sector development resulting in reductions in public sector service budgets and staff (Basu et al. 2012).

The experience of the United States, the most thoroughly privatized and commercialized health system among developed countries, should be a caution. The United States spends twice as much on health care costs per person than most other advanced countries, but leaves millions of persons uncovered. In comparative studies based on measurers of quality, efficiency, access, equity, and health lives, the United States has ranked last among developed countries. While there was room for improvement in every country, the United States stood out as not getting good value for its health care expenditure (Davis et al. 2010).

Factors Affecting the Impact of Privatization on the Right to Health

Research suggests that the impact of privatization and contracting out of services on the right to health depends on a number of factors. The following section highlights some of these.

Strength of the Government's Continuing Commitment to the Right to Health

The extent of the continuing commitment of a state to its right to health obligations and more broadly to universal health coverage affects the potential impact of privatization. The expectations and demands of citizens regarding the implementation of their health rights constitute another factor. A related feature is whether the health system continues to be treated as a core social institution existing for the benefit of the society or health services are conceptualized more as a commodity appropriate to buy and sell like other commodities.

A number of countries appear to be moving away from a commitment to the right to health or universal and equal health provision or at least significantly qualifying it. For example, there is research on Canada, a single-payer health system ostensibly with universal coverage, revealing that health care is increasingly being portrayed as a consumer commodity and as a business that can be a source of profit (Armstrong 2002, 16–43). Some Canadian analysts express concern about the undermining of a commitment to social citizenship based on "a relationship of members of society to each other through the state that recognizes a positive obligation of the state to ensure the conditions exist for the realization of the shared dignity of all human beings" (Cameron 2007, 163). Critics claim that the entitlements once designed to enable all social classes to participate fully in social life are being displaced by a notion of market citizenship based on a sense of the legally equal but self-reliant and self-interested seller and buyer of classical liberalism (Young et al. 2007, 2–8). Other analysts point to the increasing legitimization of two-tiered health care as a considered policy option (Flood 2014, 95) and a process of "passive privatization" of Canadian health care. The latter development includes allowing user fees or extra billing for publicly insured care and permitting increasing numbers of ostensibly "necessary" health goods and services to silently fall into the privately financed basket (Flood 2014, 83).

In other cases, cut backs in health entitlements reflect policies imposed on countries. During the Great Recession several European countries – Greece, Portugal, Spain, and Ireland – which were unable to refinance government debt or to bail out overindebted banks sought assistance from the European Central Bank and the International Monetary fund. The loans that were provided had austerity conditions imposed that required cutting health spending. The resulting demise of their universal health care systems left many of their citizens responsible for their own health care at a time when many of them were unemployed or otherwise suffering from severe economic problems (Karanikolos et al. 2013).

Type of System into which Private Health Care Is Introduced

As Jean Dréze and Amartya Sen point out in their recently published book on India, introducing private health services in a health system with the solid foundations of universal public health has quite different implications than relying on private health care where the state provides little in terms of decent health facilities. In the few Indian states with adequate public health services, such as Kerala, private health facilities can provide additional options for the newly rich without directly harming other population groups. But elsewhere, such as in northern Indian states, where inadequate funding has undermined public health provision, poor people have no choice but to rely on poor quality and often expensive private care (2013, 38).

Similarly, research suggests that contracting out the provision of health services can be an acceptable alternative to public provision if certain conditions are met: (a) real competition exists between competent and substantial private providers; (b) there is adequate government capacity to assess needs and to negotiate and monitor contract terms; (c) the legal and political environment facilitates enforcing regulations and resisting patronage and corruption; and (d) the interests of low-income groups are defended within the political and health systems. These conditions exist in the developed countries that have had relative success in contracting out health services, such as France, Germany, and Belgium, but are absent in most developing countries, perhaps with the exception of a few urban centers in middle-income countries. Moreover, unlike in Europe the poor usually play little role in shaping health care policies or setting budgets in developing countries.

Degree of Privatization

A health system in which privatization is used selectively and strategically to accomplish specific objectives, as in the case of many European countries, is very different from one in which privatization occurs in a wholesale and indiscriminant manner as in the United States. The appropriate type and level of privatization also depend on the government's objectives. In this regard an International Monetary Fund-sponsored study notes that an ethic of social solidarity is incompatible with allowing private health insurers to perform the function of collecting premium contributions and engaging in risk pooling (Gupta et al. 2012, 11). The situation whereby a government has chosen to rely on private sector provision for some types of health service provision rather than invest in the development of public services also is often problematic. In Brazil, for example, the systematic underfinancing of the public sector has been a major barrier to building a truly universal system capable of providing comprehensive health care services to all members of society (Global Health Watch 2014, 117–118).

Capacity and Willingness to Regulate the Private Sector

The capacity and willingness of the state to regulate the private sector and try to ensure its adherence to human rights principles constitute critical factors. Most high-income countries have an extensive and effective regulatory system built up over many decades that regulates prices, quality, levels of service, and citizen's entitlements (World Health Organization 2010a, para 5). If the government is committed to doing so, these capacities can be brought to bear to require that the private sector operate in a manner consistent with human rights norms. However, having the capacity to regulate the private sector does not necessarily mean a government will do so. In Canada, for example, provincial regulators have primarily focused their attention on publicly financed health care, making little effort to regulate privately financed care, despite the documented need for regulation and oversight of private care facilities (Flood 2014, 81).

Brigit Toebes work on the reorganization of health services in the Dutch health care system, which privatized the provision of health insurance (2006), shows the care the government initially took to try to protect access to and the affordability of basic health services. Elements of the reform package included guaranteed issue, community rating, sliding-scale income-based subsidies for the purchase of insurance, price competition for a standardized basic benefits package, and risk equalization for insurers. Her evaluation was conducted too close to the implementation of the changes to assess their impact, but Toebes still had several concerns. Later research completed two years after the reform showed that the reform had not compromised the Dutch tradition of universal coverage. Subsidies for purchasing insurance were available when the premium was greater than 5 percent of individual or household income. Consistent with the Dutch tradition of solidarity, the system entailed an explicit redistribution from the healthy to the sick and from the young to the old (Rosenau and Lako 2008, 1046). On the negative side, however, there were rises in consumer premiums (Rosenau and Lako 2008, 1040), mixed consumer satisfaction, and concern with insufficient transparency about quality of care from providers and medication (Rosenau and Lako 2008, 1044–1046). At that time policy analysts believed that several additional problems might emerge: the basic benefits package may be eroded; risk selection may be practiced even though it is not legal; the precedent of privatizing basic insurance may lead to the privatization of other health insurance programs (Rosenau and Lako 2008, 1048), possibly with more detrimental consequences for the right to health.

In contrast, the lack of institutional capacity characteristic of many low- and middle-income countries constrains constructive engagement with and regulation of private sector health providers (De Groote et al. 2005). In part this reflects the understaffing and underfunding of regulatory institutions, often a consequence of past disinvestment in the health sector (WHO 2010b, para 17). The inadequate registration of private providers leaves a critical gap of knowledge. In addition, regulations are often inappropriate or outdated and enforcement is weak (World Bank 2011, xvi). Thus, the states where public provision of health care has failed to provide the minimum standards of decent universal and affordable health care are those least able to oversee that private sector providers do so. Even Gregg Bloche, who is generally supportive of private provision, acknowledges that privatization is most risky in societies where public provision is least able to fulfill its human rights obligations (Bloche 2005, 217).

As noted in the brief discussion of the Colombian health care system, even in health systems recognizing the right to health, privatization of health provision in the absence of an effective regulatory capacity is likely to be problematic. In 1993, under pressure from the international financial institutions and local demand for better and more equitable health services, the government undertook an overhaul of the health system. Consistent with neoliberal policy prescriptions, the reform adopted in Colombia relied on private health providers and insurers, which were to be subject to the strict regulation of government agencies. The reform led to the unprecedented expansion of coverage from 21 percent of the population in 1993 to 92 percent in 2009. But it also precipitated a regulatory crisis because the Ministry of Health and the Superintendence of Health, the government agency that was assigned primary responsibility for regulating the health sector, failed to discipline health insurance companies and providers when they refused patients the pharmaceuticals and medical procedures to which they were legally entitled. This situation then provided incentives for these companies, which were paid the same capitation fee regardless of their failure to deliver services, to continue to deny health entitlements. In response, the ease of filing a *tutela* claim, an expedited injunction for a citizen to seek judicial protection when their rights are threatened by the state or a third party, unleashed an unprecedented wave of health rights-based litigation. Between 1999 and 2013 more than one million Colombians went to court to seek judgments against private health insurance companies, most of which were granted and the cost then reimbursed by the Ministry of Health. Because this tsunami of litigation threatened the stability of the health system, as well as overwhelming the legal system, the Constitutional Court intervened, and in 2008 the Constitutional Court issued a judgment ordering the Ministry of Health and other regulatory agencies to adopt a wide range of regulatory measures to protect the right to health. Although many of these measures have been instituted, they have not been successful in curbing litigation for health entitlements, presumably because the private insurance companies are still refusing to provide relevant health benefits (Lamprea 2014; Lamprea et al. forthcoming).

Affordability

General Comment 14 requires that health care be affordable and articulates a stringent standard of what affordability entails. According to GC 14,

> payment for health-care services, as well as services related to the underlying determinants of health has to be based on the principle of equity, ensuring that these services, whether privately or publicly provided, are affordable for all, including socially disadvantaged groups. Equity demands that poorer households should not be disproportionately burdened with health expenses as compared to richer households (CESCR 2000, para 12 (b)).

Financial arrangements determine which people can afford to use private health services when they need them, assuming that they are accessible. It is therefore problematic that in many cases privatization has led to increased out-of-pocket payments for health goods and services (Grover 2012, para 3) and increased their cost. The incidence of financial catastrophe associated with direct payments for health services, calculated as the proportion of people who spend more than 40 percent of their incomes, can be high. Research suggests that households with a disabled member, those with children, and those with elderly members are particularly vulnerable to catastrophic health expenditures. According to WHO, the reduction of the incidence of catastrophic health costs requires that reliance on direct payments falls to less than 15 to 20 percent of total health expenditures, a goal achieved primarily by high-income countries (WHO 2010b, 40–42).

Increasingly, there has also been greater awareness in the human rights community of the importance of health costs also being affordable to the government. For example, General Comment 14 recognizes that investments in health should not disproportionately favor expensive curative care health services, which are often accessible only to a small, privileged fraction of the population, rather than expenditures on primary and preventive health care, which are lower in cost and have the potential of benefiting a far larger part of the population. It also notes that inappropriate health resource allocation can lead to discrimination that may not be overt (CESCR 2000, para 19). Anand Grover adds that investment in primary health care services is more cost efficient because it prevents illness and promotes general health, which in turn reduces the need for more costly secondary and tertiary care. The resulting savings can then be reinvested in the health system, potentially in the form of additional subsidies for the poor (Grover 2012, para 12).

The structural impact of privatization on the health sector is therefore of concern. As Anand Grover recognizes, in many cases privatization has led to disproportionate investment in secondary and tertiary care sectors at the expense of primary care. He also mentions that privatization tends to increase disparity in the availability of health facilities, goods, and services among rural, remote, and urban areas (2012, para 3). Selective privatization, whereby those who are affluent can opt out of the public health system to seek private insurance and private health services is also problematic because it often leads to a two tier health system whereby the privileged obtain a higher quality of health care. Also it may reduce pressure on the government to improve the quality of health services provided by the public health sector.

Concluding Reflections

Health systems with health care provision and financing divided between public and private providers pose significant issues for the realization of a human rights approach. Privatization can be inimical to the values that underlie and sustain a human rights approach. It can also reduce access to health facilities and services, particularly for the poorer segments of the population. By fragmenting the health system, private sector provision can complicate governmental efforts to formulate and implement national health plans. Research has shown that when the public sector relies on private actors to provide basic services it often results in public resources being directed to profits rather than being used to extend access to and/ or improve the quality of service. Additionally, when the private sector provides health services on behalf of, or in place of, the state, it can make it more difficult for citizens to hold either their governments or the provider accountable.

It is important that the health and human rights community take cognizance of the issues raised by private health provision and contribute to deliberations about the future of health systems. However, the health and human rights community appears to be poorly prepared to deal with the dilemmas and difficulties that private health provision and financing pose for human rights-based approaches to health. There is little in international human rights law, key human rights interpretative documents, or human rights research that addresses the challenges of mixed or predominantly private health systems in any depth. Reiterating that states remain responsible for ensuring that private providers act in accordance with human rights norms is only a beginning. There is a need to offer specifics as to how this might be accomplished.

The extent and nature of the difficulties reliance on private health provision and insurance impose for implementation of a human rights-based approach to health within a specific health system depend on a number of factors. Several are particularly important. First and foremost is whether a state retains a commitment to the right to health and the achievement of universal health coverage. Second is whether it frames a national health strategy and plan of action to take steps toward the realization of the right to health that explicitly defines and appropriately restricts the role of the private sector in the health system. Equally important is a third factor, whether the plan includes provisions to lessen the equity impact of financing private health services to assure affordability and protect health access, most particularly of low-income groups. Governments also need to be willing and able to establish a regulatory framework and monitoring capability to attempt to assure that private institutions conform to human rights standards. The dilemma is that policies to reduce the inimical human rights impacts of private sector provision require capabilities to regulate and monitor health systems, which many countries lack. Also countries with the weakest health systems and consequently the greatest reliance on the private sector are particularly likely to have limited abilities to do so.

Importantly, data do not support claims often made by private sector advocates that private health sector institutions are more efficient, accountable, or effective than public sector institutions. Instead studies point to the importance of public sector provision, particularly at the level of primary care. One conclusion that can be drawn is that public sector subsidies that underwrite the costs of private health provision in some countries are a poor investment. Public sector investments in private health provision also tend to be inimical to realizing a human rights approach, particularly when it comes at the expense of investments strengthening the public health sector. For this reason the various proposals to rely on private health provision to achieve universal coverage in poor- and middle-income countries, as will be discussed in Chapter Eight, are problematic from a human rights perspective.

To date, the topic of the impact of private health institutions on the realization of the right to health has not been given sufficient attention by members of the human rights community working on health issues. In one of his reports, Anand Grover states that "The right to health approach to health financing recognizes that an appropriate balance must be achieved between public and private financing for health, as well as between public and private administration of health facilities, goods and services" (2012, para 3). What should the specifics of this balance be? How should the relationship between the public and private sectors vary depending on characteristics of the country and its health goals? It is critical that the human rights community address these important topics.

References

Abadia, Cesar Ernesto and Oveido, Diana G. (2009) "Bureaucratic Itineraries in Colombia: A Theoretical and Methodological Tool to Assess Managed Health Care Systems," *Social Science and Medicine* 68 (6): 153–160.
Armstrong, Pat (2002) "The Context for Health Care Reform in Canada," in Pat Armstrong, Carol Amaratunga, Jocelyn Bernier, Karen Grant, and Ann

Pederson, eds., *Exposing Privatization: Women and Health Care Reform in Canada*, Aurora, ON: Garamond Press, pp. 11–48.

Arts, Wil and Verburg, Rudi (2001) "Modernisation, Solidarity and Care in Europe: The Sociologist's Tale," in Ruud Ter Meulen, Wil Arts, and Ruud Muffels, eds., *Solidarity in Health and Social Care in Europe*, Dordrecht, Boston, and London: Kluwer Academic Publishers, pp. 15–39.

Barr, Donald A. (2007) *Introduction to U.S. Health Policy: The Organization, Financing and Delivery of Health Care in America*, 2nd ed., Baltimore: The Johns Hopkins University Press.

Basu, Sanjay, Andrews, Jason, Kishore, Sandeep, Panjabi, Rajesh, and Stuckler, David (2012) "Comparative Performance of Private and Public Healthcare Systems in Low-and Middle-Income Countries: A Systematic Review," *PLoS Medicine* 9 (6): e1001244, doi:10.1371/jouenL.PMWS.1001244.

Birdsall, Nancy and Nellis, John (2003) "Winners and Losers: Assessing the Distribution Impact of Privatization," *World Development* 31 (10): 1617–1633.

Bloche, M. Gregg (2005) "Is Privatisation of Health Care a Human Rights Problem?" in Koen De Feyter and Felip Gómez Isa, eds., *Privatisation and Human Rights in the Age of Globalisation*, Antwerp and Oxford: Intersentia, pp. 207–228.

Buchanan, Allen (2009) *Justice & Health Care: Selected Essays*, Oxford and New York: Oxford University Press.

Bueno de Mesquita, Judith and Kismödi, Eszter (2012) "Maternal Mortality and Human Rights: Landmark Decision by United Nations Human Rights Body," *Bulletin of the World Health Organization* 90: 79–79A, doi:10.2471/BLT.11.101410.

Cameron, Barbara (2007) "Accounting for Rights and Money in the Canadian Social Union," in Margaret Young, Susan B. Boyd, Gwen Brodsky, and Shelagh Day, eds., *Poverty: Rights, Social Citizenship, and Legal Activism*, Vancouver and Toronto: UBC Press, pp. 162–180.

CESCR (Committee on Economic, Social and Cultural Rights) (1990) General Comment No. 3, The Nature of States parties' Obligations, U.N. Doc. E/1991/23, annex III at 86 (1990), reprinted in Compilation of General Comments and General Recommendations Adopted by Human Rights Treaty Bodies, U.N. Doc. HRI/GEN/1, Rev. 6 at 14 (2003).

(2000) General Comment No. 14: The Right to the Highest Attainable Standard of Health (article 12 of the International Covenant on Economic, Social and Cultural Rights), U.N. Doc. E/C.12/2000/4.

Chaoulli v. Quebec (Attorney General), no. 29272, Supreme Court of Canada 130 CRR (2d) 99, 2005 CRR LEXIS 76.

Committee on the Rights of the Child (2002) Day of General Discussion, Summary Record (Partial) of the 813th Meeting, U.N. Doc. CRC/C/SR.813.

(2013a) General Comment No. 15 (2013) on the Right of the Child to the Enjoyment of the Highest Attainable Standard of Health (art. 24), U.N. Doc. CRC/C/GC/15.

(2013b) General Comment No. 16 (2013) on State Obligations Regarding the Impact of the Business Sector on Children's Rights, U.N. Doc. CRC/CGC/16.

Committee to Eliminate All Forms of Discrimination Against Women (CEDAW) (1999) General Recommendation No. 24: Women and health (Article 12)

Commonwealth Fund (2010) *International Profiles of Health Care Systems*, Commonwealth Fund pub. No. 1417, New York City, www.common wealthfund.org/...Fund%20Report/2.../

Cook, Rebecca J. (2013) "Human Rights and Maternal Health: Exploring the Effectiveness of the *Alyne* Decision," *Journal of Law, Medicine & Ethics* 41 (1): 103–123.

Council of the European Union (2011) Directive on Cross-border Health Care, adopted Brussels, February 28, 2011 (7056/11).

Dahlgren, Göran (2008) "Neoliberal Reforms in Swedish Primary Health Care: For Whom and for What Purpose?" *International Journal of Health Services* 38 (4): 697–715.

(2012) Profit Driven Health Sector Reforms: Experiences from Sweden," background paper for the 15th Turkish National Public Health Congress, October 2–6.

Davis, Karen, Schoen, Cathy, and Stremikis (2010) *Mirror, Mirror on the Wall: How the Performance of the U.S. Health Care System Compares Internationally 2010 Update*, New York: The Commonwealth Fund.

De Groote, Tony, De Paepe, Pierre, and Unger, Jean-Pierre (2005) "Colombia: In Vivo Test of Health Sector Privatization in the Development World," *International Journal of Health Services* 35 (1): 125–141.

De Feyter, Koen and Gómez Isa, Felipe, eds. (2005) *Privatisation and Human Rights in the Age of Globalisation,* Antwerp and Oxford: Intersentia.

den Exeter, Andre (2010) "Health System Reforms in the Netherlands: From Public to Private and Its Effects on Equal Access to Health Care," *European Journal of Health Law* 17: 223–233.

Dréze, Jean and Sen, Amartya (2013) *An Uncertain Glory: India and Its Contradictions*, Princeton: Princeton University Press.

Ferraz, Octavio L. Motta (2011) "Brazil: Health Inequalities, Rights, and Courts: The Social Impact of the Judicialization of Health," in Alicia Ely Yamin and Siri Gloppen, eds., *Litigating Health Rights: Can Courts Bring More Justice to Health*, Cambridge: Harvard University Press, pp. 132–154.

Flood, Colleen M. (2014) "Litigating Health Rights in Canada; A White Night for Equity," in Colleen M. Flood and Aeyal Gross, eds., *The Right to Health at the Public/Private Divide: A Global Comparative Study*, New York: Cambridge University Press, pp. 79–106.

Gevers, Josette, Gelissen, John, Arts, Wil, and Muffels, Rudd (2001) "Popular Support for Health Care in Europe: Review of the Evidence of Cross-national Surveys," in Ruud Ter Meulen, Wil Arts, and Ruud Muffels, eds., *Solidarity in Health and Social Care in Europe*, Dordrecht, Boston, and London: Kluwer Academic Publishers, pp. 41–76.

Gilson, Lucy, Doherty, Jane, and Loewenson, Rene (2011) "Challenging Inequity Through Health Systems," in Jennifer H. Lee and Ritu Sadana, eds., *Improving Equity in Health by Addressing Social Determinants*, Geneva: World Health Organization, pp. 196–230.

Global Health Watch (2014) *Global Health Watch: An Alternative World Health Report*, London: Zed Books for the People's Health Movement, Medact, Medico International, Third World Network, Health Action International, and ALAMES.

Gloppen, Siri and Roseman, Mindy Jane (2011) "Introduction: Can Litigation Bring Justice to Health?" in Alicia Ely Yamin and Siri Gloppen, eds., *Litigating Health Rights: Can Courts Bring More Justice to Health*, Cambridge: Harvard University Press, pp. 1–16.

Gómez Isa, Felipe (2005) "Globalisation, Privatisation and Human Rights," in Koen De Feyter and Felipe Gómez Isa, eds., *Privatisation and Human Rights in the Age of Globalisation*, Antwerp and Oxford: Intersentia, pp. 9–32.

Gross, Aeyal (2013) "Is There a Human Right to Private Health Care," *Journal of Law, Medicine & Ethics* 41 (1): 138–146.

(2014) "The Right to Health in Israel between Solidarity and Neoliberalism," in Colleen M. Flood and Aeyal Gross, eds., *The Right to Health at the Public/Private Divide: A Global Comparative Study*, New York: Cambridge University Press, pp. 159–187.

Grover, Anand (2012) Interim Report of the Special Rapporteur on the Right of Everyone to the Enjoyment of the Highest Attainable Standard of Physical and Mental Health to the United Nations General Assembly, U.N. Doc. A/67/150.

Gupta, Sanjeev, Clements, Benedict, and Coady, David (2012) "The Challenge of Health Care Reform in Advanced and Emerging Economies," in Sanjeev Gupta, Benedict Clements, and David Coady, eds., *The Economics of Public Health Care Reform in Advanced and Emerging Economies*, Washington, DC: International Monetary Fund, IMF Publications, pp. 3–22.

HJC 4253/02 *Kiryati et v the Attorney General* (2009).

Holmes, David (2013) "All Change for the NHS in England as Legislation Takes Effect," *The Lancet* 381: 1169–1170.

Homedes, Núria and Ugalde, Antonio (2005) "Why Neoliberal Health Reforms Have Failed in Latin America," *Health Policy* 71: 83–96.

International Finance Corporation (2007) *The Business of Health in Africa: Partnering with the Private Sector to Improve People's Lives*, Washington, DC: The World Bank Group.

Karanikolos, Marina, Mladovsky, Philipa, Cylus, Jonathan, Thomson, Sara, et al. (2013) "Financial Crisis, Austerity, and Health in Europe," *The Lancet* 381: 1323–1331.

Lamprea, Everaldo (2014) "Colombia's Right-to-Health Litigation in a Context of Health Care Reform," in Colleen M. Flood and Aeyal Gross, eds., *The Right to Health at the Public/Private Divide: A Global Comparative Study*, New York: Cambridge University Press, pp. 131–158.

Lamprea, Everaldo, Forman, Lisa, and Chapman, Audrey (forthcoming 2016) "Structural Reform Litigation, Regulation and the Right to Health in Colombia," in David Zaring and Francesca Bignami, eds., *Comparative Law and Regulation*, Cheltenham and Camberley, UK: Edward Elgar Publishers.

Levcovitz, Eduardo (2007) Processes of Change and Challenges for Health Systems Based on the Renewed PHC Strategy. VII Regional Forum: Strengthening PHC-Based Health Systems, PAHO.

Maarse, Hans (2006) "The Privatization of Health Care in Europe: An Eight-Country Analysis," *Journal of Health Politics*, 31 (5): 981–1014.

Mackintosh, Maureen (2006) "Commercialisation, Inequality, and the Limits to Transition in Health Care: A Polanyian Framework for Policy Analysis," *Journal of International Development* 18: 393–406.

Marriott, Anna (2009) "Blind Optimism: Challenging the Myths about Private Health Care in Poor Countries," Oxfam Briefing Paper No. 125.

McDonald, David A. and Ruiters, Greg (2012) *Alternatives to Privatization: Public Options for Essential Services in the Global South*, New York and Capetown: Routledge/Taylor & Francis and Human Sciences Research Council.

Meulen, Ruud Ter, Arts, Wil and Muffels, Ruud (2001) "Solidarity, Health and Social Care in Europe: Introduction to the Volume," in Ruud Ter Meulen, Wil Arts, and Ruud Muffels, eds., *Solidarity in Health and Social Care in Europe*, Dordrecht, Boston, and London: Kluwer Academic Publishers, pp. 1–11.

Meulen, Ruud Ter and Maarse, Hans (2008) "Increasing Individual Responsibility in Dutch Health Care: Is Solidarity Losing Ground?" *Journal of Medicine and Philosophy* 33: 262–279.

Mills, Anne, Brugha, Ruairi, Hanson, Kara, and McPake, Barbara (2002) "What Can Be Done about the Private Health Sector in Low-income Countries?" *Bulletin of the World Health Organization* 80 (4): 325–330.

Mossialos, Elias and Wenzl, Martin, eds. (2015) *2014 International Profiles of Health Systems*, New York: The Commonwealth Fund, www.commonwealthfund .org/publications/fund-reports/2013/nov....

O'Connell, Paul (2010) "The Human Right to Health in an Age of Market Hegemony," in John Harrington and Maria Stuttaford, eds., *Global Health and Human Rights: Legal and Philosophical Perspectives*, London and New York: Routledge, pp. 190–209.

Paim, Jamilson, Travassos, Claudia, Almeida, Celia, Bahia, Ligia, Macinko, James (2011) "The Brazilian Health System: History, Advances, and Challenges," *The Lancet* 377: 1778–1797.

Pellegrino, Edmund D. (1999) "The Commodification of Medical and Health Care: The Moral Consequences of a Paradigm Shift from a Professional to a Market Ethic," *Journal of Medicine and Philosophy* 24 (3): 243–266.

Propper, Carol and Green, Katherine (1999) A Larger Role for the Private Sector in Health Care? A Review of the Arguments, CMPO Working Paper No. 99/009, Centre for Market and Public Organisation, University of Bristol.

Rosen, Bruce and Samuel, Hadar (2009) "Israel: Health System," *Health Systems in Transition* 11 (2), European Observatory on Health Systems and Policies, www.euro.who.int_data/.../E92608.pdf

Rosenau, Pauline Vaillancourt and Lako, Christiaan J. (2008) "An Experiment with Regulated Competition and Individual Mandates for Universal Health Care: The New Dutch Health Insurance System," *Journal of Health Politics, Policy and Law* 33 (6): 1031–1055.

Rudra, Nita (2008) *Globalization and the Race to the Bottom in Developing Countries: Who Really Gets Hurt?* Cambridge, England, and New York: Cambridge University Press.

Saltman, Richard B. and Cahn, Zachary (2013) "Restructuring Health Systems for an Era of Prolonged Austerity: An Essay," *BMJ* 346:f3972.

Sengupta, Amit (2013) Universal Health Care in India: Making It Public, Making It a Reality, Municipal Services Project Occasional Paper No. 19, www .municipalservicesproject.org.

Smith, Elizabeth, Brugha Ruairi, and Zwi, Anthony (2005) *Working with Private Sector Providers for Better Health Care: An Introductory Guide*, London: Options Consultancy Services Ltd. And London School of Hygiene and Tropical Medicine, www.who.int/management/parternships/private/privatesectorguide.pdf

Toebes, Brigit (2006) "The Right to Health and the Privatization of National Health Systems: A Case Study of the Netherlands," *Health and Human Rights* 9 (1): 102–127.

UNRISD (United Nations Research Institute for Social Development) (2007) "Commercialization and Globalization of Health Care: Lessons from UNRISD Research," UNRISD Research and Policy Brief 7.

USAID (United States Agency for International Development) (2012) USAID's Global Health Strategic Framework: Better Health for Development, Washington, D.C., www.usaid.gov.

Waitzkin, Howard, Jasso-Aguilar, Rebeca, and Iriat, Celia (2007) "Privatization of Health Services in Less Developed Countries: An Empirical Response to the Proposals of the World Bank and the Wharton School," *International Journal of Health Services* 37 (2): 205–227.

World Bank (2004) *World Development Report: Making Services Work for Poor People*, Washington, DC: World Bank.

(2009) World Bank Responds to New Oxfam Health Report, web.worldbank .org>Topics>Health.

(2011) *Healthy Partnerships: How Governments Can Engage the Private Sector to Improve Health in Africa*, Washington, DC: World Bank and International Finance Corporation.

World Health Organization (WHO) (2007) *Everybody's Business: Strengthening Health Systems to Improve Health Outcome*, Geneva: WHO.

(2010a) *The World Health Report: Health Systems Financing, The Path to Universal Coverage*, Geneva: WHO.

(2010b) Strengthening the Capacity of Governments to Constructively Engage the Private Sector in Providing Essential Health-Care Services, report by the Secretariat, Sixty-Third World Health Assembly, A63/25.

Yamin, Alicia Ely, Parra-Vera, Oscar, and Gianella, Camilia (2011) "Colombia/ Judicial Protection of the Right to Health: An Elusive Promise?" in Alicia Ely Yamin and Siri Gloppen, *Litigating Health Rights: Can Courts Bring More Justice to Health?* Cambridge, MA: Harvard University Press, pp. 103–131.

Yamin, Alicia Ely and Norheim, Ole Frithjof (2014) "Taking Equality Seriously: Applying Human Rights Frameworks to Priority Setting in Health," *Human Rights Quarterly* 36 (2): 296–324.

Young, Margot, Boyd, Susan, Brodsky, Gwen, and Selagh Day, eds. (2007) *Poverty: Rights, Social Citizenship, Legal Activism*, Vancouver and Toronto: UBC Press.

5

Globalization, Health, and Human Rights

The human rights paradigm identifies states as the primary duty bearer for the fulfillment of human rights. A human rights approach generally assumes that states can fulfill their rights-based obligations if they have a commitment to do so. Because economic and social rights are linked with the availability of resources, allowance is made for lack of sufficient economic resources, and states are given the option of realizing rights gradually. Failure to implement human rights commitments is often attributed to the absence of political will or insufficient dedication to human rights.

While human rights advocates may sometimes be correct, the situation is more complicated than this model assumes. In the contemporary globalized world, states are interwoven into a variety of types of economic and political relationships that limit their independence and constrain their ability to formulate and implement health policies. The Lancet-University of Oslo Commission on Global Governance for Health observes that "Nation states are responsible for respecting, protecting, and fulfilling their populations' right to health, but with globalization many important determinants of health lie beyond any single government's control and are now inherently global" (Ottersen et al. 2014). Moreover, it is often difficult for states to engage in policy-making on health protection or human rights matters without taking into account how it will affect their economic competitiveness, attractiveness to foreign investors, implementation of international trading agreements, and in the case of some countries, possibilities for negotiating new loans with the World Bank and the

This chapter builds on several of my earlier articles on health, human rights and globalization: Audrey R. Chapman (2009) "Globalization, Human Rights, and the Social Determinants of Health," *Bioethics* 23: 97–111; Ted Schrecker, Audrey R. Chapman, Ronald Labonté, and Robert De Vogli, (2010) "Advancing health equity in the global marketplace: How human rights can help," *Social Science & Medicine* 71: 1520–1526; Audrey R. Chapman and Salil D. Benegal (2013) "Globalization and the Right to Health," in Lance Minkler, ed., *The Status of Economic and Social Rights: A Global Overview*, New York: Cambridge University Press, pp. 61–85.

International Monetary Fund. The manner in which the 2007 U.S. financial crisis precipitated the global economic crisis, its impact on the economies of Europe, and the health systems toll of the austerity policies that several of the countries, particularly Greece, were required to adopt as a condition for needed loans show that even developed countries cannot escape the health effects of global trends (Karanikolas et al. 2013).

Globalization, a process characterized by the growing interdependence of the world's people, which involves the integration of economies, culture, technologies, and governance, has altered the political, economic, and health landscape. While globalization is not a new phenomenon, the rapidity and degree to which states are being drawn into a global economy, polity, and culture is a new development. Also new, the hegemony of the market economy constitutes the characteristic feature of contemporary globalization. As Rhoda Howard-Hassmann comments, "although globalization includes political, social, and cultural aspects, the chief impetus and beneficiary of globalization is capitalism" (2010, 7). She identifies the following as some of the key aspects of globalization: the expanding world market and the importance of international trade and capital flows; the centrality of transnational corporations; the role of institutions of global governance, particularly international financial institutions established to regulate the market and also international human rights bodies; travel, migration, communications, and global culture; the rise of a global civil society, including international nongovernmental organizations, global social movements, and private social actors, some of which are dedicated to human rights (2010, 8).

Neoliberal economic thought and policy prescriptions have infused contemporary forms of globalization just as they are shaping national economic systems and policies. As Paul O'Connell points out, the age of globalization is better understood as being an age of market hegemony during which all of the governments of the world, whether through ideological commitment or under externally imposed pressures of market discipline, embraced and implemented neoliberal policy prescriptions (2007). The implications of neoliberal economic doctrine for a human rights approach to health were discussed in Chapter Three. To reiterate, proponents of neoliberalism believe that markets and market principles are the most appropriate basis for organizing most areas of economic and social life, including the health sector, regardless of the ethical, human rights, and distributional consequences. Neoliberalism favors a reduction in the role of the state in favor of according the market free reign. Neoliberalism's policy agenda advocates minimizing economic regulation, reducing expenditures on public goods such as health systems, decreasing state budgets, and transferring responsibility for the social services formerly provided by the state, such as health care, education, and basic social services, to the private sector (Gómez Isa 2005, 13).

This chapter will explore the manner in which neoliberal globalization affects the realization of a human rights approach to health. Arguably, the right to health is one of the economic and social rights most affected by the globalization process. It will begin with a brief overview of international economic trends and a brief discussion of human rights assessments of globalization. The next section will consider the impact of globalization on health status, health systems, and the availability of health personnel in poor countries. The chapter will then consider the impact of transnational actors on the right to health including the World Health Organization (WHO), corporations, the World Bank, the World Trade Organization (WTO) and its International Agreement on Trade-Related Aspects of Intellectual Property Rights (TRIPS), and international aid donors. This will be followed by a section reviewing how globalization has affected the social determinants of health. The final section of the chapter will detail human rights responses and assess their potential effectiveness.

Economic Context

Global market integration is shrinking the ability of governments to make decisions about health without taking into consideration such factors as economic competitiveness, credit worthiness, debt payments to external creditors, and complying with trade agreement conditions, even when these impose health-negative effects. Over the past few decades countries have been integrated into an international trading system and global marketplace characterized by the reorganization of production across multiple national borders. This economic system, particularly its promotion of market fundamentalism and a form of super capitalism, erodes the values important to a human rights approach and reorders social and political priorities away from human welfare.

Transnational corporations unanchored in particular countries and largely free of regulation from any national or international actors increasingly dominate the economic landscape. According to Gary Teeple, until the 1970s the expansion of capitalism always came in the form of national capital, that is capital with particular territorial and historical roots, but then capitalism began to become independent of national political and economic regulations and restrictions (Teeple 2000, 175). Embodied in the form of the transnational corporation, capital is increasingly free of national loyalties, controls, and interests (Teeple 2000, 179). The speed with which investors can rapidly move money in and out of national economies has placed most countries in an economically competitive environment where powerful economic actors and international investors can condition investment on the elimination of onerous regulations, reduced labor protection measures to lower costs, and trade liberalization policies that open the country to foreign investment. Many of these policies have human rights implications.

To date, globalization has disproportionately benefited the countries and economic entities with the resources and the power to shape the rules under which the international economic system functions. Entities unable to compete in or marginalized by the new and sometimes brutal competitive economic order have suffered. Globalization has tended to increase economic inequality, insecurity, and vulnerability of the poorer segments of the population. Richard Falk characterizes these developments as resulting in a form of "predatory globalization" because he believes the ideas and dynamics guiding global policy are pushing states toward cruelty and irresponsibility, particularly with regard to the social agenda (1999).

Economic globalization has also subjected developed countries to deleterious economic forces. Since 2008, many countries have struggled with flat growth rates and soaring unemployment brought on by the Great Recession. This financial crisis exacerbated long-term structural forces. Developed countries increasingly have postindustrial service-oriented economies that cannot replicate the high growth rates of the manufacturing led economies of the post–World War II period. Depending on how they are managed, reduced public resources can have significant implications for the health sector, particularly in countries where the public sector has been the main source of health funding (Saltman and Cahn 2013). Although economic crises and their countermeasures have pronounced unintended effects on public health, these have been little acknowledged or addressed by policymakers (Karanikolos et al. 2013; Kentikelenis et al. 2014).

Economic inequalities have risen significantly since the early 1990s reflecting increasing concentrations of income, resources, and wealth both between and within countries (Birdsall 2005). The richest 5 percent of the global income distribution has gained substantially over the globalization period, while the poorest 90 percent have lost ground, with the losses most severe in the poorest quarter. Sub-Saharan Africa, already the poorest region of the world, has been the least competitive and suffered the most. Currently, the poorer two-thirds of humanity hold only 4 percent of global private wealth and have merely 6 percent of global household income (Bhalotra and Pogge 2012, 13).

It is sometimes claimed that globalization stimulates global economic growth and over the long term will thereby lead to widely shared improvements in population health. Developments associated with globalization have led to a rising standard of living for several hundred million people in Asia. However, between 1981 and 2005, a period during which the value of the world's economic product quadrupled, progress in reducing poverty, particularly in the poorest countries, was modest. The notable exception was China (Schrecker 2011, 156). It is also worth noting that half of the poverty reduction in China occurred before that country embraced global market reforms. Moreover, economic growth in China did not lead to improvements in access to health care. Instead, because growth coincided with the rapid marketization of health care provision it has resulted in significant declines in access and affordability (Labonté et al. 2011, 266–267).

Human Rights Assessments of Globalization

To date, much of the human rights assessment of the impact of globalization has depended more on views about capitalism and neoliberalism than on globalization per se. While some human rights analysts identify both negative and positive features in contemporary globalization, most are basically critical, particularly of its interconnections with neoliberal economic policies. Rhoda Howard-Hassmann, who has a predominantly positive view of globalization, is an exception. In contrast with many human rights advocates, she also believes that capitalism is a necessary, though not sufficient, prerequisite for democracy and the realization of human rights (Howard-Hassmann 2010, 127).

Howard-Hassmann characterizes globalization as the "second great transformation," which is transforming the entire world from agricultural to industrial societies (2010, 33–40). She recognizes that globalization often has short-term deleterious impacts on human rights, but argues that it also brings about "human rights leapfrogging" that diffuses the conception of human rights. By so doing, she believes that globalization enables human rights advocates to confront negative aspects of industrialization. She acknowledges globalization's tendency to exacerbate economic inequality across and within countries but balances it against globalization's claimed reduction in world poverty levels and its potential to increase economic growth rates and thereby contribute to the realization of social and economic rights (2010, 16). Although she cautions that it is premature to draw conclusions as to whether globalization will benefit or harm human rights, she is basically optimistic (Howard-Hassmann 2005, 2010). In response to the critics who blame globalization for adverse conditions for fulfilling economic and social rights, she argues that many of the decisions that affect human rights were made by sovereign national governments and not by abstract economic forces (2010, 14). However, this claim fails to acknowledge the impact of the global economic system and the demands of the World Bank and other nonstate actors that will be discussed later in this chapter.

On the other side of the issue, several human rights advocates raise central questions about the impact of globalization, particularly neoliberal globalization, on human rights. Paul O'Connell argues that it is not possible to be committed to the protection of human rights and at the same time acquiesce to the dominant model of globalization. According to O'Connell, the conditions for the violation of human rights are structurally embedded in the neoliberal globalization program (O'Connell 2007). Thomas Pogge contends that the organization of the global economy is fundamentally unjust and that the severe poverty it fosters represents a violation of the fundamental duty to avoid doing harm, specifically to avoid human rights violations that are unavoidably associated with severe poverty (Pogge 2002, 2007). Ted Schrecker describes channels of influence linking the global marketplace with routine violations of economic and social rights. He contends that recent trends in globalization underscore the urgency of a human rights challenge to the global marketplace while offering a pessimistic assessment of the likelihood of its success in fundamentally transforming policies to be consistent with human rights requirements (Schrecker 2011).

Impact of Globalization on Health and Health Systems

Global Health Status

Reflecting the inequalities in economic status noted above, there are also significant health inequalities within and between countries and regions. The 2008 report of the WHO Commission on the Social Determinants of Health noted the following about the disparities in life opportunities and health status between rich and poor countries and between the rich and poor within countries: "Our children have dramatically different life chances depending on where they were born. In Japan or Sweden they can expect to live more than 80 years; in Brazil, 72 years; India, 63 years; and in one of several African countries, fewer than 50 years. And within countries, the differences in life chances are dramatic and are seen worldwide. The poorest of the poor have high levels of illness and premature mortality" (Commission on the Social Determinants of Health 2008, VI). Using language rarely seen in a WHO report, the Commission also protested that "social injustice is killing people on a large-scale" (Commission on the Social Determinants of Health 2008, vi).

The Commission on Global Governance for Health identified the following global health gaps: despite the existence of adequate global food production nearly a billion people are chronically hungry and more than a third of deaths among children under five years are attributable to malnutrition; 1.5 billion people face threats to their physical integrity with their health being undermined by extreme psychological stress as well as by direct bodily harm; life expectancy differs by twenty-one years between the highest ranking and lowest ranking countries on the human development index and even in countries successful in reducing rates of child death the difference in mortality is increasing between the least and most deprived quintiles of children; more than 80 percent of the world's population is not covered by adequate social protection; the number of unemployed workers is soaring, and of those who work, 854 million people, mostly in sub-Saharan Africa and southeast Asia, are forced to survive on less than $2.00 a day; worldwide women still face obstacles and inequalities with respect to reproductive and sexual rights (Ottersen et al. 2014).

Nevertheless, there have been noteworthy improvements in global health during the past half century: impressive gains in life expectancy, the eradication of smallpox, declines in the incidence of polio and measles, and successes in reducing the toll of the HIV/AIDS epidemic. These gains have been attributed to a variety of socioeconomic factors, public policies, and improved health care. However, these improvements have not been distributed equally among or within countries. In some countries – especially in sub-Saharan Africa and the former Soviet Union – there have even been reversals in life expectancy. Within many countries, some social groups have benefited while the health status of others has stagnated or worsened (Anand and Peter 2003, 1).

Funding increases for the health sector stimulated by the Millennium Development Goals process and new programs initiatives the MDGs encouraged have played a role in improving health status in a number of poor and middle-income countries. Of the eight major Millennium Development Goals, three goals applied directly to health – the goals to reduce child mortality, maternal mortality, and the incidence of infectious disease. Other goals related to improving access to health determinants like water and sanitation, and the improved availability of medicines, were included as a target under the global partnership for development goal. However, the outcomes were uneven within and across countries. Goals relating to reducing child mortality, water, and infectious diseases made significant progress while goals relating to maternal mortality, sanitation, and essential medicines had much smaller gains (United Nations 2012). Moreover, the Millennium Development goals were focused on country level improvements, and even in those countries showing improvement benefits did not accrue to all sectors of the population.

The 2010 Global Burden of Disease study (Lozano et al. 2012) on causes of death for 187 countries reveals major shifts in health trends around the world since 1990. There has been a broad shift in most regions of the world, except in Africa, from the highest incidence of mortality moving away from communicable diseases toward noncommunicable diseases. Four noncommunicable diseases – cardiovascular disease, cancer, respiratory disease, and diabetes - now account for 63 percent of annual global deaths. Along with their associated human suffering, noncommunicable diseases take a toll on development and impose rising health care costs and lost productivity. While sometimes portrayed as a first-world problem, 85 percent of the 35 million people who die annually from noncommunicable diseases now live in low- and middle-income countries (Thomas and Gostin 2013, 16). However, in sub-Saharan Africa, in contrast with other regions, communicable, maternal, neonatal, and nutritional causes still account for 76 percent of premature mortality. Whereas infectious disease and childhood illnesses related to malnutrition were once primary causes of death across the globe, today children living outside of sub-Saharan Africa are more likely to suffer from eating too much than too little food, much of which is unhealthy. As children survive into an unhealthy adulthood, disability is causing a greater burden and greater fraction of the burden of disease (Lozano et al. 2010).

The globalization of communicable diseases remains a key public health concern. The HIV/AIDS epidemic has had significant effects on the pattern of disease, particularly in eastern and southern sub-Saharan Africa. Not only have other new infectious diseases emerged, for example Ebola and SARS, but familiar ones, like cholera and tuberculosis, have returned, sometimes in more virulent form, with the burden falling primarily on poor countries (Labonté et al. 2011, 268). The increasingly transnational nature of health concerns is exemplified by the near-instantaneous spread of novel pathogens through air travel. As an example, within weeks of the initial outbreak in Guangdong, China of a new coronavirus responsible for severe acute respiratory syndrome (SARS), it was identified in thirty-seven additional countries. Similar rapid transmission patterns took place with H1N1 influenza and with recurrent outbreaks of malaria (Kruk 2012, 1–2). The very quick spread of Ebola across borders in West Africa with occasional cases brought to Europe and the United States provides another instance.

There is evidence that global trade patterns are linked with a rise in the incidence of noncommunicable diseases in low- and middle-income countries, posing an additional challenge to countries still facing high burdens of communicable diseases. The linkage is partly attributable to global trade and investment policies that have the effect of diffusing western products and lifestyles leading to the increasing consumption of unhealthy products. The increasing exposure to unhealthy commodities by transnational corporations looking for new markets has been termed "manufacturing epidemics" (Stuckler et al. 2012). The list includes soft drinks and processed foods that are high in salt, fat, and sugar, as well as tobacco and alcohol products. The global rise of transnational food-and-drink companies, along with neoliberal policies opening markets to trade and foreign investment, has created environments conducive to the widespread distribution of unhealthy commodities. Significant penetration by multinational processed food manufacturers into food environments in low- and middle-income countries has resulted in consumption of unhealthy products at levels reaching, and in some cases exceeding, those in high-income countries. Tobacco and alcohol manufacturers have also targeted low- and middle-income markets with sales in them then increasing substantially (Stuckler et al. 2012). The displacement of traditional long-established food systems and dietary patterns by ultra-processed products manufactured by transnational food corporations has increased the incidence of obesity and other chronic diseases (Monteiro and Cannon 2012). Public health professionals have been slow to respond to such nutritional threats in high- and low-income countries. One reason is the belated recognition of the importance of obesity to the burden of disease. Another factor is the difficulty of tackling vested interests, particularly powerful "big food" companies with strong ties to and influence over national governments (Stuckler and Nestle 2012).

Over the past thirty-five years of intensified market integration, some prior trends of health improvement have slowed or reversed, particularly in the poorest countries, with growing health inequalities and reduced access to health care (Labonté et al. 2007). The health gap between the worst and best-off groups is increasing: affluent populations are increasingly healthier and living longer while poorer populations have higher rates of illness and are dying at a younger age (Gostin and Hodge 2007). Econometric analysis using data on 136 countries suggests that on a global level the effects of market-oriented economic policies between 1980 and 2000 canceled out much of the progress toward better health, as measured by life expectancy at birth, that would have resulted from medical progress if social and economic trends had continued on their 1960–1980 trajectory. In two regions, sub-Saharan Africa and the transitional economies exposed to the full rigors of the global marketplace after the fall of the Soviet Union, neoliberal policies contributed to a substantial decline in life expectancy. In the case of sub-Saharan Africa, only half of the loss was explained by the HIV epidemic, itself not unconnected to globalization (Cornia et al. 2009). Rick Rowden makes the point that in the past decreases in life expectancy of these magnitudes have been associated with plagues, famines, or natural catastrophes. While acknowledging the role of HIV/AIDS in reducing life expectancy, Rowden attributes most of the decreases during the past two decades as primarily the result of policy changes (2009, 153).

Impact on Health Access and Health Systems

The World Health Organization's 2007 report opens with the observation that "Health outcomes are unacceptably low across much of the developing world, and the persistence of deep inequalities in health status is a problem from which no country in world is exempt. At the centre of this human crisis is a failure of health systems" (2007, 1). Years of low financing of health systems, partly as a result of the pressures to defund health care and privatize health services imposed by international financial institutions, and partly also due to the crushing debt burden on many poor countries and lower government revenues resulting from trade liberalization measures, have significantly weakened public health institutions in these countries. It seems questionable, therefore, at this point in time whether most governments, particularly in poor- and middle-income states, have the institutional and infrastructure capabilities and medical and health staff to meet the requirements imposed by the right to health.

Policies advocated by international financial institutions (IFIs) have been a major contributor to this situation. A 1985 World Bank policy paper "Paying for Health Services in Developing Countries: An Overview" advocated focusing on prices and markets as the best strategy to improve the efficiency of health care. The paper also promoted the privatization of health care. It suggested that user fees are better for the poor since they provide improvements on the supply side while dismissing concerns about the ability and willingness of poor people to pay user fees (Rowden 2009, 147–148). By 1987, the Bank was committed to a neoliberal approach to health care. This market approach became a key part of its structural adjustment programs, discussed below, particularly during the 1990s (Rowden 2009, 149). The World Bank's influential 1993 report, *Investing in Health*, reiterated the neoliberal agenda. The World Bank's 2004 *World Development Report: Making Services Work for Poor People* continued to endorse the basic neoliberal approach, advising that governments should decrease their role as public service providers and instead encourage private health care providers to sell services to their wealthier citizens while contracting out with for-profit private companies and not-for-profit private providers to deliver health services for poorer citizens (Rowden 2009, 151).

Impact of Globalization on the Availability of Health Personnel in Poor Countries

The availability of sufficient numbers of trained health personnel is essential to the provision of adequate and accessible health services. Currently there is a critical global shortage of trained health care workers. In 2006, the World Health Organization (WHO) estimated there were 2.4 million too few physicians, nurses, and midwives to provide essential health interventions. By 2013 WHO's estimate was that the figure stood at a deficit of 7.2 million health care workers and would increase to 12.9 million by 2035 (World Health Organization 2013). WHO has concluded that health workforce shortages have replaced system financing needs as the most serious obstacle to realizing the right to health within countries (WHO 2006, 20).

As might be assumed, the problem is most severe in poor countries. There is often an inverse correlation between need for and the availability of health workers: countries with the greatest burden of disease have the fewest workers and those with the lowest relative need, such as the United States, Canada, and the European countries, have the highest numbers. According to WHO, fifty-seven countries, mostly in sub-Saharan Africa, but also a few in Asia, including India, Indonesia, and Bangladesh, face crippling health workforce shortages (WHO 2006).

Globalization has intensified the problem by facilitating the emigration of health professionals from poor to higher-income countries. Not only do many low-income countries face serious shortages of health care workers, but when governments try to rectify the situation by investing scarce resources in training, many of their best trained health care personnel migrate from the country to accept positions elsewhere, usually in wealthier countries. Hospitals, governments, and health institutions in developed countries attempt to fill vacancies by recruiting well-trained doctors and nurses from poor countries. Health professionals in poor countries are encouraged to emigrate by the higher salaries, better working conditions, greater opportunities for postgraduate training, and better prospects for advancement in affluent countries (O'Brien and Gostin 2011, 19–42). These factors have resulted in a brain drain from developing to developed countries. A 2010 survey of physicians in the United States conducted by the American Medical Association found that 15 percent of those in active practice were from lower-income countries. International medical graduates constitute an even greater part of the physician work force in several other developed countries, including Canada (23 percent), Australia (27 percent), and the United Kingdom (28 percent) (Torrey and Torrey 2012). Other sources have come up with even higher numbers.

Migration has had a particularly damaging effect on the health systems of many sub-Saharan countries where a critical shortage of doctors, nurses, and midwives has been compounded by the continent bearing the greatest burden of HIV/AIDS epidemic (UNAIDS 2010). While Africa suffers 24 percent of the global burden of disease, it has only 2 percent of the global supply of doctors (Mills et al. 2011). The case of Ghana, a low middle-income country with relatively good medical training conducted in English, is a case in point. In 2003, Ghana adopted a National Health Insurance Act with the goal of moving toward universal health coverage. However, the country has been hampered by human capital constraints: despite its educational investments, the supply of trained medical personnel in Ghana is lower than the average in sub-Saharan Africa and less than half the levels recommended by WHO (Rockefeller Foundation 2010, 34). The problem is that about 70 percent of doctors trained there leave the country within three years of qualifying (Rowden 2009, 34).

When poor countries with limited resources invest in the education of health care workers so as to improve their people's access to health, only to have them leave to practice in developed countries, these countries are, in effect, subsidizing health systems in wealthier countries, something they cannot afford to do. The International Organization for Migration estimates that developing nations spend U.S. $500 million each year to educate health workers who then leave to work in North America, Western Europe, and South Asia (Kuehn 2007). An analysis of the financial cost of doctors emigrating from the nine sub-Saharan countries most affected by HIV/AIDS estimates that the countries lost more than $2 billion of investment through the emigration of trained doctors, with South Africa and Zimbabwe having the greatest losses (Mills et al. 2011).

In 2010, WHO adopted a code of practice on the international recruitment of health personnel, which seeks to establish and promote principles, standards, and practice for the ethical international recruitment of health care workers. The code calls on member states to balance the relationship between the individual rights of health personnel to leave their home countries with the right of source countries to achieve the highest attainable standard of health of their populations (World Health Organization 2010, article 3.4). It urges that recruitment arrangements should especially benefit developing countries and countries with economies in transition through the provision of effective and appropriate technical assistance, support for training appropriate to their disease profiles, support for capacity building in the development of appropriate regulatory frameworks, and access to specialized training and the support of return migration, both temporary or permanent (World Health Organization 2010, art. 5.2). Other studies have made similar recommendations, including for recipient countries to provide financial compensation to reimburse the costs of the training of health professionals they recruit from elsewhere (Mills et al. 2011; O'Brien and Gostin 2011).

But it seems unlikely that it will be possible to rectify this unjust situation unless and until all countries accept responsibility to train sufficient numbers of health care personnel for their own needs, particularly the developed countries that are the current beneficiaries of this brain drain. Their current predatory practice of recruiting health personnel from countries that can ill afford to lose them constitutes a violation of the international obligations related to the right to health (CESCR 2000, para 39).

On the other side of the equation, the source countries from which the health personnel are being filched have the responsibility to improve conditions of service that currently encourage health workers to emigrate. There is an internationally recognized human right to the enjoyment of just and favorable conditions of work (International Covenant on Economic, Social and Cultural Rights 1966, article 7). Very poor working conditions can incline even idealistic and committed medical professionals to look for employment opportunities elsewhere. The health systems of many poor and some middle-income countries are characterized by poor salaries for health professionals and often with delayed remuneration, large workloads of far too many patients, lack of adequate medicines and equipment, disorganized health management, poor access to continued training and development opportunities, and workplace violence (O'Brien and Gostin 2011, 33). At least some of these can be rectified, and they will have to be if the government is committed to moving toward realization of the right to health.

Impact of Transnational Actors on the Right to Health

Globalization has strengthened the influence of a variety of international institutions and actors in shaping health policy while it has constrained the independence of governments, particularly those governments that are aid dependent. In the "post-Westphalian" world order, the policy space for all governments, particularly small, weak, and aid-dependent states, has shrunk. Transnational corporations, international financial institutions, and the World Trade Organization, all of which are not legally bound by human rights law or norms, have been ascending in influence. This section will sketch the impact of several of these international actors on health systems and the realization of the right to health.

World Health Organization

WHO has not significantly increased its responsibilities and influence in the changing global health order, at least up to the present time. While the WHO has played an important role in a number of international health initiatives, such as coordinating a robust global response to H1N1 influenza, and has taken the initiative on some significant policy issues, for example, by establishing the Commission on the Social Determinants of Health and by enacting the Framework Convention on Tobacco Control, its severe budget constraints and ineffective organizational structure have limited its potential to play an ongoing leadership role (Kruk 2012, 4). WHO is financed both by member states' assessed contributions and by supplementary donations. Since the 1980s, there has been almost no real growth in WHO's regular budget and this has made the WHO increasingly reliant on donations. Only one-fourth of WHO's total budget is currently covered by assessed contributions (Sangorgio 2013, 4). Declining contributions as a result of the global recession have required the organization to further cut its budget. Its two-year budget issued in 2014 was only $3.98

billion or about $2 billion per year. In comparison, the budget for the U.S. Centers for Disease Control and Prevention (CDC) was about $6 billion for 2013 alone (Fink 2014).

The WHO's ineffective response to the Ebola crisis reflects these cuts and the toll they have taken on the organization, as well as its bureaucratic ineffectiveness. In response to the cuts, WHO dissolved its epidemic and pandemic response department and divided its duties among other departments. In 2014, as the Ebola crisis in West Africa developed, WHO's entire unit devoted to the science of pandemic and epidemic diseases had only fifty-two regular employees, only one of whom was a technical expert on Ebola and other hemorrhagic diseases, and a separate section responsible for emergency response was reduced from ninety-four to thirty-four employees. Although the WHO hoped to compensate by strengthening the ability of member countries to respond to public health threats on their own, fewer than a third of the countries in Africa had programs to detect and manage infectious diseases in 2014 (Fink 2014).

WHO's flaws also contribute to its marginalization. Critics charge that WHO is too focused on technical matters and vertical programs, too bureaucratic, too wedded to a traditional biomedical disease model, and insufficiently involved with civil society. In the past, WHO was unable, and it continues to be reluctant, to use the power of international law. The rise of a plethora of nonstate actors and the development of major global health initiatives driven by public-private partnerships, foundations, and other non-UN entities, in part because of disillusionment with WHO, have further diminished the importance of WHO and other health-related UN organizations. Initiatives such as the Global Fund and the Joint UN Program on HIV/AIDS (UNAIDS) have taken away WHO's purview over major diseases (Ng and Ruger 2011, 4). The entry of the well resourced Bill & Melinda Gates Foundation and the Clinton Foundation into global health funding has made private philanthropies major actors.

Nor has WHO been an active proponent of a human rights approach. The preamble to the WHO Constitution states that "the enjoyment of the highest attainable standard of health is one of the fundamental rights of every human being." However, human rights have not played a significant role in guiding the overall work of WHO. WHO's early years were marked by the Secretariat's active involvement in drafting human rights treaty law and cooperative efforts with other UN agencies to expand human rights frameworks for public health, but to avoid controversy WHO chose to reposition itself during the Cold War as a purely technical organization focusing on medical issues. In the 1980s, WHO rediscovered the importance of human rights in responding to the HIV/AIDs pandemic. However, subsequent initiatives to incorporate human rights law in the work of WHO suffered from insufficient investment of resources and isolation in the Secretariat (Meier and Onzivu 2014, 180–183). Benjamin Meier's analysis of the history of WHO's involvement with the right to health documents WHO's institutional neglect of human rights and the squandered opportunities for WHO to provide leadership in advancing a rights-based approach to health (2010). According to Meier, "the WHO Secretariat remains structurally limited in efforts to advance health-related human rights, with an institutional structure beholden to state political priorities, distant from the international legal system, and governed by medico-technical approaches to health" (Meier and Onzivu 2014, 185). In one of his final reports as Special Rapporteur on the right to health, Paul Hunt also lamented the failure of WHO to provide leadership in this field. Writing in 2007, Hunt characterized the health and human rights agenda within WHO as "marginal, contested, and severely under-resourced" (2007, para 50).

Despite all of its inadequacies the global health community continues to look to WHO as the leading global health coordinator because there are no viable alternatives. There are currently proposals, as there have been at other points in the past, to strengthen WHO by giving it a stronger mandate, increasing its budget, and providing it with enforcement powers (Ng and Ruger 2011, 4). Whether states that have been reluctant in the past to increase the power of the WHO will now decide it is in their interest to do so is difficult to anticipate.

Transnational Corporations

Transnational corporations, which operate across multiple countries and regions, are growing in power and playing an increasingly powerful role on the world stage. Globalization and market liberalization have enabled transnational corporations to enter into otherwise closed domestic markets, influence domestic and international law making, and infringe upon states' policy space (Grover 2014, para 36). Although transnational corporations can contribute economically by creating jobs and raising incomes, they can also harm health through dangerous working conditions, inadequate pay, environmental pollution, and producing goods, like tobacco, that are a threat to health (Ottersen et al. 2014). Corporations have directly perpetrated serious human rights violations, including to the right to health, particularly in developing and least developed countries. The dilemma is that states have been unable to regulate these corporations other than on a voluntary basis to prevent them from violating the right to health (Grover 2014, para 36). Moreover, the asymmetry of economic power between many of these corporations and their host governments has enabled transnational corporations and their domestic subsidiaries to evade responsibility.

To provide some sense of the differential in resources between transnational corporations and governments, of the world's 100 largest economic entities in 2009, forty-four were corporations. Corporations comprised an even larger proportion of the top 150 economic entities, 59 percent. Together the forty-four companies identified as among the 100 largest economic entities generated revenues equivalent to more than 11 percent of global GDP. Their combined revenues were larger than the combined economies of 155 countries – all the countries in the world with the exception of the largest forty countries. In many cases, the economic clout and impact of these global corporations exceed the influence of the nations that host them, particularly in the case of smaller and poorer states, enabling them to sway their host countries' economic and political policies (Keys and Malnight 2012). Morever, some of the largest and most powerful corporations are in sectors with health implications. The combined market capitalization of the five largest tobacco corporations is more than U.S. $400 billion; the figure for the five largest beverage firms is more than U.S. $600 billion; and for the five largest pharmaceutical firms it rises to more than U.S. $800 billion (Ottersen et al. 2014).

Gary Teeple (2000) links the ascendance of the concentrated monopoly capitalism associated with corporate globalization to the increasing income and wealth inequalities and the weakening of social infrastructure in many countries. According to his analysis, transnational corporations actively apply their increasing power to oppose welfare state policies in order to reduce their labor costs. The increasing ability of transnational corporations to shift investments across the globe pressures national governments to accede to their demands. National governments that cannot resist the power of these corporations then become complicit in processes that result in deteriorating social, health, and economic conditions.

Transnational corporations have also played an important role in shaping and influencing some global institutions. Importantly, business networks, led by twelve CEO's of U.S. based multinational corporations, four of whom were pharmaceutical companies, were the main driving force behind the development of the TRIPS Agreement, whose role is described below. Concerned about the extent to which foreign governments would protect U.S. patents, these companies sought the support of the U.S. government in pressuring foreign governments to adopt and enforce strict patent protection laws. In contrast with human rights activists, who were not given a voice during the negotiations of the TRIPS agreement, there was a strong presence of business networks, including on some government delegations. Working with their European and Japanese counterparts, U.S. based corporations achieved an intellectual property code that was a wholesale reflection of the private sector's interests. According to one analyst, "It would not be an overstatement to conclude that TRIPS was hijacked by the private sector" (Alkoby 2012, 56). The success of these corporations has been attributed to the economic power they wield, their lobbying activity and the institutional access it brings, and their strategy in framing the issue of intellectual property protection as a solution for the U.S. trade deficit and thereby as beneficial for the U.S. economy. Once TRIPS was adopted, these same networks sought to assure that countries complied with its provisions by pressing the U.S. government to impose sanctions against violating countries and to bring complaints in international adjudicative bodies (Alkoby 2012, 55–58). The U.S. government has continued actively to represent the interests of major corporations in promoting the implementation of strong intellectual property regimes even though the health needs of most of the world's population are not well-served by patent-based pharmaceutical markets (Outterson 2008, 279). Chapter Seven will discuss this subject in greater depth.

World Bank Policies

Policies advocated by international financial institutions (IFIs) and made a precondition of financial aid have been a major contributor to the adoption of neoliberal approaches to health systems. A 1985 World Bank policy paper "Paying for Health Services in Developing Countries: An Overview" advocated for focusing on prices and markets as the best strategy to improve the efficiency of health care. The paper also promoted the privatization of health care. It contended that user fees would benefit the poor by providing improvements on the supply side while dismissing concerns about the ability and willingness of poor people to pay user fees (Rowden 2009, 147–148). By 1987 the Bank was committed to a neoliberal approach to health care. This market approach became a key part of its structural adjustment programs, discussed below, particularly during the 1990s (Rowden 2009, 149). The World Bank's influential 1993 report, *Investing in Health*, reiterated the neoliberal agenda. The World Bank's

2004 *World Development Report: Making Services Work for Poor People* continued to endorse the basic neoliberal approach advising that governments should decrease their role as public service providers and instead encourage private health care providers to sell services to their wealthier citizens while contracting out with for-profit private companies and not-for-profit private providers to deliver health services for poorer citizens (Rowden 2009, 151).

The imposition of user fees has been a central component of market prescriptions for health care. By 1998 about 40 percent of the World Banks' health, nutrition, and population projects, nearly 75 percent of which were in Africa, required the introduction or increased application of user fees (Lister and Labonté 2009, 190). As noted in Chapter Three, user fees and other cost recovery mechanisms have decreased access to health care for the poor (Katz 2005; UNICEF 2008; Oxfam International 2009; Rowden 2009, 160–163).

Structural Adjustment Programs (SAPs) are the conditions imposed by the World Bank and International Monetary Fund (IMF) on developing countries as the prerequisite for obtaining a new loan or for having the interest rates lowered on existing loans. Under structural adjustment, the economic model current from the early 1980s until the late 1990s, the IMF and World Bank imposed austerity policies on borrowers, ostensibly to end their fiscal imbalances, and required states to adopt a market orientation as well as to open their borders to foreign investment. More recently, the World Bank has moved from structural adjustment to a nominal focus on poverty reduction, but there is often little practical change. Rigid ceilings on public health and other social services expenditures imposed by the Bank's Medium-Term Expenditure Frameworks continue to restrict adequate funding for the realization of economic, social, and cultural rights. Almost all of the Poverty Reduction Strategy Papers (PRSPs), the national planning frameworks that are now a precondition for Bank concessional lending, include or refer to an existing Medium-Term Expenditure Framework. Once included in a PRSP, countries cannot adapt the limits on funding, even if a new essential need arises (Ooms and Hammonds 2008, note 76, p.3).

The PRSP process generally fails to take obligations related to the right to health into account (Chapman 2009, 110–111). Paul Hunt cites a 2002 WHO preliminary study of ten full PRSPs and three interim PRSPs, which found that none even mentioned health as a human right (Dodd and Hinselwood 2002). Nor did they provide much evidence of efforts to adapt national health strategies to meet the needs of the poorest groups. Very few of the PRSPS incorporated any health indicators that could monitor the impact on poor people or geographic regions. No PRSP included plans to include poor people in a participatory monitoring process (Hunt 2003, para 71).

Structural adjustment policies (SAPs) have impacted health-related policies and inhibited progressive realization of the right to health in three main ways. First, by weakening the public health sector, these policies have encouraged wealthier demographics to opt out of state-provided health care and turn to the private sector (Barrientos 2000). This has led to increasingly fragmented health care systems with little coordination and declining coverage in terms of meeting essential needs or providing for a majority of the population. Second, there has been a larger-scale ontological and policy shift in governments' approach to health care services, with the focus shifting away from goals of universal access and greater emphasis being placed on cost recovery mechanisms such as user fees, which have often acted as exclusionary barriers, reducing equity and limiting coverage to only those able to afford it.

Thirdly, SAPs have had an indirect impact on health care policies and outcomes by worsening the distribution of economic gains as well as reducing the size of the overall "economic pie" in many cases (Stiglitz 2003; Abouharb and Cingranelli 2007), hindering the abilities of people in much of the developing world to pay for their own health needs. Actions targeting price subsidies or worsening protections for other economic rights such as the right to work in developing countries such as Mozambique, Nigeria, and Nicaragua (Abouharb and Cingranelli 2007, 140) have increased the cost burden on the poor for basic goods such as fuels, transportation, and food. States have also often been pressured to privatize and commodify essential social determinants of health such as water and sanitation services (Alexander 2005).

Large-scale panel data confirm these trends. In an analysis of 131 developing countries, Abouharb and Cingranelli (2007) found that implementation of World Bank and IMF structural agreements reduced government respect for the economic and social welfare of their citizens, contributing to a deterioration of the situation for the majority of the population in these countries. Specifically, user fees when privatizing water, health care, and education led to a greater marginalization of poor and vulnerable groups and hindered realization of basic economic rights. SAPs and shifts toward investor friendly, globally integrated economies led to reduced subsidies as states were forced to reduce public spending and the transfers of enterprises such as water and sanitation utilities to private investors increased inequity while creating natural monopolistic markets that saw reduced efficiency and responsiveness.

A multicountry review by the Structural Adjustment Participatory Review International Network (SAPRIN) reached similar conclusions. The study (SAPRIN 2004) found that a number of major problems were either caused or exacerbated by adjustment programs. According to the study, adjustment policies contributed to the impoverishment and marginalization of local populations, while increasing economic inequality. Simultaneously, trade liberalization, financial sector liberalization, and the weakening of state support and demand for local goods and services devastated local industries, particularly the small and medium-sized enterprises that provide the bulk of national employment. Additionally, neoliberal structural and sectoral policy reforms in the agricultural and mining sectors undermined the viability of small farms, weakened food security, and damaged the natural environment. Further, the privatization of public utilities and services usually resulted in significant price increases for the public. Of particular relevance to economic and social rights, the SAPRIN review concluded that the quality of education and health care has generally declined as a result of pressure to reduce public expenditures and that cost sharing schemes have imposed serious constraints on access by poor people to health care and education.

World Trade Organization, TRIPS, and Other Trade Agreements

As noted in Chapter Three, neoliberal policies promote trade liberalization to eliminate trade barriers and to facilitate the flow of capital and goods across national borders. Neoliberalism advocates permitting foreign investment in all sectors of the economy even if doing so results in the displacement of domestic economic actors. These principles have been incorporated in a series of bilateral, regional, and global trade agreements often involving both industrialized and developing countries. So-called free trade has often come at a significant price for the economies of both developed and developing countries by dislocating key economic sectors, displacing workers, and disadvantaging communities hurt by foreign competition. Major transnational corporations have frequently been the winners gaining new markets, higher profits, expanded investment rights, and increased political power from the agreements. Various bilateral and multilateral trade agreements, most importantly the international Agreement on Trade-Related Aspects of Intellectual Property Rights and more recently the various "Trips Plus" free trade agreements, have also had a deleterious impact on individual and population health. An article in *The Lancet* noted, "the ability of governments worldwide to introduce and implement public health policies and laws is being threatened by trade and investment treaties that privilege investors over governments and provide avenues for international corporations to challenge democratically enacted public health policies in different countries" (Gleeson and Friel 2013, 1507). The same could be said of the endangerment of health-related human rights protections.

World Trade Organization

The World Trade Organization (WTO) was established in 1995. It has four major roles: (1) to promote the progressive opening of domestic markets to international trade; (2) to ensure the trade rules negotiated by members of the WTO are respected; (3) to settle disputes among members; and (4) to monitor and review trade policies of members to assess whether they are abiding by WTO rules. As of April 2015, 161 countries had become members of the WTO, about the same number that have ratified the International Covenant on Economic, Social and Cultural Rights. However, in contrast with the UN international human rights system, the obligation to abide by all of the WTO agreements is backed up by dispute settlement mechanisms that have the power to impose significant economic penalties. Members may file complaints against other members claiming they have been harmed by violations of WTO agreements that first go to arbitration and then, if not resolved, are decided by a panel of three experts. Once a definitive ruling is issued, the losing party must comply; if it does not do so, the country is subject to sanctions. Since 1995, more than 400 complaints have been filed by WTO members (WTO website 2015).

TRIPS Agreement

Economic globalization in recent decades has been accompanied by the internationalization of intellectual property institutions and standards. Not only have intellectual property regimes become globalized, but the scope of the subject matter subject to intellectual property claims has also been expanded and standards have become more rigorous. These trends were accelerated by the adoption of the international Agreement on Trade-Related Aspects of Intellectual Property Rights (TRIPS) in 1995. All members of the WTO are automatically subject to the provisions of the

TRIPS Agreement. The minimum standards of intellectual property protection stipulated by the TRIPS Agreement have made it far more difficult for individual countries to tailor levels of intellectual property protection to fit their development needs and to protect human rights.

As will be discussed in greater detail in Chapter Six, the TRIPS Agreement affects access to medicines, a key component of the right to health, in several ways. It obligates WTO members to grant patents in all fields of technology, including extending patent protection to pharmaceuticals, something few poor countries had previously done, and requires all countries to permit foreign entities to patent their products and processes. When large pharmaceutical corporations acquire patent rights globally, including in poor countries, it allows them to charge prices substantially higher than marginal costs. Although patent protection is often justified as providing a stimulus for research and development, this is rarely the case in countries lacking capital and the required scientific and technological infrastructure for pharmaceutical research (Correa 2009, 270). The TRIPS Agreement also restricts the right of governments to grant compulsory licenses to allow local manufacturers to produce patented products or processes without the consent of the patent owner. By requiring pharmaceutical patents it also cut off the exports of cheap generic drugs from countries like India to other poor countries, as they have become subject to TRIP rules. The implications can be shown in figures on the prices of patented antiretrovirals (ARVs) to treat AIDS. In 2000, the cost per patient per year often exceeded $10,000. The next year Indian generic firms made the same ARV treatment available for less than U.S. $400, and competition lowered the originator's and the generic drug prices thereafter. Indian generic manufacturers were able to make the ARVs cheaply because India did not then recognize pharmaceutical product patents, but TRIPS required India to become compliant with its standards in 2005 (Correa 2009, 272).

Concerns about the impact of the TRIPS Agreement on access to medicines and more broadly on public health led to the drafting of a supplementary document, the Doha Ministerial Declaration on TRIPS and Public Health (World Trade Organization 2001). The Doha Declaration recognized the gravity of the public health problems afflicting many developing countries and least developed countries, especially from HIV/AIDS, tuberculosis, malaria, and other epidemics (para 1), and agreed that the TRIPS Agreement should not prevent members from taking measures to protect public health (para 4). But the main solution it offered is to affirm the right of countries to take advantage of the flexibilities of the

TRIPS Agreement, particularly the right of countries to grant compulsory licenses in national emergencies. The Doha Agreement did not resolve the knotty issue of how WTO members with insufficient or no manufacturing capacity can take advantage of the flexibilities. Although a subsequent WTO agreement sought to address this issue, the mechanism is so cumbersome that its provisions are very difficult to use. It also depends on the willingness of a country to manufacture the product to fill the compulsory license of a second country (Correa 2009, 277).

TRIPS Plus Agreements

Free trade agreements that impose even more onerous conditions, including higher standards of intellectual protection than those incorporated in the TRIPS Agreement (and therefore are often referred to as Trips Plus agreements), have proliferated in recent years. A recent examination of 165 free trade agreements in force or under negotiation found that a majority involving the United States had pharma-related provisions that undermine the ability of signatories to utilize the flexibilities in the TRIPS Agreement (Global Health Watch 2014, 292). These provisions can enable pharmaceutical companies to challenge the patent laws of host states even when the patent laws are compliant with the TRIPS agreement.

Many of these free trade agreements incorporate investors' rights that may also affect states' ability to introduce health laws in the public interest. Several high profile cases are currently being litigated. After Uruguay had entered into a bilateral investment agreement with Switzerland, it adopted public health measures on the packaging and advertisement of cigarettes pursuant to the WHO Framework Convention on Tobacco Control. Even though those measures were consistent with the public health exception in the bilateral investment agreement, Philip Morris International initiated a dispute against Uruguay, claiming its law breached the guarantee of fair and equitable treatment (Grover 2014, para 54). Philip Morris Asia has challenged Australia's tobacco plain packaging laws. Tobacco companies have also commenced investor-state actions against Uruguay and Norway (Gleeson and Friel 2013, 1507). States may also be vulnerable to being sued through dispute settlement mechanisms when they breach an obligation under an agreement in order to comply with their human rights obligations. In one such case, the Ethyl Corporation submitted a claim against a public health decision by the Government of Canada to impose a trade ban on a controversial gasoline additive produced by the corporation (Grover 2014, para 55).

Human rights and public health advocates have concerns that the costs of litigation, which can amount to millions of dollars, along with the threat of an adverse judgment, which could also have significant financial implications, will have a deterrent effect on governments considering the introduction of new laws to regulate industry in order to protect public health (Gleeson and Friel 2013, 1507). It is therefore important that states review trade agreements under negotiation and review or renegotiate international investment agreements to ensure they have the right to change law and policies in furtherance of human rights. Some forty states have already begun renegotiating bilateral investment treaties to reduce their vulnerability and to limit investor rights (Grover 2014, para 59).

International Aid

Article 2.1 of the International Covenant on Economic, Social and Cultural Rights (1966) makes realization of rights contingent on the maximum of available resources. Over the past fifteen to twenty years there has been an unprecedented rise in public foreign aid and private philanthropic giving, resulting in billions of additional dollars being directed to addressing the health needs of middle-income and poor countries. It is estimated that total foreign assistance for health programs rose from U.S. $8 billion in 1995 to U.S. $31.3 billion in 2013. Across regional groups, sub-Saharan Africa received the largest share of development assistance for health. Nevertheless, countries with the highest disease burdens often do not receive the most aid (Dieleman et al. 2013, 10).

In terms of where the development assistance for health was invested, the HIV/AIDS sector was the beneficiary of the most substantial share among health focus areas. The share of development assistance targeting maternal, newborn, and child health also grew substantially during this period. However, other potential targets, as for example noncommunicable diseases and tobacco control, received little funding (Dieleman et al. 2013, 10). While some programs directed toward tackling specific diseases have had significant beneficial results, for example the eradication of small pox in the 1970s and more recently a reduction in the incidence of polio, the onchocerciasis control program, Chagas disease control, guinea worm reduction, and improvements in access to treatment services for HIV/AIDS, malaria, and tuberculosis in some countries, others have failed to do so (Ng and Ruger 2011, 11). Also, the greater availability of giving for health has generally not strengthened the health systems of recipient countries. In large part this is because donors have typically neglected population-wide services and focused primarily on improving financial or physical health services to programs addressing specific diseases and seeking to improve maternal and child health.

The revolution in global health funding has been stimulated in large part by efforts to promote achievement of the health-related Millennium Development Goal targets and commitments to funding HIV/AIDS programs. In the process, the investment in improving health in developing countries has given rise to the proliferation of global health funding mechanisms and donors. These include multilateral organizations such as the Global Fund to Fight AIDS, Tuberculosis and Malaria; the World Bank's Multi-Country AIDS Program (MAP); and the GAVI Alliance. There are also new bilateral aid programs, one example of which is the U.S. President's Emergency Plan for AIDS Relief (PEPFAR); and the involvement of private philanthropic foundations, most notably the Gates Foundation. All of these donors have sought to influence the policies of recipient countries, sometimes in conflicting ways and often without reference to the host country's own priorities or the involvement of civil society. In addition, this proliferation of initiatives has occurred with little effort among the donors to coordinate their programs and projects.

Importantly, these donors have promoted disease-based vertical programs that have tended to weaken health systems in recipient countries and generate problems resulting from the lack of integration of services. For example, a study of the impact of external funding earmarked for HIV/AIDS control in resource-poor countries provided by the Global Fund to Fight AIDS, TB and Malaria, the World Bank Multi-country AIDS Program, and the U.S. President's Emergency Plan for AIDS Relief (PEPFAR) documented that the funding distracted recipient governments from coordinated efforts to strengthen their health systems and led to the establishment of parallel bodies and processes for planning, management, monitoring, and evaluation that were poorly coordinated and aligned with national systems. The additional workload that the external AIDS funding imposed strained public sector health workers, already overworked because of staff shortages (Biesma et al. 2009). Some critics claim that global health funding has drawn attention away from health problems of the poor, weakened already fragile public health systems, attracted health professionals away from vital infrastructure positions, contributed to the brain drain, and failed to reach the populations in greatest need (Moon and Omole 2013). Donor influence on priority-setting and their lack of accountability has also been criticized (Sridhar 2010). Others have a more positive view of the benefits of this influx of money (Bates and Boateng

2007; de Waal 2007; Sachs 2007), but even so, it is indisputable that this funding has further fragmented the health system and weakened the public health institutions on which the implementation of the right to health depends.

Multiple donors have created yet other problems. According to Anand Grover, the second Special Rapporteur for the right to health, poorly coordinated donor interventions have led to redundant spending, inefficient allocation of health funds, and the failure of initiatives to address domestic health needs effectively (2012, para 30). He contrasts this fragmentation with the operation of the Global Fund and the International Drug Purchase Facility (UNITAID), which have successfully pooled resources from donor states and through innovative financing mechanisms allocated funds and resources based on need to recipient countries (Grover 2012, para 32).

Importantly, donor aid for health does not necessarily result in greater public health spending. In many instances the macroeconomic conditions attached to loans from international financial institutions require states to use these funds to build up their reserves. Additionally the influx of foreign funding has often led to decreased domestic government spending on health. Ministries of finance tend to reduce funding to government ministries that spend money on health when large amounts of development assistance for this purpose are given to the government. Studies of health spending in low- and middle-income countries show that for every U.S. $1 provided in development assistance for health programs, government health expenditures from domestic resources were reduced by $0.43 to $1.14 of their own money (Lu et al. 2011; Institute for Health Metrics and Evaluation 2012). Because foreign assistance goes disproportionately to fight AIDS and other infectious diseases, core health programs like obstetrical care and public health institutions particularly lose out when governments shift money from health to other budget areas.

Impact of Globalization on the Social Determinants of Health

In many regions of the world the most valuable steps toward improvement of health are not the provision of medical services but improvements in the social determinants of health or what General Comment 14 refers to as the "underlying determinants of health," such as access to safe and potable water and adequate sanitation, an adequate supply of safe food, and healthy occupational and environmental conditions (CESCR 2000: para 11). As noted in Chapter Two, the general comment identifies the provision of most of these underlying determinants as core health obligations of the state, whose implementation is not subject to resource constraints (CESCR 2000: para 43).

In 2008, the WHO Commission on the Social Determinants of Health published a report, *Closing the Gap in a Generation Through Action on the Social Determinants of Health* (2008), which will be discussed in greater detail in Chapter Six. The report is unequivocal in its condemnation of the disparities in life opportunities and health status between rich and poor countries and between the rich and poor within countries. The Commission ascribes these differentials to "a toxic combination of poor social policies and programmes, unfair economic arrangements, and bad politics" (Commission on the Social Determinants of Health 2008:26). Many of the poor social policies, unfair economic arrangements, and bad politics that the Commission criticizes reflect neoliberal policies.

Research conducted by the Globalization Knowledge Network, one of the nine networks established to gather and analyze data for the Commission on the Social Determinants of Health, identifies several, often interacting, pathways leading from globalization to changes in the social determinants of health, with detrimental consequences for health equity (Labonté et al. 2007). The manner in which globalization affects the social determinants of health includes the following:[1]

- Perhaps most importantly, given the strong and pervasive link between poverty and health (Braveman and Gruskin 2003), globalization has rendered many poor people in low-income countries even poorer (Birdsall 2005). According to WHO, "Poverty wields its destructive influence at every stage of human life, from the moment of conception to the grave. It conspires with the most deadly and painful diseases to bring a wretched existence to all those who suffer from it" (WHO 1995). Trade liberalization, the lowering of barriers to imports, and the global reorganization of production also tend to increase the economic vulnerability of large numbers of poor people (Labonté et al. 2007, 10–11, 46–52).
- Globalization is gradually leading to the emergence of a global labor market characterized by growing inequalities between skilled and unskilled workers both within and across national borders. Global economic integration and the development of a global labor force are

---

[1] The description of the impact of globalization on the social determinants of health is based closely on Audrey R. Chapman (2009) "Globalization, Human Rights, and the Social Determinants of Health," *Bioethics* 23 (2): 98–99.

generating increased pressures for labor market flexibility with detrimental effects on economic security for many workers. As countries compete for foreign investment and outsourced production, the need to appear business-friendly affects their ability to adopt and implement labor standards, protecting workers' interests, strict health and safety regulations, and redistributive social policies (Labonté et al. 2007, 46–52).

- Lack of access to safe water is linked with poverty and economic insecurity as well as being detrimental to health outcomes, particularly through causing diarrheal diseases. Like health services, the neoliberal model treats water as a commodity. During the past two decades transnational corporations have emerged as major actors in the water sector. International Monetary Fund (IMF) loan agreements with many of the smallest, poorest, and most debt-ridden countries have included conditions requiring water privatization or full cost recovery policies. Private provision of services to meet basic needs, like water and sanitation, invariably leads to escalating costs and inequitable access (Katz 2005). A market-based approach also deters investments to expand water service delivery to previously unserved or underserved areas and to set affordable rates (Labonté et al. 2007, 108–111).

- Trade reforms that lower trade barriers, as neoliberal ideology advocates be instituted, can be damaging to food security in the short and medium term unless countered by policies designed to offset the negative effects (Labonté et al. 2007, 108–111). Evidence suggests that diets have been influenced by three important changes in the food system: the growth of transnational food companies, including supermarkets; liberalization of international food trade and foreign direct investment; and global food advertising and promotion. All three affect diets by altering the availability, prices, and desirability of different foods (Hawkes et al. 2009, 241). Increased global trade in food products appears to be associated with changes in diet and nutrition in many low- and middle-income countries away from traditional foods grown locally to store-bought foods, many of which are processed and high in sugars and carbohydrates, but the manner in which global food trade is affecting different segments of the population in poor- and middle-income countries is not well researched (Hawkes et al. 2009, 258).

Declines in public revenues from tariff reductions, the growing burden of public debt, and public policies promoted by multilateral organizations and increasingly adopted by governments all further constrain the ability of many developing countries to meet basic needs related to the social determinants of health (Labonté et al. 2007, 92–113).

Human Rights Initiatives to Respond to Globalization

That the human rights paradigm focuses on states as the primary, often exclusive, duty bearer for the fulfillment of human rights constitutes an important constraint on the human rights response to globalization. The human rights community has sought ways to extend the purview of the human rights model by assigning governments the responsibility of protecting the rights of citizens from violations by third-party actors, including transnational corporations. Whether governments are motivated and able to do so, however, is at issue in a global system in which corporations often have greater resources and power than their host governments. Further complicating the equation, corporations are not recognized as directly subject to international human rights law. This latter issue will be discussed at greater length in Chapter Seven on Access to Medicines as a Human Right.

As already noted, in a global system many states, particularly poor ones, have significant constraints on both their ability and their freedom to implement human rights obligations, or, to describe the situation in another way, global market integration is shrinking national policy space. Global policy space has been defined as the extent to which national decision-making for health and the social determinants of health can be made without subordination to considerations such as economic growth, maintaining payments to external creditors, or complying with trade agreement conditions even when these impose health-negative effects (Labonté et al. 2007, 52–53). Developed countries can also be subject to externally imposed economic policies. Several governments in Europe affected by the 2008 financial crisis have had to adopt stringent austerity policies that affected the health sector in order to obtain needed loans. Or to put the matter another way, these high-income countries were treated in much the same way by European and international lenders as the international financial institutions have historically dealt with low- and middle-income countries.

A different viewpoint has also been put forward, namely, that some states may use these seeming conflicts between the demands of global institutions and national commitments strategically as a way to avoid their obligations and to render themselves unaccountable both to their citizens and to international institutions (Randeria 2007). Whether or not one agrees with this assessment, there is ample evidence that when there are conflicts between the demands imposed by the WTO, IMF, or the World Bank and the requirements necessary to realize human rights obligations, virtually all governments tend to neglect their human rights commitments. The ability of the WTO to impose trade sanctions and the IMF and World Bank to eliminate eligibility for loans offers incentives to do so. In contrast, international human rights institutions, which primarily rely on "naming and shaming," lack comparable sanctions to promote accountability.

Response to Globalization within UN Human Rights Mechanisms

As states' available resources for social spending have diminished and their autonomy has been increasingly impinged on by the policies of international financial institutions, requirements of trade agreements, and competition for markets and investments, protection and fulfillment of the right to health has stagnated in much of the developing world, and many industrialized countries have cut back on the health entitlements. The Committee on Economic, Social and Cultural Rights has been aware of these deleterious developments and the issues they raise. Its 1999 statement on globalization mentions the increasing reliance upon the free market, deregulation of a range of activities, the growth in the influence of international financial markets and institutions in shaping national policy priorities, the privatization of various functions previously considered to be the exclusive domain in the state, and a diminution in the role of the state and the size of its budget (CESCR 1999: para 2). While the Committee avers that none of these developments is necessarily incompatible with the principles of the Covenant or with the related obligations of governments, it acknowledges that "taken together, however, and if not complemented by appropriate additional policies globalization risks downgrading the central place accorded to human rights by the United Nations Charter in general and the International Bill of Rights in particular," especially in relation to economic and social rights (CESCR 1999: para 3).

Various UN special rapporteurs have also addressed the impact of globalization on human rights. Miloon Kothari, a former UN Special Rapporteur on the right to adequate housing, detailed how macroeconomic factors associated with globalization reduce the resources available for social spending on essential social services that are integral to fulfilling economic, social, and cultural rights (2002, para 51). He also pointed out that privatization of essential social services, like water delivery, impedes the implementation of human rights obligations related to ensuring the availability and affordability of services to vulnerable groups and reduces or eliminates the accountability, transparency, and opportunities for the participation of the community in decision-making, which are essential components of the human rights approach.

In 2003, Paul Hunt, who was then the Special Rapporteur on the right to health, conducted a mission to the World Trade Organization and held meetings with the WTO secretariat and the chairpersons of three of its councils. The main aim of his mission was modest: to enhance the quality of dialogue between the human rights/right to health and trade communities (Hunt 2004, para 70). His consultations tended to confirm that the right to health is not well understood among some of those working on trade issues, just as trade is not well understood among some of those working on human rights (Hunt 2004, para 13). Given the support he found for designing a methodology for right-to-health impact assessments in the context of trade agreements, he recommended that urgent attention be given to this issue (Hunt 2004, para 72). He also proposed that the Human Rights Commission consider requesting a report on how technical assistance provided by the Office of the High Commissioner for Human Rights, WTO, WHO, and the World Intellectual Property Organization could ensure that the progressive liberalization of trade is most conducive to the progressive realization of the right to health (Hunt 2004, para 74). On policy matters, he emphasized the need for states to establish effective mechanisms within their governments that enhance policy coherence between health, human rights, and trade. He reminded states to take their national and international human rights obligations into account, including those relating to the right to health, when formulating trade policies (Hunt 2004, para 79). He additionally cautioned states about enacting "TRIPS plus" intellectual property legislation that goes beyond TRIPs provisions without first understanding the impact of such legislation on the protection of the right to health. Conversely, he advocated that wealthy countries should not pressure a developing country to implement "TRIPS plus" legislation unless reliable evidence confirms it will enhance enjoyment of the right to health (Hunt 2004, para 82). These recommendations, however, have not been implemented.

Human rights advocates have sought to influence the policies, practices, and operations of various international organizations, particularly international financial institutions and the WTO, through leveraging the human rights obligations of member states. The Committee often reminds state parties, particularly those from developed countries, of the need to do all they can to ensure that the policies and decisions of those organizations are in conformity with their obligations to the Covenant (CESCR 2002, para 26). And the Committee offers similar advice to poor countries that are the recipients of aid, underscoring the importance of integrating human rights, including economic, social, and cultural rights, in the formulation of their Poverty Reduction Strategy Papers for the World Bank (CESCR 2001, 2002, 2004).

Human rights advocates have also argued that the realms of trade, finance, and investment are not exempt from human rights principles. The CESCR made such a statement in its 1998 statement on globalization (CESCR 1998, para 5) and called on the IMF and World Bank to pay enhanced attention to respect for economic, social, and cultural rights in their activities (CESCR 1998, para 7). The statement is upbeat about the impact of globalization, asserting that all of the risks can be guarded against, or compensated for, if appropriate policies are put in place, but the Committee concedes that most governments are not doing so (CESCR 1998: para 4).

When Olivier De Schutter served as the Special Rapporteur on the right to food, he proposed four mechanisms to avoid or overcome conflicts between trade law, investment law, and human rights law while ensuring the primacy of human rights: (1) the insertion of clauses and flexibilities in trade and investment treaties allowing states to comply with their human rights obligations without being liable for economic sanctions; (2) conducting human rights impact assessments to evaluate the potential impact of trade and investment agreements that are being negotiated before approving them; (3) "harmonization through interpretation" so as to interpret trade and investment agreements as being coherent with human rights obligations to the fullest extent possible; and (4) "sunset" clauses based on human rights impact assessments done after new rules take effect that allow for a revision of a treaty where it appears to have a negative impact on human rights (2009). He has also prepared a set of principles on human rights impact assessments of trade and investment agreements aimed at providing states with guidance on how best to ensure that the trade and investment agreements they conclude are consistent with their obligations under international human rights instruments (De Schutter 2011). While this agenda could contribute toward reducing the deleterious impact of globalization on human rights, it does not appear to have been widely adopted.

Extraterritorial Obligations of States

Another way the human rights community has sought to respond to globalization is through identifying extraterritorial obligations of states. General Comment 14 includes a section detailing international human rights obligations related to the right to health that builds on the stipulation in Article 2.1 of the ICESCR that all state parties are "to take steps, individually and through international assistance and cooperation, especially economic and technical, towards the full realization of the rights recognized in the Covenant" (1966). According to the general comment, to comply with their human rights obligations related to the right to health, state parties have to respect the enjoyment of the right to health, and to prevent third parties from violating the right in other countries if they are able to do so. Depending on the availability of resources, states should provide necessary aid to help facilitate access to essential health facilities, goods, and services. Yet another responsibility identified is that state parties should ensure that the right to health is given attention in international trade agreements and should take steps to prevent international agreements from adversely affecting the right to health. The general comment further directs states that are members of international financial institutions, notably the International Monetary Fund, the World Bank, and regional developments banks, to pay greater attention to the protection of the right to health in the lending policies, credit agreements, and international measures of these institutions (CESCR 2000, para 39).

The general comment also sets down a series of collective responsibilities of state parties to cooperate in providing disaster relief and humanitarian assistance in times of emergency, including assistance to refugees and internally displaced persons to the maximum of its capabilities. Given that some diseases are transmissible beyond state borders, the general comment maintains that international community also has a collective responsibility to aid poorer developing states develop adequate responses to address these health problems (CESCR 2000, para 40). According to the general comment, states should also refrain at all times from imposing embargoes or similar measures that result in restrictions on adequate medicines and medical equipment (CESCR 2000, para 41).

These norms and policies are not currently informing states' policies. Moreover, the obligations identified do not address the structural issues that have given rise to current health inequities. Nor do they provide anything near the compensatory measures now required to begin to undo the ravages of neoliberal globalization on health systems and the right to health.

There are a number of recent initiatives focusing on cross-border health and human rights initiatives but none as yet have had significant impact. The Joint Action and Learning Initiative on National and Global Responsibilities for Health (JALI) was launched by a coalition of civil society and academics in the hope of developing a post Millennium Development Goal (MDG) framework for global health rooted in the right to health and aimed at securing universal health coverage for all people (Gostin et al. 2011). Using broad partnerships and an inclusive consultation process, one objective of JALI is to clarify the health services to which everyone is entitled under the right to health. The organizers of JALI also hope to provide the impetus for the adoption of a global agreement, such as a Framework Convention on Public Health, which would set priorities, clarify national and international responsibilities, ensure accountability, and develop an institutional framework and governance structure to achieve these objectives. Recognizing that resource-poor states lack the capacity to provide all of their people even with core health goods and services, let alone a fuller realization of the right to health, the JALI coalition envisions the need for aid beyond development assistance, but is not specific as to the forms it would take. The coalition takes a hopeful stance that states will agree to greater accountability and coordination of health policies despite acknowledging that many countries currently fail to adhere to existing commitments. Its hopefulness comes in part from the belief that the framework of mutual responsibilities that emerges from JALI will prove attractive to both Southern and Northern governments. It also vests its hope in the possibilities of social mobilization, as the AIDS movement has done.

Like the JALI coalition, Anand Grover has been concerned with the need for sustainable international funding for health for low-income states that lack adequate funds and resources for health. He has proposed that the global paradigm of international assistance for health be shifted from a donor-based charity regime toward an obligatory system based on the principle of solidarity. To that end he recommended the creation of treaty-based global pooling mechanisms under which states would incur legal obligations to contribute to the pool according to their ability to pay and through which funds would be allocated based on need. To be consistent with a human rights approach, he envisioned all funding and programmatic processes would be transparent and include the active and informed participation of civil society and the affected communities (Grover 2014, para 33).

Social and Political Mobilization

Globalization has contributed to the diffusion of human rights norms and provided new and expanded space for civil society, including human rights nongovernmental organizations (NGOs) and citizens' social movements. The transformation of the global communications network by electronic means through e-mail and the Internet has facilitated civil society's capacity to organize. It has also enabled citizens to become generators of knowledge about social issues and to form transnational advocacy networks (Howard-Hassmann 2010, 100–105). As of 2007, there were approximately 3,000 nongovernmental organizations (NGOS), including human rights NGOs, with formal consultative status at various UN agencies. Human rights NGOs can therefore be seen as part of global governance in that they insert private citizens' organizations into discussions of norms, rules, and institutional responsibilities of states and international organizations (Howard-Hassmann 2010, 106).

Globalization has sped up both capitalist expansion and resistance to neoliberal globalization (Howard-Hassmann 2010, 112). Nongovernmental organizations are considered by many to be the most legitimate and effective organizations to make known the claims of those adversely affected by globalization. Human rights groups have protested against the neoliberal policies of governments, human rights infractions of transnational corporations, and the requirements of international financial institutions (Howard-Hassmann 2010, 113).

There is a fundamental dilemma in how to frame a strategy to bring about change. Rhoda Howard-Hassmann believes the most effective social movements and NGOs critical of globalization have tended to focus on specific abuses of economic human rights, especially by transnational corporations, while diffuse social movements that seek to overhaul the entire system of global trade have had far less marked success (2010, 110). Nevertheless, specific infractions often reflect underlying structural problems. Moreover, Howard-Hassmann also acknowledges that reform often occurs when those in power seriously engage with moderates to stave off criticisms by more radical groups (2010, 114).

In the past twenty years, the human rights movement has expanded and become more involved with the protection and promotion of health issues. A broad range of issues with health implications, as for example, water privatization, oil contamination, exploitation of indigenous lanes, and the impact of trade agreements on access to medicine, are now being contested as rights issues (Yamin 2008). International NGOs like Amnesty International that formerly focused on civil and political rights are now more vested in health and human rights. Organizations of medical professionals such as Médecins San Frontières, Partners in Health, Doctors for Global Health, and other humanitarian organizations increasingly use human rights as an advocacy tool (Hunt 2007, para 15).

There have been a series of initiatives, some having real impact, to improve access to essential medicines. Opposition to TRIPS first became visible in the street protests during the WTO Seattle Ministerial Conference in 1999. Networks of activists calling on governments to ensure access to essential drugs and reexamine institutional arrangements impeding access to essential medicines even gained the support of WHO and the UN Development Program (Alkoby 2012, 56). In 2001, a global campaign led by Oxfam, Médecins San Frontières, and other organizations, which collected some 250,000 signatures on a petition, convinced the Pharmaceutical Manufacturers of South Africa to withdraw its legal suit, which had been filed on behalf of thirty-nine major drug companies seeking to forestall implementation of the South African government's 1997 Medicines Act to enable the country to import cheaper alternatives to branded medicines (Alkoby 2012, 56). Pressure from nongovernmental organizations concerned with the access of poor countries to essential medicines contributed to the formulation of the 2001 Doha Declarations clarifying that "The TRIPS agreement does not and should not prevent Members from taking measures to protect public health" (World Trade Organization 2001) and the subsequent decision (August 2003) permitting countries producing generic copies of patented drugs under compulsory license to export these drugs to countries with little or no manufacturing capacity (Alkoby 2012, 57).

Human rights considerations have also played an important role in international campaigns by AIDS activists. Recognizing that low-income countries highly affected by HIV/AIDS are unable to finance treatment, AIDS activists pressured the international community to create the Global Fund to fight AIDS, Tuberculosis, and Malaria. The Fund has been characterized as "nothing more than a tool for compliance with the transnational obligation to fulfill an essential part of the core content of the right to health" (Ooms and Hammonds 2008, 161). The political declaration adopted by governments at the June 2006 UN General Assembly

High Level Meeting on AIDS affirms that the full realization of all human rights and fundamental freedoms for all is an essential element in the global response to the HIV/AIDS pandemic (General Assembly 2006, para 11), and on this basis commits the global community to pursue all necessary efforts to scale up country-driven, sustainable, and comprehensive responses for prevention, treatment, care, and support, with the full participation of people living with HIV and vulnerable groups (General Assembly 2006, para 19).

The potential foundation of an international health and human rights movement is beginning to develop. The People's Health Movement, a global network of grassroots health activists, civil society organizations, and academic institutions working on health-related issues, was formed in 2000. The People's Charter for Health, drafted at its inaugural 2000 assembly, recognizes health as a fundamental human right; identifies "inequality, poverty, exploitation, violence and injustice" as the main drivers of ill health and the deaths of poor and marginalized people, and calls for "Health for ALL Now." Echoing the 1978 Alma Ata Declaration, the Charter calls for universal, comprehensive primary health care as the basis for formulating policies related to health. It recognizes the importance of social action to press for social and economic rights and of participatory approaches to address social injustices. It also stresses the importance of tackling the broader social and economic determinants for health (People's Charter for Health 2000). The People's Health Movement has chapters in countries in South Asia, Africa, South and Central America, North America, and Europe.

The People's Health Movement Right to Health and Health Care Campaign, launched in 2005, seeks to use a participatory process that both informs people about their right to health and involves them in preparing the assessment of the right to health care in their country. It consists of three phases. The first involves grassroots organizations carrying out rights-based assessments of national health policies utilizing an assessment guide prepared by the People's Health Movement. The guide specifically deals with structural and globally prevalent health systems' issues such as privatization, inequity, and the lack of access, using a rights-based framework. In the second phase, the participants in the national assessments will be linked in a global mobilization around the right to health through a series of regional assemblies to share assessments and action plans, facilitate a dialogue with national health policy makers on the implementation of health rights-based changes in the health system, and make recommendations for how the People's Health Movement as a global movement should support national demands for compliance with right to health and health care commitments. The third phase of the campaign will be to mobilize for the universal recognition of the right to health and to mobilize for implementation of the plans developed by the regional assemblies (Turiano and Smith 2008). Whether the People's Health Movement becomes an effective international force able to confront inequitable health policies remains to be seen.

Conclusion

Globalization has had a significant impact on health systems and on the potential of realizing rights-based approaches to health. It has impacted the incidence and patterns of diseases, the health status of communities, the structure and capabilities of health systems, the availability of health personnel, and the roles of states, nongovernmental organizations, and global actors regarding health issues. To date, globalization has disproportionately benefited the countries and economic entities with the resources and the power and increased economic and health disparities within and between countries. Neoliberal policies have also reduced the resources available to invest in promoting a rights-based approach to health. In the global system, many states, particularly poor ones, have significant constraints on both their ability and their freedom to implement human rights obligations.

While a human rights approach potentially offers an alternative and compelling paradigm to counter neoliberal globalization, to date, it has not been able to do so. Many factors reduce the potential counterweight human rights might exert, including, and specifically, the state-centric nature of the human rights approach, weakening political commitments to promoting and protecting health rights on the part of some states, and reduced institutional and economic resources to do so. Also, the human rights community has not yet developed a truly effective strategy for dealing with globalization. Human rights advocates have asserted the priority of human rights obligations over the requirements of economic treaties and agreements apparently without convincing relevant actors. Civil society actors have sought to influence the policies, practices, and operations of various international organizations, particularly international financial institutions, but with very sporadic success. The absence of the ability to impose human rights sanctions of the kind that the WTO and the World Bank have at their disposal places human rights institutions at a significant disadvantage.

The hope for the future is that human rights will inspire more effective civil society efforts to counter the deleterious impacts of the globalization on health. It is sometimes observed that human rights are claimed through mobilization from the bottom and not granted from the top. Campaigns against the adverse effects of globalization on health may give rise to more successful efforts to reclaim a rights-based approach to health. The further development of the People's Health Movement may be one promising possibility, but it is too soon to know.

References

Abouharb, M. Rodwan and Cingranelli, David (2007) *Human Rights and Structural Adjustment*, New York: Cambridge University Press.

Alexander, Nancy (2005) "The Roles of the IMF, World Bank and WTO in Liberalization and Privatization of the Water Services Sector," *Citizen's Network on Essential Services*, http://servicesforall.org.

Alkoby, Asher (2012) "Improving Access to Essential Medicines: International Law and Normative Change," in Lisa Forman and Jillian Clare Kohler, eds., *Access to Medicines as a Human Right*, Toronto: University of Toronto Press, pp. 46–74.

Anand, Sudhir and Peter, Fabienne (2003) "Introduction," in Sudhir Anand, Fabienne Peter, and Amartya Sen, eds., *Public Health, Ethics, and Equity*, Oxford and New York: Oxford University Press, pp. 1–12.

Barrientos, Armando (2000) "Getting Better After Neoliberalism: Shifts and Challenges of Health Policy in Chile," in Peter Lloyd Sherlock, ed., *Healthcare Reform & Poverty in Latin America*, London: Institute of Latin American Studies, pp. 94–111.

Bates, Roger and Boateng, Katherine (2007) "How to Promote Global Health," A Foreign Affairs Roundtable, www.foreignaffairs.com/discussions/roundtables/how-to-promote-global-health.

Bhalotra, Sonia Radhika and Pogge, Thomas (2012) "Ethical and Economic Perspectives on Global Health Interventions," IZA Policy Paper No. 38, Bonn, Germany, fttp.iza.org/pp38.pdf.

Biesma, Regien, Brugha, Ruairi, Harmer, Andrew, Walsh, Aisling, et al. (2009) "The Effects of Global Health Initiatives on Country Health Systems: A Review of the Evidence from HIV/AIDS Control," *Epidemiology and Public Health Medicine Articles: Royal College of Surgeons in Ireland*, e-publications @ RCSI: 240–252.

Birdsall, Nancy (2005) "Debt and Development: How to Provide Efficient, Effective Assistance to the World's Poorest Countries," Working Paper, Washington, DC: Center for Global Development.

Braveman, P. and Gruskin, S. (2003) "Defining Equity in Health," *Journal of Epidemiology and Community Health* 57: 254–258.

CEGAA (The Centre for Economic Governance and AIDS in Africa) and RESULTS Educational Fund (REF) (2009) "Evidence of the Impact of IMF Fiscal and Monetary Policies on the Capacity to Address HIV/AIDS and TB Crises in Kenya, Tanzania and Zambia."

CESCR (Committee on Economic, Social and Cultural Rights) (1999) Statement on Globalization, U.N. Doc. E/C.12/1999/9.

(2000) General Comment No. 14: The Right to the Highest Attainable Standard of Health (article 12 of the International Covenant on Economic, Social and Cultural Rights), U.N. Doc. E/C.12/2000/4.

(2001) Report on the Twenty-Fifth, Twenty-Sixth and Twenty-Seventh Sessions. 23 April–11 May 2001, 13–31 August 2001 and 12–30 November 2001, U.N. Doc E/C.12/2001/17.

(2002a) Concluding Observations United Kingdom of Great Britain and Northern Ireland, the Crown Dependencies and the Oversees Territories. U.N. Doc. E/C/12/1Add.79.

(2002b) Report on the Twenty-Fifth, Twenty-Sixth and Twenty-Seventh Sessions. April 23–May 11, 2001, August 13–31, 2001 and November 12–30, 2001, U.N. Doc. E/C/2002/22.

(2004) Concluding Observations on Azerbaijan, U.N. Doc. E/C.12/1/Add.104.

Chapman, Audrey R. (2009) "Globalization, Human Rights, and the Social Determinants of Health," *Bioethics* 23 (2): 97–111.

Chapman, Audrey R. and Benegal, Salil D. (2013) "Globalization and the Right to Health," in Lance Minkler, ed., *The State of Economic and Social Rights: A Global Overview*, New York: Cambridge University Press, pp. 61–85.

Commission on the Social Determinants of Health (2008) *Closing the Gap in a Generation: Health Equity Through Action on the Social Determinants of Health*, Geneva: World Health Organization.

Cornia, Giovanni Andrea, Rosignoli, Stefano, and Tiberti, Luca (2009) "An Empirical Investigation of the Relation between Globalization and Health," in Ronald Labonté, Ted Schrecker, Corinne Packer, and Vivien Runnels, eds., *Globalization and Health: Pathways, Evidence and Policy*, New York and London: Routledge, pp. 34–62.

Correa, Carlos M. (2009) "Intellectual Property Rights and Inequalities in Health Outcomes," in Ronald Labonté, Ted Schrecker, Corinne Packer, and Vivien Runnels, eds., *Globalization and Health: Pathways, Evidence and Policy*, New York and London: Routledge, pp. 263–288.

De Schutter, Olivier (2009) "A Human Rights Approach to Trade and Investment Policies," in Sophia Murphy and Armin Paasch, eds., *The Global Food Challenge: Towards a Human Rights Approach to Trade and Investment*

Policies, Ecumenical Advocacy Alliance (EAA), FoodFirst Information and Action Network (FIAN), and Others.

(2011) Report of the Special Rapporteur on the Right to Food: Guiding Principles on Human Rights Impact Assessments of Trade and Investment Agreements, United Nations General Assembly, U.N. Doc. A/HRC/19/59/Add.5.

de Waal, Alex (2007) "Major Challenges/Minor Response," A Foreign Affairs Roundtable, www.foreignaffairs.com/discussions/roundtables/how-to-promote-global-health.

DfID (Department for International Development, UK) (2004) "The Case for Abolition of User Fees for Primary Health Services," London: Health Systems Resource Centre, Department for International Development.

Dieleman, Joseph, Murray, Christopher J. L., and Haakenstad, Anne (2013) Financing Global Health 2013: Transition in an Age of Austerity, University of Washington: Institute for Health Metrics and Evaluation, www.healthdata .org/.../financing-global-health-2013-transition-age-auste...

Dodd, Glen and Hinselwood, Steve (2002) "PRSPS: Their Significance for Health," draft presented to the WHO Meeting of Interested Parties.

Falk, Richard (1999) *Predatory Globalization: A Critique*, Cambridge, UK: Polity.

(2008) *Law in an Emerging Global Village: A Post-Westphalian Perspective*, New York: Transnational Publishers Inc.

Fink, Sheri (2014) "Cuts at W.H.O. Hurt Response to Ebola Crisis," *The New York Times*, September 4, A1.

Freedman, Lynn P., Waldman, Ronald J., de Pinho, Helen, Wirth, Meg E. et al. (2007) *Who's Got the Power? Transforming Health Systems for Women and Children*, London and Sterling, VA: Earthscan and the Un Millennium Project.

General Assembly (2006) Political Declaration on HIV/AIDS, U.N. Doc. A/ RES/60/262.

Gleeson, Debrah and Friel, Sharon (2013) "Emerging Threats to Public Health from Regional Trade Agreements," *The Lancet* 381: 1507–1509.

Global Health Watch (2014) *Global Health Watch 4: An Alternative World Health Report*, London and New York: Zed Publishing Company for the People's Health Movement, Medact, and the Global Equity Gauge Alliance.

Gómez Isa, Felipe (2005) "Globalisation, Privatisation and Human Rights," in De Feyter Koen and Gómez Isa, Felipe, eds., *Privatisation and Human Rights in the Age of Globalisation,* Antwerp and Oxford: Intersentia, pp. 9–32.

Gostin, Lawrence O., Friedman, Eric A., Ooms, Gorik, Gelauer, Thomas, et al. (2011) "The Joint Action and Learning Initiative: Towards a Global Agreement on National and Global Responsibilities for Health," *PLOS Medicine* 8 (5): e100103.

Gostin, Lawrence O. and Hodge, James G., Jr. (2007) "Global Health Law, Ethics, and Policy," *The Journal of Law, Medicine & Ethics* 35: 519–525.

Grover, Anand (2012) Interim Report of the Special Rapporteur on the Right of Everyone to the Enjoyment of the Highest Attainable Standard of Physical and Mental Health to the United Nations General Assembly, U.N. Doc. A/67/150.

(2014) Report of the Special Rapporteur on the Right of Everyone to the Enjoyment of the Highest Attainable Standard of Physical and Mental Health, General Assembly, U.N. Doc. A/69/299.

Hawkes, Corinna, Chopra, Mickey, and Friel, Sharon (2009) "Globalization, Trade, and the Nutrition Transition," in Ronald Labonté, Ted Schrecker, Corinne Packer, and Vivien Runnels, eds., *Globalization and Health: Pathways, Evidence and Policy*, New York and London: Routledge, pp. 2235–2262.

Howard-Hassmann, Rhoda E. (2005) "The Second Great Transformation: Human Rights Leapfrogging in the Era of Globalization," *Human Rights Quarterly* 27 (1): 1–40.

(2010) *Can Globalization Promote Human Rights?* Philadelphia: University of Pennsylvania Press.

Hunt, Paul (2003) Report of the Special Rapporteur on the Right of Everyone to the Enjoyment of the Highest Attainable Standard of Physical and Mental Health to the Commission on Human Rights. U.N. Doc. E/CN.4/2003/58.

(2004) Report of the Special Rapporteur on the Right of Everyone to the Enjoyment of the Highest Attainable Standard of Physical and Mental Health to the Commission on Human Rights. U.N. Doc. E/CN.4/2004/49/Add.1.

(2007) Report of the Special Rapporteur on the Right of Everyone to the Enjoyment of the Highest Attainable Standard of Physical and Mental Health to the Human Rights Council, U.N. Doc. A/HRC/4/28.

(2008) Draft Guidelines for Pharmaceutical Corporations, www2.ohchr.org/English/issues/health/right/docs/draftguid150508.doc.

Institute for Health Metrics and Evaluation (2012) Financing Global Health 2012: The End of the Golden Age? Seattle: University of Washington, www.healthdata.org/pol.

International Covenant on Economic, Social and Cultural Rights (ICESCR) (1966) United Nations General Assembly Resolution 2200 A (XXI) of December 16, 1966, 21 U.N. GAOR Supp. (No. 16) at 49, U.N. Doc. A/6316, entered into force January 3, 1976.

Karankolos, Marina, Mladovsky, Philipa, Cylus, Jonathan, and Thomson, Sarah (2013) "Financial Crisis, Austerity, and Health in Europe," *The Lancet* 381: 1323–1331.

Katz, Alison (2005) "The Sachs Report: Investing in Health for Economic Development – or Increasing the Size of the Crumbs from the Rich Man's Table?" *International Journal of Health Services* 35 (1): 171–188.

Kentikelenis, Alexander, Karanikolos, Marina, Reeves, Aaron, McKee, Martin, Stuckler, David (2014) "Greece's Health Crisis: From Austerity to Denialism," *The Lancet* 383: 748–753.

Keys, Tracey and Malnight, Thomas (2012) "Corporate Clout: The Influence of the World's Largest 100 Economic Entities," www.scribd.com/.../Corporate-Clout-the-Worlds-100-Largest-Eco...

Kothari, Miloon (2002) *Report of the Special Rapporteur on Adequate Housing as a Component of the Right to an Adequate Standard of Living*, U.N. Doc. E/CN.4/2002/59.

Kruk, Margaret E. (2012) "Globalisation and Global Health Governance: Implications for Public Health," *Global Public Health: An International Journal for Research, Policy and Practice* (May): 1–9, http://dx.doi.org/10.10 80/17441692.2012.689313.

Kuehn, Bridget M. (2007) "Global Shortages of Health Workers, Brain Drain Stress on Developing Countries," *JAMA* 298: 1853–1855.

Labonté, Ronald, Mohindra, Kate, and Schrecker, Ted (2011) "The Growing Impact of Globalization for Health and Public Health Practice," *The Annual Review of Public Health,* 32 263–283, www.publhealth.annualreviews.org.

Labonté, Ronald, Schrecker, Ted, Blouin, Chantal, Chopra, Mickey, Lee Kelley, et al. (2007) *Towards Health Equitable Globalisation: Rights, Regulation, and Redistribution. Final Report to the Commission on Social Determinants of Health Globalization Knowledge Network*, www.who.int/social_determinants/resources/gkn_report_06_2007.pdf.

Levcovitz, Eduardo (2007) Processes of Change and Challenges for Health Systems Based on the Renewed PHC Strategy. VII Regional Forum: Strengthening PHC-Based Health Systems, PAHO.

Lister, John and Labonté, Ronald (2009) "Globalization and Health Systems Change," in Ronald Labonté, Ted Ronald, Corinne Schrecker, Corinne Packer, and Vivien Runnels, eds., *Globalization and Health: Pathways, Evidence and Policy*, New York and London: Routledge, pp. 181–212.

Lozano, Rafeal, Naghavi, Mohsin, Foreman, Kyle, Lim, Stephen et al. (2012) "Global and Regional Mortality: Causes of Death for 20 Age Groups and the Global Burden of Disease in 2010," *The Lancet* 380: 2095–2128.

Lu, Chunling, Schneider, Matthew T., Gulbins, Paul, Leach-Kemon, Katherine (2011) "Public Finance for Health in Developing Countries: A Cross-national Systematic Analysis," *The Lancet* 375 (9723): 1375–1387.

Meier, Benjamin Mason (2010) "The World Health Organization, the Evolution of Human Rights, and the Failure to Achieve Health for All," in John Harrington and Maria Suttaford, eds., *Global Health and Human Rights: Legal and Philosophical Perspectives*, Abingdon, Oxon, and New York: Routledge, pp, 163–189.

Meier, Benjamin Mason and Onzivu, William (2014) "The Evolution of Human Rights in the World Health Organization Policy and the Future of Human Rights in Global Health Governance," *Public Health* 128: 179–187.

Mills, Edward J., Kanters, Steve, Hagopian, Amy, Bansback, Nick, et al. (2011) "The Financial Cost of Doctors Emigrating from Sub-Saharan Africa: Human Capital Analysis," *British Medical Journal* 343: d7031. doi: 10.1136/bmj.d7031.

Monteiro, Carlos A. and Cannon, Geoffrey (2012) "The Impact of Transnational 'Big Food' Companies on the South: A View from Brazil," *PLOS Medicine* 9 (7), e1001252, DOI:10.1371/journL.P.MWS.1001252.

Moon, Suerie and Omole, Oluwatosin (2013) Development Assistance for Health: Critiques and Proposals for Change, Chatham House Working Group on Financing, Paper 1, www.chathamhouse.org/.../Global%20Health/041.

Ng, Nora Y. and Ruger, Jennifer Prah (2011) "Global Health Governance at a Crossroads," *Global Health Governance* III (2): 1–37.

O'Brien, Paula and Gostin, Lawrence O. (2011) Health Worker Shortages and Inequalities, Milbank Memorial Fund Report.

O'Connell, Paul (2007) "On Reconciling Irreconcilables: Neoliberal Globalisation and Human Rights," *Human Rights Law Review* 3: 483–509.

Ooms, Gorik and Hammonds, Rachel (2008) "Correcting Globalisation in Health: Transnational Entitlements versus the Ethical Imperative of Reducing Aid-dependency," *Public Health Ethics* 1 (2): 154–170.

Ottersen, Ole Petter, Dasgupta, Jashodhara, Blouin, Chantal, Buss, Paulo, et al. (2014) "The Political Origins of Health Inequity: Prospects for Change," The Lancet-University of Oslo Commission on Global Governance for Health, *The Lancet,* 383 (9917): 630–667.

Outterson, Kevin (2008) "Should Access to Medicines and TRIPS Flexibilities Be Limited to Specific Diseases?" *American Journal of Law & Medicine* 34: 279–301.

People's Health Movement (2000) People's Charter for Health, www.phmovement .org>Home>Charters & Declarations.

Pogge, Thomas (2002) *World Poverty and Human Rights*, Cambridge: Polity.

Randeria, Shalini (2007) "Globalization of Law: Environmental Justice, World Bank, NGOs and the Cunning State in India," *Current Society* 51: 305–328.

Rodrik, Dani (2006) "Goodbye Washington Consensus, Hello Washington Consensus," *Journal of Economic Literature* 44: 973–987.

Rockefeller Foundation (2010) *Catalyzing Change: The System Reform Costs of Universal Health Coverage*, New York, www.rockefellerfoundation .org.

Rowden, Rick (2009) *The Deadly Ideas of Neoliberalism: How the IMF Has Undermined Public Health and the Fight Against AIDS,* London and New York: Zed Books.

Sachs, Jeffrey D. (2007) "Beware False Tradeoffs," A Foreign Affairs Roundtable, deps.washington.edu/.../GarrettForeignAffairs...

Saltman, Richard B. and Cahn, Zachary (2013) "Restructuring Health Systems for an Era of Prolonged Austerity: An Essay," *British Medical Journal* 346: f3972 doi: 10.1136/bmj.f3972.

Sangorgio, Miriam (2013) "Upcoming 66th World Health Assembly: Main Topics of Discussion," *The Health Diplomacy Monitor* 4 (3): 3–5.

SAPRIN (Structural Adjustment Participatory Review International Network) (2004) *Structural Adjustment: The SAPRIN REPORT: The Policy Roots of Economic Crisis, Poverty, and Inequality*, London: Zed Books.

Schrecker, Ted (2011) "The Health Case for Economic and Social Rights Against the Global Marketplace," *Journal of Human Rights* 10 (2): 151–177.

Schrecker, Ted, Chapman, Audrey R., Labonte, Ronald, and De Vogli, Roberto (2010) "Advancing Health Equity in the Global Marketplace: How Human Rights Can Help," *Social Science & Medicine* 71: 1520–1526.

Sridhar, Devi (2010) "Seven Challenges in International Development Assistance for Health and Ways Forward," *Journal of Law, Medicine & Ethics* 38 (3)2–12.

Stiglitz, Joseph (2003) *Globalization and Its Discontents*, New York: WW Norton & Co.

Stuckler, David and Nestle, Marion (2012) "Big Food, Food Systems, and Global Health," *PLOS Medicine* 9 (6), e1001242, doi:10.1371/journal .pmed.1001242.

Stuckler, David, McKee Martin, Ebrahim Shah, and Basu, Sanjay (2012) "Manufacturing Epidemics: The Role of Global Producers in Increased Consumption of Unhealthy Commodities Including Processed Foods, Alcohol, and Tobacco," *PLOS Medicine* 9 (6), e1001235, doi:10.1371/journal .pmed.1001235.

Teeple, Gary (2000) *Globalization and the Decline of Social Reform into the Twenty-First Century*, Aurora, ON: Garamond Press.

Thomas, Bryan and Gostin, Lawrence O. (2013) "Tacking the Global NCD Crisis: Innovations in Law and Governance," *The Journal of Law, Medicine & Ethics* 41 (1): 16–27.

Torrey, E. Fuller and Torrey, Barbara Boyle (2012) "The U.S. Distribution from Lower Income Countries," *PLOS One* 7 (3): e33076. doi:10.1371/journal .pone.0033076.

Turiano, Laura and Smith, Lanny (2008) "The Catalytic Synergy of Health and Human Rights: The People's Health Movement and the Right to Health and Health Care Campaign," *Health and Human Rights* 10 (1): 137–147.

UNAIDS (2010) Report on the global AIDS epidemic 2010, www.unaids .org.../20101...

UNICEF (2008) "Nationwide Needs Assessment or Emergency Obstetric and Newborn Services in Sierra Leone," Reproductive and Child Health Programme, Ministry of Health and Sanitation.

United Nations (1948) Universal Declaration of Human Rights, adopted 10 December 1948. United Nations General Assembly Res. 217 A (III), www .un.org/en/documents/udhr/.

(2012) Millennium Development Goals Report, 2012, New York: United Nations.

World Bank (1993) *World Development Report 1993: Investing in Health*, New York: Oxford University Press.

(2004) *World Development Report: Making Services Work for Poor People*, Washington, DC: World Bank.

World Health Organization (1958) Preamble to the Constitution, in *The First Ten Years of the World Health Organization*, Geneva: WHO.

(1995) *The World Health Report 1995: Bridging the Gaps*, www.who.int/whr/ 1995/en/

(2006) *The World Health Report 2006 – Working Together for Health*, Geneva: WHO, www.who.int/whr/2006/en/.

(2007) *The World Health Report 2007: Everybody's Business: Strengthening Health Systems to Improve Health Outcomes*. Geneva: WHO, http://who.int/ healthsystems/strategy/everybodys_business.pdf.

(2008) *The World Health Report: Primary Health Care – Now More Than Ever.* Geneva: WHO, www.who.int/whr/2008/en/index.html.

(2010) International Recruitment of Health Personnel: Draft Global Code of Practice, A63/8.

(2011) "Pharmaceutical Industry," www.who.int/trade/glossary/story073/en/ index.html.

(2013) A Universal Truth: No Health without a Workforce, Geneva, http://eee .eho.int/workforce.

World Trade Organization (2001) Declaration on the TRIPS Agreement and Public Health, Ministerial Conference, Fourth Session, Doha, WT/MIN(01)/ DEC/W2.

Yamin, Alicia Ely (2008) "Beyond Compassion: The Central Accountability in Applying a Human Rights Framework to Health," *Health and Human Rights* 10(2): 1–20.

6

Achieving Improved Access to Medicines

Access to medicines, particularly essential medicines, is fundamental to the right to health, but there are many obstacles to its realization in the neoliberal era in which private for-profit corporations control the pharmaceutical sector and market mechanisms govern decisions about what kinds of medicines are developed and how they are priced. Currently, it is estimated that some 2 billion people, one-third of the world's population, most of whom live in low- and middle-income countries, lack access to essential medicines. Many more people in both developed and developing countries cannot afford the high prices charged for many pharmaceuticals. The lack of availability and access to potentially life-giving essential medicines and drugs is both a significant ethical and human rights issue.

This chapter will explore the factors contributing to this situation. The chapter will also examine the role and responsibilities of both governments and pharmaceutical corporations. In addition, the chapter will review how civil society and human rights-based advocacy have responded to these constraints. The chapter has sections that address the following topics: essential medicines, intellectual property (IP) laws and access to medicines, prices and cost of medicines, corporate responsibility issues, advocacy efforts, and the international human rights responsibilities of governments.

Access to Medicines as a Human Rights Requirement

Providing access to medicines, particularly essential medicines, constitutes a fundamental component of realizing the right to health. Provision of medical care in the event of sickness, as well as the prevention, treatment, and control of disease, are central features of the right to health that depend on access to appropriate medicines when needed. The availability and appropriate use of pharmaceuticals and vaccines can reduce morbidity and mortality rates and enhance the quality of life. As Anand Grover, the second Special Rapporteur on the right to health, specified in his 2009 report, states have an obligation under the right to health to ensure that medicines are available, financially affordable, and physically accessible to everyone in their jurisdiction (Grover 2009, para 11). General Comment 14 (GC 14) identifies the provision of essential drugs, as defined under the WHO Action Program on Essential Drugs, as a core obligation of state parties to the International Covenant on Economic, Social and Cultural Rights (CESCR 2000, para 43 d). Essential drugs refer to the medicines that address the priority needs of the population. The general comment also designates the provision of immunizations against the major diseases occurring in the community to be an obligation of comparative priority (CESCR 2000, para 44). Additionally, the Committee on Economic, Social and Cultural Rights (CESCR) has drawn attention many times, including in GC 14, to the responsibility of developed states to contribute to the full realization of health in resource-deprived countries through international assistance and cooperation (CESCR 2000, para 38). This obligation includes facilitating access to medicines and, by extension, to their development in cases where no drugs exist to treat medical problems prevalent in low-income countries.

It is noteworthy that in 2013 the Human Rights Council adopted a resolution on access to medicines in the context of the enjoyment of the highest attainable standard of physical and mental health (Human Rights Council 2013). The resolution recognizes that access to medicines is one of the fundamental elements in achieving progressively the full realization of the right to the enjoyment of the highest attainable standard of physical and mental health. It also urges states to undertake a wide range of policy initiatives toward that goal, many of which will be discussed in this chapter.

Accessibility of medicines has four components from a human rights perspective: first, medicines must be available in all parts of the country, not just in a few urban centers. Second, medicines must be affordable to all, including those living in poverty. This is likely to require both cost controls to limit the prices charged and programs to subsidize the cost of some more expensive medicines, particularly in developing countries. Third, medicines must be accessible without discrimination on any of the prohibited grounds (race, color, sex, language, political or other opinion, national or social origin, property, birth, or other status). And fourth, reliable information about medicines must be accessible to patients and health professionals in order for them to be able to make well-informed decisions (Grover 2009 para 20). The World Health Organization (WHO) defines the appropriate use of medicines to require that "patients receive medicines appropriate to their clinical needs, in doses that meet their own individual requirements, for an adequate period of time, and at the lowest cost to them and their communities" (cited in Bigdeli et al. 2014, 22).

Assurance of the quality of medicines is another important component of the right to medicines in order to protect the population from exposure to impure, counterfeit, and potentially harmful medicines and to avoid the waste of resources on ineffective medicines. Unfortunately, substandard medicines are common in developing countries. This situation reflects inadequate regulation of the pharmaceutical sector. For example, only about one in three drug regulatory agencies in Africa function adequately. Some foreign manufacturers take advantage of this situation by exporting substandard medicines they cannot sell on the closely regulated domestic markets in developed countries, and some domestic manufacturers and distributors knowingly sell impure medicines because of the small probability they will be discovered and prosecuted. This situation has led to a number of tragic incidents, such as when contamination of one type of medicine in Pakistan resulted in more than 100 deaths. In Rwanda, it has been shown that 20 percent of the hypertensive medicines purchased on the market were of substandard quality and 79 percent were insufficiently stable (Hogerzeil et al. 2013, 682). Rwanda recently witnessed a significant rise in confirmed malaria cases because a type of bed net that had been widely distributed across the country turned out to be of substandard quality and thus had low bioefficacy (Binagwaho et al. 2015).

Improving access to medicines was also implicit in several Millennium Development Goals (MDGs), the set of eight goals that 191 United Nations member states agreed to achieve in 2000 and, in the case of developed countries, to help poor states realize by 2015. Three of the goals were health related. MDG 4 was a commitment by countries to reduce child mortality by two-thirds in 2015 below 1990 levels, including by expanding programs of immunization. MDG 5 entailed improving maternal health and included the targets of reducing maternal mortality ratio by three-fourths from 1990 levels and providing universal access to reproductive care. MDG 6 focussed on combatting HIV/AIDs, malaria, tuberculosis, and other diseases with the subgoal of achieving universal access to treatment for those who need it. In addition, MDG 8, to develop global partnerships for development, included the subgoal, in cooperation with pharmaceutical companies, to provide access to affordable essential medicines in developing countries.

Lack of Access to Medicines

There is a global crisis in the availability of essential medicines and the ability of the majority of people to afford access to needed medicines. Currently, approximately two billion people, some one-third of the world's population, do not have access to the medicines necessary for their health care. Moreover, there has been little improvement in the availability and affordability of medicines in developing countries in recent years (MDG Gap Task Force Report 2012, xvi). Individuals across the globe are afflicted by, and some also die from, diseases that are preventable or curable because they cannot gain access to and/or afford appropriate medicines.

The burden of paying for pharmaceuticals is particularly onerous in low- and middle-income countries where 50 to 90 percent of the cost of medicines is usually paid for by the patient or the patient's family (Hunt and Khosla 2010). More than 100 million people fall into poverty annually because of high health care costs, with the cost of medicines frequently constituting the most important component of out-of-pocket costs. Many people in industrialized countries also cannot afford lifesaving, but costly, drugs, particularly when health systems or health insurance do not underwrite drug costs or require high co-pays for medicines. If the price of pharmaceuticals continues to rise, the problem of the affordability of medicines will intensify. This issue will be further discussed in the chapter.

As the burden of disease globally shifts from infectious to noncommunicable diseases (NCDs) such as cardiovascular diseases, chronic respiratory diseases, diabetes, and cancer, yet another problem is that access to medicines and vaccines to prevent and treat NCDs is very low worldwide. The situation exists even though most NCDs can be treated with a small range of off-patent and relatively inexpensive medicines. There is a risk that some generic medicines are so cheap that they are no longer commercially appealing and might therefore cease being produced (Hogerzeil et al. 2013, 682). As might be anticipated, large disparities exist between high-income, middle-income, and low-income countries and within countries in access to medicines for NCDs as well as for infectious and acute diseases. According to The Lancet NCD Action Group, mean availability of essential medicines in thirty-six low-income and middle-income countries in the public sector was about 36 percent for NCDs versus 54 percent for acute diseases, and 55 percent versus 66 percent in the private sector (but at a much higher price) (Hogerzeil et al. 2013, 680).

It is estimated that improving access to essential medicines could save some 10 million lives each year. Providing meaningful incentives for the development of new medications for the world's poor could reduce the disease burden even further (Grover 2009, para 14). The often cited figure 10/90 refers to the pattern in which only 10 percent of global funds for research and development are invested in the diseases affecting less developed countries, in which 90 percent of the global disease burden occurs. Studies indicate that of the 1,556 new medicines developed between 1975 and 1999, only forty-six were for neglected diseases in poor countries, and between 2000 and mid-2009 only twenty-six new medicines and vaccines addressing neglected diseases were marketed (MDG Gap Task Force Report 2012, 71).

Brief Overview of the Factors Affecting Access to Medicines

The Working Group on Access to Essential Medicines in the United Nations Millennium Project identified six barriers to access to essential medicines: inadequate national commitment, inadequate human resources, failure of the international community to keep its promises to developing countries, lack of coordination of international aid, obstacles created by the Trade-Related Aspects of Intellectual Property Rights (TRIPS) Agreement, and the current incentive structure for research and development of medicines and vaccines, which places priority on the health needs of developed countries (MDG Gap Task Force Report 2008, 42). Some of these factors were mentioned in earlier chapters and will be further discussed here. Importantly, the analysis of the Working Group on Access to Essential Medicines in the United Nations Millennium Project omits two significant factors, the dominant role of for-profit private corporations in the pharmaceutical sector and the escalating cost of medicines. Both issues will be considered in this chapter.

To provide a brief overview of the six factors identified by the Working Group on Access to Essential Medicines in the United Nations Millennium Project, many of which will be better documented later in this chapter, inadequate national commitment is reflected in the insufficient investment in the health sector in general and in essential medicine programs in particular in many low- and middle-income countries, and there are cutbacks in support for coverage for pharmaceuticals in some high-income countries. Inadequate national commitment also leads to various types of policy failures affecting access to medicines. As noted in the previous chapter, the shortage of sufficient numbers of trained health personnel for the medical and health sector is a pervasive global problem further complicated by the brain drain from developing to developed countries. Very few high-income countries have taken their international right to health obligations seriously. Also important, the failure of developed countries to implement commitments made some forty years ago to provide a level of development assistance equal to 0.7 percent of their gross national income has failed to increase and in some cases decreased the level of bilateral and multilateral aid made available to resource-deprived countries for health sector programs. The implications of the lack of coordination of international aid donors for the health sector, which were discussed in Chapter Four, have the similar consequences for the availability of needed medicines: it drains time and energy of Ministry of Health staff, often reflects the priorities of donors rather than the recipient country, and contributes to the uneven availability of needed medicines. The strict IP requirements of the Agreement on Trade-Related Aspects of Intellectual Property Rights constitute an important impediment to access to medicines and raise the cost of drugs.

The incentive structure skews research and development of medicines and vaccines in the one trillion dollar a year pharmaceutical sector (Statista 2015) to those products that can bring the greatest profits. The private for-profit companies that dominate the pharmaceutical sector focus on products for markets in developed countries, particularly the United States, which alone accounts for two-fifths of global sales (Statista 2015), because these markets are considered to be more profitable. Conversely, neglect of the medical needs of the much larger number of people who live in poor countries reflects the assessment that products for diseases and medical conditions prevalent in poor countries will not be as profitable. It is assumed that poor people and low-income countries cannot afford high-priced pharmaceuticals.

The incentive structure also discourages investment in high priority but potentially low profit pharmaceuticals needed in developed countries. The current lack of a pipeline for new antibiotics to replace the antibiotics being rendered ineffective by drug-resistant bacteria constitutes one example. In the past decade, most large pharmaceutical companies have withdrawn from the antibiotic field because the profit margins for these drugs were considered too low to be attractive. A recent worst-case scenario anticipates there may be 10 million deaths per year by 2050 due to antimicrobial resistance to current drugs and the absence of effective substitutes (Servick 2015).

The profit-orientation of drug companies has other detrimental consequences. Financial incentives have generated a business model that encourages the development of "me-too" drugs, which are products that largely duplicate the composition and the mechanism of action of existing drugs with little additional therapeutic benefit, because such drugs are less expensive to develop and viewed as offering substantial profits. Producing me-too drugs focuses research and development resources on drugs for conditions for which treatment options exist and contributes to the neglect of other conditions that may have more pressing public health importance. Moreover, more options in a therapeutic class do not usually bring price reductions (Gagne and Chouduhry 2011). The profit orientation also encourages massive investments in promotional activities directed at physicians and advertising in countries where doing so is permissible. Analysts estimate that drug companies invest at least twice as much money in promoting sales as in research to produce new pharmaceuticals (Gagnon 2013). The focus on profits also encourages pharmaceutical companies to overprice their medicines, sometimes exorbitantly, so as to increase their profit margins. A later section of the chapter will provide examples and discuss their consequences. The misalignment between these financial incentives and public health needs has been termed the corruption of pharmaceutical markets (Rodwin 2010; Gagnon 2013; Light et al. 2013).

The tremendous economic resources and profits of the major pharmaceutical corporations, particularly the top twenty corporations currently remaining after a period of mergers and consolidation,[1] have conferred considerable political power. The major pharmaceutical companies and the associations representing them have been highly effective in recruiting governments, particularly a series of U.S. administrations, to support their commercial interests in domestic and international policy forums. The aggressive lobbying of the U.S. government by a group of pharmaceutical corporations played an important role in the development of the TRIPS Agreement and subsequent free-trade pacts that have imposed strict IP requirements on developing countries and thereby limited the availability of affordable medicines (Dutfield 2008, 114–115; Alkoby 2012, 55). That the corporations make sizeable political contributions, which amounted to over U.S. $21 million in the U.S. federal elections in 2012 (Jorgensen 2013, 561), also contributes to the responsiveness of U.S. policy makers to their demands. While the policy support and corporate welfare granted to

---

[1] Of these twenty major corporations, seven have their parent company in the United States (Johnson & Johnson, Pfizer, Merck, Eli Lilly, Bristol-Myers Squibb, AbbVie, and Gilead Sciences Inc.), nine in Europe (La Roche, GlaxoSmithKline, Novartis, Sanofi, AstraZeneca, Novo Nordisk, Bayer AG, Merck KGaA, and Boehringen Ingelheim), and four in Japan (Eisai Co, Astrellas Pharma, Daiichi Sankyo, and Takeda Pharmaceutical Company) (Access to Medicine Foundation 2014).

the industry are justified as promoting a public good – the development of medications to reduce suffering and death – pharmaceutical firms often make huge profits with drugs that do not much improve public health and that sometimes are unsafe or are prescribed without need (Jorgensen 2013, 562).

Essential Medicines

The Framework

Essential medicines, as defined by the WHO, are those that satisfy the priority health care needs of the population. According to Hans Hogerzeil of the WHO, WHO has developed its essential medicines program according to principles consistent with a rights-based approach. The program has focused on sustainable, universal access to essential medicines through the development of national medicines policies based on the principles of nondiscrimination and care for the poor and disadvantaged. It has also emphasized the careful selection of essential medicines, good quality assurance, good procurement and supply management procedures, and rational use according to evidence-based clinical guidelines to optimize the value of limited government funds (Hogerzeil 2006, 371–372).

WHO produced its first model list of 205 essential medicines to provide guidance to member countries in 1977. Subsequently, the list has been updated every two years by an expert committee and in the process has been expanded on an ongoing basis. The first model list of essential medicines for children came in 2007 (World Health Organization 2008). While the earliest iterations of the essential medicines list excluded medicines that were covered by patents, it is no longer the case. In 2002, WHO removed the absence of patent protection as a criterion for selection and instead placed emphasis on effectiveness, safety, and comparable cost effectiveness. As a result, expensive drugs, like antiretrovirals (ARVs) for HIV/AIDS, were listed irrespective of their high cost (World Health Organization 2003; Hogerzeil 2004). In 2015, WHO added three new treatments for hepatitis C, a variety of additional cancer treatments, and medicines for multidrug resistant tuberculosis, all of which are very expensive. In fact, WHO acknowledged that some of these medicines are even too costly for high-income countries (Media Centre 2015). Hence, essential medicines are not cheap medicines for poor people in developing countries. They are the most cost effective treatment for a given condition (World Health Organization 2003; Hogerzeil 2004).

The implementation of the essential medicines concept is meant to be adaptable to fit national disease prevalence and priorities. Determining which medicines are considered to be essential is a national responsibility based on a systematic evaluation of needs, comparative efficacy, safety, and value of medicines. By 2000, 156 mostly developing countries had published national essential medicines lists. Hans Hogerzeil has also argued that middle- and high-income countries, which also face problems of increasing demand and rising medicine costs, should adopt the concept of essential medicines in order to provide the scientific and public health basis for pharmaceutical expenditures. The benefit in doing so would enable these countries to respond in a more integrated way to the increasing costs of medicines and would help control the spiraling cost of drugs (Hogerzeil 2004). He envisions that a national medicine policy potentially relevant for developed countries would include such elements as additional criteria for market approval (comparison with best available treatment, comparative cost effectiveness); evidence-based national clinical guidelines; insurance and reimbursement policies, with the type and level of reimbursement focused on essential drugs; state subsidies (direct supply, subsidy, or subsidized insurance for poor and disadvantaged people); patent policies (balance between innovation and equitable access to essential medicines); price controls; evaluation of the advantages of local production as compared with importation; public information and education about medicine use; and investment in research and development (Hogerzeil 2004, 1171).

While other health policy experts agree that rising costs of drugs is a universal problem, they believe that most developed countries already apply many of the principles of the essential medicines concept to improve care and to manage costs. They also question whether people will accept the need for restrictions to improve wider access in countries where most medicines are already readily available (Reidenberg and Walley 2004). They are partially correct that many countries with health care entitlements incorporate some elements of the essential medicines concept, but they tend to do so from an economic rather than a human rights or equity perspective. There are also outliers like the United States which lack the legislative authority to take costs into account in making decisions about what treatments to cover in government sponsored programs (Congressional Budget Office 2007, 30–31).

Essential medicines "are intended to be available at all times in functioning health systems, in adequate amounts, in the appropriate dosage forms, with assured quality and adequate information, and at an affordable price" (World Health Organization n.d.). Therefore, it is a human rights obligation for governments to develop an essential medicines program with the necessary infrastructure and policies to do so. To be able to do so entails establishing a monitoring system to determine disease prevalence as the basis for national priorities; an evaluation system to assess the efficacy, safety, and comparative cost of medicines; an institution charged with regulatory approval; and a purchasing and distribution system able to keep essential medicines stocked in public sector health facilities. To keep essential drugs affordable, governments also have the responsibility to institute price control mechanisms and to subsidize the cost of essential drugs when necessary to make them affordable to patients who need them. Other specifically human rights elements include a mechanism for consulting all beneficiaries such as patients' organizations, rural communities and professionals in government, universities, and professional associations; mechanisms for transparency and accountability that use indicators and targets and specify the roles and responsibilities of the various stakeholders; mechanisms to assure equal access of the main vulnerable groups to essential medicines through ongoing monitoring based on disaggregated statistics, especially girls, women, children, people living in poverty, rural communities, indigenous communities, minorities, immigrants, the elderly, prisoners, and people with disabilities; and mechanisms for safeguards and redress of human rights violations (Hogerzeil 2006).

However, according to WHO, many lower- and middle-income countries lack the necessary infrastructure for an effective essential medicines program. One key element that is frequently missing is a regulatory system able to evaluate medicines (WHO 2008, para 8). Selection of products for procurement therefore can fail to comply with appropriate methods. There are poor linkages between national medicines lists, the medicines actually purchased and supplied, and those prescribed to patients (WHO 2008, 11). The infrastructure and human resources to support their medical supply systems are also generally neglected resulting in duplication, inefficiencies, and failures to provide and distribute the medicines (WHO 2008, para 10). WHO additionally identifies the frequent problem of counterfeit medical products that put human lives at risk and undermine the credibility of health systems (WHO 2008, para 12).

Inadequate financing by the government also contributes to the low availability of medicines in the public sector in many countries. The next chapter will discuss the more general problem of public underspending on health in many lower- and middle-income countries and how this inhibits access to health care. Here it is relevant to note that inadequate financing affects the provision of medicines. Average per capita spending on medicines in high-income countries can be 100-times higher than in low-income countries (Hunt and Khosla 2008, 99). According to WHO figures, national per capita spending on medicines by the public sector averages from $0.04 to $187.30 among poor- and middle-income countries.

Access, Availability, Prices, and Affordability of Essential Medicines

Access has been defined as having essential medicines continuously available and affordable at public or private health facilities or medicine outlets that are within one hour's walk from the homes of the population (United Nations Development Group, 2003). As noted above, GC 14 defined access to essential medicines as a core obligation. In addition, the 1978 Alma-Ata conference identified provision of essential medicines as one of the eight key components of primary health care (WHO/UNICEF 1978).

Being placed on a country's essential medicines list implies these medicines should be made available and affordable to all patients who need them, but in developing countries this often is not the case. Surveys and reports have documented an ongoing lack of availability of essential medicines in the public sector in poor- and lower-middle-income countries. In one survey of the twenty-seven developing countries for which data were available, average public sector availability was only 34.9 percent. (It is possible that some public sector facilities may not be expected to stock all the essential medicines on the list.) Since health facilities in the public sector generally provide medicines at lower cost, they play a critical role in providing access to medicines for the poor. When medicines are not available in the public sector, patients either have to purchase them in the private sector at a much higher cost or forego treatment (WHO n.d., 36).

Other surveys have also indicated similar trends. An analysis of adjusted data from forty-five surveys in thirty-six countries collected using the WHO/Health Action International methodology showed that the average availability of generic medicines in the public sector ranged from 29 percent in Africa to 54 percent in the Americas. Private sector availability of generics was an average of 50 percent. Originator brands were less available than generics in low-income countries (27 percent) and middle-income countries (44 percent) than upper-middle-income countries (62 percent). Moreover, patients in these countries often pay considerably higher prices than the baseline international reference price, even for generic medicines in the public sector. The median procurement prices for fifteen generics were one to eleven times the international reference price. (International reference prices are the average prices offered by not-for-profit companies to developing countries.) Private sector patients had to pay nine to twenty-five times the international reference price for the lowest priced generics and more than twenty times the international reference price for originator products (Cameron et al. 2009).

A 2009 report written by the MDG Gap Task Force cited data that showed that in the public sector generic medicines were only available in 38 percent of facilities surveyed and on average cost 250 percent more than the international reference price. In the private sector, those same medicines were available in nearly two-thirds of facilities (63 percent), but at a far higher cost – on average 610 percent of the international reference price (MDG Gap Task Force Report 2009, 51–55).

Affordability of essential medicines depends on a number of factors including the price of the medicines, the household income, and the regimen and duration of the treatment. The WHO sets its affordability benchmark for the pricing of medicines at one day's wages for the lowest paid government worker. However, many workers in these economies earn substantially less than this benchmark or are unemployed (MDG Gap Task Force Report 2012, 61–62). Prices often render essential medicines unaffordable, especially for chronic diseases requiring ongoing treatment.

For example, research on the cost of drugs in Malaysia essential to basic health care showed that these drugs have been priced out of the reach of the poor. An international team of researchers using the methodology developed by WHO and Health Action International collected price and availability data in twenty public hospitals, thirty-two private sector pharmacies, and twenty dispensing doctors' clinics in four regions of western Malaysia. It found that the availability of medicines was poor with only 25 percent of generic medicines obtainable on average through the public sector. The prices of both patented and generic drugs were on average considerably higher than international reference prices, ranging from 2.4 times the international reference price for innovator brands accessed through public hospitals to sixteen times the international reference price for innovator brands accessed through private pharmacies. Even more problematically, some dispensing doctors were selling generic drugs at 310 times their real cost (Babar et al. 2007). The prices for medicines in Malaysia were found to be higher than other middle-income countries, likely because the government allows market forces to determine drug prices. Another factor in Malaysia and other countries as well is that markups by wholesalers and retailers added to the cost. The country also fails to subsidize or cushion the cost of medicines for the poor (Babar et al. 2007). Similar problems with the cost of essential drugs exist elsewhere (MDG Gap Task Force Report 2012, 61–62).

The combination of the low availability and high prices of essential medicines contravenes human rights standards as well as the principles of the WHO essential medicines program. The need for governments to adopt systematic policies to lower the prices of essential medicines and increase their availability is central to their right to health obligations.

Many regulatory measures can help to reduce the prices of medicines, including abolishing tariffs and eliminating or at least significantly reducing taxes on medicines, controlling markups of prices, and facilitating the use of trade policy flexibilities. Developing local production capabilities, wherever possible, could also lower prices (MDG Gap Task Force Report 2013, 62-72). More will be said about trade policy flexibilities later in this chapter. Furthermore, in a poor country it may require providing free or deeply subsidized pharmaceuticals at least to those sectors of the population otherwise unable to afford them. The central government in India has considered providing free drugs at state-run hospitals (Bajaj 2012), but the government decided not to do so. Instead, the central government proposed that it would subsidize state governments willing to implement such a program. However, implementation at the state level is likely to be uneven and confined primarily to the more progressive states (Nagarajan 2015).

Intellectual Property Laws and Access to Medicines

Intellectual Property Law as an Impediment to Access to Medicines

Public health and human rights experts, including Anand Grover, have identified IP laws, particularly the global minimum standards established under the 1994 Agreement on TRIPS, as a significant impediment to greater access to medicines and as a major contributor to their high cost (Grover 2009; Grover 2011, para 7). Patents, the most common form of IP applied to pharmaceuticals, accord patent holders the right to exclude others from making, using, selling, offering to sell, or importing the patented invention into a country where it is protected. In recent years industrialized countries, led by the United States, have pushed for increased global protection of IP. The establishment of the World Trade

Organization (WTO) in 1994 and the coming into force of the TRIPS Agreement soon afterward have strengthened the global character of IP regimes. The TRIPS Agreement both sets mandatory minimum standards for national protection of IP and requires that patents be available for all "inventions" in all fields of technology if they are new, involve an inventive step, and are capable of industrial application (World Trade Organization 1994, art. 8). Membership in the WTO, which is linked with acceptance of the TRIPS Agreement, also makes countries subject to enforcement measures, including potential trade sanctions, for failure to comply with TRIPS standards.

Historically, IP law governing patents, copyrights, and trademarks was developed on a national basis, with considerable diversity in the nature and stringency of protections. In many countries, pharmaceuticals were exempted from IP protections. Patents, through which the state grants a monopoly to the inventor for a specified period of time, currently usually twenty years, in turn for the disclosure of the invention, had been applied to pharmaceutical products in some high-income countries prior to the formulation of the TRIPS Agreement, but it was rarely covered under the patent laws in lower- and middle-income countries. Prior to the adoption of TRIPS, approximately fifty countries did not have any form of patent protection for medicines, and in other cases, India for example, their laws permitted patents for the process involved in developing a pharmaceutical but not the product (Helfer and Austin 2011, 120). Despite their misgivings, a large number of developing countries eventually decided to join the WTO and thereby accept the TRIPS standards in the hopes of receiving trade concessions, to become more attractive for foreign investment, and to be eligible for potential technology transfers.

The pharmaceutical industry makes two primary justifications for stronger IP protections: first that IP provides an incentive to develop innovative drugs, and second, that IP encourages investment because it enables industry to recoup the funds it spends on research and development (Grabowski et al. 2015). However, strict IP standards do not necessarily equate with the development of innovative pharmaceuticals. Even though the number of patents awarded for pharmaceuticals in industrialized countries has increased in recent years, the number of truly innovative drugs has not. So few new molecular entities (compounds without precedents among approved drug products) have been launched each year and so few of the newly patented products offer a true therapeutic advance over existing products that some analysts have written about an innovation crisis (Gagnon 2013).

Moreover, whatever the situation in developed countries, patents do not stimulate innovation in or on behalf of poor countries because patents only work as incentives where profitable markets exist (Correa 2009, 270). The small market for medicines in developing countries, particularly the lower-income countries, is not viewed by companies as potentially profitable. The expert Commission on Intellectual Property Rights created by the UK Department for International Development concluded that patent protection hardly plays any role in stimulating research on diseases prevalent in developing countries, except for the diseases where there is also a substantial market in developed countries (Commission on Intellectual Property 2002, 13). Instead, "In countries lacking capital and required scientific and technological infrastructure, patents operate as a levy collection mechanism and not as a stimulus of local R&D" (Correa 2009, 272). It is therefore not surprising that between 1975 and 2004 only 21 of the 1556 new chemical entities marketed were targeted at poor country diseases like malaria and Biharzia (Malpani and Kamal-Yanni 2006).

Developing countries generally believe that it is not in their economic interest to implement stronger patent laws. Strict IP models appropriate for advanced market economies tend to disadvantage less developed countries because IP protection usually increases the cost of products, constrains product development, and restricts access (Grover 2009, para 23). Patented drugs tend to be considerably more expensive than their unpatented generic counterparts because the monopoly accorded to patent holders for production and use confers the freedom to price their products at arbitrary, often high levels that often put drugs beyond the means of the poor.

The evolution of the prices of patented ARVs provides an example. In 2000, the cost of treatment per patient per year for patented ARVs, then the only option, was more than U.S. $10,000. The next year Cipla, an Indian generic firm, made the same ARVs available for less than U.S. $400 per patient, and the prices of both the originator's and generic ARVs have continued to fall. Indian drug makers were able to produce generic versions of the ARVs because at the time India did not grant pharmaceutical product patents. However, as of January 1, 2005 India was required to become fully TRIPS compliant (Correa 2009, 272). Abiding by TRIPS standards will prevent Indian manufacturers from marketing generic forms of new patented medicines unless they do so with a license granted by the patent holder.

When the TRIPS Agreement was formulated, some low- and middle-income countries lobbied to have the agreement incorporate a number of flexibilities to mitigate the adverse impact of a strong patent regime on access to medicines, and the TRIPS Agreement does include a number of such provisions or flexibilities. Article 1 established the principle that member states can determine the appropriate method for implementing TRIPS within their own legal systems. Article 30 of the treaty authorizes "limited exceptions" to exclusive patent rights, provided that such exceptions do not unreasonably conflict with the normal exploitation of the patent (World Trade Organization 1994, art. 30). Some countries have used this exception, sometimes referred to as the Bolar provision, to allow the manufacturers of generic drugs utilize patented inventions before their expiration without the patent owner's permission to assist with applications for marketing approval so that their generic version can be marketed as soon as the patent expires (WTO 2006). Article 31 permits governments to issue compulsory licenses that authorize the use of a patented product or process without the owner's consent, but subject to the payment of adequate remuneration and numerous procedural requirements, such as prior efforts to negotiate with the patent owner for a voluntary license. This requirement may be waived in a national emergency, other circumstances of extreme urgency, or in cases of public noncommercial use (World Trade Organization 1994, art. 31.b). A related provision, article 31 (f) has the further qualification that uses under a compulsory license must be predominantly for the supply of the domestic market. This is problematic for countries with little or no local pharmaceutical manufacturing capacity, which therefore cannot produce generic drugs themselves (Helfer and Austin 2011, 123). Another provision permits countries to engage in the practice of parallel importing when a patented product is offered in another market at a lower cost (World Trade Organization 1994, art. 6). Additionally, article 27 allows member states to exclude certain categories of inventions from patentability whose commercial exploitation is considered to be detrimental to human life or health (World Trade Organization 1994, art. 27).

The TRIPS Agreement also granted developing countries the right to delay deadlines for implementation. Developing countries had until 2000, and those countries that did not previously grant product patent protection in certain areas of technology, such as pharmaceuticals, had an additional five years to comply with the TRIPS requirements in those areas (Grover 2009, 28). Least developed countries (a UN classification for the most economically impoverished countries with weak human assets) originally had until January 2006 to implement TRIPS. This deadline was then extended to July 2013 and then to 2021 or when the countries ceased to be in the least developed countries category (World Trade Organization 2013). The importance of the transition period is that the absence of product patents on medicines can help to establish local manufacturing capacity, promote generic manufacturing, and facilitate the import of affordable medicines from other countries (Grover 2009, 31). Many countries, however, do not take advantage of these options.

Under TRIPS governments also retain some discretion to tailor patent requirements to meet their public health needs. For example, by adopting a narrow definition of novelty they can exclude some medicines from patentability, such as additional uses of existing medicines (second-use patents) (Helfer and Austin 2011, 120). It is also possible to draft patent laws to prevent patent holders from making slight changes in their formulations and then receiving a new patent in order to extend their period of exclusivity (termed "evergreening" a patent). India has done so with some success.

The Doha Declaration

Few poor and middle-income countries have been able to take advantage of the TRIPS flexibilities described above. The requirements of applying the TRIPS flexibilities are complex and onerous, and many developing countries have lacked the requisite legal capability and appropriate laws. Additionally, multinational pharmaceutical corporations have sought to block initiatives to produce or import low-cost medicines in both developed and developing countries. Strategies have included suing competitors by claiming patent infringement and filing lawsuits against governments on the grounds that their laws violate World Trade Organization requirements. For example, when India incorporated strict patentability criteria in order to address the "evergreening" of patents, the pharmaceutical company Novartis challenged this public health safeguard in the Madras High Court alleging it was a violation of TRIPS. The provision was upheld as a fulfillment of the right to health obligations of the government (Grover 2009, para 60). When South Africa approved legislation in 1997 allowing importation of affordable medicines and increased use of quality generic drugs, thirty-nine multinational pharmaceutical companies sued and blocked implementation of the law for three years, initially with the tacit support of the U.S. government. In 2001, the case was dropped in the face of severe international condemnation (Forman 2008).

Despite the clear right of all WTO member countries to take advantage of the TRIPS flexibilities, the U.S. government has consistently expressed its displeasure whenever other governments have adopted measures to prioritize public health in ways that limit the IP rights of U.S. businesses, as for example, through engaging in compulsory licensing and parallel importation (Dutfield 2008, 115). European governments have also sometimes applied diplomatic pressure and threatened to impose trade sanctions or file complaints against the country in the WTO when countries have sought to apply TRIP flexibilities (Dutfield 2008; Malpani and Kamal-Yanni 2006). In 1996, when South Africa adopted a new National Drugs Policy to ensure an adequate and reliable supply of safe, cost-effective drugs of acceptable quality, the U.S. government placed South Africa on its Special 301 Watch List, which is a precursor to having trade sanctions imposed.

The United States and to a lesser extent the EU have also sought to counter the TRIPS flexibilities by negotiating a series of bilateral and multilateral trade agreements, sometimes referred to as TRIPS plus treaties, that impose more expansive and stringent IP protection rules than those in TRIPS in exchange for trade concessions. These agreements often require developing countries to implement TRIPS fully before the end of its specified transition periods, or require such countries to conform to the requirements of other multilateral IP agreements (Helfer and Austin 2011, 40).

As new threats to public health emerged, particularly the global HIV/AIDS crisis, it became increasingly important to address the detrimental effect of the TRIPS Agreement on access to affordable medicines. Developing countries' trade representatives, supported by widespread public outrage, insisted that the public health consequences of TRIPS should be addressed as part of a development round negotiation of new trade rules scheduled to be launched in Doha in 2001. These efforts produced the Doha Declaration on TRIPS and Public Health, which affirms that the flexibilities of the TRIPS Agreement "can and should be interpreted and implemented in a manner supportive of WTO Members' right to protect public health and, in particular, to promote access to medicines for all" (World Trade Organization 2001, para 4). It also acknowledges the right of all countries to issue compulsory licenses to produce low-cost drugs in national health emergencies and for those countries to be able to determine when they have need for doing so.

The Doha Declaration additionally instructed WTO members to find a solution for countries with insufficient generic manufacturing capacity to take advantage of the right to issue compulsory licenses to produce affordable medicines in national health emergencies. In 2003, the TRIPS Council waived the domestic use requirement for compulsory licenses,

and in 2005 it made the waiver permanent by adopting a formal amendment to TRIPS that will become effective when ratified by two-thirds of the
WTO's member states. However, the waiver is subject to complex procedures and notification rules that make it difficult to use (Helfer and Austin
2011, 123–124). Moreover, thus far only a few countries have enacted
legislation to implement the WTO decision as potential exporters under
compulsory license to countries without manufacturing capacity: Canada,
China, Norway, India, the Netherlands, and Iceland. As of 2011 the system
had only been used in one case, the supply of an ARV from Canada to
Rwanda (Correa and Matthews 2011, 22).

Applications of TRIPS Flexibilities

A number of countries have incorporated provisions in their legislation
to facilitate using TRIPS flexibilities. Countries that have been able and
willing to use the TRIPS flexibilities to produce generics despite existing patent protection and/or engage in compulsory licensing and parallel importation have sometimes made dramatic breakthroughs in health
care policy. Brazil became a model in the fight against HIV/AIDS because
of the government's decision to produce generic AIDS medicines and distribute them to patients free of charge or at a subsidized rate. The Brazilian
government has threatened to issue compulsory license for overpriced
ARVs and thereby managed to lower their price, and when that strategy
has been unsuccessful, it has issued compulsory licenses.

Under their respective patent laws, India and the Philippines seek to
prevent the practice of "evergreening" by excluding new forms of known
substances unless they are significantly more efficacious, as well as excluding new (or second) uses and combinations of known substances (Grover
2009, para 35). In a 2013 case, India's top court dismissed Swiss drug
maker Novartis AG's attempt to win patent protection for its cancer drug
Gleevac. Ruling on the basis of the provision to exclude "evergreening," the
Supreme Court decided that Gleevac did not satisfy a patent's "novelty"
requirements. Pfizer's cancer drug Sutent and Roche's hepatitus C treatment Pegaxyx also lost their patented status in India in 2012 on similar
grounds (Kulkarni and Mohanty 2013).

The 2001 Kenyan Industrial Property Act contains provisions on compulsory licenses, research exceptions, and parallel importation, intended
to protect the public health system in Kenya (Oke 2013, 101). However,
the Kenyan Anti-Counterfeit Act of 2008 undermined implementation by
categorizing generics as counterfeit. In a 2012 case before the Kenyan High

Court, the petitioners, who were HIV/AIDS patients, alleged that certain sections of the Kenyan Anti-Counterfeit Act of 2008 threatened their access to essential generic drugs, thereby infringing their rights to life, dignity, and health. The UN Special Rapporteur on the right to health, Anand Grover, filed an *amicus* brief in which he agreed with the contention that the manner in which this Act was framed conflated the definition of counterfeit drugs and generic drugs. The High Court's decision, which referred both to the Kenyan Constitution, which guarantees the right to health, and General Comment 14 on the right to health, concurred with the position of the petitioners stating that the right to life, dignity, and health must take priority over IP rights when the latter could endanger the right to health (Oke 2013, 101).

Limitations of the Flexibilities in TRIPS and the Doha Agreement

Although many commentators and NGOs initially hailed the Doha Agreement as a major breakthrough for access to medicines, recent analyses have been more tempered. A paper written for UNDP concludes that the Doha Declaration does not seem to have triggered a significant increase in the use of TRIPS flexibilities to increase access to medicine (Correa and Matthews 2011, 20). A database compiled in 2012 of trends in the compulsory licensing of pharmaceuticals identified only twenty-four verified compulsory licenses initiated in seventeen countries. Most compulsory licenses were issued between 2003 and 2005, involved drugs for HIV/AIDS, and occurred in upper-middle-income countries. None occurred in least-developed or low-income countries. Compulsory licensing activity has diminished markedly since 2006 reflecting the increased number of signatory countries to TRIPS-plus Agreements with provisions blocking the use of compulsory licenses. In light of the considerable countervailing pressures against compulsory licensing and the TRIPS-plus provisions in regional and bilateral trade agreements, the authors of the study concluded that there is a low probability of continued compulsory license activity (Beall and Kuhn 2012). A second list of selected voluntary licensing agreements whereby the patent holder has given a specific country the right to produce a medicine under license, usually through the Medicines Patent Pool Foundation[2] created with the support of UNITAID in 2010,

---

[2] The Medicine Patent Pool aims to increase access to appropriate HIV medicines at an affordable price to treat patients with HIV living in developing countries.

has fourteen examples provided by nine different companies, mostly for HIV treatment (MDG Task Force Report 2013, 66, 68).

Carlos Correa and Duncan Matthews attribute the small impact of the Doha Declaration to a number of factors. First, many countries prematurely changed their patent laws to the TRIPS standards before the end of the transition period for developing countries and before fully recognizing the impact doing so would have on access to medicines. Most countries have also been reluctant to review adopted legislation to incorporate additional flexibilities. India, the Philippines, and China have been the exceptions. Second, a significant number of developing countries have entered into free trade agreements and other bilateral agreements that incorporate Trips-plus provisions that affect access to medicines. These agreements typically include extension of patent terms to compensate for delays in the examination of a patent application, requirements that prevent the marketing approval of generic versions of a medicine when patents relating to it exist, requirements to grant patents for second indications of pharmaceuticals, and enhanced enforcement provisions, as for example, allowing custom authorities to seize goods on suspicion of infringement of a patent in cases of importation or exportation. Third, some developing countries (not involved in free trade agreements) have not received appropriate technical assistance and capacity-building to be able to fully understand and incorporate TRIPS flexibilities (Correa and Matthews 2011, 20–21).

Also relevant to understanding the small impact of the Doha Agreement, the United States and the EU have continued their bullying tactics to discourage countries from using TRIPS flexibilities. For example, in 2007, after Thailand issued compulsory licenses for HIV and heart disease medicine to meet its human rights obligations to provide universal access to medicines, it too was placed on the U.S. Special 301 Priority Watch List (Grover 2009, paras 57 and 58), and the EU Trade Commissioner sent a letter to the Minister of Commerce of Thailand claiming that the TRIPS Agreement did not justify a systematic policy of applying for compulsory licenses whenever medicines exceed certain prices (Grover 2009, footnote 60). The United States and EU have also continued to promote trade agreements with TRIPS-plus provisions. The recently concluded Trans-Pacific Partnership Agreement, which involves twelve countries including the United States, Canada, Japan, Australia, and eight middle-income countries, contains particularly stringent limitations on the ability of governments to balance IP enforcement with the public interest (UNITAID 2014).

Other analysts have identified additional factors. Many countries continue to be stymied by deficient administrative, legal, and regulatory capacity as well as by the restrictions of their trade agreements. Local production, particularly in low-income countries, still confronts a number of obstacles, including lack of infrastructure, lack of qualified human resources, lack of appropriate raw materials, and the small size of the potential market in many countries. Pharmaceutical companies continue to use multiple strategies to block entry of affordable generic medicines, such as the filing of numerous patent applications for the same medicine and seeking to extend the life of a patent by making a small change in the original patented molecule. Countries have failed to incorporate TRIPS flexibilities into country laws on IP, have done so very inadequately, or lack the human and financial resources to ensure the flexibilities are actually used. Many of these countries also lack an adequate system to examine patents so as to determine which should be allowed. High-income countries also undermine implementation of the TRIPS flexibilities by working for harmonization of the process of examining patent applications in order to impose their standards of patent examination on the rest of the world (Malpani and Kamal-Yanni 2006; Dutfied 2008; Global Health Watch 2014, 288–295). Also important, through years of technical assistance and programs of cooperation to patent offices in developing countries, the three leading global patent offices in the United States, EU, and Japan have also promoted a pro-patenting perspective in them (Drahos 2008).

The Cost of Medicines

Patents contribute to high drug prices. Conferring market exclusivity to the patent holder for up to twenty years gives pharmaceutical companies free reign to price their medicines as high as they think the market can bear. Escalating prices, particularly for newer drugs but also even for some generic medicines, has made many medicines increasingly unaffordable both for governments and for patients. High drug costs are also a central reason for patients' nonadherence to appropriate treatment regimes with essential medicines (Gagne and Choudhry 2011, 711).

Price tags for drugs entering the U.S. market are particularly high, particularly for newer medicines and specialty drugs, because of U.S. government policies to leave pricing to the market and refrain from negotiating drug prices, imposing price controls, or engaging in bulk purchasing of drugs even for federally funded programs like Medicare. A *New York Times* editorial critical of runaway drug prices indicated that the list price of one year's supply of Kalydeco, a cystic fibrosis drug, is $311,000. A standard course of treatment with Blincyto, a leukemia drug, is about $178,000 (The Editorial Board 2015). Newer cancer drugs average more than $100,000 per year. A 2013 editorial in the journal *Blood* castigating drug makers for promoting an unsustainable pricing strategy and highlighting the plight of a growing cadre of leukemia patients who can no longer afford to pay for their treatments was signed by over 100 leading cancer specialists from more than fifteen countries (Editorial 2013). Even generic drug prices are soaring. Some of the low-cost generic drugs that helped restrain health care costs for decades are experiencing unexpected price hikes of up to 8,000 percent (Perrone 2014). Moreover, the arbitrariness of these prices is shown by the fact that a drug can cost $200 one day and more than $1,300 the next

The high prices of medicines impose serious financial pressure on health systems. On average, current pharmaceutical expenditures in lower- and middle-income countries account for more than a quarter of total health expenditures (30 percent in low-income countries and 28 percent in lower middle-income countries), with some countries devoting up to two-thirds of their health expenditures on pharmaceuticals (Bigdeli et al. 2014, 33). The figures for high-income countries are somewhat lower. United States spending on prescription drugs accounts for a tenth of the country's total health spending, and if over-the-counter medicines were also calculated it would be higher (The Editorial Board 2015). In Europe, the spending on pharmaceuticals in 2010 ranged from 10 percent in the Netherlands to 19 percent in Spain (Ruggeri and Nolte 2013, 22). High expenditures on medicines in some situations can threaten the sustainability of a country's health system. It did so in Ghana when in 2008, three years following the implementation of the National Health Insurance Scheme, spending on medicines consumed nearly half of the scheme's expenditures (Bigdeli et al. 2014, 33). It has also been reported that the high price of medicines in the United States is straining the budgets of federal programs like Medicare and Medicaid and the budgets of many states (The Editorial Board 2015).

Unfortunately, in low- and middle-income countries, where people can least afford to pay for medicines, 50 to 90 percent of the cost is borne by the patient (Grover 2011, para 5). In comparison, in many high-income countries, at least until recently, over 70 percent of the cost of medicines has been publicly funded. Where the cost of medicines is borne by patients and their families it can further impoverish already disadvantaged populations and block equitable access to medicines (Hunt and Khosla 2008, 107).

But even in high-income countries, paying in full for medicines or meeting the co-payments on expensive pharmaceuticals can bankrupt patients and their families. Data indicate that in 2014 out-of-pocket spending on drugs in developed countries ranged from a low of U.S. $295 in Denmark to U.S. $718 in Japan and U.S. $1010 in the United States, and these figures do not include medicines not purchased because of their high cost (Mossialos et al. 2015, p. 7). Covering co-payments for high priced drugs can be devastating. In the United States, for example, around half of all insured patients are now responsible for 30 percent of their drugs' costs through co-payments. As an editorial in *Nature Biotechnology* commented, 30 percent of a single $100,000 drug is a crippling burden, made even more unsustainable because many patients take more than one drug (Editorial 2013).

How government programs, private insurers, and individuals will be able to pay the costs of new Hepatitis C medicines provides a case in point of the dilemmas high cost wonder drugs raise. Hepatitis C, the most common blood borne infection in the United States, which affects 130 to 150 million people worldwide, is a chronic disease that can lead to serious liver problems including cirrhosis (scarring) of the liver, liver cancers, and liver failure (Media Centre 2014). Three newly developed medications, Gilead Science's Sovaldi and Harvoni and AbbVie's Vikeira Pak, are highly effective in treating Hepatitis C and can cure most cases in twelve weeks with few side effects. As noted earlier in the chapter, WHO recently placed the new Hepatitis C drugs on its essential medicines list making provision of these drugs a right to health obligation. However, at their list price the drugs cost between U.S. $84,000 and U.S. $95,000 per patient plus the additional cost of the medicines taken along with them. In the United States, it is estimated that about 5 million people suffer from Hepatitis C, many of whom are poor and eligible for Medicare or in the prison population, whose medical needs are also covered by state governments. Projections are that full coverage of this population would cost state governments collectively more than $55 billion per year and overwhelm state budgets. As a consequence, states are rationing access and limiting eligibility to the sickest patients (Ollove 2014; Silverman 2014). Private insurance companies appear to be doing the same. Although Gilead is offering Sovaldi at discounted rates in Europe and in many developing countries, the price is still far too high to make it widely accessible.

Pharmaceutical companies try to justify their high prices by claiming that research to discover and develop new medicines entails high costs and high risks. PhRMA, the U.S. pharmaceutical trade association, claimed the average cost of new drug development was $1.32 billion in 2006 (cited in Light and Warburton 2011, 3). Another estimate done in 2003 at the Tufts Center for the Study of Drug Development in Boston, an institution that has received substantial industry funding, using proprietary data submitted by drug companies, was $802 million per drug (cited in Light and Warburton 2011, 3). However, an analysis has taken issue with the sampling and the methodologies used in arriving at these figures.[3] After correcting for these errors and using data based on independent sources, Donald Light and Rebecca Warburton concluded that research and development cost companies a median of only $43.4 million per new drug (Light and Warburton 2011).

Government involvement to negotiate and control pharmaceutical pricing practices is essential to achieve public health and human rights objectives. Most European countries employ some form of direct price controls for reimbursable medicines whose costs are covered by pubic payers either fully or partially. Price controls involve setting a fixed maximum price for a medicinal product. Governments also use other measures to lower the price, such as price negotiation, bulk purchasing, or public procurement at a fixed price (Ruggeri and Nolte 2013). Price differentials between the United States and European countries attest to the ability of these policies to lower costs. As an example, prices of multiple sclerosis drugs available in the United States are two to three times greater than the list prices in Canada, Australia, or Britain (The Editorial Board 2015).

The Role and Responsibility of the Pharmaceutical Industry

In the human rights paradigm, states/governments have the obligation to regulate private sector actors to encourage them to act consistently with human rights norms and to prevent them from committing human rights violations, but in the case of the major pharmaceutical corporations, their influence and power from their size, assets, and profits make it difficult

---

[3] The methodological issues cited in Light and Warburton, 2011, include particularly the inclusion of the "cost of capital," that is, the costs of returns from funds that would have been invested in the stock market were the research and development not undertaken, the failure to take tax breaks into account, the inflation of trial costs, and the exaggerated length of time included for preclinical research and clinical trials.

to do so. The total level of pharmaceutical revenues worldwide is nearly one trillion U.S. dollars (Statistica 2015). It has been estimated that the collective worth of the world's top five drug companies is twice the combined gross national product of all sub-Saharan African states. Moreover, pharmaceutical profits, whether calculated as a percentage of assets or a percentage of revenues, are among the highest of any commercial sector (Global Health Watch 2009). To protect these profits, the companies seek to bring their wealth to bear to influence the levers of Western power.

As the transnational pharmaceutical companies have grown in economic power and political influence, the international human rights community has become increasingly concerned about the disparities between the industry's level of profits and influence on the one side and its failure to contribute more to social benefit and public health. Their critique of the industry intensified when the TRIPS Agreement, whose provisions were influenced by the intensive lobbying by some of these companies, resulted in the inability of millions of people infected with HIV and AIDS to be able to access expensive ARV medicines protected under TRIPS rules (Forman and Kohler 2012b, 8). Subsequently, efforts by developing countries' governments to reduce the price of these drugs by allowing for generic substitution or using parallel importation of the drugs from countries where their prices were lower encountered strong resistance both from the multinational corporate patent holders and the host countries of these corporations (Alkoby 2012, 54). Public interest groups have criticized pharmaceutical companies for setting prices too high and thereby blocking access to lifesaving medicines, imbalanced research and development priorities, petitioning for stricter IP standards such as the TRIPS plus agreements that eliminate the flexibilities in TRIPS and the Doha Agreement, inappropriate drug promotion, problematic clinical trials, and other practices that are viewed as obstructing states' ability to discharge right to health responsibilities (Hunt and Khosla 2008, 109).

Over time, concerns in the human rights community have translated into increasing calls for state regulation of the corporations, something that is difficult to effectively achieve given the disparity in resources and power between governments in poor- and middle-income countries and these companies and the tendency of the governments in the United States and Europe, with greater resources and power, to support the industry rather than accord primacy to the public interest in increasing access to affordable medicines. It has also engendered a debate about the human rights responsibilities of these corporations (Forman and Kohler 2012b, 5). General Comment 14, while recognizing that only states are parties to the

ICESCR and thus legally bound by its provisions, also asserts that all members of society, including the private business sector, have responsibilities for the realization of the right to health (CESCR 2000, para 42).

The claim that corporations have "hard" or binding obligations under international human rights law is controversial because, at least as originally formulated, international human rights law does not directly apply to nonstate actors. John Ruggie, when he served as the UN Secretary-General's special representative relating to human rights and corporations, took the position that no binding international law presently placed duties on corporations. His later reports nonetheless stated that corporations do hold duties to respect human rights and not infringe on the rights of others (Forman and Kohler 2012, 6–7). When the issue of their human rights responsibilities is raised, corporations have tended to argue that their primary or sole responsibility is to their shareholders. Corporations also cite the contributions they make to human welfare through the development of new medicines. While human rights advocates, as for example, Patricia Illingworth, acknowledge that pharmaceutical corporations have an obligation to shareholders, they also believe that this obligation does not exempt them from a special duty to provide aid to further the right to essential medicines of people in the developing world. She justifies her position by virtue of the moral character of health care needs, health as a human right, and the unique capacity of pharmaceutical companies to render aid (Illingworth 2012).

Discussions in a variety of forums have given rise to a proliferation of "soft" (nonbinding) codes of corporate conduct, some written by the companies themselves and others, like the United Nations Global Compact, that are the outcome of multilateral negotiations. The Global Compact is a UN initiative to encourage businesses to adopt socially responsible policies, including respect for human rights, and to report on their implementation. The UN reports there are over 8,000 corporate participants in the Global Compact (United Nations Global Compact Homepage, 2015).

When Paul Hunt was the Special Rapporteur for the right to medicine, he undertook the most comprehensive and significant of the initiatives to develop a code outlining the human rights responsibilities of pharmaceutical corporations. The Human Rights Guidelines for Pharmaceutical Companies in Relation to Access to Medicines were published by the UN in 2008 after a process that included consultations with representatives of pharmaceutical corporations, the WHO, investor groups, and the International Federation of Pharmaceutical Manufacturers and Associations, as well as various UN agencies, academics, and civil society groups. The pharmaceutical sector also had an opportunity to comment on a draft of the guidelines, and several did so (Hunt 2008; Khosla and Hunt 2012, 29–30).

The guidelines begin from the premise that while states have the primary responsibility to enhance access to medicine this is a shared responsibility. Moreover, by virtue of being granted a monopoly power through the granting of patents, pharmaceutical companies have certain social responsibilities, among them the human rights responsibility to make medicines available and accessible. Hence the guidelines call for formal, express recognition of the importance of human rights and the right to health as a firm foundation of the company's policies and activities on access to medicine. Some of the guidelines refer to human rights standards like equality and nondiscrimination and the importance of transparency and accountability and their relevance to the activities of pharmaceutical companies. To that end, the guidelines encompass items for broad disclosure on policies regarding pricing and discount arrangements, the quantity and value of drug donations along with the tax exemptions arising from the donations, and for lobbying and advocacy at the regional, national, and international levels that impact on access to medicines. Others deal with the adoption of socially responsible policies that some corporations already claim they have adopted in their reports, but in contrast with the current self-monitoring and reporting, the guidelines call for an external monitoring mechanism independent of the companies. The guidelines require that companies should make a public commitment to contribute to research and development for neglected diseases through either in-house research and development or by supporting research and development by other agencies. On the important issue of patents and licensing, the guidelines aim to ensure that companies do not interfere with TRIPS flexibilities and respect the right of countries to use TRIPS provisions for compulsory licensing and parallel importing for the purpose of promoting access to medicines. The guidelines further commit corporations to stop lobbying for IP standards stricter than the protections in the TRIPS Agreement. Additionally, the guidelines have a provision that companies should not apply for patents in low- or middle-income countries on trivial modifications of existing medicines (Hunt 2008, Khosla and Hunt 2012).

Unsurprisingly, the guidelines failed to obtain support from the industry. In their response to the guidelines, several companies did acknowledge a responsibility to respect and protect at least the health of their employees but rejected having a societal mandate to care for the sick (PLoS Medicine Editors 2010). The Merck Vice President for

Global Health Policy and Corporate Responsibility did concede that pharmaceutical corporations have a subsidiary role to play in promoting public health. However, she claimed that Merck was already doing so through its core capability of researching, developing, and producing medicines and vaccines to address unmet needs and in helping in their distribution. She also pointed to the contributions Merck and other pharmaceutical corporations were already making to help foster access to medicines in emerging and least developed countries, such as implementing innovative differential pricing frameworks that reflect levels of economic development and disease burden and granting voluntary licenses to generic companies to improve access to selective medicines in resource-limited settings (Ritter 2010).

When a UN sponsored expert consultation on access to medicines as a fundamental component of the right to health was held in 2010 pursuant to a Human Rights Council resolution on that subject, none of the pharmaceutical companies invited opted to participate. One corporation, Novartis, did submit a letter in which it regretted not being available (Grover 2011, para 2).

Nevertheless, in recent years, some pharmaceutical corporations have become more responsive to the need to address the gap in access to medicines in developing countries. The Access to Medicines Index, an independent initiative funded by the Gates Foundation, tracks the efforts of the twenty leading pharmaceutical companies to provide access to medicines, vaccines, and technologies for preventing, diagnosing, and treating disease in 103 countries. Its 2014 edition reports that these companies are doing somewhat more to improve access to medicine in developing countries and identifies 327 potentially relevant products in the drug pipeline. Another of its key findings is that more companies are paying attention to socioeconomic factors, such as people's ability to pay, by tailoring their prices between countries and within countries. However, the report also acknowledges that progress is uneven in terms of what individual companies have accomplished. Five of the top twenty companies account for more than half the drugs in the pipeline, and more than half the new products target only five diseases: lower respiratory infections, diabetes, hepatitis, HIV/AIDS, and malaria. All of these, with the exception of malaria, also have markets in upper-income countries. Importantly, company support for pro-access IP law modification is very limited, and private lobbying continues against flexibilities in the TRIPS agreement. While pro-access licensing agreements that facilitate the entry of generic versions of their products are increasing in number,

the overwhelming majority of licenses are still only for HIV/AIDS products. Furthermore, claims of commitment to ethical behavior do not
necessarily correlate with performance. All of the top twenty companies have codes of conduct governing bribery and corruption, but in the
two-year period preceding the 2014 Access to Medicines report, eighteen of the companies were the subject of settlements or fines for corrupt
behavior, unethical marketing, or breaches of competition law (Access
to Medicines Foundation 2014, 10–13).

Public Interest Advocacy and Mobilization

The human rights community has been part of a coalition of public interest groups seeking to change public policies to improve access to medicines. One view of these initiatives is that public advocacy and action on
pharmaceuticals have been effective in bringing attention to these issues
and influencing agenda-setting, but it has had a more limited role in
influencing solutions through changes in global policies (Koivusalo and
Mackintosh 2009). Others stress the role of various civil society groups in
the AIDS activism, which helped to facilitate access to generic versions of
patented medicines on a large scale: "New approaches to achieving innovation and access to medicines are possible today because of the previous
decade of activism that demanded a change in the way we approach intellectual property and public health. The political and civil society mobilization catalyzed by HIV/AIDS was at the forefront of these changes" (Hoen
et al. 2011).

To briefly review these initiatives, until the late 1990s the potential effect
of TRIPS on access to medicines was little understood, and there was not
much interest in IP issues among the public health or human rights communities. The 1998 lawsuit of forty-one drug companies to try to block the
South African government's Medicine Act, which aimed to make low-cost
medicines more readily available in that country, mentioned earlier in this
chapter, brought these issues to their attention. "Big Pharma vs. Nelson
Mandela shocked the world's conscience. It was a call to action that pulled
many different actors onto the stage" (Hoen et al. 2011). A global campaign against the lawsuit conveyed the message that efforts by the pharmaceutical companies to protect their profits meant that people with AIDS
in developing countries would die. It was highly successful in garnering
publicity and collecting signatures on a petition. Faced with a public relations disaster, pharmaceutical companies withdrew their case (Alkoby
2012, 56).

In 1999, a group of NGOs and AIDS activists held a conference at the UN in Geneva to discuss how flexibilities in IP law, such as compulsory licensing, could be used to increase the availability of low-cost generic medicines for HIV/AIDS in the developing world.

Opposition to TRIPS first became publicly visible in 1999 in the street protests during the WTO Seattle Ministerial Conference. After Seattle activists attracted support from the UN Development Programme, the WHO called upon governments to ensure access to essential medicines and to review institutional arrangements impeding access to essential medicines. Also of note, in 2001, the Indian generic medicines producer Cipla first offered a triple-combination of generic ARVs at the much reduced price of $350 per patient per year, thus highlighting the much higher cost of patented medicines (Hoen et al. 2011).

In contrast with the strong involvement of business networks, human rights activists were not given a voice in the WTO during the Doha Declaration negotiations (Alkoby 2012, 58). Nevertheless, the public interest campaign preceding the event likely contributed indirectly to the affirmation in the Doha text that "The TRIPS agreement does not and should not prevent Members from taking measures to protect public health" (World Trade Organization 2001). Since Doha, activists networks have continued a sporadic attack on IP norms, IP producing countries, pharmaceutical companies, and sometimes the WTO as illegitimate through acts of shaming and social sanctioning of states (Alkoby 2012 58–59).

South Africa's Treatment Action Campaign (TAC) comprises a landmark movement in which human rights and civil society groups succeeded in changing public policy to improve access to medicines, in this case for HIV/AIDS sufferers. Although South Africa is one of the countries most affected by the HIV/AIDS epidemic and the South African constitution recognizes the right to access health care, the administration of President Thabo Mbeki refused to make ARV treatment available in public health facilities. In 1998, a nongovernmental human rights organization, the TAC, launched a campaign to secure the right of access to treatment for AIDS and to lower the costs of ARVs through a combination of protests, mobilization, and legal action. Initially it demanded that the South African government introduce a national program to prevent mother-to-child HIV transmission. The TAC also argued that the excessive pricing of essential medicines by multinational pharmaceutical companies violated a range of rights entrenched in the South African constitution. Working closely with progressive lawyers, the TAC also filed a series of legal cases that went up through the judicial system to the

Constitutional Court, which resulted in judgments supporting the TAC's claims. And when the government refused to implement the judgments, the TAC mobilized its supporters, many of whom were AIDS patients, and conducted a series of marches, rallies, and media events. Unlike academics or human rights advocates who take up human rights issues out of conscience, the TAC sought to build a people's movement and through its education and mobilization succeeded in galvanizing a social movement made up of people who were predominantly poor, black, and living with HIV (Heywood 2009).

Overall, however, the public advocacy activities of the human rights community have been dwarfed by the role of Médecins Sans Frontières (MSF). In 1999, after being awarded a Nobel Peace Prize in recognition of its pioneering humanitarian work across several continents, MSF launched a medicines access campaign to push for access to and the development of life saving and life prolonging medicines, diagnostic tests, and vaccines. This ongoing campaign has worked along a variety of tracks: (1) to challenge the high cost of existing drugs, such as those used to treat HIV/AIDS, and work to reduce the costs; (2) to stimulate research into new medicines for neglected diseases; and (3) to develop newer and simpler models of care. MSF has had successes on all three dimensions of its access campaign that have reflected its persistence, resources, medical knowledge and expertise, and credibility. Notably, it was prominent in the development of large-scale treatment programs for HIV/AIDS with lower-cost ARVs. It also cofounded the Drugs for Neglected Diseases initiative and proposed the creation of a medicines patent pool, which was officially established in 2010 as a UN-supported organization to improve access to appropriate, affordable HIV medicines and technologies for people in developing countries (MSF 2015).

International Obligations

General Comment 14 delineates a series of international obligations relevant to the availability of medicines. As in the International Covenant on Economic, Social and Cultural Rights and its earlier General Comment No. 3, the Committee drew attention to the obligation of states parties to recognize the essential role of international cooperation and comply with their commitment to take joint and separate action to achieve the full realization of the right to health in resource-deprived countries (CESCR 2000, Para 38). GC 14 also underscores that to comply with their international obligations state parties have to respect the enjoyment of the right to health in other countries in a variety of ways and prevent third parties from violating the right in other countries when they are able to influence these third parties through legal or political means. It identifies the need for those states with the resources to do so to facilitate access to essential health facilities, goods, and services in other countries whenever possible and to ensure the right to health is given due attention in international agreements (CESCR 2000, para 39). According to GC 14, states also have joint and individual responsibilities to cooperate in providing disaster relief and humanitarian assistance in times of emergency (CESCR 2000, para 40).

How should the performance of developed countries in fulfilling these obligations be evaluated? On the one hand, the United States and several of the European governments have contributed considerable funds to support health programs in resource deprived countries, some of which has gone to support the availability of medicines, through bilateral and multilateral aid programs. High-income countries have also played an important role in bringing about new financing mechanisms for medicines, particularly for AIDS, tuberculosis, and malaria, such as the Global Fund, PEPFAR (The U.S. President's Emergency Plan for AIDS Relief), and UNITAID, which have played an important role in increasing access to medicines, and have contributed large sums of money to fund these organizations. The Global Fund to Fight AIDS, Tuberculosis, and Malaria invests nearly U.S. $4 billion each year, 95 percent of it donated by developed countries' governments, in programs run by local experts in the countries most in need. The United States is the top donor ahead of France, the United Kingdom, Germany, Japan, and the European Community (Global Fund website 2015). As of September 30, 2014, PEPFAR reports it was supporting life-saving ARV treatment for 7.7 million persons worldwide and funding HIV testing and counseling for more than 14 million women (PEPFAR website 2015). The U.S. National Institutes of Health also sponsors a long-standing program of research devoted to better understanding, treating, and preventing neglected tropical diseases including support for the discovery and development of drugs for these diseases (National Institute of Allergy and Infectious Diseases website 2015).

That said, the level of this development assistance falls considerably short of the 0.7 percent of the gross national income developed countries committed to provide in 1970 at the UN General Assembly. Few countries, other than Denmark, Norway, Sweden, and the Netherlands, are reaching that goal. The United States, often the largest donor in terms of the dollar amount of foreign aid provided, ranks among the lowest in the percentage of its gross national income devoted to foreign assistance. Moreover, critics claim that aid systems often fail to benefit their recipients because the programs are based on the interests of donors instead of the needs of recipients; too little aid reaches the countries that need it most; and all too often much of this aid is wasted because recipients must use overpriced goods and services from donor countries. They also point out that the inflow of international aid is often much less than the outflow from developing countries as a result of their trade deficit, primarily with developed countries (Shah 2014).

Moreover, many of the most promising initiatives to improve access to medicines come from nongovernmental organizations, foundations, and philanthropic organizations and not through official governmental channels. The Bill and Melinda Gates Foundation has made some $33 billion in grants since its inception in 2000, a significant portion of which went to initiatives related to developing medicines for neglected diseases or increasing access to medicines in developing countries. Its nearly $4 billion in grants in 2014 included $1.5 billion to the GAVI Alliance, which seeks to improve access to new and underused vaccines for children in the poorest countries, and $456 million to the Path Malaria Vaccine Initiative to accelerate malaria vaccine development (Bill and Melinda Gates Foundation website 2015). The Global Fund to Fight AIDS, Tuberculosis, and Malaria, which is a public-private partnership, invests nearly U.S. $4 billion per year to support programs run by local experts to improve access to treatments in the countries most in need (The Global Fund website 2015). UNITAID is an international drug purchasing facility supported by a north/south membership, which is funded by a small levy on airline tickets and contributions of governments and the Gates Foundation. It negotiates reductions in purchasing prices with manufacturers and then distributes the drugs. It currently funds projects in ninety-four countries (UNITAID website 2015). The Global Vaccine Initiative (GAVI) links public and private initiatives in the shared goal of creating equal access to new and underused vaccines by children living in the poorest countries (GAVI website 2015). The Drugs for Neglected Diseases initiative is a patient-driven, nonprofit research and development organization. Set up in 2003 by Médecine Sans Frontières, by 2015 it had six new treatments for neglected diseases in preclinical and clinical development (Drugs for Neglected Diseases initiative website 2015).

In assessing whether high-income countries are fulfilling their international human rights obligations, the various ways in which the policies of key powerful countries, particularly the United States, constitute an impediment to the realization of the right of access to medicines should be taken into account. Their strong support for the strict IP system benefits drug companies at the expense of the public welfare in low- and middle-income countries, and the population of their own countries as well. The United States in particular threatens to use trade sanctions and actively promotes free trade pacts that impose TRIPS-plus requirements on countries that preclude the use of the flexibilities in the TRIPS Agreement. High medicine prices resulting from the monopoly prices charged by pharmaceutical companies for patent-protected medicines often make medicines unaffordable particularly in developing countries. However, while U.S. policies clearly violate the right to medicines, it is important to remember that the United States is not a state party to the ICESCR. Nor does it recognize the right to health as a binding obligation. However, it could be argued that the obligation to not violate internationally recognized human rights law derives from customary international law and from the human rights requirements in other international human rights instruments that the United States has ratified and which have some health provisions, as for example, the International Convention on the Elimination of All Forms of Racial Discrimination (1969). Moreover, political policies that harm the health of billions of people worldwide so as to secure greater profits for a few corporations constitute an egregious ethical violation.

Concluding Reflections

Access to appropriate medicines, particularly essential medicines that are financially affordable, of good quality, and physically available in sufficient quantities to everyone on a nondiscriminatory basis is a central component of the right to health. However, as noted in this chapter, some two billion people, one-third of the world's population, most of whom live in low- and middle-income countries, lack access to the medicines necessary for their health care, and there has been little improvement in the availability and affordability of medicines in developing countries in recent years (MDG Gap Task Force Report 2012, xvi). Many people in industrialized countries also cannot afford life-saving but costly drugs, particularly in those countries that do not underwrite drug costs through universal insurance coverage or other types of health entitlements or have high co-payment requirements. As a consequence, individuals across the globe are afflicted by, and many also die from, diseases that are preventable or curable because they cannot gain access to and/or afford appropriate medicines. In addition, more than 100 million people fall into poverty annually because of high health care costs, and the cost of medicines represents an important factor.

Significant structural issues underlie the disparity between health needs and access to medicines. The availability of drugs is dependent on market mechanisms that skew incentives to develop the drugs anticipated to bring the greatest profits. As a consequence, pharmaceutical development is focused on markets in developed countries and on potentially high-profit medicines for those countries rather than efforts to address the priority medical needs of the majority of people. Financial incentives have also generated a business model that encourages the development of "me-too" drugs, which are slight variations of existing drugs with little additional therapeutic benefit. Further, pharmaceutical companies price their medicines to make them ever more costly so as to increase their profit margins even when research and development costs do not warrant such high prices.

Strict IP regimes, particularly the global minimum standards established under the 1994 TRIPS Agreement, constitute a significant impediment to greater access to medicines and a major contributor to their high cost. Despite the claims made to justify the IP monopolies, strict IP standards do not equate with the development of innovative and needed pharmaceuticals. Even though the number of patents awarded in industrialized countries has increased in recent years, the number of truly innovative drugs has not. Moreover, whatever the situation in advanced economies, patents do not stimulate the development of appropriate medicines suited to the needs of developing countries because patents only work as incentives where potentially profitable markets exist.

Furthermore, it has been difficult for low- and middle-income countries to take advantage of the flexibilities in the TRIPS Agreement despite the advantages of doing so in order to increase access to medicines. The requirements of applying the TRIPS flexibilities are complex and onerous, and many developing countries have lacked the requisite legal capability and appropriate laws. More important though, the proliferation of TRIPS-plus free trade agreements that the United States and to a lesser extent the EU governments have concluded with developing countries restrict and in some cases eliminate the ability to implement any TRIPS flexibilities. Additionally, multinational pharmaceutical corporations, frequently supported by the United States and EU governments, have sought to block initiatives to produce or import low-cost medicines through legal action.

Critics of the patent-based system have proposed replacing it with alternative mechanisms that could better balance innovation incentives with access to affordable medicines. One possibility that has been identified would be to provide much larger public subsidies for biomedical research and clinical trials or to substitute government research and development of drugs for the current reliance on private pharmaceutical companies (Grabowski et al. 2015, 307–308). Presumably, under these schemes increased government spending and government-sponsored research would not proceed as it does now in the United States and many other developed countries, with researchers who receive government grants having the right to patent their inventions and license them for development and marketing to private industry. A second proposal is to establish a prize system for specific types of drug innovations with competitors agreeing to forego patenting their products. A third proposed initiative is a Health Impact Fund, a voluntary pay-for-performance scheme under which drug developers would forego patents and agree to sell their products at low prices. In exchange, developers would receive ten annual payments based on the health impact or contribution of their products. This latter proposal has the advantage of incentivizing the development of products that have the potential of benefiting large numbers of people in poor countries (Gootendorst et al. 2011).

Others take issue with these proposals claiming they present both theoretical and practical problems. Evaluating the potential contributions and limitations of these proposals is outside the scope of this chapter. Nevertheless, even critics acknowledge that greater government funding provided as a supplement to the present system, as for example, to incentivize the development of new antibiotics, could address important unmet needs and gaps (Grabowski et al. 2015, 308). Some critics also concede that a carefully designed voluntary prize system could make a valuable contribution as a supplement to the patent system (Grabowski et al. 2015, 309). At a minimum, governments in developed countries have both an ethical responsibility and a human rights obligation to invest significant resources in pharmaceutical development, particularly for high priority medicines otherwise unlikely to become available. This obligation extends both to medicines needed in their own countries and in developing countries lacking a pharmaceutical research infrastructure. The proposals for introducing prizes and a Health Impact Fund deserve further exploration through limited trials.

The current market-based and patent-supported system of pharmaceutical development clearly has increased the wealth, power, and influence of the major corporations that dominate the pharmaceutical industry. In the human rights paradigm, states have the responsibility to regulate the conduct of nonstate actors to prevent human rights violations, but the power and resources vested in the major pharmaceutical companies and their operations across national borders make it difficult to do so. Moreover, some of the most powerful states with a greater potential to control Big Pharma companies instead aid and abet them. Some human rights advocates have therefore sought to place primary responsibility or at least co-responsibility for rectifying the current lack of access to medicines on these companies. Claims that pharmaceutical corporations have an obligation to further the right to essential medicines, particularly for people in the developing world, reflect the importance of health care needs, the recognition of the right to health, and the unique capacity of pharmaceutical companies to render aid. However, the contention that corporations have "hard" or binding obligations under international human rights law has not been widely accepted because, at least as originally formulated, international human rights law does not directly apply to nonstate actors. Moreover, pharmaceutical companies argue they have primary or sole responsibility to their shareholders, and they have resisted acknowledging they have direct human rights obligations to other members of society.

Although the right to health incorporates a series of obligations for states in conjunction with ensuring access to medicines, most states have been negligent in fulfilling these obligations. Therefore, it is proposed here that serious initiatives to improve the right to medicines require states, particularly the states that are state parties to the ICESCR, to develop and implement policies focused on the following:

Adopting an explicit human rights framework for the development of laws and policies: To acknowledge their human rights responsibilities to make needed and particularly needed essential medicines available to members of their population, particularly those individuals and groups that are economically deprived and otherwise vulnerable, countries, particularly those that are state parties to the ICESCR, should incorporate a right to health perspective into the development of their legislation dealing with access to medicines including their patent law and adopt relevant policies to implement this commitment.

Establishing the necessary infrastructure and policies for an effective essential drugs program: Doing so requires establishing a monitoring system able to determine disease prevalence as the basis for national priorities; an evaluation system to assess the efficacy, safety, and comparative cost of medicines; an institution charged with regulatory approval; and a purchasing and distribution system able to keep essential medicines stocked in public sector health facilities. To keep essential drugs affordable, governments also have the responsibility to institute price control mechanisms and to subsidize the cost of essential drugs when necessary to make them affordable to patients who need them. Other specifically human rights elements include a mechanism for consulting all beneficiaries such as patients' organizations and rural communities as well as government, universities, and professional associations; mechanisms for transparency and accountability that use indicators and targets and specify the roles and responsibilities of the various stakeholders; mechanisms to assure equal access of the main vulnerable groups to essential medicines through ongoing monitoring based on disaggregated statistics, especially women, children, people living in poverty, rural communities, indigenous communities, minorities, immigrants, the elderly, prisoners, and people with disabilities; and mechanisms for safeguards and redress of human rights violations (Hogerzeil 2006). Clearly many countries lack these capabilities and will need technical assistance and financial aid to develop an effective essential medicines program. It should be an international priority to provide these requirements. A national medicine policy potentially relevant for developed countries would include such additional elements as strict criteria for market approval (including comparison with best available treatment and comparative cost-effectiveness benefits); evidence-based national clinical guidelines; insurance and reimbursement policies with the type and level of reimbursement focused on essential drugs; state subsidies (direct supply, subsidies that reduce the cost, or subsidized insurance for poor and disadvantaged people); patent policies that balance innovation and equitable access to essential medicines; price controls; evaluation of the advantages of local production as compared with importation; public information and education about medicine use; and investment in research and development (Hogerzeil 2004, 1171).

Investing sufficient funds in the procurement of essential medicines: At this time the precise figures for countries at varying levels of development to have sufficient funds for the procurement of essential medicines have not been determined. Nevertheless, it is clear that many poor- and middle-income countries are not investing sufficient funds in health expenditures in general and medicines in particular. Developed countries with the potential for research and development of needed drugs also have the responsibility of channeling funds to do so both for the use of their populations and for neglected diseases in other countries. In addition, developed countries have the additional responsibility to provide aid to bilateral and multilateral programs to underwrite the purchase of medicines for poor countries.

Enacting measures to control the prices of medicines: Many regulatory measures can help to reduce the prices of medicines. In countries relying on imports, these include abolishing tariffs and eliminating or at least significantly reducing taxes on medicines, controlling markups of prices, and facilitating the use of trade policy flexibilities. Developing local production capabilities, wherever possible, could also lower prices (MDG Gap Task Force Report 2013, 62). Countries with pharmaceutical production capabilities need to develop public policies that encourage the strategic production of needed pharmaceuticals at a reasonable cost. Implementing price controls or price limits on medicines constitutes another measure. Many countries fail to adopt these policies and leave pricing to market mechanisms. In those situations, public policies contribute to the high price of pharmaceuticals.

Adopting appropriate intellectual property laws consistent with human rights principles: Despite all of its problems, it seems unlikely that there will be major changes to the current patent system in the near future. In his 2009 report to the Human Rights Council, Anand Grover made a series of recommendations as to how states could better proceed through the IP thicket to make medicines available, acceptable, and of good quality to reach ailing populations without discrimination. His recommendations, which this author supports, included the following:

- States need to take steps to facilitate the use of TRIPS flexibilities. To do so, developing countries and less developed countries should review their laws and policies and consider whether they have made full use of TRIPS flexibilities, and if necessary, consider amending their laws and policies to make full use of the flexibilities (Grover 2009, para 97). However, this recommendation does not take into account the extent to which states have agreed to abide by Trips-plus standards that restrict the use of these flexibilities. The options in such situations would be to try to amend the Trips-plus agreement or for the affected countries to refuse to abide by these unfair stipulations.
- Least developed countries should make full use of the transition period and revoke or suspend patent laws adopted to conform to TRIPS requirements, if necessary, for the balance of the period. He also proposed that less developed countries should consider asking for a further

extension of the transition period (Grover 2009, para 98). This subsequently occurred, and the transition period was extended for the least developed countries but not for other poor countries.

- Least developed countries should use the transition period to explore options to establish local manufacturing capabilities (Grover 2009, para 99).
- Developing and least developed countries should establish high patentability standards and institute exclusions from patentability, such as new forms and new or second uses in order to address evergreening[4] and facilitate generic entry of medicines (Grover 2009, para 100).
- Developing and least developed countries should provide for parallel importation with simplified procedures in their national laws (Grover 2009, para 101) in order to facilitate its use.
- Developing and least developed countries need to incorporate all the possible grounds upon which compulsory licenses may be issued in their patent laws (Grover 2009, para 102).
- Developing and least developed countries should incorporate both Bolar[5] and research, experimental, and educational exceptions[6] in their patent laws and explore how other limited exceptions could further promote access to medicines (Grover 2009, para 104).
- Developing and least developed countries should seek international assistance in building capacity to implement TRIPS flexibilities to promote the right to health, as for example, from WHO and other United Nations bodies (Grover 2009, para 106).
- Developing and least developed countries should actively promote the participation of individuals and communities in decision-making processes relating to TRIPS and TRIPS flexibilities. These countries should also conduct impact assessments of TRIPS and TRIPS flexibilities (Grover 2009, para 107).
- Developing and least developed countries should not introduce TRIPS-plus standards in their national laws. Developed countries should not encourage developing and least developed countries to enter

---

[4] Evergreening refers to a strategy by which pharmaceutical companies with patents about to expire seek to secure new patents by making minor modifications in the product.

[5] The Bolar exemption is a form of research exemption to rights conferred by patents that allow generic manufacturers to use elements of an original manufacturers approval of a product whose patent is about to expire for preparing its own product for regulatory approval.

[6] Exemptions in patent law allow for protections from infringement of patents for limited purposes. A research exemption typically allows researchers to use a product under patent to seek to understand it better or for efforts to develop a new product.

into TRIPS-plus free trade agreements and should be mindful of other actions that may infringe upon the right to health (Grover 2009, para 108). It would seem more appropriate to categorically recommend that developed countries not engage in actions that may infringe on the right to health.

- All future technical assistance and cooperation by developed countries, WHO, and the World Intellectual Property Organizations to developing countries and least developed countries (presumably related to IP issues) should be based on the obligation to respect, protect, and fulfill the right to health (Grover 2009, para 109).

To respect and implement international obligations related to the right to health: As noted in this chapter, the right to health incorporates key international components that require all state parties to comply with international obligations to respect the enjoyment of the right to health in other countries. For the reasons discussed in this chapter, countries responsible for establishing and upholding the current international system of strict IP requirements, particularly those hampering access to medicines through negotiating free trade agreements with Trips-plus intellectual property standards, are in effect violating the right to essential medicines. Unfortunately, the primary violator, the United States, has not ratified the ICESCR. Nor does it recognize the right to health as a binding human rights obligation. Nevertheless, its policies, which prioritize corporate profits over human welfare, deserve strong censure on ethical as well as human rights grounds.

References

Access to Medicines Foundation (2014) *The Access to Medicine Index 2014*, Haarlem: Access to Medicines Foundation, www.accesstomedicinesindex.org/.

Alkoby, Asher (2012, "Improving Access to Essential Medicines: International Law and Normative Change," in Lisa Forman and Jillian Clare Kohler, eds., *Access to Medicines as a Human Right: Implications for Pharmaceutical Industry Responsibility*, Toronto, Buffalo, and London: University of Toronto Press, pp. 46–74.

Babar, Zaheer Ud Din, Ibrahim, Mohamed Izham Mohamed, Singh, Harpal, Burkal, Nadeem Irfan, et al. (2007) "Evaluating Drug Prices, Availability, Affordability, and Price Components: Implications for Access to Drugs in Malaysia," *PLoS Medicine* 4 (3): e82. doi:10:1371/journal.pmed.0040082.

Bajaj, Vikas (2012) "India Weighs Providing Free Drugs at State-Run Hospitals," *The New York Times*, July 6, Business Day, pp. 1–2.

Beall, Reed and Kuhn, Randall (2012) "Trends in Compulsory Licensing of Pharmaceuticals since the Doha Declaration: A Database Analysis," *PLoS Medicine* 9 (1): e1001154.

Bigdeli, Maryam, Peters, David H., and Wagner, Anita K. (2014) *Medicines in Health Systems: Advancing Access, Affordability and Appropriate Use*, Geneva: Alliance for health Policy and Systems Research and the World Health Organization.

Bill and Melinda Gates Foundation (2015), www.gatesfoundation.org/

Binagwaho, Agnès, Freeman, Richard, Scott, Kirstin, Badrichani, Anne, et al. (2015) "Improving International Accountability – a Tool for Protecting Health as a Basic Human Right," *Health and Human Rights Journal*, published online 4/15, www.hhrjournal.org/...impoving-interna

Cameron, A., Ewen, M., Ross-Degnan, D., Ball, P., et al. (2009) "Medicine Prices, Availability, and Affordability in 36 Developing and Middle-income Countries: A Secondary Analysis," *The Lancet* 373 (9659): 240–249.

CESCR (Committee on Economic, Social and Cultural Rights) (2000) General Comment 14: The Right to the Highest Attainable Standard of Health, U.N. Doc. E.C.12.2000.4.EN.

Commission on Intellectual Property Rights (2002) Integrating Intellectual Property Rights and Development Policy: Report of the Commission on Intellectual Property Rights, London.

Congressional Budget Office (2007) Research on the Comparative Effectiveness of Medical Treatments: Issues and Options for an Expanded Federal Role, Washington, DC: U.S. Government, www.cbo.gov/sites/default/files/12-18-comparativeeffectiveness.pdf.

Correa, Carlos M. (2009) "Intellectual Property Rights and Inequalities in Health Outcomes," in Ronald Labonté, Ted Schrecker, Corrine Packer, and Vivien Runnels, eds., *Globalization and Health: Pathways, Evidence and Policy*, New York and Abington, UK: Routledge, pp. 263–288.

Correa, Carlos M. and Matthews, Duncan (2011) The Doha Declaration Ten Years on Its Impact on Access to Medicines and the Right to Health, Discussion Paper, United Nations Development Programme, www.undp.org/...Discussion_P...

Drahos, Peter (2008) "'Trust Me': Patent Offices in Developing Countries," *American Journal of Law & Medicine* 34: 151–174.

Drugs for Neglected Diseases initiative website (2015) www.dndi.org/.

Dutfield, Graham (2008) "Delivering Drugs to the Poor: Will the TRIPS Amendment Help?" *American Journal of Law & Medicine* 34: 07–124.

Editorial (2013) "What Price Affordable Access?" *Nature Biotechnology* 31 (6): 467.

Forman, Lisa (2008) "'Rights' and Wrongs: What Utility for the Right to Health in Reforming Trade Rules on Medicines?" *Health and Human Rights* 10: 37–48.

Forman, Lisa and Kohler, Jillian Clare (2012) "Introduction: Access to Medicines as a Human Right – What Does It Mean for Pharmaceutical Industry

Responsibilities," in Lisa Forman and Jillian Clare Kohler, eds., *Access to Medicines as a Human Right: Implications for Pharmaceutical Industry Responsibility*, Toronto, Buffalo, and London: University of Toronto Press, pp. 3–24.

Gagne, Joshua J. and Choudhry, Niteesh K. (2011) "How Many 'Me Too' Drugs Is Too Many?" *JAMA* 305 (7): 711–712.

Gagnon, Marc-André (2013) "Corruption of Pharmaceutical Markets: Addressing the Misalignment of Financial Incentives and Public Health," *Journal of Law, Medicine & Ethics* 41: 571–580.

GAVI the Vaccine Alliance Website 92015) www.gavi.org/.

Global Health Watch (2006) *Global Health Watch 2005–2006: An Alternative World Health Report*, London: Zed Publishing Company for the People's Health Movement, Medact, Medico International, Third World Network, Health Action International, and Asociación Latinoamericana de Medicina Social.

(2009) *Global Health Watch 2: An Alternative World Report*, London: Zed Publishing Company for the People's Health Movement, Medact, and the Global Equity Gauge.

(2014) *Global Health Watch 4: An Alternative World Health Report*, London and New York: Zed Publishing Company for the People's Health Movement, Medact, and the Global Equity Gauge Alliance.

Gootendorst, Paul, Hollis, Aidan, Levine, David K., Pogge, Thomas, et al. (2011) "New Approaches to Rewarding Pharmaceutical Innovation," *Canadian Medical Association Journal* 183 (6): 681–685.

Grabowski, Henry G., DiMasi, Joseph A., and Long, Genia (2015) "The Roles of Patents and Research and Development Incentives in Biopharmaceutical Innovation," *Health Affairs* 34 (2): 302–310.

Grover, Anand (2009) Report of the Special Rapporteur on the Right of Everyone to the Enjoyment of the Highest Attainable Standard of Physical and Mental Health, Human Rights Council, A/HRC/11/12.

(2011) Report of the Special Rapporteur on the Right of Everyone to the Enjoyment of the Highest Attainable Standard of Physical and Mental Health, Expert Consultation on Access to Medicines as a Fundamental Component of the Right to Health, Human Rights Council, A/HRC/17/43.

Helfer, Laurence R. and Austin, Graeme W. (2011) *Human Rights and Intellectual Property: Mapping the Global Interface*, New York and Melbourne: Cambridge University Press.

Heywood, Mark (2009) "South Africa's Treatment Action Campaign: Combining Law and Social Mobilization to Realize the Right to Health," *Journal of Human Rights Practice* 1 (1): 14–16, doi: 10.1093.

Hoen, Ellen't, Berger, Jonathan, Calmy, Alexandra, and Moon Suerie (2011) "Driving a Decade of Change: HIV/AIDS, Patents and Access to Medicines for All," *Journal of the International AIDS Society* 14:15, www.jiasociety.org/content/14/1/15.

Hogerzeil, Hans V. (2004) "The Concept of Essential Medicines: Lessons for Rich Countries," *British Medical Journal* 329: 1169–1172.

(2006) "Essential Medicines and Human Rights: What Can They Learn from Each Other," *Bulletin of the World Health Organization* 84 (5): 371–375.

Hogerzeil, Hans V., Liberman, Jonathan, Wirtz, Veronika, Kishore Sandeep P., et al. (2013) "Promotion of Access to Essential Medicine for Non-communicable Diseases: Practical Implications of the UN Political Declaration," *The Lancet* 281: 680–689.

Human Rights Council (2013) Access to Medicines in the Context of the Right of Everyone to the Enjoyment of the Highest Attainable Standard of Physical and Mental Health, Twenty-third session, agenda item 3, A/HRC/23/L.10/Rev.1.

Hunt, Paul (2008) Report of the Special Rapporteur on the Right of Everyone to the Enjoyment of the Highest Attainable Standard of Physical and Mental Health, UN Doc. A/63/263.

Hunt, Paul and Khosla, Rajat (2008) "The Human Right to Medicines," *Sur* 5 (8): 99–116.

Hunt, Paul and Khosla, Rajat (2010) "Are Drug Companies Living Up to Their Human Rights Responsibilities? The Perspective of the Former United Nations Special Rapporteur (2002–2008)," *PLoS Medicine* 7 (9): e1000330.

Illingworth, Patricia (2012) "Corporate Social Responsibility and the Right to Essential Medicines," Lisa Forman and Jillian Clare Kohler, eds., *Access to Medicines as a Human Right: Implications for Pharmaceutical Industry Responsibility*, Toronto, Buffalo, and London: University of Toronto Press, pp. 75–88.

International Convention on the Elimination of All Forms of Racial Discrimination (1969) United Nations General Assembly Resolution 2106 (XX) of December 21, 1965, Annex 20 U.N. GAOR Supp (No 14) at 47, U.N. Doc. A/6014, entered into force on January 4, 1969.

Jorgensen, Paul D. (2013) "Pharmaceuticals, Political Money, and Public Policy: A Theoretical and Empirical Agenda," *The Journal of Law, Medicine & Ethics* 4 (3): 561–570.

Khosla, Rajat and Hunt, Paul (2012) "Human Rights Responsibilities of Pharmaceutical Companies in Relation to Access to Medicines," in Lisa Forman and Jillian Clare Kohler, eds., *Access to Medicines as a Human Right: Implications for Pharmaceutical Industry Responsibility*, Toronto, Buffalo, and London: University of Toronto Press, pp. 25–45.

Koivusalo, Meri and Mackintosh, Maureen (2009) "Global Public Action in Health and Pharmaceutical Policies: Politics and Policy Priorities," Innovation Knowledge Development Working Paper No. 45, The Open University.

Kulkarni, Kaustubh and Mohanty, Suchitra (2013) "Novartis Loses Landmark India Cancer Drug Patent Case," *Reuters Business and Financial News*, www.reuters .com.assets/print?aid=USBRE93002120130401.

Light, Donald W., Lexchin, Joel, and Darrow, Jonathan J. (2013) "Institutional Corruption of Pharmaceuticals and the Myth of Safe and Effective Drugs," *The Journal of Law, Medicine & Ethics* 41: 590–600.

Light, Donald W. and Warburton, Rebecca (2011) "Demythologizing the High Costs of Pharmaceutical Research," *BioSocieties*, The London School of Economics and Political Science 1745–8552: 1–17.

Malpani, Rohit and Kamal-Yanni, Mohga (2006) Patents versus Patients: Five Years after the Doha Declaration, Oxfam International, Oxfam Briefing Paper 95.

MDG Gap Task Force Report (2008) *Delivering on the Global Partnership for Achieving the MDGs*, New York: United Nations Publications.

(2009) *Strengthening the Global Partnership for Development in a Time of Crisis*, New York: United Nations Publications.

(2012) *The Global Partnership for Development: Making Rhetoric a Reality*, New York: United Nations Publications.

MDG Gap Force Report (2013) *The Challenges We Face*, New York: United Nations Publications.

Médecin Sans Frontières (MSF) (2015) Website: The Access Campaign, www .msfacess.org/TheAccessCampaign.

Media Centre (2014) Hepatitis C, fact sheet no. 164, Geneva: World Health Organization.

(2015) "WHO Moves to Improve Access to Lifesaving Medicines for Hepatitis C, Drug-resistant TB and Cancers," Geneva: World Health Organization, www .who.int/mediacentre/news/releases/2015/new-essential-medicines-list/en/.

Mossialos, Elias, Wenzl, Martin, Osborn, Robin, and Anderson, Chloe, eds. (2015) *International Profiles of Health Systems*, 2014, New York: Commonwealth Fund.

Nagarajan, Rmea (2015) "Free Drugs Plan Gets a Quiet Burial," *Times of India*, http://timesof india.com/india/free-drugs-plam-gets-a-quiet-burial/ articleshow/4680931.com.

National Institute of Allergy and Infectious Disease Website (2015) www.niad.nih...

Oke, Emmanuel Kolawole (2013) "Incorporating a Right to Health Perspective into the Resolution of Patent Law Disputes," *Health and Human Rights* 15 (2): 97–107.

Ollove, Michael (2014) "Could New Hepatitis C Drugs Bust State Budgets?" *USA Today*, March 3, www.usatoday.com/story/news/nation/2014/03/03/ stateline-hepat...

Perrone, Matthew (2014) "Soaring Drug Prices Draw Senate Scrutiny," Associated Press, November 20, www.sanders.semate.gpv/newsroom/must-read/ soaring-generic-d...

PLoS Medicine Editors (2010) "Drug Companies Should Be Held More Accountable for Their Human Rights Responsibilities," *PLoS Medicine* 7 (9): E1000344.

Reidenberg, Marcus M. and Walley, Tom (2004) "Commentary: The Pros and Cons of Essential Medicines for Rich Countries," *British Medical Journal* 329: 1172.

Ritter, Geralyn (2010) "Are Drug Companies Living Up to Their Human Rights Responsibilities: The Merck Perspective," *PLoS Medicine* 7 (9): e1000343.

Rodwin, Marc A. (2013) "Introduction: Institutional Corruption and the Pharmaceutical Industry," *The Journal of Law, Medicine & Ethics* 41: 544–552.

Ruggeri, Kai and Nolte, Ellen (2013) Pharmaceutical Pricing: The Use of External Reference Pricing, Rand Europe, www.rand.org.

Servick, Kelly (2015) "The Drug Push," *Science* 348 (6237): 850–853.

Shah, Anup (2014) "Foreign Aid for Development Assistance," *Global Issues*, www .globalissues.org.

Silverman, Ed (2014) "Will Gilead's Hepatitis C Drug Bust State Budgets?" *WSJ Pharmalot*, July 17, http://blogs.wsj.com/pharmalot/2014/07/17/will-gileads-hepatitis-c-dr...

Statista (2015) The Statistics Portal, www.statista.com/topics/1764/global-pharmaceutical-industry/

The Editorial Board (2015) "Runaway Drug Prices," *The New York Times*, May 5, A22.

The Global Fund website (2015) www.theglobalfund.org...

United Nations Development Group (2003) *Indicators for Monitoring the Millennium Development Goals*, New York: United Nations.

United Nations Human Rights Council (2013) Access to Medicines in the Context of the Right of Everyone to the Enjoyment of the Highest Attainable Standard of Physical and Mental Health, A/HRC/23/L.10/ Rev.1.

UNITAID (2014) *The Trans-Pacific Partnership Agreement: Implications for Access to Medicines and Public Health*, Geneva: UNITAID Secretariat, www.unitaid.eu.

UNITAID website (2015) www.unitaid.eu/who/about-unitaid.

WHO/UNICEF (1978) Primary Health Care: Report of the International Conference on Primary Health Care, Alma-Ata, USSR, September 6–12. Health for all, series 1: Geneva: World Health Organization.

World Health Organization (n.d.) Access to Affordable Essential Medicines. www .who.int/medicines/.../MDG08ChapterE...

(2003) The Selection and Use of Essential Medicines," Report of the WHO Expert Committee 2002.

(2004) What Are Essential Medicines? www.who.int/topic/essential_medicines/ en/l.

(2008) WHO Medicines Strategy 2008–2013, working draft. www.who.int/ medicines/publications/medicines_strategy.

World Health Organization, Health Action International (2003) *Medicine Prices – a New Approach to Measurement*, Geneva: World Health Organization, http:// whqlibdoc.who.int/hq/2003/WHO EDM PAR 2003.2.pdf.

World Trade Organization (1994) Agreement on Trade-Related Aspects of Intellectual Property Rights, 1869 U.N.T.S. 299.

(2001) Ministerial Conference Fourth Session, Doha, November 9–14, Declaration on the TRIPS Agreement and Public Health, T/MIN(01)/DEC/2.

(2013) "Responding to Least Developed Countries' Special Needs in ip," www .wto.org/english/tratop-?e/trips._e/ldc/e.htm.

7

The Social Determinants of Health, Health Equity, and Human Rights

There is increasing documentation that health status, both on an individual and on the community level, is shaped by a wide range of nonmedical factors. Work in social epidemiology, social medicine, and medical sociology has shown that the social determinants of health, the social and economic conditions in which people grow, live, work, and age, affect their opportunities to lead healthy lives. Research also links economic inequalities and social disparities with health outcomes. Two well-known studies of inequalities in health status in Britain, one by a working group appointed in 1977 (Townsend and Davidson 1982) and a second in 1997 (Marmot 1999), found that inequalities of health status in lower level occupational groups, as compared with those in the higher level groups, persisted at all stages of life despite universal access to health services through the National Health Service. The researchers attributed the continuing disparities primarily to social and economic factors such as income, work (or lack of it), environmental conditions, education, housing, transport, and what are now termed "life-style" issues that remained outside the ambit of national health policy. More recently, the landmark report of the World Health Organization's Commission on the Social Determinants of Health (CSDH), *Closing the gap in a generation: Health equity through action on the social determinants of health* (CSDH 2008), has provided greater visibility for the significant role of the social determinants of health in shaping health outcomes and thereby contributing to existing and growing health inequalities both within and between societies.

Studies have also demonstrated correlations between specific social determinants and health outcomes. Research in many parts of the world has documented that income has a striking association with health. In many poor countries, such as Ghana, India, or Guatemala, children born into the poorest 20 percent of households have more than double the risk of mortality in the first year of life compared to children born into the richest 20 percent (Watkins 2014, 2250). The income–health relationship also holds for high-income countries. U.S. adults living in poverty are more than five times as likely to report being in fair or poor health as adults with incomes at four times the federal poverty level or higher (Woolf and Braveman 2011, 1853–1854). An extensive literature also provides evidence of large health disparities among individuals with different levels of education. Research based in the developing world has identified educational status, especially of the mother, as a major predictor of health outcomes (Gakidou et al. 2010). In the high-income countries, the United States for example, the gradient in health outcomes correlated with levels of educational attainment has become steeper over the last four decades resulting in larger health status differentials between Americans with high- and low-educational attainment (Zimmerman and Woolf 2014).

Improvements in the social determinants of health are essential to improve health status. To provide a few examples, provision of a safe, reliable, affordable, and easily accessible water supply for the billion people in developing countries that lack the basic requirements for a safe water supply would be a vital contribution to their better health (Hunter et al. 2010). Social protection programs, such as conditional cash transfer programs which transfer cash to poor households have been shown to increase health service utilization rates and improve health outcomes and nutritional status, especially among children, and lower childhood mortality (Lagarde et al. 2009; Rasella et al. 2013). A major research study seeking to identify why Americans have a shorter life expectancy and poorer health outcomes than sixteen comparable high-income or peer countries linked the U.S. health disadvantage with the relative lack of investment in and support for improvements in the social determinants of health (Woolf and Aron 2013). Citing the mounting scientific evidence, the most recent Healthy People initiative, a national agenda to set priorities for health promotion and disease prevention, coordinated federally by the U.S. Department of Health and Human Services, embraces a social determinants perspective. Specifically, the 2020 plan emphasizes such factors as poverty, education, and numerous aspects of the social structure (Koh et al. 2011).

These studies take on added importance for human rights in a world where after three decades of neoliberal policies inequalities are on a steep upward trajectory, and many governments, both those in rich and poor countries, appear reluctant to advance an equity agenda. Chapter Three documented trends in income inequality in recent years in both developing and developed countries. Nevertheless, at a time when inequality around the world is rising, when disparities linked to wealth and opportunity are under challenge from social protest movements, and many governments stand accused by their citizens of favoring vested interests ahead of the public good, few governments, regardless of the situation in their countries, seem inclined to consider the major policy changes that would be required to address these problems (Watkins 2014, 2248).

Given the importance of the social determinants to health status and outcomes, it becomes important to evaluate the potential relevance of the right to health paradigm to this approach. On the positive side, the framing of the right to health has always been broader than just a right of access to health care. The Universal Declaration of Human Rights enumerates a right to a standard of living adequate for health and well-being (Universal Declaration 1948, article 25). Article 12 of ICESCR directs state parties to the improvement of all aspects of environmental and industrial hygiene (1966, Article 12.b) and the prevention, treatment, and control of epidemic, endemic, occupational, and other diseases (1966, Article 12.c). Article 24 (c) of the more recently drafted Convention on the Rights of the Child (1989) stipulates that the right to health includes access to nutritious food, clean drinking water, and environmental sanitation. Importantly, the Committee on Economic, Social and Cultural Rights' (CESCR) General Comment 14 interprets the right to health as an inclusive right extending not only to timely and appropriate health care but also to the underlying determinants of health. These, according to the text, include access to safe and potable water and adequate sanitation, an adequate supply of safe food, nutrition and housing, healthy occupational and environmental conditions, and access to health-related education and information (CESCR 2000, para 11). Providing these underlying determinants is considered to be a core obligation that is immediately realizable and not dependent on the availability of resources (CESCR 2000, para 43). In addition, the general comment avers that both biological and sociocultural factors play a significant role in influencing health (CESCR 2000, paras 18–20). In 2002, the Committee also took the unprecedented step of adopting a general comment on the right to water, a right that is not explicitly enumerated in the International Covenant from which the Committee derives its mandate, in part because it viewed access to clean water as inextricably related to the right to health (CESCR 2002).

On the negative side, rights-based approaches to health, with some notable exceptions, have not engaged in a meaningful way with the growing body of research that shows the significant impact of the social determinants of health and health inequalities on health status and population health. Many in the human rights community continue to equate the right to health solely or primarily with the availability of medical care. Paul

Hunt, the first Special Rapporteur on the right to the enjoyment of the high-est standard of physical and mental health, lamented that there is a "definite tendency in some Governments, international organizations and elsewhere to devote a disproportionate amount of attention and resources to medical care at the expense of the underlying determinants of health" (Hunt 2007, para 48). This focus, which also includes many working on health and human rights issues, likely reflects the influence of the current biomedical paradigm. The biomedical model centers on the individual rather than the commu-nity, promotes a curative rather than a preventive approach, and investigates the immediate biological, and sometimes behavioral, causes of illness while neglecting or discounting the role of the social determinants (Ottersen et al. 2014). While there is a small but growing group of human rights scholars and practitioners addressing issues related to the social determinants of health (Braveman and Gruskin 2003; Hunt 2004, 2005, 2007; London 2007; Yamin 2008; MacNaughton 2009, 2013; Wilson 2009; Schrecker et al. 2010; Yamin and Irwin 2010), they are definitely a minority in the field. An excessive focus on the individual at the expense of the community as the sole rights holder and the relative neglect of the public health dimensions of the right to health have contributed to inattention to the social determinants of health.

It is also important to note that on the other side of the disciplinary divide many of those working in the social medicine and social epidemiology fields have been reluctant to acknowledge their common ground with the human rights community. There are important exceptions who have done so (Farmer 2003; Solar and Irwin 2007; Braveman 2010; Rasanathan et al. 2010). Notably, the CSDH rejected its secretariat's recommendation that it adopt a rights-based approach as an appropriate conceptual framework to advance toward health equity through action on the social determinants of health (Solar and Irwin 2007, 7–9). Even when the CSDH report (2008) uses rights-based terminology, it rarely cites relevant international human rights instruments or notes the potential contributions of human rights institutions or advocacy. Its failure to incorporate an explicit human rights approach weakened the line of reasoning in some sections of its report, par-ticularly when it deals with empowerment, and diminished the likelihood of fulfilling its mandate to foster a global movement to promote health equity.

This chapter explores the importance of the social determinants of health and economic inequalities for the realization of a rights-based approach to health.[1] It proposes that there are six changes that will be

---

[1] This chapter builds on some of my previous work on the social determinants of health including the following: Chapman, Audrey R. (2009) "Globalization, human rights, and

necessary to incorporate a more meaningful consideration of the social determinants of health and equity concerns into a rights-based approach:

(1) To begin with, it will be necessary to engage more consistently with the findings of research from social medicine and social epidemiology. The field of social medicine, which is closely linked with public health, seeks to understand how social and economic conditions impact health, disease, and the practice of medicine. Social epidemiology focuses on identifying and documenting disparities in health outcomes through a multitude of factors, including gender, ethnicity, socioeconomic status, education, and area of residence (Rasanathan et al. 2010). *Closing the gap in a generation* (CSDH 2008) offers a good starting point because it builds upon and synthesizes major findings in the fields of social medicine and social epidemiology from countries at all levels of income and development.

(2) It is important to give greater emphasis to the collective dimensions of the right to health. An "absolutist focus" on conceptualizing human rights as only encompassing the rights of individuals is inimical to addressing differences in population health outcomes, the role of the social determinants of health, and health equity issues (Rasanathan et al. 2010). Although rights-based approaches to health already deal with some collective elements, this has not percolated back into the understanding of the right as a collective as well as an individual right.

(3) Despite widespread affirmation of the foundational principle of human rights that all human beings are equal in dignity and worth and therefore entitled to equal rights, work on the right to health has not invested sufficient attention to the systemic and structural causes of health inequalities and health inequities and identified those that are avoidable by reasonable policy changes. To be able to do so will require the human rights field to deal more systematically with economic inequalities and the manner in which social and economic standing, that is, social class and social status, affects health outcomes.

the social determinants of health," *Bioethics* 23 (2): 97–111; Chapman, Audrey R. (2010) "The social determinants of health, health equity, and human rights," *Health and Human Rights* 12 (2): 17–30; Schrecker, Ted, Chapman, Audrey R., Labonté, Ronald, and De Vogli, Roberto (2010) "Advancing health equity in the global marketplace: how human rights can help," *Social Science & Medicine* 71: 1520–1526; Chapman, Audrey R. (2011) "Missed opportunities: the human rights gap in the report of the commission on social determinants of health," *Journal of Human Rights* 10 (2): 132–150.

(4) In a related manner, human rights requires a more expansive and substantive conception of equality. The concept of equality, which in human rights law is now based on equality of dignity, legal standing, and legal status, should be broadened to incorporate substantive equality.

(5) All of this then leads to identifying and seeking to rectify the inequitable distribution of power, money, and resources in the way society is organized, as for example, the pervasive inequalities between women and men and the manner in which the affluent use their economic and political power to shape policies that advantage them at the expense of the middle class and the poor. With some important exceptions, the human rights community has generally been hesitant to deal directly with the political and economic power structure of society. But real change requires going beyond identifying those who have been the victims of discrimination and disempowerment and seeking redress to identifying the sources of the deprivation and exclusion and trying to change the system.

(6) Policies that affect the social determinants of health often originate outside the health sector. Therefore, to improve access to the social determinants of health, it is necessary to formulate health policies in a more multisectoral framework and to assess the implications of policies made in other sectors on health status. CSDH advocates for policy coherence – mechanisms to support health equity in all policies (2008). Health impact analysis, particularly when done in a human rights framework, offers an important tool for assessing the health implications of public policies proposed in other sectors.

The CSDH Report: *Closing the Gap in a Generation*

The WHO launched the Commission on Social Determinants of Health (CSDH) in March 2005 with a mandate to marshal evidence on what can be done to promote health equity and to foster a global movement to achieve it. Specifically, the CSDH was tasked with collecting, collating, and synthesizing global evidence on the social determinants of health and their impact on health inequity from countries at all levels of income and development, and with making recommendations on actions to address this inequity (CSDH 2008, 1.) To pursue its mandate the Commission established a series of subject-matter working groups, termed "knowledge networks," on nine topics: globalization, early childhood development, employment conditions, women and gender equity, social exclusion, health systems, priority public health conditions, urban settings, and measurement and evidence,[2] each of which wrote a report that was then synthesized into a final report by the CSDH. The major contributions of *Closing the gap* are the visibility it gives to the social determinants of health, its justice-oriented trajectory, the extensive research it marshals, and its body of recommendations.

As noted in Chapter Five, the Commission's final report is unequivocal in its condemnation of the disparities in life opportunities and health status between rich and poor countries and between the rich and poor within countries. Beyond describing and criticizing these differences, the CSDH protests that "It does not have to be this way and it is not right that it should be like this. Where systematic differences in health are judged to be avoidable by reasonable action they are, quite simply, unfair ... Putting right these inequities – the huge and remediable differences in health between and within countries – is a matter of social justice ... Social injustice is killing people on a grand scale" (2008, vi). The Commission ascribes these differentials to "a toxic combination of poor social policies and programmes, unfair economic arrangements, and bad politics" (CSDH 2008, 26). The report makes three overarching recommendations: (1) improve the conditions of daily life – the circumstances in which people are born, grow, live, work, and age; (2) tackle the inequitable distribution of power, money, and resources that serve as the structural drivers of those conditions of daily life – globally, nationally, and locally; and (3) measure the problem, evaluate actions, expand the knowledge base in order to understand the problem and assess the impact of action and raise public awareness about the social determinants of health (CSDH 2008, 2, 26).

The goals of the human rights community are congruent with some, but not all, of these objectives. Certainly ongoing efforts to implement the full range of economic, social, and cultural rights seek to improve the conditions of daily life, although human rights initiatives are rarely described as such. Although *Closing the gap* avoids using human rights formulations, many of its concerns and commitment to achieve its first goal overlap with the content of the economic, social, and cultural rights enumerated in the International Covenant on Economic, Social and Cultural Rights (ICESCR 1966) and elaborated in the CESCR's subsequent general comments. Similarly, there is considerable overlap between the third of CSDH's overarching recommendations, to improve measurement of the problem

---

[2] The reports of the knowledge networks, and in some cases additional supporting documentation, are available at http:www.who.int/socialdeterminants/en.

and expand the knowledge base to understand the problem and assess the impact of actions, and the long-term commitment of the human rights community to monitoring in order to evaluate the status of the realization of human rights.

However, the second of the CSDH's overarching recommendations, to tackle the unequal distributions of power, money, and resources that serve as the structural drivers of inequitable conditions of daily life, breaks ground not trodden by the human rights community. As one of the subsequent sections of this chapter discusses, the human rights community has often been negligent in raising problematic structural issues and in addressing the resultant distribution of power, money, and resources. Nevertheless, there are no inherent reasons why it should not do so.

Social Determinants and the Underlying Determinants of Health

The conceptualization of the social determinants of health by the CSDH reflects recent thinking in the social medicine literature whereby the social determinants are viewed as a community attribute as well as a factor influencing individual health status (Diderichsen et al. 2001, 14). *Closing the gap* argues that the poor health of the poor, the social gradient in health within countries, and the marked health inequities between countries are caused by differences in the immediate, visible circumstances of peoples' lives – their access to health care, schools, and education, their conditions of work and leisure, their homes, communities, towns, or cities – and their concomitant chances of leading flourishing lives (CSDH 2008, 1). In turn, the CSDH contends that these inequalities reflect the unequal distribution of power, income, goods, and services, globally and nationally, which are then translated into inequitable social policies and programs, unfair economic arrangements, and bad politics (2008, 1). The CSDH views both the conditions of daily life and the underlying structural determinants shaping them as together constituting the social determinants of health.

Paul Hunt has claimed that a rights-based approach to health, at least as it has developed in recent years, also incorporates concern with the social determinants of health (2009, 38). From the outset Paul Hunt's reports as Special Rapporteur portrayed the right to health as necessarily incorporating the underlying determinants while acknowledging that this expansive view is not universally accepted. His 2007 report to the General Assembly has a section on two key underlying determinants, safe water and adequate sanitation, characterizing them as essential for the realization of the right to health and of other human rights as well (paras 45–69). Similarly his 2008 report observes that an effective and integrated health system, encompassing health care and the underlying determinants of health, is central to the right to health (para 15). When mentioning the establishment of the CSDH in his 2005 report to the UN General Assembly, he proffered that "There is considerable congruity between the Commission's mandate and the 'underlying determinants of health' dimension of the right to health, as well as other interconnected human rights such as adequate housing, food and water" (Hunt 2005, para 7).

Hunt is correct up to a point, but there also are significant differences between the way the two communities have conceptualized and approached this subject as well as the relative emphasis they accord. The difference in the terminology usually used – social determinants of health on one side and underlying determinants of health on the other – reflects other divergences in perspective. The approach to the underlying determinants by members of the human rights community tends to be narrower both in concept and in emphasis from the role the social determinants of health play in the social epidemiology and social medicine fields as reflected by the CSDH report. The CSDH has a far broader, more comprehensive, and better integrated understanding of the role of social determinants than the human rights community does of the underlying determinants. The focus of a rights-based approach, including its treatment of the underlying determinants, tends to be on identifying the state's obligations and assessing the extent to which they are being fulfilled. Human rights work only very secondarily considers the role of the underlying determinants as factors that determine the health status and outcomes of individuals and communities. And two critical social determinants, income and social class, are often missing from human rights discourse. In addition, human rights analysis tends to consider the underlying determinants of health individually and sequentially, thus missing the impact their interacting and cumulative effects can have on individuals and communities. Nor does a human rights approach link inadequacies and injustices in the distribution of the social determinants to a structural analysis of the way political, social, and economic forces in society shape life opportunities, as the CSDH tries to do.

Importantly, the relative emphasis given to these determinants also differs quite considerably in the two communities. For example, of the sixty-five paragraphs in the CESCR's general comment interpreting the right to health, only five mention the underlying determinants of health. Much of the remainder of the general comment addresses obligations of the state related to the health system and health services. Moreover, the references to the underlying determinants tend to be on lists without an explication of their influence on health outcomes. In contrast, the CSDH treats the health system as just another social determinant and confines its discussion of health services primarily to a single chapter of the seventeen chapters in its report.

Closing the gap, as well as the extensive body of research and publications on which it rests, makes a compelling case for viewing health systems and the people they serve within a wide social context. One of the implications of the CSDH report, and more broadly the findings of the social medicine and social epidemiology fields, is that societies cannot improve the health status of their populations and reduce significant health inequalities solely or primarily by increasing the resources devoted to medical services. While necessary and significant, investments to improve availability of health services and to enhance their quality and relevance cannot compensate for significant disparities in access to the social determinants of health. Therefore, social and economic policies that invest in the social determinants of health, more than just a narrow focus on health systems, constitute a more promising health policy approach. If the goal of the right to health is to improve health status in a society, particularly of vulnerable groups, then it is vitally important for those working on rights-based approaches to health to pay far greater attention to the conditions in which people grow, live, work, and age and to understand better how they shape health and well-being.

There are a variety of ways through which rights-based approaches to health can incorporate a more robust treatment of social determinants. Some human rights theorists have already called for a transformative engagement between health and human rights and the work in social epidemiology and social medicine (Yamin and Irwin 2010). Efforts to apply the findings of research on the social determinants of health would provide a starting point. A more vigorous effort to address inequalities and inequities in health outcomes, as advocated in the next sections, would also require greater attention to reducing disparities in access to the social determinants of health and require research and planning to achieve this objective.

Recovering the Collective Dimensions of the Right to Health

Additionally, a robust approach to the social determinants of health and to equity requires according greater emphasis to the collective dimensions of the right to health. Social determinants are social conditions that affect entire communities. Therefore, as noted above, an "absolutist focus" on the right to health as an individual right is inimical to addressing differences in population health outcomes, the role of the social determinants of health, and health equity issues (Rasanathan et al. 2010). Like other human rights, particularly economic, social, and cultural rights, the right to health has always had important collective or social dimensions whether or not they have been recognized by human rights analysts. Chapter Two discussed the social or collective components of the right and their recognition in General Comment 14. But like other human rights, the right to health is frequently portrayed solely or primarily as an individual right.

Benjamin Meier, collaborating with two different coauthors, has written a series of articles seeking to reinterpret the obligations related to the right to health from a collective perspective. These articles are premised on the belief the right to health advanced in ICESCR is a limited, atomized right that focuses on individual access to health care at the expense of collective health promotion and disease prevention (Meier and Mori 2005, 117), which I think is a more extreme characterization than is warranted. His first article, written with Larisa Mori (2005), argues that a society-based collective right to public health that complements the individual human right to health is a necessary precondition for fulfilling health rights in an age of globalization because globalization has created new underlying determinants of health unaccounted for by a limited individual right to health (2005, 104).

Two subsequent articles, written with Ashley Fox, recommend utilizing the collective right to development to realize the social determinants of health. Contending that even the expansive language of General Comment 14 is insufficient to establish a right to effective public health systems, they instead propose employing the collective right to development to achieve the goals of the right to health. Their thesis is the collective right to development, transcending the right to health's focus on the individual, offers public health actors an opportunity to allocate public goods for the public's health so as to ensure that economic growth improves health (Meier and Fox 2010, 260; Fox and Meier 2009, 122). They identify ways in which the right to development can operate as a "vector" of individual economic, social, cultural, civil, and political rights. As a vector or composite right, the right to development can enable these interconnected rights to be realized together within an integrated framework (Fox and Meier 2009, 119).

However, Meier and Fox overlook several important considerations. The first is that the right to health is not and never has exclusively been an individual right. Granted its public health components have often been neglected, but they are there to build upon. The second is that the right to development does not have the international standing and status of the right to health. So if the goal is to promote the highest attainable standard of health, it seems far preferable to conceptualize and strengthen the collective dimensions of that right.

Health Inequalities and Inequities

Inequalities in health describe differences in health status independent of any assessment of their cause or fairness. In contrast, the term equity is an ethical concept grounded in principles of distributive justice connoting fairness or social justice (Braveman and Gruskin 2003, 254). As Paula Braveman explains, health equity is the principle or goal motivating efforts to reduce or eliminate health disparities by improving the health of the economically and socially disadvantaged. Progress is measured by whether these disparities are narrowed, static, or widening over time (2013). In much of the literature on health inequalities and health justice, health inequalities that are avoidable and unnecessary are considered to be unjust and unfair and labeled as inequities (Dahlgren and Whitehead 1991; Daniels 2008; Braveman et al. 2011). The dilemma is determining and reaching agreement on which health inequalities are avoidable and unnecessary.

According to the CSDH, promoting health equity has two important components: improving average health and eliminating avoidable inequalities in health within countries. Much like a human rights approach, the CSDH report states that in both cases the emphasis should be on improving the health status of the worst off. However, the CSDH goes beyond a human rights approach in two significant ways: the first is its strategy to tackle the underlying structural determinants that generate stratification and social class divisions in a society and that define individual socioeconomic position within hierarchies of power, prestige, and access to resources,[3] and the second, its goal of bringing the worst off to the level of the best (CSDH 2008, 29).

One of the goals of the CSDH is to explicate the pathways that explain health disparities and inequities. According to the CSDH, the social determinants of health inequalities operate through a set of intermediary

---

[3] This strategy and its rationale are most clearly defined in the conceptual framework document prepared by the CSDH secretariat (Solar and Irwin 2007, 34–45).

determinants of health to shape health outcomes. The three categories of intermediary determinants of health identified are (1) material circumstances (such factors as housing and neighborhood quality, the financial means to buy healthy food, warm clothing, etc., and the physical work environment), (2) psychosocial circumstances (such factors as psychosocial stressors, stressful living circumstances and relationships, and social support and coping styles or the lack thereof), and (3) behavioral and biological factors (including nutrition, physical activity, tobacco consumption, and alcohol consumption). All of these are distributed differently among constituent social groups (Solar and Irwin 2007, note 7, 34–35).

The CSDH also implicates structural determinants or structural drivers in health inequalities and inequities. It proposes that social, economic, and political mechanisms within a particular society give rise to a set of sociopolitical positions whereby populations are stratified according to income, gender, education, occupation, race, ethnicity, and other factors. In turn, these socioeconomic positions shape specific determinants of health status reflective of people's place within social hierarchies (2008, 49). Fundamental inequalities in the social determinants of health result from the unequal distribution of power, income, goods, and services, globally and nationally (2008, note 2, p. 1). These differentials translate into inequitable social policies and programs, unfair economic arrangements, and bad policies that perpetuate the inequalities (2008, 1).

Building on the work in social medicine and social epidemiology, the CSDH report highlights the concept of a "social gradient" in health, that is, the systematic correlation between social standing and health outcomes. It provides evidence that across different types of societies lower social and economic status correlates with worse health outcomes. As one ascends the socioeconomic ladder, advances in social standing are paralleled by improvements in health. To put the matter another way, the relationship between socioeconomic standing and health is on a continuous gradient. Those second from the top have worse health than those at the top, and so on down the social hierarchy. This not only means that the poor have worse health than the rich, but the middle class have worse health than those who are more affluent than they are as well. The CSDH asserts that this relationship holds for people in poor and rich countries alike, even in better-off countries where living conditions among the poorest groups are far above any absolute poverty line (2008, 30–34).

Recommendations outlined in the report seek to reduce the slope of the social gradient, break the link between position in the social hierarchy and health outcomes, and improve the life opportunities and health status for those who are the worst off (2008, 20–31). Some of the proposals put forward overlap with the agenda of the human rights community. One CSDH strategy, for example, is to promote health status by making investments in early childhood development (defined as prenatal to eight years of age) and to promote access to education (2008, 3–4, 50–59). Other recommendations go beyond a human rights approach. For example, the CSDH maintains that the most effective way to promote greater equality in health status is to change the underlying causes of inequality – the social and political structures, policies, and mechanisms that shape the unfair and inequitable distribution of and access to power, wealth, and other necessary resources (2008, 109, 142, 155). A human rights approach usually focuses on more modest and incremental policy changes.

In contrast with the CSDH, a human rights approach tends to focus on formal equality rather than substantive equality, that is, equality of opportunity rather than equality of outcomes. Human rights analysis rarely considers inequalities in economic status and social class to be problematic unless they directly interfere with the realization of human rights or are implicated in differential treatment by the state. This reflects a difference in perspective about the kinds of inequalities that matter and what should be done about them. Human rights law is concerned with disparities in the enjoyment of rights rather than differentials in social position, access to resources, and political power. It does not usually correlate how these differentials affect the enjoyment of rights. There are a variety of reasons why this is the case.

Perhaps foremost, the emphasis in the human rights paradigm is on equality of dignity, legal standing, and legal status, and not equality in social or economic position. A human rights approach is grounded on the affirmation that "All human beings are born free and equal in dignity and rights" (Universal Declaration, article 1). Nondiscrimination, together with equality before the law and equal protection of the law, constitute core human rights principles (Human Rights Committee 1994, article 1). Discrimination "constitutes any distinction, exclusion, restriction or preference or other differential treatment that is directly or indirectly based on the prohibited grounds of discrimination and which has the intention or effect of mollifying or impairing the recognition, enjoyment, or exercise, on an equal footing of Covenant rights" (CESCR 2009, para 7). International human rights law requires that state parties implement the specific human rights enumerated in instruments they have ratified without distinctions of any kind or preferences based on race, color, sex, language, religion, political or other opinion, national or social origin, property, birth, or other status (International Covenant on Economic, Social and Cultural Rights 1966, article 2 and International Covenant on Civil and Political Rights 1966, article 2).

To what extent can nondiscrimination, equality before the law, and equal protection of the law, even if fully respected, bring about a more equalitarian society? Here it is helpful to cite Albie Sachs, an antiapartheid activist and later a member of South Africa's Constitutional Court for fifteen years. He argues that the equal protection principle is not sufficient to compensate for the status of disadvantaged persons who had been forced by racial discrimination to live in conditions of gross inequality, not even when coupled with affirmative action. According to Sachs, equal protection coupled with affirmative action could greatly assist the emerging new black middle class in South Africa, but not the desperately poor, because these principles do not require positive action on the part of the state to enable people to live in conditions consistent with at least minimum standards of human dignity (Sachs 2009, 169–170).

Gillian MacNaughton's analysis of equality and nondiscrimination in international human rights law provides further illumination of the limitations of these concepts for addressing economic and social inequalities. She observes that although equality and nondiscrimination are separate principles, legal scholars and UN treaty bodies have tended to conflate the two, thereby reducing their potential for addressing social inequalities (2009, 47). She explains that interpretations of equality are usually stated in the negative form as nondiscrimination, which prohibits differences in treatment upon a number of expressly prohibited grounds. In contrast, a positive interpretation of equality would require that everyone be treated in the same manner unless explicit justification is provided. Additionally, when legal scholars and courts describe relationships between equality and social rights they rarely identify poverty and economic status as prohibited grounds of discrimination under international human rights law (MacNaughton 2009, 47–48). Referring to the drafting history of the equality of law provision in the Universal Declaration and the International Covenant on Civil and Political Rights, MacNaughton shows that the intention was to assure that the law would be applied in the same manner to all. To put the matter another way, the equality provision was aimed at formal equality in the way laws are to be enforced. It was not meant to provide a guarantee of substantive equality or to offer a mandate to address underlying inequalities in power and socioeconomic and political status that preclude equal enjoyment of rights (MacNaughton 2009, 50).

A related issue is the question of who is the subject of equality under international human rights law, that is, "who is to be equal to whom." Alicia Yamin observes there is a tension in international human rights law between group-based human status and individual human treatment. While she acknowledges that inequalities within a group can be significant, she cautions that focusing on individual as opposed to group rights may be deleterious in achieving meaningful empowerment of people from disadvantaged groups (2009, 3–4). She notes that formal equality, which historically has been a central goal of human rights struggles, does not necessarily address underlying inequalities in power, access, and socioeconomic circumstances. Therefore, for her the question in achieving substantive equality "is not how to treat people in the same way but what is required for people in fundamentally different circumstances to actually have equal enjoyment of their rights" (2009, 6).

It should also be noted that the interpretation of economic, social, and cultural rights has additional elements with implications for social and economic inequalities. To compensate for rights fulfillment being conditional on the availability of resources in a state, the CESCR specifies that every state party, regardless of the resources available, ensure satisfaction of at least minimum essential levels of each right (CESCR 1990, para 10). The minimum essential levels or core obligations defined by the Committee in relationship to individual rights, particularly the right to health (CESCR 2000, paras 43–44), are quite extensive. It includes the duty "to ensure access to the minimum essential food which is nutritionally adequate and safe, to ensure freedom from hunger to everyone" (CESCR 2000, para 43 (b)); and "to ensure access to basic shelter, housing and sanitation, and an adequate supply of safe and potable water" (CESCR 2000, 43 (c)). If states were to implement these core obligations, the status and well-being of poor and disadvantaged individuals and groups would be significantly improved but still would not be equal. As Yamin points out, even if converted into effective strategies, the provision of a minimum essential level of health care, housing, education, and the like would reduce absolute deprivation, whereas equality is a matter of relative deprivation (Yamin 2009, 2).

Like the prescriptions of the CSDH, the human rights community historically has accorded priority to the status and needs of the most disadvantaged and vulnerable individuals and communities. Because a human right is a universal entitlement, its implementation is measured particularly by the degree to which it benefits those who hitherto have been the most disadvantaged and vulnerable and brings them up to mainstream standards. The Committee stipulates that even in times of severe resources constraints, whatever the cause, the vulnerable members of society can and indeed must be protected, for example, by the adoption of relatively low-cost targeted programs (CESCR 1990, para 12). The dilemma is that few countries appear to take this prescription seriously.

In recent years the human rights community has begun to accord greater attention to poverty as a human rights problem (Bengoa and Sanchez-Robles 2003; Pogge 2007). Some analysts working on health and human rights issues recognize that the strong and pervasive links between poverty and health mean that a commitment to improving health status necessarily implies a commitment to reducing poverty and the social disadvantages associated with it (Braveman and Gruskin 2003). Work in the human rights field has also highlighted that poverty entails more than just a lack of financial resources. It is also about the discrimination and disempowerment affecting disadvantaged groups – women, racial and ethnic minorities, disabled persons, and others – who are disproportionately represented among the economic disadvantaged, but also, as a consequence, the groups whose effective enjoyment of rights is most impaired and therefore require some means of redress (Yamin and Norheim 2014, 297–298). However, there is little conceptual clarity in the human rights communities as to whether poverty or extreme poverty is a violation of human rights, a violation of one right, namely, the right to an adequate standard of living or a right to development, or a cause or consequence of human rights violations (Costa 2008). Much of the work on poverty and human rights has addressed how to design, implement, and monitor a poverty reduction strategy through a human rights-based approach rather than assessing the impact of poverty on human rights (Hunt et al. 2003). Moreover, there has been little in-depth research on poverty and health from a human rights perspective.

Moreover, rather than being simply a problem of poverty or marginalization, as significant as these issues are, social and economic standing correlates with the health gradient in a society, which affects all classes from the top to bottom of society. To put this relationship another way, the social and economic ladder that exists in all societies gives rise to a parallel health status ladder. Some 200 peer-reviewed studies associate differences in economic status with a gradient in life expectancy, birth weight, rates of infant and child mortality, height, self-reported health, and vulnerability to AIDS, depression, mental illness, and obesity (Wilkinson and Pickett 2009). Data also indicate there is a continuous gradient in death rates: the higher people's economic and social status, the longer they live (Wilkinson 2005). Significantly, data from a wide variety of sources reveal that health differences between various classes have increased during the last few decades (Wilkinson 2005). This means that even if it were possible to eliminate all of the health problems associated with poverty and discrimination, the greater part of health inequalities would persist (Wilkinson 2005, 16).

Yet another important set of findings that argues for the importance of the human rights community investing more attention to equality as a determinant of health status and advocating for policies promoting greater equality is that it has been shown that more equal societies have better health (Subramanian and Kawachi 2004; Lynch et al. 2004; Wilkinson and Pickett 2006, 2009). Some twenty years ago the editor of the *British Medical Journal* wrote, "The big idea is that what matters in determining mortality and health in a society is less the overall wealth of that society and more how evenly wealth is distributed. The more equally wealth is distributed the better the health of that society" (Editor 1996). In *The Spirit Level: Why Greater Equality Makes Societies Stronger*, Richard Wilkinson and Kate Pickett also document both that more equal societies are correlated with better health outcomes and, the converse, that more unequal societies are associated with lower life expectancy, higher rates of infant mortality, greater rates of depression, greater obesity, a higher incidence of mental illness, higher rates of drug and alcohol addiction, and other poor health indicators (2009, 19, 81). While the benefits of greater equality in a society extend to everyone, they tend to be greatest among the poor (Wilkinson and Pickett 2009). Moreover, more egalitarian societies tend to have greater social trust and ability to cooperate, to be less violent, and less likely to discriminate against vulnerable groups, whether women or religious, racial, or ethnic minorities (Wilkinson 2005, chapters 1 and 2), thereby offering a social environment more conducive to promoting human rights.

So how might a rights-based approach to health incorporate a more sustained commitment to and promotion of substantive equality of health and social status? Gillian MacNaughton proposes that equality and non-discrimination might be more effectively employed for this purpose by recognizing poverty itself as a status and one-to-one or individual-level equality as a complement to social rights. A prohibition against discrimination on the basis of economic status might also help in securing a more equal distribution of financing for economic and social rights. In addition, she observes that there is support for both of these approaches in the International Bill of Human Rights. For example, one-to-one equality is recognized in civil and political rights in conjunction with such rights as the right to vote (2009, 49, 52).

Another proposal Alicia Yamin and Ole Frithjof Norheim put forward in a recent article on "Taking Equality Seriously" (2014, 308) is to adopt what has been termed a "Rawlsian maxi-min approach to equality" based on the principles articulated in John Rawls's well known *A Theory of Justice* (1971). Such an approach would ensure that the worst off would be given priority and benefit as much as possible from any changed allocation of health facilities, goods, and services. Indeed the very legitimacy of a proposed policy or institutional change would be evaluated on the basis of how much benefit it would bring to those who are disadvantaged. Although this approach would most likely improve the well-being of the poor and marginalized groups, it would not result in substantive equality (Yamin and Norheim 2014, 309).

However, before the human rights community could make a meaningful contribution there would first be a need to try to come to greater consensus about which inequalities in health constitute inequities and how egalitarian a society must be to provide a social order in which human rights can be realized. One step toward determining which inequalities constitute inequities from a human rights perspective could be to examine how specific inequalities are produced and whether governments and other actors can be held accountable for redress (Yamin and Norheim 2014, 308). It is relevant to note that the source of many of the inequalities of wealth and health violates established human rights principles. Given the focus of human rights on combating discrimination, it should be a small step to acknowledge that inequalities rooted in circumstances over which individuals and groups have no control such as their race, sex, or ethnic origin, constitute a source of unfair and unjust social disparity (Watkins 2014, 2249). Similarly health inequalities stemming from one's position on the societal social or economic ladder should be seen as unfair and unjust. Additionally, an examination of the sources of inequality requires a structural analysis to identify patterns rather than to simply catalogue single human rights violations. It would also be important to consider which of the inequalities constitute inequities from a human rights perspective.

If the human rights community wants to improve health status and health outcomes throughout the society, as well as to protect the interests of vulnerable and disadvantaged groups, it will need to pay more attention to inequalities in social, economic, and political status and their underlying causes and mechanisms. In this context, the economic and social impacts of the neoliberal policies discussed in Chapter Three are significant impediments. As noted there, during the past thirty years of following neoliberal policy prescriptions, economic inequalities have grown more marked both within and between countries. These trends reflect both the dynamics of capital accumulation under advanced capitalism and the neoliberal economic and political policies governments have adopted that reduce economic regulation and promote the interests of the affluent.

Beyond undertaking a structural analysis or coming to greater agreement about which inequalities constitute inequities from a human rights perspective, there is a need for human rights practitioners and analysts to advocate for the political policies to correct current inequities and to create greater equality of opportunity. An effective equity-based program would also require systematically addressing the social determinants of a wide set of economic and social sectors that have a bearing on health. An equity-based health approach would benefit from rights-based social protection measures to address poverty and food insecurity, as for example, through cash and food transfers to help the poorest sectors of the population (Watkins 2014, 2251–2253).

There are also various health systems and health policy-related measures that have been identified as having significant equity impact. These include reducing, and if possible eliminating, out-of-pocket payments for health services that impoverish an estimated 100 million people a year, establishing large-scale pooling of risk and resources financed through progressive taxation and mandatory prepayment, moving toward meaningful universal health coverage based on a comprehensive package of progressively financed health services for all, and strengthening the health system particularly at the primary care level. These will be discussed in greater depth in Chapter Eight as critical components of universal health coverage.

Power, Money, and Resources

One of the CSDH's principles of action is the need to address the inequitable distributions of power, money, and resources in the way society is organized, as for example, the pervasive inequalities between men and women (2008, 2). According to the Commission, inequities or avoidable inequalities in power interact across four main dimensions – political, economic, social, and cultural – and together they constitute a continuum along which groups are excluded or included to varying degrees. As conceptualized by the CSDH, the political dimension comprises formal rights embedded in legislation, constitutional provisions, policies, and the conditions under which rights are exercised, such as access to safe water, sanitation, shelter, health care, and education (2008, 155), but strangely not the formal power structure of the society, the nature of the government, or the character of the major political actors. The economic dimension is constituted by access to and distribution of material resources necessary to sustain life, and the social dimension by proximal relationships of support and solidarity, such as friendship, family, clan, community, and movements. Finally, the cultural dimension relates to the extent to which a diversity of values, norms, and ways of living with relevance for the health of all are accepted and respected (2008, 155–156).

The CSDH appreciated that any serious effort to reduce health inequities and to challenge and change the unfair distribution of social resources would necessarily involve transforming the distribution of power within a society and more broadly in the global system. Nevertheless, it seemed reluctant to identify the neoliberal policies exacerbating the inequalities and injustice or to directly confront them.

The CSDH report offers both top-down and bottom-up strategies for addressing the power imbalances that have led to health inequalities and inequities. Like a human rights approach, it advocates on behalf of a strong public sector and strengthened governance. Importantly, many of its recommendations related to power, resources, and money go well beyond those offered in human rights documents in their objectives and specificity. Believing that every aspect of government and the economy has the potential to affect health and health equity, the report puts forward an integrative approach to health equity across all areas of the government, and not just within the health sector (2008, 10). The CSDH advocates for a strong public sector that is committed, capable, and adequately financed to fund action across the social determinants of health. While human rights law is neutral on the issue of the privatization of health and other social services, with the caveat that private provision not reduce the availability, accessibility, acceptability, and quality of health facilities, goods, and services (CESCR 2000, paras 12, 24, 35), the CSDH argues that it is essential to have strong public sector leadership, public financing, and universal public health service provision to be able to make progress toward health equity (2008, chapter 11). Similarly, while General Comment 14 briefly stipulates that health facilities, goods, and services must be affordable for all (CESCR 2000, para 12.b), the Commission has an entire chapter on the importance of public financing through progressive taxation so as to provide adequate resources on an equitable basis to fund programs across the social determinants of health and universal health system services (2008, chapter 11).

Much like a human rights approach, the report also recognizes that civil society actors can be powerful drivers for positive social, political, and economic changes that affect health equity. *Closing the gap* devotes a chapter to political empowerment, inclusion, and voice. It offers two reasons for doing so. First, inclusion, agency, and voice are vital to social well-being and equitable health (CSDH 2008, 155). Second, political empowerment is identified as an important strategy for changing the distribution of power within society and global regions, especially in favor of disenfranchised groups and nations (CSDH 2008, 155). According to the report, political empowerment for health and health equity requires strengthening the fairness by which all groups in a society are included or represented in decision-making about these matters. In turn, the ability to do so depends on the existence of social structures supported by the government that mandate and ensure the right of groups to be heard and represent themselves (CSDH 2008, 158). "It is clear that community or civil society action on health inequities cannot be separated from the responsibility of the state to guarantee a comprehensive set of rights and ensure the fair distribution of essential material and social goods among population groups" (CSDH 2008, 165).

Empowerment and the active participation of disadvantaged and vulnerable persons and communities in order to enable them to have control over the decisions that affect their lives and health are central to the contemporary interpretation of the human rights paradigm. A human rights regime balances state responsibility as the ultimate guardian of its population's welfare with the empowerment of the individuals who are the holders of rights. This empowerment rests on an expanding notion of the requirements of human dignity and the affirmation of the principles of consultation, participation, transparency, and accountability for entitlements and freedoms as essential components of a human rights approach. Together these can change the self-perception of hitherto powerless constituencies into more activist rights holders. Therefore, rights approaches increasingly recognize the role of agency on the part of vulnerable groups to enable them to realize their socioeconomic rights. There is also increasing realization within the human rights community that sole reliance on a legal framework for rights is insufficient and disempowering; without community mobilization, claims to rights can be ignored (London 2007).

To put the matter another way, "A fundamental distinction of a human rights approach to development and policy-making that affects health is that it aims to enable those who are most impacted by poverty, patriarchy, and disease to be active participants in constructing the solutions to their problems" (Yamin 2009, 6). International human rights law emphasizes the central importance of participation in relationship to the right to health per se and to women's reproductive and sexual health, children's health, indigenous health, and the health dimensions of disabilities in particular (Yamin 2009, 6). Participation has been called "the right of right" because it allows members of society to claim their other rights (Halabi 2009), to challenge political arrangements and decisions that prevent us from having power over the decisions and processes that shape our lives and our health, and if need be to confront what Paul Farmer has termed "pathologies of power" that impose political and economic injustice, suffering, and illness (Farmer 2003).

The CSDH secretariat, aware that the human rights paradigm advocates for the empowerment of disadvantaged communities in order to enable them to exercise greater control over the factors that determine their health, had argued for adoption of a human rights framework for the report (Solar and Irwin 2007, 7–9). But the members of the Commission rejected doing so just as they steadfastly refused to acknowledge their common ground with a human rights framework or cite relevant human rights norms and instruments throughout the report (Chapman 2011). As a result, *Closing the gap* borrows the principles of empowerment and voice from human rights without incorporating the conceptual foundation of a human rights approach or offering a compelling rationale. What results is an uncomfortable hybrid in which advocacy of community empowerment is grafted onto a report that focuses primarily on top–down initiatives through changes in government policy.

The limitations of the CSDH's conception of empowerment can be seen through the lens of Alicia Yamin's work on participation (also referred to as empowerment) in rights-based approaches to health, which identifies three ways of thinking about domination and participation-as-empowerment. The first is a liberal understanding in which there is an overarching concern for ensuring fair processes of participation that enable competing groups to express their voices so that no one group may impose its will on others. In a second, participatory approaches go beyond formal inclusion to determine the content of decision making, that is, which issues that affect health are placed on the agenda to be decided. A third also includes sensitivity to the need for oppressed groups to have the means to shape perceptions of their own interests as input to the policymaking agenda. This entails their overcoming or escaping from the internalized cultural, social, and ideological forms of domination that prevent them from doing so (Yamin 2009, 5, 13–14).

The CSDH's interpretation of empowerment approximates what Yamin characterizes as a liberal understanding and suffers from many of its limitations. Unfortunately, so does the approach of some human rights activists. As Yamin explains, a liberal understanding typically assumes a level playing field in which the ability to express ones' views can potentially be effective as input for change. However, the CSDH's own analysis of structural inequalities recognizes this is far from the situation in most societies, particularly those that are the most unequal and have the greatest inequities. A liberal construal of participation fails to accord sufficient sensitivity to the power relations in which participatory processes are embedded and which determine which of the issues that affect health are put on the agenda to be decided (Yamin 2009, 5, 7).

The CSDH's thesis that efforts to promote greater health equity often require changes in the power structure of a society raises an important issue and something that the human rights community often overlooks. This is not to say that all rights-based work on health lacks awareness that "health is a reflection of power relations as much as biological or behavioral factors" (Yamin 2009, 6). However, the human rights community tends to neglect the manner in which the top-down organization of power across the political, economic, and social systems affects the realization of human rights. All too often human rights actors attribute failures to follow human rights prescriptions to a lack of political will on the part of the government rather than analyzing the underlying national and international power dynamics and structural determinants that block implementation.

More consistent attention to power dynamics would be an important complement to other human rights modes of analysis. As Alicia Yamin observes, the way power is conceptualized in a rights framework is linked both to notions of participation and more fundamentally to how we understand the purpose and meaning of human rights themselves (Yamin 2009, 5). Structural analysis of the way that social, economic, and political structures of societies intersect with the fulfillment of rights would be an appropriate starting point. The human rights community would also do well to invest greater effort to determine what kinds of political structures, institutions, and modes of financing are conducive to the fulfillment of specific social and economic rights.

However, an affirmation of the importance of empowerment and participation in the abstract does not necessarily translate easily into concrete initiatives to change policies or to improve access to beneficial social determinants. Organizing and mobilizing communities and groups for political change is difficult for a wide variety of reasons. A study of barriers to efforts to improve access to urban services for the poor identified internal divisions within the community; a low willingness to pay for improved water, sanitation, and hygiene infrastructure because people do not fully understand their value or contributions to improved health; coordination problems; and bureaucratic hurdles as factors affecting initiatives (Duflo et al. 2012). Chapter Five pointed out some of the problems that globalization and the role of transnational corporations impose for the social determinants of health. When foreign corporations control the availability or play a role in setting the costs and supply of vital social determinants like water and food, it is difficult for local communities to challenge or influence policies. Trade liberalization and the terms of free trade agreements also constrain the parameters of public health policies to limit exposure to harmful products, as for example, prohibiting imports of tobacco and placing warning labels on these products.

Public interest litigation to improve access to the social determinants of health is a strategy that has been used successfully in a number of situations. Human rights-related litigation on health issues has generally been characterized by the prevalence of individual claims for the provision of curative treatments without cost, most often medicines, by litigants from middle- and upper-class backgrounds, and not efforts to improve the basic preconditions or social determinants of health for a wider community of beneficiaries that include the poor. These lawsuits have been criticized for promoting inequality because they benefit a small number of plaintiffs, most of whom are privileged, who get more from the health system than the rest of the population (Yamin 2014). Nevertheless, there are instances where public law litigation has been used successfully for lawsuits involving water and sanitation public policies that improve access for the poor. One review of 258 cases in Brazil, generally filed by public prosecutors on behalf of municipalities and communities, found that courts were favorable to 76 percent of claims for sanitation services. A favorable judgment can launch social change processes, and social mobilization was often important in the implementation of the judicial decisions (Barcellos 2014).

There are also examples of litigation being used to improve access to specific social determinants in South Africa. In the Mazibuko case, poor residents in one township in Soweto challenged the city's policy on water rights seeking an increase in the free water made available each month to account holders on the grounds that the current policy violated the right to sufficient water under the constitution and the Water Services Act.

The litigants also sought an order that the installation of prepayment water meters in the township was unlawful. This latter claim was supported by the Anti-Privatisation Forum, a social movement comprised of community-based organizations and activists seeking to halt the commodification of basic needs. The Anti-Privatisation Forum organized mass action, including mass marches to offices of the city and the service provider. Although the High Court ruled in favor of the litigants, the Constitutional Court overturned the judgment on appeal (Cooper 2011, 205–207).

The Right to Food Campaign is an informal network of organizations and individuals committed to the realization of the right to food in India. It is an outgrowth of public interest litigation on the right to food, which demands a series of policies to be adopted to prevent hunger and starvation. It began with a writ petition submitted to the Supreme Court in 2001. The case has been handled by an advisory group consisting of representative from the People's Union for Civil Liberties, the Human Rights Law Network, and individuals active in the campaign. Supreme Court hearings have been held at regular intervals and the Supreme Court has issued interim orders from time to time. For example, the Supreme Court directed the Indian government to introduce cooked mid-day meals in all primary schools (Right to Food Campaign 2012). In 2013, the central government passed a law acknowledging a legal right to food that allots qualified households five kilograms of grain each month at subsidized prices. However, critics don't believe the ordinance is doing enough to enforce the right (Kajouee 2014).

Coordination Across Sectors and Health Impact Assessments of Government Policies

As the CSDH recognized, every aspect of government and the economy – finance, education, housing, employment, and transport – has the potential to affect health and health equity, even when health may not be the focus of policies in these areas. Therefore, it proposed that a policy agenda that seeks to address the social determinants of health from a pro-equity perspective should have an ongoing relationship between health and other sectors at global, national, and local levels (2008, 111). However, achieving policy coherence on health so that different government departments' policies complement rather than contradict each other on the achievement of health goals is difficult to achieve. There are significant barriers to intersectoral coordinated policy and action among health and nonhealth sectors.

Many low- and middle-income countries may lack the capacity to do so, especially those that have a continuing silo focus on disease-centered approaches to health. Intersectoral action on health also confronts a fundamental tension with the structural framework in which the government operates and the competing mandates between government departments (CSDH 2008, 110).

To begin to overcome these barriers CSDH made several recommendations. First, it emphasized the importance of national leadership on this issue. Second, it proposed that national governments establish a whole-of-government mechanism concerned with health and health equity that is chaired at the highest political level possible and accountable to parliament (CSDH 2008, 112). Third, when the institution of such a mechanism to promote intersectoral coordination on health is not feasible it suggested attention to the nature of policy and action within sectors (2008, 113). Fourth, the Commission recommended that the monitoring of social determinants and health equity indicators be institutionalized and health equity impact assessment of all government policies, including finance, be conducted (2008, 115). Fifth, the Commission advised that the health sector expand its programs in health promotion, disease prevention, and health care to include a social determinants of health approach (2008, 116).

So how could a rights-based approach to health promote greater intersectoral coordination and assessment of the health implications of policies outside the health sector? Importantly, many of the key social determinants of health identified in the CSDH report – access to nutritious food, safe working conditions, adequate housing, clean water and education – are enumerated as rights or components of rights in the ICESCR. A human rights approach could build from the principle of the indivisibility and interdependence of rights to develop a more integrated perspective on the role the realization of these rights play in health outcomes. General Comment 14 specifies that the right to health is closely related to, and dependent upon, the realization of other human rights, among them the rights to food, housing, work, and education (CESCR 2000, para 3). To date, however, indivisibility tends to be more of a rhetorical affirmation than a lens through which to analyze and advocate for the right to health. What is needed is greater attention to interpreting the right to health, and specifically the achievement of the social determinants of health, through this interdependent lens.

Additionally, health impact assessment within a human rights framework offers an important tool for predicting the potential consequences of a proposed policy, program, or project on the enjoyment of specific human rights. It could be applied for the purpose of informing policy makers of the likely impact of initiatives in other sectors on the right to health. Impact assessments are used in other fields. Environmental impact assessments constitute one example that has been employed for several decades. But human rights impact assessment is a much newer concept.

Paul Hunt presented a brief overview of a methodology for human rights impact assessment in one of his reports to the General Assembly (2007, paras 33–44) and a more expanded analysis in an article written with Gillian MacNaughton (Hunt and MacNaughton 2006). The first part of the methodology sets out seven general principles for performing a rights-based impact assessment. These are to: (1) use an explicit human rights framework; (2) aim for progressive realization of human rights as expeditiously and effectively as possible; (3) promote equality and non-discrimination at all stages and in all aspects of the impact assessment; (4) ensure meaningful participation by all stakeholders; (5) provide information to all parties potentially affected by the policy and protect the right of everyone to freely express ideas; (6) establish accessible and transparent mechanisms to hold the state accountable; and (7) recognize the interdependence of all human rights (Hunt 2007, para 40; Hunt and MacNaughton 2006). The second part of the methodology proposes six steps for integrating the right to health into existing impact assessments and also could be used to assess the right to health impact of proposed policies in other sectors. The steps are: (1) to begin by performing a pre-liminary check to determine whether or not a full-scale right to health impact assessment is necessary; (2) if it is determined appropriate to go forward, to prepare an assessment plan and distribute information on the policy and plan to all stakeholders; (3) to collect information on potential right to health impacts of the proposed policy; (4) to prepare a draft report comparing these potential impacts with the state's legal obligations arising from the right to health; (5) to distribute the draft report and engage stake-holders in evaluating the options; and (6) to prepare a final report detailing the decision made, the rationale, and a framework for implementation and evaluation (Hunt 2007, para 41).

Concluding Reflections

This chapter has argued that realization of a right to health requires investing greater attention to the social determinants of health and health inequalities. It provided data showing the links between social determinants and health status and outcomes. It proposed that for rights-based approaches to health to incorporate a more robust treatment of the social determinants it will be necessary for those working on these issues to engage more consistently with the findings of research from social medicine and social epidemiology. Through dialogue with the final report of the WHO Commission on the Social Determinants of Health, the chapter began the process of doing so.

The chapter also discussed the need for the human rights field, and more specifically those working on health and human rights issues and policies, to focus greater attention on the manner in which social class and economic status affect health outcomes. To be able to do so, the chapter called for the human rights field to adopt a more expansive and substantive conception of equality than the current human rights approach based primarily on assessing legal standing and legal status as they affect equality of dignity. The chapter cited data showing a correlation between the social and economic hierarchies and the health gradient in a society, which affects all classes from the top to bottom of society. It also identified data that show that the more equally wealth is distributed, the better the health of that society is and conversely studies that show more unequal societies are associated with lower life expectancy, higher rates of infant mortality, greater rates of depression, greater obesity, and a higher incidence of mental illness, and drug and alcohol addiction.

The implication of this analysis is that health and human rights practitioners should advocate for measures to bring about greater societal equality and fairer access to the social determinants of health as a path to more equal and equitable health outcomes. However, in order to effectively rectify health inequalities and inequities, it is first necessary to understand the manner in which they are produced and whether governments and other actors can be held accountable for redress. This agenda leads to the need for the human rights community to address the structural drivers of health inequalities and inequities. As the CSDH report notes, fundamental inequalities in the social determinants of health result from an unequal distribution of power, income, goods, and services, which then translate into inequitable social policies, unfair economic arrangements, and bad policies that perpetuate the inequalities (2008, 1).

This agenda raises the question of how to effectively advocate for fundamental changes leading to greater health equity. To be able to do so, it will be necessary to take on the neoliberal economic establishment and the neoliberal political order. More specifically, the human rights community will need to counter the underlying assumptions of neoliberalism, to reveal the skewed distribution of the beneficiaries of neoliberal policies in favor of the affluent and powerful, and to seek to bring about a return to something more closely approximating the social welfare orientation of governments in the decades following World War II.

I realize the menu of changes recommended in this chapter is very demanding and would require a fundamental reorientation of the health and human rights field. I also acknowledge that there would be a need for a great deal of new work to address structural issues related to the distribution of resources and power from a human rights perspective. Additionally, going forward with these prescriptions would also necessitate extensive discussions within the health and human rights community to try to reach greater consensus about many thorny issues, such as what health equity and equality of access to health care and health services entail. It would also be important to address and try to reach greater consensus within the human rights community and across disciplines working on health equity issues as to which health inequalities constitute inequities and which of these are avoidable by reasonable policy changes.

While I realize what I am proposing would have to surmount many hurdles and might not be palatable to many in the human rights community, it is important to keep in mind the importance of doing so. Reducing avoidable health inequalities and improving the life prospects of the poor and disadvantaged is literally a matter of life and death for millions of people. Hopefully a shared commitment to ameliorate some of the brutal health inequalities in the world in which we live will provide an incentive to go in the directions outlined in this chapter.

References

Barcellos, Ana Paula de (2014) "Sanitation Rights, Public Law Litigation, and Inequality: A Case Study from Brazil," *Health and Human Rights Journal* 16 (2):35–46.

Bengoa, Maarta and Sanchez-Robles (2003) "Foreign Direct Investment, Economic Freedom and Growth: New Evidence from Latin America," *European Journal of Political Economy* 19: 529–543.

Braveman, Paula (2010) "Social Conditions, Health Equity, and Human Rights," *Health and Human Rights* 12 (2): 31–48.

Braveman, Paula and Gruskin, Sofia (2003) "Poverty, Equity, Human Rights, and Health," *Bulletin of the World Health Organization* 81: 539–545.

Braveman, Paula, Kumanyika, Shiriki, Fielding, Jonathan, LaVeist, Thomas, et al. (2011) "Health Disparities and Health Equity: The Issue Is Justice," *American Journal of Public Health* 101, Supplement 1: S149–S155.

CESCR (Committee on Economic, Social and Cultural Rights) (1990) General Comment 3: The Nature of States Parties Obligations (Art. 2, para. 1 of the Covenant), contained in U.N. Doc. E/1991/23.

(2000) General Comment No. 14: The Right to the Highest Attainable Standard of Health, U.N. Doc. E/C.12/2000/4, www2.ohchr.org/english/bodies/cescr/comments.htm.

(2002) General Comment 15: The Right to Water (arts. 11 and 12 of the International Covenant on Economic, Social and Cultural Rights, U.N. Doc. E/C.12/2002/11.

(2009) General Comment No. 20: Non-Discrimination in Economic, Social and Cultural Rights (art. 2, para. 2), U.N. Doc. E/C.12/GC/20.

Chapman, Audrey R. (2010) "The Social Determinants of Health, Health Equity, and Human Rights," *Health and Human Rights* 12 (2): 17–30.

(2011) "Missed Opportunities: The Human Rights Gap in the Report of the Commission on Social Determinants of Health," *Journal of Human Rights* 10 (2): 132–150.

Convention on the Elimination of Discrimination against Women (1979) adopted by the United Nations General Assembly resolution 34/180 on 18 December 1979, entered into force on 3 September 1981.

Convention on the Rights of the Child (1989) adopted by the United Nations General Assembly on 20 November, entered into force on 2 September 1990, U.N. Doc. A/RES/44/25.

Cooper, Carole (2011) "South Africa/Health Rights Litigation: Cautious Constitutionalism," in Alicia Ely Yamin and Siri Gloppen, eds., *Litigating Health Rights: Can Courts Bring More Justice to Health*, Cambridge, MA: Harvard University Press, pp. 190–231.

Costa, Fernanda Doz (2008) "Poverty and Human Rights: From Rhetoric to Legal Obligations, a Critical Account of Conceptual Frameworks," *Sur* 5: 80–108.

CSDH (Commission on the Social Determinants of Health) (2008) *Closing the Gap in a Generation: Health Equity through Action on the Social Determinants of Health*, Geneva: World Health Organization.

Dahlgren, Göran and Whitehead, Margaret (1991) Policies and Strategies to Promote Social Equity in Health: Background Document to WHO – Strategy Paper for Europe.

Daniels, Norman (2008) *Just Health: Meeting Health Needs Fairly*, Cambridge: Cambridge University Press.

Diderichsen, Finn, Evans, Timothy, and Whitehead, Margaret (2001) "The Social Basis of Disparities in Health," in Timothy Evans, Margaret Whitehead, Finn Diderichsen, Abbas Buiya, and Meg Wirth, eds., *Challenging Inequalities in Health: From Ethics to Action,* Oxford and New York: Oxford University Press.

Duflo, Esther, Galiani, Sebastian, and Mobarak, Mushfiq (2012) Improving Access to Urban Services for the Poor: Open Issues and a Framework for a Future

Research Agenda, J-PAL Urban Services Review Paper, Abdul Latif Jameel Poverty Action Lab, Cambridge, MA.

Editor (1996) "Editor's Choice," *British Medical Journal* 312 (7072), doi:http://dx.doi.org/10.1136/bmj.312.7037.0, www.bmj.com/conntent/312/7037/0.

Farmer, Paul (2003) *Pathologies of Power: Health, Human Rights, and the New War on the Poor*, Berkeley and Los Angeles: University of California Press.

Fox, Ashley M. and Meier, Benjamin Mason (2009) "Health as Freedom: Addressing Social Determinants of Global Health Inequities through the Human Right to Development," *Bioethics* 23 (2): 112–122.

Gakidou, Emmanuela, Cowling, Krycia, Lozano, Rafael, and Murray, Christopher J. L. (2010) "Increased Educational Attainment and Its Effect on Child Mortality in 175 Countries between 1970 and 2009: A Systematic Analysis," *The Lancet* 376: 959–974.

Globalisation Knowledge Network (Ronald Labonté, lead author) (2007) *Towards Health-Equitable Globalisation: Rights, Regulation and Redistribution: Final Report to the Commission on Social Determinants*, www.who.int/...gkn_final_report_042008.pd...

Halabi, Sam Foster (2009) "Participation and the Right to Health: Lessons from Indonesia," *Health and Human Rights* 11 (1): 49–59.

Human Rights Committee (1994) General Comment No. 18: Non-discrimination, adopted on 10/11/89, Compilation of General Comments and General Recommendations Adopted by Human Rights Treaty Bodies, U.N. Doc. HRI/GEN/1/Rev. 1 at 26.

Hunt, Paul (2004) Report of the Special Rapporteur on the Right of Everyone to the Highest Attainable Standard of Health, U.N.Doc. A/59/422.

(2005) Report of the Special Rapporteur on the Right of Everyone to the Highest Attainable Standard of Physical and Mental Health. Sixtieth session of the United Nations General Assembly, U.N. Doc. A/60/348.

(2007) Report of the Special Rapporteur on the Right of Everyone to the Highest Attainable Standard of Physical and Mental Health. Sixty-second session of the United Nations General Assembly, 8August, U.N. Doc. A/62/150.

Hunt, Paul and MacNaughton, Gillian (2006) "Impact Assessments, Poverty and Human Rights: A Case Study Using the Right to the Highest Attainable Standard of Health," Health and Human Rights Working Paper Series No. 6, World Health Organization and UNESCO, www.who.int/...Series_6_Impact%20Assessm

Hunt, Paul, Nowak, Manfred, and Osmani, Siddiq (2003) Principles and Guidelines for a Human Rights Approach to Poverty Reduction Strategies, Office of the United Nations High Commissioner for Human Rights, HR/PUB/04/1, www2.ohchr.org/english/issues/poverty/guideline.htm.

Hunter, Paul R., MacDonald, Alan M., and Carter Richard C. (2010) "Water Supply and Health," *PLoS Medicine* 7 (11): e1000361.

International Covenant on Civil and Political Rights (1966) Adopted 12 December 1966, 999 U.N.T.S. 171 (entered into force 23 March 1976), G.A. Res. 2200 (XXI), 21 U.N. GAOR, Supp. (No. 16) at 52, U.N. Doc. A/6316.

International Covenant on Economic, Social and Cultural Rights (1966) adopted and opened for signature, ratification and accession by United Nations General Assembly Resolution 2200A (XXI) of 16December 1966, (entered into force on 3 January 1976), U.N. Doc. A/6316.

Kajouee, Shereen (2014) India Upholds Legal Right to Food, Human Rights brief, Center for Human Rights and Humanitarian Law, 21 (1), http://hrbrief.org/author/shereen.kajouee.

Koh, Howard K., Piotrowski, Julie J., Kumanyika, Shiriki, and Fielding, Jonathan E. (2011) "Healthy People: A 2020 Vision for the Social Determinants Approach," *Health Education & Behavior* 38: 551–557.

Lagard, M., Haines, A. and Palmer, N. (2009a). The Impact of Conditional Cash Transfers on Health Outcomes and Use of Health Services in Low and Middle Income Countries, The Cochrane Collaboration. apps.who.int/rhl/reviews/CD008137.pdf.

London, Leslie (2007) "Issues of Equity Are Also Issues of Rights: Lessons from Experiences in Southern Africa," *BMC Public Health* 7, www.biomedcentral.com/1471-2458/7/14.

Lynch, John L., Smith, George D., Harper, Sam, Hillemeier, Marianne, et al. (2004) "Is Income Inequality a Determinant of Population Health? Part I. A Systematic Review," *Milbank Quarterly* 82: 5–99.

MacNaughton, Gillian (2009) "Untangling Equality and Non-discrimination to Promote the Right to Health Care for All," *Health and Human Rights* 11 (2): 47–63.

(2013) "Beyond a Minimum Threshold: The Right to Social Equality," in Lanse Minkler, ed., *The State of Economic and Social Human Rights: A Global Overview,* New York: Cambridge University Press, pp. 271–305.

Marmot, Michael (1999) "Acting on the Evidence to Reduce Inequalities in Health," *Health Affairs* 18: 42–45.

Meier, Benjamin Mason and Fox, Ashley M. (2010) "International Obligations through Collective Rights: Moving from Foreign Health Assistance to Global Health Governance," *Health and Human Rights* 12 (1): 61–72.

Meier, Benjamin Mason and Mori, Larisa M. (2005) "The Highest Attainable Standard: Advancing a Collective Human Right to Public Health," *Columbia Human Rights Law Review* 37 (1): 101–147.

Minister of Health and Others v Treatment Action Campaign and Others (No2) 2002 (5) SA 721 (CC).

Ottersen, Ole Petter, Dasgupta, Jashodhara, Blouin, Chantal, Buss, Paulo, et al. (2014) "The Political Origins of Health Inequity: Prospects for Change," *The Lancet,* 383 (9917): 630–667.

Pogge, Thomas, ed. (2007) *Freedom from Poverty as a Human Right: Who Owes What to the Very Poor?* Oxford: Oxford University Press and New York: UNESCO.

Rasanathan, Kumanan, Norenhag, Johanna, and Valentine, Nicole (2010) "Realizing Human Rights-based Approaches for Action on the Social Determinants of Health," *Health and Human Rights* 12 (2): 49–59.

Rawls, John (1971) *A Theory of Justice*, Cambridge, MA: Harvard University Press.

Report of the Special Rapporteur on the right of everyone to the enjoyment of the highest attainable standard of physical and mental health, Paul Hunt, Sixty-second session of the United Nations General Assembly, August 8, 2007, U.N. Doc. A/62/150.

Report of the Special Rapporteur on the right of everyone to the enjoyment of the highest attainable standard of physical and mental health, January 2008, U.N. Doc. A/HRC/7/11.

Right to Food Campaign (2012) Legal Action: Introduction, www.righttofoodindia .org/case/case.html.

Sachs, Albie (2009) *The Strange Alchemy of Life and Law,* Oxford and New York: Oxford University Press.

Schrecker, Ted, Chapman, Audrey R., Labonté, Ronald, and De Vogli, Roberto (2010) "Advancing Health Equity in the Global Marketplace: How Human Rights Can Help," *Social Science & Medicine* 71: 1520–1526.

Solar, Orielle and Irwin, Alec (2007) "A Conceptual Framework for Action on the Social Determinants of Health: Discussion Paper for the Commission on Social Determinants of Health," Secretariat Commission on Social Determinants of Health, www.who.int/social_determinants/.../en/.

Subramanian, S. V. and Kawachi, Ichiro (2004) "Income Inequality and Health: What Have We Learned So Far?" *Epidemiology Review* 26 (1): 78–91.

Townsend, Peter and Davidson, Nick (1982) "Introduction to the Pelican Edition," in Douglas Black, Cyril Smith, and Peter Townsend, eds., *Inequalities in Health: The Black Report*, Middlesex, pp. 13–16, England and New York, NY: Harmondsworth.

Universal Declaration of Human Rights (1948) adopted by the United Nations General Assembly Resolution 217A (III).

Watkins, Kevin (2014) "Leaving No One Behind: An Agenda for Equity," *The Lancet* 384: 2248–2255.

Wilkinson, Richard G. (2005) *The Impact of Inequality: How to Make Sick Societies Healthier*, New York: The New Press.

Wilkinson, Richard G. and Pickett, Kate E. (2006) "Income Inequality and Population Health: A Review and Explanation of the Evidence," *Social Science and Medicine* 62: 1768–1784.

Wilkinson, Richard and Pickett, Kate (2009) *The Spirit Level: Why Greater Equality Makes Societies Stronger More Equal Societies Almost Always Do Better*, New York, Berlin, and London: Bloomsbury Press.

Wilson, Barbara (2009) "Social Determinants of Health from a Rights-based Approach," in Andrew Clapham and Mary Robinson, eds., *Health: A Human Rights Perspective*, Vol. 3, pp. 60–79, available at www.swisshumanrightsbook.com/SHRB/shrb_03.html.

Woolf, Steven H. and Aron, Laudan, eds. (2013) *US Health in International Perspective: Shorter Lives, Poorer Health*, Washington, DC: National Academies Press.

Woolf, Steven H. and Braveman, Paula (2011) "Where Health Disparities Begin: The Role of Social and Economic Determinants – and Why Current Policies May Make Matters Worse," *Health Affairs* 30 (10): 1852–1859. doi: 10.1377/hlthaff.2011.0685.

Yamin, Alicia E. (2008) "Will We Take Suffering Seriously? Reflections on What Applying a Human Rights Framework to Health Means and Why We Should Care," *Health and Human Rights* 10 (1): 1–19.

(2009) "Shades of Dignity: Exploring the Demands of Equality in Applying Human Rights Frameworks to Health," *Health and Human Rights* 11 (2): 1–18.

(2014) "Promoting Equity in Health: What Role for Court?" *Health and Human Rights* 16 (2): E1–E9.

Yamin, Alicia Ely and Irwin, Alec (2010) "Collaborative Imperatives, Elusive Dialogues," *Health and Human Rights* 12 (2): 1–2.

Yamin, Alicia Ely and Norheim, Frithjof Ole (2014) "Taking Equality Seriously: Applying Human Rights Frameworks to Priority Setting in Health," *Human Rights Quarterly* 36: 296–324.

Zimmerman, Emily and Woolf, Steven H. (2014) "Understanding the Relationship between Education and Health," Discussion Paper, Institute of Medicine, Washington, DC, www.iom.edi/understandingtherelationship.

8

Right to Health Perspectives on
Universal Health Coverage

One of the most hopeful global health policy developments in recent years is the growing interest in and commitment to achieving universal health coverage (UHC). The World Health Assembly defined UHC "as access to key promotive, preventive, curative and rehabilitative health interventions for all at an affordable cost, thereby achieving equity in access" (World Health Assembly 2005). In 2011, the World Health Assembly urged member states "to aim for affordable universal coverage and access for all citizens on the basis of equity and solidarity" (World Health Assembly 2011, para 2). UHC is also incorporated in the Sustainable Development Goals adopted by the United Nations in September 2015 as part of the omnibus health goal to ensure healthy lives and promote well-being for all at all ages. Target 3.8 is to "achieve universal health coverage, including financial risk protection, access to quality essential health-care services and access to safe, effective, quality and affordable medicines and vaccines for all" (United Nations 2015). There are also initiatives to provide assistance for countries committed to progress toward that goal. In 2010, the World Health Organization's annual report was devoted to health system financing to enable countries to advance toward UHC (World Health Organization 2010). Since 2010, more than seventy countries have requested advice and support from the World Health Organization (WHO) regarding reforms required to progress toward UHC (WHO Consultative Group on Equity and Universal Health Coverage 2014, ix).

UHC can be considered to be an expression of the right to health. The preamble in the 2011 World Assembly resolution specifically links the achievement of UHC to article 25.1 of the Universal Declaration of Human Rights, which recognizes the right to a standard of living adequate for health and well-being including medical care (United Nations 1948). At its core UHC entails a commitment to enable everyone in the society, regardless of their economic status, social and ethnic background, age, geographic location, or gender, to be able to access the health care they need without suffering financial hardship. In addition, UHC advocates generally characterize health as a public good and acknowledge that the state has the responsibility to ensure access to health services, which are two major components of the right to health (Sengupta 2013, 8). Significant progress toward UHC, consistent with the requirements of the right to health, would have the potential of enabling the one billion people estimated to not have access to the health services they need each year to obtain them (Brearley et al. 2013, 16). Those who are the poorest and most disadvantaged, the groups most likely to suffer ill health and premature death and who are the least likely to have access to good quality health services and protection against health-related financial risks, would benefit the most (Brearley et al. 2013, 5).

UHC has been identified as potentially the third global health transition, the first being public health improvements such as basic sewage and sanitation and the second being the epidemiological transition that reduced the toll of communicable diseases (Rodin and de Ferranti 2012). Moreover, some experts believe that universal health care is not an idealistic goal that remains out of reach for all but the richest nations. They point to the progress a number of poor- and middle-income countries have made at relatively low cost through their pioneering public policies (Sen 2015). A Rockefeller Foundation report also proposes that the cost of transitioning toward UHC may be lower than assumed and therefore more feasible (2010, 11).

While the growing support for UHC is a welcome development, it does not necessarily mean there will be meaningful progress toward this goal in any specific country even when there are policy commitments to do so. It is important to have awareness of the complexity and requirements for UHC so that favoring UHC involves more than just rhetoric. Moving toward UHC entails a long-term process of progressive realization that requires advancing on several fronts for all people: increasing the proportion of the population that enjoys health protection, particularly the population groups that hitherto have lacked access to services; improving the available range of services provided to address people's health needs effectively; and increasing the proportion of the costs covered through government funding, pooling, and prepayment mechanisms. All of these components involve complex challenges (World Health Organization 2008b, 25–26; World Health Organization and The World Bank 2013a). Many countries may lack the resources, the capabilities, and the commitment for sustained progress.

Moreover, there is the possibility that efforts to move toward UHC may not result in the establishment of an equitable health system. As two health policy researchers warn, "beware – universal coverage is much more difficult to achieve than to advocate. And people who are poor could well gain little until the final stages of the transition from advocacy to achievement, if that coverage were to display a trickle-down pattern of spread marked by increases first in better-off groups and only later in poorer ones" (Gwatkin and Ergo 2010, 2160). In such a situation, especially if the expansion were to be stalled as has happened in a number of countries, the health status of vulnerable communities could even grow worse absolutely or relatively.

To cite a specific example of one country's stumble on the path to UHC, Ghana's frequently lauded National Health Insurance Scheme was introduced in 2004 with the intention of delivering UHC. However, ten years later the National Health Insurance Scheme still covered only 36 percent of the population with the remaining 64 percent continuing to rely on out-of-pocket payments to fund their health care (Averill and Marriott 2013, 19). Moreover, the design of Ghana's program, which requires the ongoing payment of contributions, is likely to make it difficult to expand coverage beyond workers in the formal sector. Some of the other countries often cited as success stories – Mexico, Thailand, Sri Lanka, Malaysia, and Brazil – have made more progress toward UHC, but their performance still falls short, especially when evaluated from a human rights perspective. Even some of the European countries long considered to be universal health care systems – Britain, France, Germany, the Scandinavian countries, Canada, the Netherlands, and Switzerland – have some human rights deficiencies, and problematically some of them are in the process of cutting back their health entitlements.

Importantly, not all potential paths to a universal health system are consistent with human rights requirements, even ones that result in significant health expansion. For example, some countries have prioritized expansion of a broad package of health services to workers in the formal sector and their families leaving coverage for those in the informal sector and the unemployed to a later stage of health expansion. This later stage may be deferred indefinitely. This approach violates the human rights standard of giving priority to the worst off. It also contravenes the principles proposed by the WHO Consultative Group on Equity and Universal Health Coverage for the expansion of health coverage (2014, 11, 17).

Somewhat ironically, UHC has become prominent on the global health agenda at a time when the impact of the neoliberal policies identified in previous chapters of this book makes this goal more difficult to achieve. Health systems that have received inadequate funding for a prolonged period are likely to lack the capabilities to provide effective health services to an expanded population. To bypass weak public health systems, some donor agencies and countries are opting for expansion of health delivery through private providers and funding via private health insurance. This approach reflects neoliberal policies but is inconsistent with human rights requirements for achieving UHC. Moreover, health systems that have relied on private health provision are ill suited to cover underserved populations without a significant makeover. Therefore, there is a risk that UHC may become more of a slogan than a reality.

The previous chapter highlighted the importance of redressing inequalities in the social determinants of health as a contribution toward reducing inequalities and improving health status. This chapter focuses on a second key requirement for the realization of a right to health, providing timely and affordable access to needed health services for all members of society within a well-functioning health system. The chapter first conceptualizes the requirements for the realization of UHC from a right to health perspective. It then explores the rationale and the status of each of these components so as to identify the barriers and problems that will need to be overcome.

Conceptualizing the Right to Health Requirements of Universal Health Coverage

There are a variety of conceptions of UHC, not all of which incorporate human rights norms. UHC consistent with the requirements of a right to health would include the following elements:

- Health care reforms designed to achieve universal access to essential health services would be placed within the context of a national effort to provide equitable access to the social determinants of health.
- Access to essential health services and public health protections would be made a legal entitlement with adequate means of seeking redress to challenge failures to provide statutory benefits.
- The coverage would be based on a true universality covering all residents of a country regardless of their legal status.
- There would be explicit attention to equity considerations in the design of the universal health system and throughout the process of expanding coverage, especially to instituting measures that would reduce barriers for low-income groups, rural populations, women, and other vulnerable groups that are disadvantaged in terms of service coverage and health.

- An equitable and progressive system of health funding for financial risk protection would be put in place to eliminate or at least significantly reduce financial barriers, especially for poor and disadvantaged groups. The system would provide for compulsory prepayment and the establishment of large risk pools in order to facilitate cross-subsidization. The government would cover the health costs of people who cannot afford to contribute.
- Sufficient funding would be provided for strengthening the health system so as to expand health coverage and provide a publicly funded package of priority health services based on people's needs. To do so would require lower- and middle-income countries devoting at least 5 percent of GDP and 15 percent of the total government budget to health in the medium term.
- Health system strengthening would be accorded priority in order to make good quality health services widely available, especially in currently underserved communities and with a greater balance achieved between rural and urban areas.
- There would be opportunities for consultation with and the participation of the population in the design of the path to UHC and the determination of packages of benefits.
- The process for pursuing progressive realization of UHC would first expand coverage for high-priority services to everyone with special efforts to ensure that disadvantaged groups are reached.
- A uniform package of health service benefits closely linked to the population's needs would be universally provided by the government.
- An improved data monitoring system would be put in place to evaluate the distributional effects of efforts to achieve UHC and improve health outcomes with the capacity to track and assess data on a disaggregated basis so as to be able to identify and undertake corrective action when necessary.

Prioritizing the Social Determinants of Health

As the previous chapter discussed, efforts to improve access to the social determinants of health and address inequalities in the distribution of resources and in the living and working conditions in a society are essential to achieving the right to health. In countries with widespread access to at least basic health services, the provision of sufficient good quality food, water, shelter, sanitation, and education, consistent with the obligations outlined in the various general comments drafted by the Committee on Economic, Social and Cultural Rights to conceptualize the requirements of economic and social rights, would likely have a greater impact on improving public health status than provision of a wider range of health care services. Nevertheless, discussions of progressive reforms to achieve universal health care frequently neglect the importance of the social determinants of health.

For example, in a 2011 series in *The Lancet* on achieving universal health care in India only the author of the final article mentions the importance of the social determinants and the broader social context in which the reforms would take place. Ravi Narayan underscores that meaningful health care reforms and efforts to build an integrated national health system have to be placed within a national effort to provide social determinants of health. He also reminds his readers that "Equity, solidarity, and public good must be central" (Narayan 2011, 883). Otherwise, he warns, curative medical care will take precedence over provisions for well-being, including preventive medicine and health promotion. In place of the top-down biomedical and techno-managerial framework presented in the other contributions to the series, he proposes a bottom-up initiative based on community involvement, civil-society engagement, and action on the social determinants (Narayan 2011).

Providing a Legal Entitlement

One of the core principles of the right to health is that countries should recognize the right to health in national law and by ratifying relevant human right treaties (CESCR 2000, para 1). Because legal recognition of the right to health is usually formulated in general terms, it also requires follow-up legal provisions to spell out what kinds of health services and facilities the government will provide or require from third parties contracted to deliver health services and how the services will be funded. Such clarifications may be provided by laws, regulations, protocols, guidelines, and/or codes of conduct (Backman et al. 2008, 2047). Legal recognition of the right to health provides a basis through which to contest government failures to provide health entitlements and a foundation for judicial decisions seeking to improve the delivery of health-related services. It also facilitates the use of nonjudicial mechanisms of accountability (Backman et al. 2008, 2076 and 2078).

Like a right to health, a commitment to UHC should be in the form of a binding legal provision. If UHC is not to be achieved immediately, which would be the situation in most countries, there should be a timeline specified for the extension of coverage. In addition, the law should specify the kind of health services and financial subsidies the government will provide.

Who Is to Be Covered

At first glance the question of who should be covered in a universal health system seems quite simple. The Merriam-Webster dictionary defines the word universal as existing or available for everyone. Beginning with the Universal Declaration of Human Rights (General Assembly 1948), human rights instruments have recognized the inherent dignity and the entitlement to equal and inalienable rights of all persons without distinctions of any kind. A right to health embodies a critical value: the acknowledgement that those goods and services that constitute essential health services and support health have to be available and accessible to all and leave no one out (Allotey et al. 2012). The United Nations Committee on Economic, Social and Cultural Rights (CESCR) has stated that "states are under the obligation to respect the right to health by, inter alia, refraining from denying or limiting equal access for all persons, including prisoners or detainees, minorities, asylum seekers and illegal immigrants, to preventive, curative and palliative health services" (CESCR 2000, para 34). According to the Committee, "all persons, irrespective of their nationality, residency or immigration status, are entitled to primary and emergency medical care" (CESCR 2008, para 37). A recent report of the UN Secretary-General on the question of the realization in all countries of economic, social, and cultural rights reiterates that migrant workers enjoy all economic and social rights enumerated in international human rights instruments and that these obligations extend to documented and undocumented migrants, refugees, and asylum seekers (Secretary-General 2014, para 50).

Although European Union member states are often identified as examples of countries ostensibly committed to the principle of universal access or UHC, few of these countries have fully universal health systems that cover every resident within their borders. Almost all European countries provide health entitlements to their citizens and some also extend partial coverage to legal foreign residents. But not many of these countries offer health entitlements to undocumented immigrants, or as they are sometimes described, irregular migrants who do not fulfill legal conditions for entry, stay, or residence (European Union Agency for Fundamental Rights 2011, 7). Even European countries with generous health benefits often provide undocumented migrants only with access to emergency care, and this care is not always granted cost-free (Wörz et al. 2006, 2). The failure to provide full health benefits to this vulnerable group is particularly problematic from a human rights perspective because their life situation often exposes them to health-impairing risks from exploitative working conditions and precarious living conditions (European Union Agency for Fundamental Rights 2011, 7). In the three countries – Belgium, Italy, and France, (and a fourth, Spain before austerity measures were imposed during the Great Recession as a condition for loans to stabilize the banking system) – where migrants in an irregular situation may access some publicly funded health services if they fulfil specific conditions, there are other types of barriers preventing them from receiving care. These barriers include complex reimbursement procedures; lack of awareness of entitlements by both health providers and beneficiaries; and fear of the risk of detection and deportation due to information passed on to the police (European Union Agency for Fundamental Rights 2011, 7).

Additionally, in several EU countries cost-sharing arrangements and administrative barriers sometimes deter health access even for legal residents and citizens. As noted in Chapter Three, a 2010 survey in eleven European countries indicated that some adults had to forego medical care because of their inability to afford user fees or pay the full cost of the services in the past year. The percentages were relatively low in some countries (5 percent in the UK, 6 percent in the Netherlands, and 10 percent in Sweden and Switzerland) but rose to 13 percent in France and 25 percent in Germany – higher than would have been anticipated for countries considered to have UHC (Thomson et al. 2013, 8). Also, complex administrative requirements can deter some vulnerable groups. The unemployed are one group with problems in meeting administrative requirements. Lack of geographical proximity to health services can also be a problem for many people.

Equity-Related Measures to Reduce Barriers for Vulnerable Groups

Equity needs to be made an explicit commitment in designing both the process by which a state plans to expand coverage of health services and the institutions of the universal health services system. Without an adequate focus on equity, vulnerable and poor populations may receive inadequate or inferior health care. For example, inequities may arise in UHC systems through disparities in the quality of care and access to specialized clinical services available to different groups depending on their socioeconomic status (Rodney and Hill 2014). Research has shown that while there is little income-related inequity in the utilization of public primary care in many countries, there is a pro-rich inequity in the utilization of specialists and in the type and quality of health services available, particularly in countries where private options are available. This relationship holds for countries in the European Union (Wörz et al. 2006, 2) as well as in many developing countries.

Universal access, which is a right to health requirement, is a concept that includes but goes beyond universal coverage. It implies "the absence of geographic, financial, organization, sociocultural, and gender-based barriers to care" (Pan American Health Organization 2007). Universal access therefore requires initiatives to remove supply-side barriers as well as demand barriers such as social exclusion and discrimination, lack of information, and the absence of decision-making power to seek health care (Ravindran 2012). It also calls for special efforts to identify vulnerable groups and to initiate efforts to reduce and eventually eliminate barriers that prevent them from gaining access to health services. Vulnerability, which is broadly described as the susceptibility to harm, often is contextual, that is, dependent on social, economic, and cultural risk factors and trends (Allotey et al. 2012). Moreover, policies aimed at promoting UHC may not benefit some groups to the same extent as others. For example, unless there is attention to gender differences, ostensibly universal health services may be inadequate for women's needs (Ravindran 2012).

To assure that vulnerable groups are fully included within and benefit from the progressive realization of UHC requires the careful design and implementation of strategies for advancing toward universal coverage that target these communities. Several components of General Comment 14 are relevant to these efforts:

- The requirement to make health facilities, goods, and services and the underlying determinants of health physically accessible to all, especially the most vulnerable or marginalized, such as women, children, adolescents, older persons, persons with disabilities, and persons with HIV/AIDS in both law and fact (CESCR 2000, para 12 (b ii)).
- The obligation that health facilities, goods, and services must be affordable for all and based on the principle of equity; it further specifies that equity demands that poorer households should not be disproportionately burdened with health expenses as compared to richer households (CESCR 2000, para 12 (b iii)).

- Health facilities, goods, and services must also be culturally appropriate for all peoples and communities and sensitive to gender and life-cycle requirements (CESCR 2000, para 12 c).
- The general comment advocates for special efforts to eliminate discrimination against women through developing and implementing a comprehensive strategy for promoting women's right to health throughout their life span, including interventions aimed at the prevention and treatment of diseases affecting women and policies to provide access to a full range of relevant and affordable health care, including sexual and reproductive services (CESCR 2000, para 21).
- The general comment also has special requirements for protecting and promoting the health of children, persons with disabilities, indigenous peoples, and older persons (CESCR 2000, paras 24–27).

A recent report of the WHO Consultative Group on Equity and Universal Health Coverage addresses key issues of fairness and equity that arise on the path to UHC. The report underscores that a commitment to fairness, equity, and respecting individuals' right to health must guide countries as they make decisions about how to expand priority services, cover more people, and reduce the burden of paying for health services (WHO Consultative Group on Equity and Universal Health Coverage 2014, x–xi). The report offers three guiding considerations for countries pursuing the goal of UHC:

- Fair distribution: Coverage and use of services should be based on need, and priority should be given to the policies benefiting the worse-off groups. In particular, no one should be denied access to high-priority services because he or she is too poor to be able to pay for them (WHO Consultative Group on Equity and Universal Health Coverage 2014, 9). Brazil's Family Health Program and Mexico's Popular Insurance initiative constitute examples of countries that have sought to reduce inequality in health coverage by initially concentrating expansion of services among the most disadvantaged groups before extending initiatives with declining subsidies to those with higher income levels (Rodney and Hill 2014).
- Cost-effectiveness: Given the limitations in available funding, priority should be given to the most cost-effective policies. Cost-effective policies and services generate large total benefits relative to cost (WHO Consultative Group on Equity and Universal Health Coverage 2014, 9). By doing so, it becomes possible to stretch scarce resources for health programs and services.

- Fair contribution: Contributions to fund the health system should be based on ability to pay and not on need, particularly for high-priority services (WHO Consultative Group on Equity and Universal Health Coverage 2014, 9–10). This principle translates into a commitment to subsidize the cost of essential health services for those too poor to afford them.

The obligations enumerated in General Comment 14 and the equity considerations discussed in the report of the WHO Consultative Group on Equity and Universal Health Coverage (2014) have significant implications for all dimensions of the financial and institutional policies adopted on the path to UHC as well as the priorities set. Subsequent sections of this chapter will apply the human rights obligations and equity considerations to the topics being discussed.

Equitable Health Funding for Financial Risk Protection

Moving toward more equitable sources of health funding is central to the achievement of universality. Realization of the right to health is dependent upon the affordability of health care both for the state to finance and for its members to be able to cover their needed health care without imposing an undue financial burden. As noted above, a much cited 2005 World Health Assembly resolution links attainment of universal coverage with the principle of financial-risk protection to ensure that the cost of care does not put people at risk of financial catastrophe and with equity in financing, which envisions households contributing to the health system based on the ability to pay. WHO has prioritized four key policy initiatives to finance UHC: reducing out-of-pocket payments; maximizing mandatory prepayment; establishing large risk pools; and using general government revenues to cover those who cannot afford to contribute (World Health Organization 2010). These proposals parallel recommendations made by Anand Grover, the second Special Rapporteur of the Right to Health on this issue (2012).

Reducing reliance on out-of-pocket (OOP) payments to pay for health goods and services, and if possible eliminating these costs for vulnerable groups, is a key priority of UHC. OOP payments is the least equitable and often a common approach to health funding. Moreover, globally the proportional share of health financing through OOP fees imposed at the point of service is highest in low-income countries where the population can least afford it (Social Protection Department 2014, 15), sometimes reaching as high as 80 percent of total health funding (Rockefeller Foundation 2010, 7). In many poor countries, neoliberal reforms, usually undertaken in response to donor pressure, introduced or increased the role of user fees in the health sector. As noted in Chapter Three, OOP fees have a disproportionate impact on the poor, who must pay considerably larger proportions of their income for health care than more affluent individuals. As a consequence, when illness strikes poor households they often experience financial catastrophe and impoverishment in order to pay for health care or are forced to forego needed care (Grover 2012, para 2). Every year some 100 million people, most of whom live in low-income countries, are pushed into poverty as a result of excessive or catastrophic spending on health care (WHO 2010, 12).

Today there is a shift in the international consensus away from the imposition of user fees in poor countries. Even the World Bank has moved away from its earlier ideologically driven approach to requiring user fees as a condition for its loan packages (Rowden 2013, 178). Studies in countries that have eliminated user fees indicate that doing so increases use of health services: in African countries the increases have ranged from 17 percent in Madagascar to 84 percent in Uganda (Lister 2013, 158). However, not all countries that imposed user fees in the 1990s in response to World Bank pressure have decreased or removed user fees. A 2006 survey of thirty-two African countries found twenty-seven still imposing fees (Lister and Labonté 2009, 190). Also, a policy decision to eliminate or reduce health fees is not an immediate panacea. In some cases, changes in policy have not been fully implemented, and in others new informal fees have been imposed to compensate for the loss of income. Additionally, a health system that has been underfunded for a prolonged period lacks the capacity to provide health services to a greatly expanded number of patients, especially when countries have not prepared adequately for the transition. For example, a study of reforms in six sub-Saharan African countries found that lack of planning and consultation resulted in poor design of the reform and weaknesses in the implementation (Meesen et al. 2011).

Reduction of fees in public facilities, even when direct payments fall to 15 to 20 percent of total health expenditure, the level WHO calculates will be sufficient to reduce the incidence of financial catastrophe and impoverishment (2010, xiv), will not necessarily eliminate the burden of catastrophic health expenditure among the poor unless there are parallel improvements in the availability and quality of care in the public health system. Results of surveys in thirty-nine low- and middle-income countries indicate that on average only 45 percent of the OOP costs of out-patient care were for payments at government facilities (WHO 2010, 50). The poor quality of health services in many public facilities drives people to use private sector health facilities, and the frequent unavailability of drugs at government facilities forces patients to purchase them from private pharmacies (Xu et al. 2006). Transport can be another major expense, especially for populations in remote rural areas (WHO 2010, 51). To compensate, some countries, primarily in Latin America, provide conditional cash transfers, whereby people receive money if they do certain specified things to improve their health, which can be used to offset transportation costs, lost income, and other expenses incurred when obtaining health care (World Health Organization 2010, 52).

Protection from catastrophic health expenditures needs to be a high priority in the progressive realization of UHC, and some health policy experts believe it is feasible to do even in poor countries. Despite its poverty, the state of Andhra Pradesh in India established a community health insurance scheme that automatically covers all families living below the poverty line (about 80 percent of its eighty-two million population). The Aarogyasri Scheme, while not comprehensive, provides coverage for catastrophic secondary and tertiary conditions. The cost of the program is entirely funded by the state government, which receives substantial aid from a variety of donors to be able to do so (Rockefeller Foundation 2010, 2–30).

Raising sufficient resources for health funding in an equitable way requires the use of tax revenues and/or the pooling of health funds collected through mandatory prepayment schemes and other mechanisms, such as insurance pools, that allow for cross-subsidization of financial risks across a population. Importantly, no country has achieved anything close to UHC through relying on voluntary insurance contributions. Public financing has played a central role in all the UHC success stories to date (Averill and Marriott 2013, 4, 25). Tax financing is particularly important for poorer countries where a large proportion of the population earns low wages and many work in the informal sector. Even some European countries with long-established social insurance schemes, for example, Germany, are finding that social insurance schemes that fund health services through members' payroll contributions are insufficient to cover the health care costs. These countries therefore have to inject general tax revenues to keep the system afloat (Averill and Marriott 2013, 14). Mandatory schemes also support cross-subsidization. Cross-subsidization is important because it facilitates the transfer of resources from wealthier individuals to poor, vulnerable, and marginalized groups and from those who have low risk factors to others with high risk factors for illness (Grover 2012, para 12). In addition, contributions need to be compulsory for those who can afford them to prevent the rich and the healthy from opting out thereby leaving the health system with insufficient funding to cover the needs of the poor and the sick (WHO 2010, xv).

As a matter of equity and to ensure that disadvantaged groups are not left behind in the path to fair progressive realization of UHC, countries at all levels of income will need to cover the health care costs of those who cannot afford to contribute (WHO 2010). It is an implication of the human rights principle of according priority to the worse off, and it also has a firm grounding in the theory of fair distribution (WHO Consultative Group on Equity and Universal Health Coverage 2014, 14–15). A study of the structure of national insurance reforms in nine developing countries in Africa and Asia, all of which are classified as low- or lower-middle income, indicated that the countries that have made sustained progress toward UHC have used tax revenues to fund health coverage for poor people and other vulnerable groups such as pregnant women and children (Lagomarsino et al. 2012, 936).

Although voluntary insurance schemes in poor countries have been shown to have low coverage rates, to be costly to administer, and to exclude the poor, some governments and donor agencies, among them the World Bank Group, the ILO, the Dutch government, and UNICEF, continue to provide encouragement and financial and technical support to initiate and attempt to expand voluntary schemes (Averill and Marriott 2013, 14). One such scheme is India's much touted Rashtriya Swasthya Bima Yojna (RSBY), the country's flagship national health insurance plan for people living below the poverty line. According to the government 50 percent of eligible households are enrolled in the 460 districts where RSBY operates, but these figures are likely to be a significant overestimation. Also problematic, male enrolment was over 1.5 times higher than female enrolment. Additionally, RSBY provides inadequate financial protection to enrollees. It only covers hospital costs in a country where 74 percent of OOP costs is expended on outpatient care and medications. Cost escalation by the private insurance companies financing RSBY in order to maximize profits is another major problem (Averill and Marriott 2013, 15).

Social health insurance, a pooling mechanism funded by compulsory prepayments collected through individual and organizational contributions, has the advantage of creating sufficiently large risk pools to allow for cross-subsidization but the disadvantage of often excluding those who are not formally employed or who cannot afford the required health insurance payments. While social health insurance has worked to achieve UHC in a number of high-income countries, the model has been much less successful in low- and middle-income countries. Developing countries typically have large-scale exclusions of those working in the informal sector and difficulty scaling up social insurance schemes to reach them and the poor. Even when social health insurance premiums and co-payments are set at a low level they often constitute a significant financial barrier. Ten years after their introduction, social health insurance schemes in Tanzania covered only 17 percent of the population; Kenya's National Hospital Insurance Fund, established nearly a half century ago, still insures only 18 percent of Kenyans; and Ghana's much heralded National Health Insurance scheme covers only 36 percent of its population. Furthermore, social health insurance schemes can be expensive to operate, especially when the government is a major employer. In 2009/10 the Government of Tanzania spent $33 million on employer insurance contributions or $83 per government employee, which was six times more than the annual per-person health expenditure for the general population (Averill and Marriott 2013, 18–20).

Reflecting neoliberal policy prescriptions, some donors and developing countries are favoring private health insurance to fund the move toward UHC. In some lower- and middle-income countries, private insurance is the only form of risk pooling available. However, even when state regulated, private health insurance frequently presents problems for equity and for human rights (Jost 2003, 11–14). One barrier is cost. In a free market system premiums for individual policies tend to be expensive, too expensive for low-income individuals to afford. Biased selection, sometimes referred to as "cherry picking" or "cream skimming," constitutes a second problem. To protect their profits, health insurers vary the potential cost and even the availability of health insurance policies depending on an applicant's health status and risk factors for illness. Higher-risk applicants, exactly the individuals who most need health insurance, face the highest rates because their health care is likely to involve the greatest reimbursement costs. In some cases, private insurers refuse to cover high-risk individuals who are not part of some larger pool of community-rated insurance and they become uninsurable.

In countries where the public health care system offers broad access to a broad range of services, the role of free market private health insurance is usually supplementary to public funding mechanisms and designed to cover additional services the publicly funded health services does not provide or requires a waiting period. The average ratio in OECD countries in 2011 was 72-to-28 in favor of public expenditures (OECD 2011). To avoid disparities in access and the quality of services, some health systems with public provision of universal coverage, Canada and Israel, for example, have prohibited citizens from opting out of the public system for covered services, but have permitted the purchase of private insurance for supplementary services not offered through the public funding mechanism, such as dental care or eye glasses. Other publicly funded systems often lack such strictures.

Some countries, for example, Germany, offer high-income individuals the option of buying private health insurance instead of participating in otherwise mandatory social insurance schemes or public sources of funding. Doing so may save money but it also tends to discourage investment in the public system and makes risk pooling less sustainable. In turn, this may reduce the overall quality and availability of public health facilities, goods, and services resulting in infringements of the right to health (Grover 2012, para 37).

There are a variety of ways that high-income countries committed to UHC reduce reliance on direct payments for private health services. These include increasing the proportion of general tax revenue needed to support and sustain the health system; underwriting the basic cost of medically necessary physician and hospital services, including those secured through the private sector; general tax revenue (Canada, Denmark, England, Italy, New Zealand, and Norway); social insurance financed by employer–employee payroll taxes and in some cases also subsidized through central taxes (France and Germany); and a regulated private insurance market with subsidies for insurance for the poor and others, like the handicapped, unemployed, and the elderly, along with government compensation to underwriters based upon a risk-adjustment formula (Netherlands and Switzerland) (Commonwealth Fund 2010). However, it should be noted that these schemes do not necessarily protect all individuals from paying high costs. Cost sharing is rising in many countries to alleviate budgetary pressures, and evidence suggests that higher co-payments have created barriers to access in some countries.

Several middle-income countries have adopted some forms of prepayment, risk pooling, catastrophic coverage, and/or financial risk protections for specific vulnerable groups. Thailand, a lower middle-income country, is sometimes cited as a model of a country that has moved toward UHC despite having significant resource constraints. In 2001, Thailand built upon a foundation of four existing health risk protection schemes to extend coverage to the more than eighteen million people then lacking health insurance. The scheme instituted provides access to subsidized health care that relies primarily on general taxation for funding. OOP expenditures for health services for many members of the population are limited, but even so, OOP expenditures as a proportion of total expenditures initially remained high, amounting to 26 percent in 2007 (Rockefeller Foundation 2010, 83) and then declining to 13 percent in 2012 (Minh et al. 2014, 5). Implementation was facilitated by having a strong political imperative and previous experience from health schemes that had partial population coverage.

Two Latin American countries, Chile and Costa Rica, have followed different approaches to financing UHC, with both achieving near-universality. Chile has maintained a dual health care system under which its citizens can opt for coverage by either the public national health insurance fund or any of the country's private health insurance funds. The public health system is funded by a universal income tax deduction equal to 7 percent of every worker's wages. Private health insurers encourage people to pay a variable extra on top of the 7 percent premium to upgrade their basic health plans. The structural segmentation of Chile's health care system has resulted in low-income and high-risk populations being serviced by the public sector, while high-income and low-risk populations are covered by the private sector. Health reforms adopted in Chile in 2005 established a list of compulsory health services applicable to both the public and private sector insurance funders that is periodically updated. According to a recent study, the negative effects of the dual system of private and public insurance include higher OOP expenditures, inequities in access to specialized care utilization, and the lower quality of public services (Ortiz Hernández and Pérez Salgado 2014).

In contrast, Costa Rica has a single national publicly funded system in which workers make contributions and the poor are covered by a non-contributory plan that is funded by the government with resources that primarily come from general taxation. A comparative analysis of the two health systems indicates that the Costa Rican health system is both less expensive and more equitable. Both countries provide access to basic services but Costa Rica has made more progress in offering comprehensive health services to everyone. Also, per capita health expenditure in Chile is considerably higher than in Costa Rica (Ortiz Hernández and Pérez Salgado 2014, 21).

Raising and Investing Sufficient Resources in Health

Financial constraints related to insufficient levels of government spending on health constitute a common barrier to making progress toward UHC in many countries. Most lower-income and many middle-income countries consider health to be a low priority sector and do not devote sufficient resources to develop an effective and equitable health system able to provide health services for all of their people.

Recent estimates of the money needed to reach the health-related Millennium Development Goals and expand health systems so as to deliver critical interventions, including for noncommunicable diseases, suggest that low-income countries need to spend a minimum of U.S. $60 per capita, nearly twice as much as the U.S. $32 per year that WHO calculated they were spending in 2010 (WHO 2010, xii). A more generous package appropriate for a middle-income country would likely cost at least three to four times as much. Investment in health systems also seeking to progress toward UHC consistent with human rights norms would require even greater resources. Many poor- and middle-income countries underspend the WHO guideline that countries invest 5 to 6 percent of their gross national product (GNP) in health (World Health Organization 2010, 50) and the figure set at the 2001 Abuja conference that countries spend 15 percent of their national budgets on health, including some where the government purports to have a commitment to UHC. In 2012, most of the ten countries in the Association of Southeast Asian Nations (ASEAN) region allocated less than 5 percent of GNP, with the exception of Cambodia and Vietnam. General government expenditure on health as a percentage of total government expenditure in 2012 was also low in these countries, ranging from 1.5 percent in Myanmar and 5.8 percent in Malaysia to 14.2 percent in Thailand (Minh et al. 2014). Some of the largest middle-income Asian countries had even lower levels of investment. In 2012, the figures for health spending in India, Bangladesh, and Pakistan as a proportion of the GDP were, respectively, 1.0 (Rao et al. 2014), 3.6, and 2.7 percent. Bangladesh and Pakistan devoted 7.7 and 4.7 percent, respectively, of total government budgetary expenditure to the health sector (Global Health Observatory Data Repository, n.d.).

In 2001, African Union countries meeting in Abuja, Nigeria, pledged to increase government funding for health to at least 15 percent of their budgets, but ten years later only one African country had reached that target. Overall, in the ten years following the meeting, twenty-six African Union countries increased the proportion of government expenditures allocated to health while eleven reduced it, and the other nine remained stable (WHO 2011). In contrast, several Latin American countries achieved the recommended targets of 5 percent of GNP and 15 percent of government budgetary spending including Argentina, Chile, Peru, and Mexico (Global Health Observatory Data Repository, no year given).

In many poor and middle-income countries, having sufficient resources for health-related expansion and for delivering needed health services requires raising more money for health both domestically as well as from donors. It also requires allocating more funds from both of these sources to health-related expenditures. According to WHO, all countries have scope to raise more money for health domestically through increasing the efficiency of revenue collection and reprioritizing government budgets, especially the majority of low- and middle-income countries with weak revenue collection systems. WHO also proposes using innovative financing mechanisms to finance health systems, such as increasing taxes on air tickets, foreign exchange transactions, and tobacco and dedicating the funds to health-related expenditures.

It is noteworthy that only eight of forty-nine countries currently classified as being in the low-income category are considered to have any prospect of generating sufficient funds for health from domestic sources alone, and others will require greater international aid targeted for health (World Health Organization 2010, xii–xiii). In recent years aid for health expenditures has increased, but it is often targeted for specific programs and it varies from year to year. Therefore, reliable multiyear commitments and transfers of aid designated more broadly for the health sector will be necessary to improve health systems and make progress toward UHC in these countries.

Building Effective and Equitable Health Systems

The underlying message of this section is that if countries are to transition to UHC, there is an urgent need to invest in health system strengthening. It is therefore disappointing that much less attention has been and continues to be devoted to the process of health system strengthening than to the financial aspects of the progressive realization of UHC. Health system strengthening requires a whole-systems approach to overcome what WHO characterizes as unfair, disjointed, and inefficient health systems focused excessively on curative services and neglecting the prevention and health promotion that WHO estimates could cut an estimated 70 percent of the global disease burden (World Health Organization 2008b).

In some countries, a very large portion of the population lives in extremely deprived areas without the availability of health services (World Health Organization 2008b, 27). Progressive realization of UHC will therefore require establishing new health care institutions in such areas, and where health services are very inadequate, the basic health care infrastructure will need to be built or rebuilt. Achieving a better balance between the availability and quality of health services between rural and urban areas constitutes another priority. Another challenge is extending coverage in countries where inequalities and patterns of exclusion result from the way health care is organized, regulated, and/or paid for by official or under-the-counter user charges (World Health Organization 2008b, 28).

The five characteristics said to underlay many of the health systems in EU countries approximate some of the important requirements of an equitable universal health system respecting human rights criteria. Their public health systems provide the primary mode of access to health care. Public funding predominates in their health systems. Participation in the health system is mandatory. Benefits coverage is broad; and access and resource allocation are on the basis of need (Wörz et al. 2006, 2). It has been suggested that the priority accorded to UHC in the EU reflects the belief that access to health care is a precondition for active membership in society (Wörz et al. 2006, 1), and this too corresponds with the right to health paradigm. However, as noted above, many of the EU countries that ostensibly respect universality do not completely fulfil its requirements, because they do not provide health coverage to migrants living in their country. Moreover, the health systems in some of these countries have other kinds of barriers to access health services.

Addressing the deficit of trained health care workers is one of the most needed and thorny requirements for strengthening health systems in order to progress toward UHC. In 2013, WHO estimated that the world has a deficit of some seven million health care workers and that by 2035 the figure would rise to 12.9 million, in part because of an ageing health workforce with staff retiring or leaving for better paid jobs without being replaced while not enough young people are entering the profession or being trained. WHO also identified internal and international migration of health workers as exacerbating regional imbalances. Currently eighty-three countries are below the basic threshold of twenty-three skilled health professionals per 10,000 people (WHO 2013).

In sub-Saharan Africa the shortages are especially acute. Data for the forty-seven countries in the African region, which together account for about 25 percent of the global burden of disease, indicate that the region has a shortage of nearly 818,000 health workers. According to 2013 data, the African region had only 1.4 percent of physicians, 2.8 percent of the nurses and midwives, 1.4 percent of the dentistry personnel, 1.6 percent of the pharmaceutical personnel, and 0.7 percent of the psychiatrists available globally. The majority of the countries had fewer than one physician per 10,000 population and 89 percent had fewer than one dentistry personnel per 10,000 population (Sambo et al. 2014). However, just 168 medical schools exist in the region; eleven countries have no medical schools and twenty-four have only one each (WHO 2013).

Moving toward UHC will also require a fundamental restructuring of the health care systems of many countries. One needed reform is additional investment of resources and personnel to rectify the significant imbalances between rural and urban populations in health coverage and access that now exist. The global deficit in rural coverage is estimated to be two- and one-half times that of urban areas. While 22 percent of the global urban population lacks health coverage, the figure rises to 56 percent of the rural population. Moreover, some 70 percent of the developing world's extremely poor people live in rural areas. The situation is aggravated by extreme health workforce shortages in rural areas. The International Labor Office estimates that only 23 percent of health workers are deployed in the rural areas to serve 50 percent of the world's population who live there (Scheil-Adlung 2015, 1–9).

A commitment to provision of people-centered primary care constitutes another component of the health system strengthening essential to progress toward UHC (World Health Organization 2008b). Comparative studies have shown that primary health care is a central feature of national health systems delivering high quality care at an affordable cost (Rawaf et al. 2008). Four decades ago the Declaration of Alma-Ata identified primary health care as key to the attainment of health for all (Declaration of Alma-Ata 1978). It still is. Primary health care is both pro-poor and pro-rural. Also, the inclusive vision of primary health care in the Declaration of Alma-Ata included attention to the social determinants of health as well as providing basic health services. This can be an important potential contribution of a strong primary health system. Moreover, health personnel trained specifically for primary health care can be recruited from local communities and are more likely to remain situated there.

There is historical evidence of the importance of primary health care as a foundation for the transition toward UHC. The Thai 2002 health care reform, often cited as a successful model of rapid health coverage expansion, was preceded by and able to leverage fifteen years of health center development that established primary health centers in rural areas (Sengupta 2013). Brazil is another country in which the development of primary health care has been central to efforts to provide universal access and comprehensive health care as well as to coordinate and expand coverage to more comprehensive levels of care. In urban areas in that country primary health clinics focus on families and communities and integrate medical care with health promotion and public health actions (Paim et al. 2011, 1788).

A comprehensive approach to primary care raises issues about how best to roll out primary care networks to fill the availability gap in currently deprived, mostly rural areas. As WHO notes, some advocate an approach in which a limited number of priority services are rolled out simultaneously to all inhabitants in deprived areas and then the services offered scaled up as resources become available. The alternative is a progressive rollout of a more comprehensive version of primary care district-by-district. Iran's progressive rollout of rural primary coverage offers an impressive example of this model. However, as WHO recognizes, this latter approach has the risk that a country will not maintain the constant effort and investment required to progressively rollout comprehensive primary care networks across the entire country (WHO 2008b, 28–30).

The achievement of universal primary care will require the investment of additional resources in primary care. Governments in countries with budget constraints will either have to be willing to increase the total resources devoted to health at the expense of another sector or to reallocate resources among levels of the health system. Currently, many countries have a disproportionate investment in tertiary health care that favors urban populations and is an inequitable use of public funds, but reallocating funds from tertiary to primary care may be politically difficult.

Expanding the delivery of health care services and developing more effective and equitable health care institutions are currently made even more challenging by the legacy of three decades of the neoliberal policies discussed in earlier chapters. After decades of inadequate funding and insufficient investment in health institutions and services, largely due to the influence of neoliberal policy prescriptions, the health systems of many countries are seriously weakened and sometimes dysfunctional. In many countries, there are serious availability constraints, including long distances to health facilities worsened by poor public transport, especially in rural areas; inadequate service provision at primary care facilities; frequent unavailability of drugs in public facilities; insufficient skilled staff, particularly doctors; and lack of diagnostic equipment in public facilities.

There are also acceptability constraints related to the lack of patients' confidence in the expertise of health staff and the poor attitudes of staff, which discourage use of facilities (Mills et al. 2012, 127). Critical shortages of health workers in the public sector remain in many countries, especially in rural settings.

Research has shown that in all the countries that have successfully transitioned to UHC the government has played a major role in financing and regulating, and in many the government has served as the direct provider of health care services (Savedoff et al. 2012, 926). Such an active, often dominant, governmental role is inconsistent with neoliberal policies designed to limit the role of government in the health sector, transfer control to the market, and provision to private companies. Although neoliberal approaches to UHC often acknowledge the need for the state to play a role in securing funding for health care and regulating the quality of health services, they rarely support having the public health sector function as the dominant health provider. The current neoliberal model of UHC prescribes a clear split between health financing and health provision that endorses the continuing role of existing private providers and allows for the entry of additional private health providers and private health management organizations. The rationale is that current health care challenges require an immediate remedy and that public health systems are too weak to do so (Sengupta 2013, 2). Therefore, instead of initiatives to rebuild and strengthen the public health sector, many countries have adopted a strategy to invest public resources in the private sector to promote the expansion of health coverage.

UHC will require a rebalancing of health systems toward greater investment in the public sector. South Africa constitutes an example. Despite a constitution entrenching the right to health, a series of policy initiatives in the years since the dismantling of apartheid in 1994 advocating for major health reforms, including framework legislation for the establishment of a National Health Insurance system, and a sufficiently high per capita health care spending level to fund universal health care, South Africa continues to have a highly inequitable health care system with poor health outcomes. Serious and persistent deficiencies in access to health care for the poor, predominantly black population reflect the disproportionate investment of resources in the private sector (60 percent of total health care funding) that serves less than 20 percent of the population, and there is also poor availability of health care workers in the public sector. (Only 30 percent of the country's health care personnel work in the public sector). Moreover, in the years since 1994 the spending gap between the public and private systems has increased and the distribution of health care workers worsened. The crisis of the availability of health care is particularly dire in areas with high poverty and in rural areas (Forman and Singh 2014, 288–300). Meaningful health care reform and progress toward UHC in South Africa will require a major redistribution of the resources and personnel between the public and private sectors, but doing so raises very difficult challenges.

India and Brazil are two other countries hampered by a strategy of relying on the private sector for achieving universal health care services. As discussed earlier in this chapter, to compensate for its historical under-investment in the public health sector, India's approach to extending coverage focuses on publicly funded but largely privately provisioned social health insurance schemes. These initiatives have further strengthened the already dominant private sector. It has also distorted the flow of resources away from primary care services and into the far more expensive and potentially profitable hospital-based tertiary care sector (Sengupta 2013, 19).

In Brazil, the Unified Health System (SUS) ostensibly provides universal coverage, free of charge, and there is a complementary family health program, *Bolsa Familia*, to provide additional services for the poor. However, in Brazil the chronic underfunding of the public health system in favor of subsidizing private health insurance and private providers has affected the quality of services in the public health system and delayed efforts to overcome regional inequalities and structural deficiencies (Hennigan 2010). To compensate for the poor quality of public health services, those who can afford to do so purchase private insurance and opt out of the public system. Private health insurance now covers about 25 percent of the population (Rao et al. 2014). Provision of secondary care is restricted in the public system and often given preferentially to individuals with private health plans (Paim et al. 2011, 1790). Hence, despite the progress that has been achieved in Brazil, studies show that access to health services still correlates with family income, and an equitable health system is still a distant goal (Guanais 2010). Also, as the private sector's market share increases, it is leading to conflicting ideologies and goals: universal access versus market segmentation (Paim et al. 2011, 1794).

Importantly, private health providers are usually not well situated to engage in health services extension to neglected communities. Offering services to poor communities and their members is usually not profitable. Therefore, well-trained and well-resourced private providers tend not to operate in disadvantaged communities and are disinclined to practice in rural areas. Hence health service extension requires opening new facilities, preferably offering integrated primary care services, rather than purchasing services from already available providers. Public health systems are more likely to be willing to invest the significant marginal costs involved in health service delivery to the most inaccessible and most disadvantaged communities (Sengupta 2013, 11).

Despite these cautions, in the short term it may be necessary to contract with private sector providers to provide some types of health services, but it would be preferable for such a policy to be viewed as a temporary measure and for it to proceed cautiously with careful oversight and regulation. It is also important that short-term contracting for private health services occurs in tandem with investments to strengthen the public sector. It has been suggested that in places where the corporate-led private health sector is strong, as for example, India, the private sector cannot be controlled by integration but has to be made to compete against a well-resourced and well-managed public system operated with public funds (Sengupta 2013, 11).

One potential approach, described as strategic purchasing, was proposed for South Africa but has broader applicability. Its elements are as follows: Purchasing of health services would be confined to situations where it would further the goals of the universal health system. Priority would be given to areas where there is not adequate public sector service delivery capacity and there are private providers available, but there would not be investment in other places where there are sufficient service providers relative to population. The process of drawing on human resources in the private sector would be undertaken in a way that is subject to the public health system ethos. An emphasis would be placed on purchasing services from primary health care providers such as general practitioners. And finally the Ministry of Health or other entity empowered to undertake strategic purchasing would be accountable for its use of public funds (Global Health Watch 2014, 123–125).

Defining and Providing Essential/Core Health Packages

Studies of country reform experience on the path to universal coverage have found that the overwhelming majority of countries making progress design and implement an explicit health benefits package (Savedoff et al. 2012; World Bank Group 2013). A 1997 WHO paper defines essential health packages as "health service interventions that are considered important and that society decides should be provided to everyone" (Tarimo 1997, 3). A recent publication of the Inter-American

Development Bank uses the terminology of health benefit plans rather than essential health benefits to refer to the same entities. It characterized health benefit plans as having three core features: (1) a minimum set of services that are guaranteed for all individuals on the grounds of equity; (2) which are financed with public resources; and (3) linked to the needs or social preferences of the population to be covered (Giedion et al. 2014, 13). These packages vary considerably in their conceptualization, the principles applied in their formulation, and their levels of comprehensiveness. In some, but not all, countries, the breadth of health services in the package corresponds with the level of development of the country and the resources available.

Absence of Clear-Cut Guidelines

Neither international human rights documents addressing the right to health nor WHO policies and publications provide clear-cut guidelines on the content of health entitlements packages. In 1990, when the UN Committee on Economic, Social and Cultural Rights first dealt with the concept of a minimum core obligation that all state parties, regardless of the resources available, are required to fulfill, it had a quite delimited and modest sense of what the minimum core obligation for the right to health would be. According to that document, all state parties are minimally obligated to provide essential primary care, but the general comment does not conceptualize what primary care should entail (CESCR 1990, para 10). General Comment 14 does not address the specific topic of the content of essential health packages, but the sections on core obligations and obligations of comparable priority offer some direction. They enumerate the need to provide essential drugs; to adopt and implement a national public health strategy addressing the health concerns of the whole population; to ensure reproductive, maternal, and child health care; to provide immunization against the major infectious diseases occurring in the community; and to take measures to prevent, treat, and control epidemic and endemic diseases (CESCR 2000, paras 43 and 44). In addition, the gender perspective in the document and its identification of a need to develop and implement a comprehensive national strategy for promoting women's right to health throughout their life, including interventions aimed at the prevention and treatment of diseases affecting women (CESCR 2000, para 21), would be significant to take into account in designing an essential health care package.

How Minimalist Can Packages Be

One question is how minimalist a package of essential health benefits can be and still be consistent with the right to health. The influential 1993 World Bank report *Investing in Health* proposed that developing countries adopt a nationally defined package of essential clinical services financed with public funds primarily as a tool for rationing publicly funded health care. It conceptualized this package of essential clinical services in minimalist terms recommending it should consist of five groups of interventions: services to ensure pregnancy-related care; family planning services; tuberculosis control; control of STDs; and care for the common serious illnesses of young children. It also mentioned it could include some treatments for minor infection and trauma, but not expensive therapies, such as costly drug therapies for HIV infection and intensive care for severely premature babies (World Bank 1993, 9–10). While the rationale of the Bank was that widespread adoption of an essential clinical package would have a tremendous positive impact on the health of people in developing countries at a reasonable cost (World Bank 1993, 1–11), the Bank had a second and at least equally important motivation. By confining public investment to these narrow purposes, the Bank was leaving the remaining types of clinical services to be financed privately. This report therefore constituted an important milestone in the Bank's support for market-based private providers in the health sector, which together with the introduction of user fees and the shrinking of government health spending saw the introduction of these packages increase rather than reduce health inequities (Mkandawire 2005).

For better or worse, many essential health care packages adopted by low-income countries are congruent with the World Bank's proposed minimalist approach and as a consequence often omit essential health services identified in General Comment 14. Few of the packages include provision of essential medicines; attention to the health needs of women; adequate coverage of measures to prevent, treat, and control relevant epidemic and endemic disease in the country; and immunization against the major infectious diseases occurring in the community. Yet another limitation is that the services identified in many low- and some middle-income countries do not subsidize some important costs, for example, transport costs and payment for medicines, which constitute barriers to service use. Moreover, the catastrophic medical costs that most often impoverish the poor are generally not covered in essential health packages (Ensor et al.

2002, 254). This latter omission is particularly problematic. It is also note-worthy that many countries adopting essential health packages do not invest sufficient resources to be able to implement a full package of the itemized services to the entire population.

Goals and Objectives for Essential Health Packages

A 2008 WHO report enumerates five goals for essential health pack-ages: priority setting on the grounds of effectiveness and relative costs, poverty reduction, equity, political empowerment and accountability, and improving service delivery (World Health Organization 2008a). In principle these goals are congruent with the right to health. But some of these goals are incompatible with one another, and many are not being realized.

A priority setting process can improve efficiency in health spending if it encourages countries to assess the effectiveness and relative cost of various potential interventions and to adopt cost-effective services so as to increase value for money at a given level of spending. However, this type of analysis is difficult to do and many countries lack the data necessary to be able to assess cost-effectiveness. Moreover, there may be other goals that require a trade-off with improving efficiency. For example, improving equity may entail investment in a high-cost expansion of service delivery to previ-ously underserved population groups (World Health Organization 2008a, 4). Countries have also included services that are not cost-effective but are benefits that people have indicated they want to receive (Giedion et al. 2014, 16). It should also be noted that despite claims that cost-effectiveness is an important rationale for developing benefit packages in EU countries, one comparative study of nine European countries (Denmark, England, France, Germany, Hungary, Italy, Poland, Spain, and the Netherlands) found that there was often no rational process reviewing the available evi-dence on specific procedures or technologies in many of the countries as the basis for updating the benefits package. Instead the decision-making process was frequently guided by lobbying activities of actors in the sys-tem (Busse et al. 2005, 50).

Political Empowerment

If there is a meaningful priority-setting process to develop an essential health package and it takes place in conjunction with public dialogue and debate about the purpose and design of the package, it can serve as

a mechanism to promote political empowerment, an important component of the right to health. As a WHO paper notes, developing an essential health package (EHP) is not just a technical exercise. "Political and
institutional processes need to be engaged, because successful implementation involves dialogue on purpose and design; decisions on financing
and delivery arrangements, and adaptation over time. Without adequate
national ownership, an EHP is unlikely to be implemented – no matter how popular it is with donors" (World Health Organization 2008a,
1). However, very few countries have managed to develop an essential
health package in such a participatory framework. More often the formulation of an essential health package is viewed as a purely technical
exercise reserved for experts and done in a nontransparent manner. Even
the process in Chile, which has been identified as one of the few examples
of the development of a national health benefit plan combining technical
expertise with public consultation to identify the public's preferences
and priorities, has been found to have a pronounced technical character
(Escobar and Bitrán 2014, 52–54).

Equity and Equality

Like human rights entitlements, a package of essential health services is
intended to be available to all members of a society regardless of their
characteristics or status and as such can potentially be an instrument to
enhance equity, especially by making the poorest and most vulnerable
members of a society eligible to receive these health services (World Health
Organization 2008a, 1). Some essential health packages, for example, the
initial package adopted in Bangladesh, have also targeted services that are
used the most and for diseases endured proportionately more by the poor
and therefore could potentially provide the most benefit for especially vulnerable groups, defined as the poor, women, and young children in rural
areas (Ensor et al. 2002).

Importantly, essential health packages cannot serve as a vehicle to promote equity or be a safety net unless the health benefits enumerated in the
package are actually available, especially to the poorest and most vulnerable members of society. Simply formulating an essential health package
is not sufficient. Essential health packages and health benefit plans do not
necessarily entail a guarantee of access to the designated health services,
and even in countries where they are intended to do so, litigation may be
necessary to overcome barriers, as for example, in Colombia and Brazil.
Also, the services identified in essential health packages and health benefit

packages may require co-payments, which can be substantial, and therefore discriminate against the poor by pricing the benefits beyond their
resources and undermining the fundamental commitments on which the
packages are based.

Delivering the essential services and pharmaceuticals specified in the
packages is a problem in many countries with fragile and inadequate
health system. For example, in Uganda 70 percent of the population in
one survey did not use a minimum-package provider even when one was
accessible, because of inadequate coverage, lack of drugs, or perceived
low quality (WHO 2008a, 10–11). In Ethiopia, despite the existence of an
essential health package, only 30 percent of children under five years with
diarrhea receive oral rehydration therapy; fewer than 10 percent of children under five years with suspected pneumonia are taken to an appropriate care provider; and only 10 percent of live births are attended by skilled
health personnel (WHO Consultative Group on Equity and Universal
Health Coverage 2014, 24).

An important right to health issue is whether to be equitable essential
health packages require absolute equality in the benefits provided to all
or just access to a minimum set of services. Many countries with essential
health packages still have significant differences in the type of quality of
health care received by those without and those with economic resources.
In Latin America, for example, many health systems have segmented
access and benefits by socioeconomic status and type of employment relationship: in those health systems individuals with formal employment
who contribute toward their health insurance have a much fuller benefit
plan than the population dependent solely on public funding (examples
include Argentina, Honduras, Mexico, and Peru). Other countries have
systems that are segmented in terms of the source of funding but still have
a single benefit plan and common governance and regulation (Chile and
Colombia) (Giedion et al. 2014, 22).

There are seeming differences in expert opinion on this point. The recommendations of the WHO Consultative Group could be interpreted as
accepting a basic minimum approach. As will be discussed in the next section, it proposed according priority to expanding coverage to everyone
in the society of those services that tend to be the most effective and to
benefit the worse off. It also characterized as ethically unacceptable the
policy of expanding coverage for low or medium priority services to some
groups before achieving near universal coverage for high priority services
(2014, xi–xii). However, the Group seemingly countenanced inequalities
in service provision beyond the basic minimum. In contrast, the one key

case where this issue was litigated using a human rights standard came to a different conclusion. In 2008, the Constitutional Court in Colombia ruled that the right to health required that all citizens be provided with a uniform benefit package and ordered that the contributory and subsidized regimes offering different types of packages be progressively unified (Judgment T-60/08, section 6.1.2).

Accountability

Because essential health packages generally provide a clear description of the types of services the government is committed to providing for all members of society they can in principle serve as a tool for holding providers accountable. For it to be effective in doing so, however, the population must know what they are entitled to receive and how to claim their benefits, and often this is a problem. Despite ongoing outreach efforts in a middle-income country with a well-established health system, household surveys have shown that less than half of the population in Chile was aware of their benefits and an even smaller number knew about specific enforceable guarantees and the option to file claims. In contrast, 88 percent of the subscribers to the private insurance system in Chile knew about the existence and specifics of the guaranteed health benefit package (Missoni and Solimano 2010, 4–5). Since Chile has a high level of educational attainment, the population in other low- and middle-income countries may have an even more limited level of awareness.

Equitable Strategies for Expanding Coverage

In most countries coverage cannot be extended to everyone immediately and choices need to be made about whom to initially give priority. A commitment to equity and fairness as well as to respecting the right to health care precludes adopting a strategy for expansion of health coverage that prioritizes those who are the easiest to reach, usually workers in the private sector and their families. Instead, it requires a policy approach that prioritizes expanding coverage for low-income groups, rural populations, and other groups currently disadvantaged in terms of service coverage, health, or both (WHO Consultative Group on Equity and Universal Health Coverage 2014, 26–27), even though these groups are more difficult to reach.

The WHO Consultative Group on Equity and Universal Health Coverage proposes a three-part strategy for countries seeking progressive realization of UHC in a manner consistent with equity principles and a human rights approach:

- First, categorize services into priority classes on the basis of such criteria as cost-effectiveness, priority to the worse off, and financial risk protection.
- Second, expand coverage for high-priority services to everyone. High-priority services are those that tend to be the most effective and to benefit the worse off. Also, institute the financial reforms related to eliminating out-of-pocket payments while increasing mandatory, progressive prepayment with pooling of funds.
- Third, as coverage is expanded, take special measures to ensure that disadvantaged groups, such as low-income groups and rural populations, are not left behind (WHO Consultative Group on Equity and Universal Health Coverage 2014, 37).

The dilemma is how to categorize services into priority classes. In some cases it may be fairly simple to evaluate medical services in terms of their effectiveness and which groups in society would benefit from their greater availability. But in other instances, perhaps the majority of situations, countries lack the data and the capacity to assess the effectiveness of various options.

Recognizing that choices will depend on context and several different pathways can be appropriate, The WHO Consultative Group on Equity and Universal Coverage nevertheless identifies a series of ethically unacceptable trade-offs:

- To expand coverage for low- or medium-priority services to some groups before there is near universal coverage for high-priority services, including eliminating out-of-pocket payments for low- or medium-priority services before eliminating out-of-pocket payments for high priority services;
- To accord priority to very costly services whose coverage will provide substantial financial protection when the health benefits are small compared to alternative, less costly services;
- To expand coverage for well-off groups before doing so for worse-off groups, including expanding coverage for those with already high coverage before groups with lower coverage;
- To first include in the universal coverage scheme only those with the ability to pay;
- To shift from out-of-pocket payment toward mandatory prepayment in a way that makes the financing system less progressive (WHO

Consultative Group on Equity and Universal Health Coverage 2014, xi–xii).

I believe it is also contrary both to ethical principles and human rights requirements to extend coverage through fashioning a two-tier health system whereby the members of the population able to contribute to the health system receive one type of health package while those subsidized by the government have to make do with a far more minimal package.

Robust Public Participation Mechanisms

Too often the transition to UHC has been viewed as a top-down initiative. However, the human rights paradigm has advocated for empowerment, participation, and accountability. The 1978 Declaration of Alma-Ata states that "The people have the right and duty to participate individually and collectively in the planning and implementation of their health care" (Declaration of Alma-Ata). General Comment 14 specifically links the right to health facilities, goods, and services with the "participation of the population in the provision of preventive and curative health services, such as the organization of the health sector, the insurance system and, in particular, participation in political decisions relating to the right to health taken at both the community and national levels" (CESCR 2000, para 17). One core obligation in GC 14 specifies the development of a national public health strategy and plan of action through a participatory and transparent process (CESCR 2000, para 43 f).

To be consistent with the right to health, a universal health care system requires robust participatory mechanisms. There is a need both to incorporate meaningful participation in the design of the essential health care packages and to involve the population more broadly in the shaping of UHC plans and institutions and the timetable and process by which the state will seek to achieve this goal.

Research studying countries that have reached UHC has found that one common feature is a political process driven by a range of social forces to improve access to health care. Countries have then responded to these social forces by creating public programs that expand access to care, improve equity, and pool the financial risks of health services across their population. For that reason countries are more likely to be successful if they recognize the importance of political action to direct expansion of coverage (Savedoff et al. 2012, 924) and encourage its development.

Data Monitoring, Evaluation, and Accountability

Accountability has been a priority norm in the right to health paradigm. Human rights law requires the state be held accountable for its actions and inactions in fulfilling its human rights obligations, how much effort it is expending (for example, in its investment of resources), and how it is going about the process. As Alicia Ely Yamin has reflected, "The accountability that human rights brings to bear converts passive recipients of health goods and services into active claims-holders, and challenges systems in which people are beholden to those wielding over them with all too much discretion" (Yamin 2008a, 13). To be able to do so requires instituting effective accountability institutional architectures into universal health systems.

Accountability necessitates having adequate monitoring and oversight, and in turn, monitoring and oversight depend on transparency about government policies and actions and the availability of relevant information. Like other elements of the right to health, progress toward UHC needs ongoing and disaggregated monitoring to assess whether all groups, particularly those who are disadvantaged and poor, are benefiting. To be consistent with human rights requirements, the collection of necessary data should be disaggregated by multiple characteristics such as sex, age, income/wealth, ethnic origin, religion, disability status, migrant status, and geographic region of residence.

A UHC monitoring framework needs to track both levels of coverage of health services and the extent of financial protection. WHO and the World Bank Group have developed a joint framework for monitoring progress toward UHC at a country level that provides an illustrative list of primary coverage and supplementary coverage indicators including indicators for communicable and noncommunicable diseases, reproductive, maternal, newborn, and child health and injuries (World Health Organization and World Bank Group 2013b). Three measures the WHO Consultative Group on Equity and Universal Health Coverage proposes to assess financial protection are the percentage of the total population that faces catastrophic health expenditure due to out-of-pocket payments, the percentage of the total population impoverished due to out-of-pocket payments, and the proportion of out-of-pocket payments relative to the total health expenditure (2014, 53).

To be able to monitor progress toward UHC effectively, it will be necessary to establish much improved health data systems in many countries. Currently there are major gaps in the availability and quality of data in many country's health information systems, and these lacunae have implications for monitoring progress toward UHC (Boerma et al. 2014). Data collection can utilize diverse methodologies, such as household surveys and research able to identify financial and nonmonetary access barriers, to inform policy corrections (Brearley et al. 2013, 53–43).

Evaluating progress also requires the development of appropriate targets and benchmarks. While UHC ultimately requires 100 percent coverage and financial protection for everyone, with everyone having access to the same publicly provided package of health benefits, a WHO/World Bank group proposes adopting the interim goal for all poor and middle-income countries of a minimum of 80 percent coverage, regardless of the level of wealth, place of residence, or sex, for 2030. The group's analysis of fifteen case studies leads them to believe this is an ambitious but achievable goal for most countries. For some preventive services, such as vaccination for particular diseases, higher targets are important and likely to be feasible (Boerma et al. 2014). The group also recommends the target that by 2030 everyone has 100 percent financial protection from out-of-pocket payments for health services (Boerma et al. 2014). These goals seem congruent with a right to health approach to universality.

Concluding Reflections

This chapter has highlighted the importance of countries moving toward UHC and doing so by implementing policies consistent with the requirements of the right to health. The discussion has often focused on the situation of lower- and middle-income countries, but these considerations apply equally to high-income countries. As the situation of the United States indicates, not all high-income countries are committed to UHC or for that matter to the right to health. Moreover, even those industrialized countries frequently identified as having achieved UHC do not necessarily comply with all of the right to health criteria identified in this chapter.

Like achieving the right to health, moving toward UHC requires a long-term process of progressive realization. Historically UHC has been achieved incrementally over long periods of time: it took Germany 127 years, Belgium 118, and Austria 79 years. In recent years, some countries have made more rapid progress toward UHC, for example, South Korea and Malaysia, and at a lower financial cost (Savedoff et al. 2012, 927). Nevertheless, most poor and many middle-income countries will require a long-term commitment, especially the many countries that will have to undertake a major extension of coverage or a restructuring of their health systems.

Unless the policies adopted to expand coverage take equity and human rights requirements into account, there is a risk they will disproportionately benefit those groups who already have access to health services and further disadvantage poor and vulnerable communities and individuals currently without access to needed health care. Moreover, inequities can arise even within universal health systems, especially when those systems countenance multitier packages tied to income and contributions. Universal health systems dependent on private health provision are also likely to advantage those with greater economic resources.

As countries embark on a journey toward UHC or seek to maintain universal health systems, it is important they adopt policies consistent with the requirements of the right to health. To do so requires the following:

- Health care reforms to improve access to essential health services and public health protections would be placed within the framework of a national effort to address access to the social determinants of health as described in Chapter Seven because meaningful health care reforms to build an integrated national health system also require a national effort to provide clean water, sanitation, nutritious food, good environmental conditions, and basic shelter. Otherwise it is likely that curative medical care will take precedence over provisions for well-being and the government will not be able to improve the health status of vulnerable groups.
- Access to essential health services and public health protections would be made a legal entitlement with an established timeline for implementation and mechanisms established for redress and accountability.
- The health system would cover and provide entitlements to all residents of a country regardless of their legal status, including minimally all long-term immigrants.
- Equity would be a priority in the design of the universal health system and throughout the process of expanding coverage. This entails explicit measures to be instituted to reduce barriers for low-income groups, rural populations, women, and other vulnerable groups that are disadvantaged in terms of service coverage and health.
- An equitable and progressive system of health funding for financial risk protection would be put in place based on the WHO's policy priorities to finance UHC: reducing out-of-pocket payments, maximizing mandatory prepayment, establishing large risk pools, and using general government revenues to cover those who cannot afford to contribute (World Health Organization 2010). In addition, poor- and middle-income countries would not rely on social insurance mechanisms more suited

to high-income countries and instead would seek to fund health services through tax funding.

- Countries would allocate sufficient funding to be able to strengthen and expand their health systems and provide a publicly funded package of priority health services based on people's needs. This requires poor and middle-income countries devoting at least 5 percent of national income and 15 percent of government expenditures to the health sector.
- Health system strengthening, preferably in a unified public health system, would be accorded priority in order to make good quality health services widely available. Priority investment would be made in currently underserved communities and in an effort to bring about a greater balance between the services available in rural and urban areas and in poor and better developed regions of the country. Governments would not rely on the private sector for the expansion of health coverage. Health system strengthening would begin with and focus on improving access to primary care.
- The process for pursing progressive realization of UHC would first expand coverage for high-priority services to everyone, with special efforts to ensure that disadvantaged groups are reached.
- A comprehensive package of health benefits would be universally provided, which is closely linked to the population's needs and defined through a process that includes a meaningful process of public consultation. The package would include provisions for preventive medical care and health promotion.
- Robust mechanisms for consultation, participation in shaping priorities, the design of the universal health system, and accountability of the government would be put in place.
- Improved data monitoring and evaluation systems would be instituted to evaluate the distributional effects of efforts to achieve UHC and improve health outcomes on a disaggregated basis so as to be able to undertake corrective action when necessary.

Having an equitable, effective, and comprehensive health system is a priority component of UHC. It is therefore disappointing that much less attention has been and continues to be devoted to the process of health system strengthening than to the financial aspects of the progressive realization of UHC. Moreover, just as past neoliberal policies have weakened health systems and been adverse to the realization of the right to health, the adoption of neoliberal approaches to achieving UHC will result in inequitable health systems unable to fulfill human rights requirements.

Contrary to neoliberal policy prescriptions, there is considerable evidence that the path to UHC requires a strong public health sector playing a major or dominant role in the delivery of health services as well as in the financing and oversight of the health system (Sengupta 2013). Therefore, it is problematic that many international agencies and funders are promoting, and in turn countries adopting, a UHC model favoring private sector health insurance and private sector health services provision. Relying on private sector insurance and health service provision for extending health coverage is more likely to reinforce rather than correct many of the current problems and inequalities that current health systems face. Moreover, even with public subsidies, few private sector providers will be inclined or positioned to make the kinds of investments necessary to extend coverage to disadvantaged and poor communities.

For these reasons UHC requires priority being given to efforts to invest in and strengthen public health systems. While the financial protection measures identified in this chapter for progressing to UHC are essential, they are not sufficient to achieve UHC. Just as WHO and other sources propose that tax and insurance contributions to finance health should be pooled, a unified system of public health provision would be less costly, more equitable, and better able to fulfil human rights requirements.

Granted this chapter has set forth demanding requirements, especially in a neoliberal era in which political and economic pressures are often pulling in other directions. To succeed will require identifying and mobilizing the groups and institutions most favorable to the provision of equitable and universal health care based on right to health requirements. As WHO reflected, "As with other entitlements that are now taken for granted in almost all high-income countries, UHC has generally been struggled for and won by social movements, not spontaneously bestowed by political leaders" (World Health Organization 2008b, 25). Countries like Brazil, which are making progress toward UHC, have placed a strong emphasis on health as a human right together with a high level of engagement by civil society toward that quest (Savedoff et al. 2012, 924). It is essential that other countries do so as well.

References

Allotey, Pascale, Verghis, Sharuna, Alvarez-Castillo, Fatima, and Reidpath, Daniel D. (2012) "Vulnerability, Equity and Universal Coverage – a Concept Note," *BMC Public Health* 12 (Suppl 1): 52, www.biomedcentral .com/1471–2458/12/61/62.

Averill, Ceri and Marriott, Anna (2013) *Universal Health Coverage: Why Health Insurance Schemes Are Leaving the Poor Behind*, Great Britain: Oxfam, www .oxfam.org.

Backman, Gunilla, Hunt, Paul, Khosa, Rajat, et al. (2008) "Health Systems and the Right to Health: An Assessment of 194 Countries," *The Lancet* 372: 2047–2085.

Boerma, Ties, Ezozenou, Patrick, Evans, David, Evans, Tim, et al. (2014) "Monitoring Progress towards Universal Health Coverage at Country and Global Levels," *PLoS Medicine* 11: e1001731.

Brearley, Lara, Marten, Robert, and O'Connell, Thomas (2013) Universal Health Coverage: A Commitment to Close the Gap, New York: The Rockefeller Foundation, Save the Children, UNICEF, and WHO, www.savethechildren .org.uk.../Universal_health.

Busse, Reinhard, Schreyögg, Jonas, and Velasco-Garrido, Marcial (2005) HealthBASKET: Synthesis Report, www.ehma.org/files/HealthBASKET-SYN-REP-051025EDIT_2pdf.

CESCR (Committee on Economic, Social and Cultural Rights) (1990) General Comment 3: The Nature of States Parties Obligations (Art. 2, para. 1 of the Covenant), contained in U.N. Doc. E/1991/23.

(2000) General Comment No. 14: The Right to the Highest Attainable Standard of Health (article 12 of the International Covenant on Economic, Social and Cultural Rights U.N. Doc. E/C.12/2000/4.

(2008) General Comment 19: The Right to Social Security, (article 19 of the International Covenant on Economic, Social and Cultural Rights U.N. Doc. E/C12/GC/19.

Commonwealth Fund (2010) *International Profiles of Health Care Systems*, Commonwealth Fund pub. No. 1417, New York City, www.common wealthfund.org/...Fund%20Report/2...

Declaration of Alma-Ata (1978) International Conference on Primary Health Care, Alma-Ata, USSR, September 6–12, www.who.int/publications/ almaata_declaration_en.pdf?ua=1.

Ensor, Tim, Dave-Sen, Peiti, Liaquat, Ali, et al. (2002) "Do Essential Service Packages Benefit the Poor? Preliminary Evidence from Bangladesh," *Health Policy and Planning* 17 (3): 247–256.

Escobar, L. and Bitrán, R. (2014) "Chile: Explicit Health Guarantees (GES)," in U. Giedion, R. Bitrán, and I. Tristao, eds., *Health Benefit Plans in Latin America: A Regional Comparison*, Washington: Inter-American Development Bank, pp. 44–75, http://publications.iabd.org/bitstream/handle/.../Health-Benefit-Plans.pdf.

European Agency for Fundamental Rights (2011) Migrants in an Irregular Situation: Access to Healthcare in 10 European Union Member States, www .fra.europa.eu.

Federal Ministry of Health (2005) Essential Health Services Package for Ethiopia, www.etharc.org/resources/download/view.download/33/80.

Forman, Lisa and Singh, Jerome Amir (2014) "The Role of Rights and Litigation in Assuring More Equitable Access to Health Care in South Africa," in Colleen M. Flood and Aeyal Gross, eds., *The Right to Health at the Public/Private Divide: A Global Comparative Study*, New York: Cambridge University Press, pp. 288–318.

Giedion, Ursula, Tristao, Ignez, Bitrán, Ricardo A. III, et al. (2014) "Making the Implicit Explicit: An Analysis of Seven Health Benefit Plans in Latin America," in Ursula Giedion, Ricardo A. Bitrán III, and Ignez Tristao, eds., *Health Benefit Plans in Latin America: A Regional Comparison*. Washington: Inter-American Development Bank, pp. 10–43, iadb.org/health.

Global Health Observatory Data Repository (n.d.) who.int/gho/data/view .main1900ALL?lang=en.

Global Health Watch: An Alternative World Health Report, 4th edition (2014) London: Zed Books for the People's Health Movement, Medact, Medico International, Third World Network, Health Action International, and ALAMES.

Grover, Anand (2012) Interim Report of the Special Rapporteur on the Right of Everyone to the Enjoyment of the Highest Attainable Standard of Physical and Mental Health to the United Nations General Assembly, U.N. Doc. A/67/150.

Guanais, Frederico C. (2010) "Health Equity in Brazil," *BMJ* 341: c6542.

   (2013) "The Combined Effects of the Expansion of Primary Health Care and Conditional Cash Transfers on Infant Mortality in Brazil, 1998-2010" *American Journal of Public Health* 103 (11): 2000–2006.

Gwatkin, Davidson R. and Ergo, Alex (2010) "Universal Health Coverage: Friend or Foe of Health Equity," *The Lancet* 377: 2160–2161.

Hennigan, Tom (2010) "Economic Success Threatens Aspirations of Brazil's Public Health System," *BMJ* 341: c5453.

Jost, Timothy Stoltzfus (2003) *Disentitlement? The Threats Facing Our Public Health-Care Programs and a Rights-Based Response*, Oxford and New York: Oxford University Press.

Judgment T-60/08, Colombia Constitutional Court (2008) ESCR-Net, www .escr-net.org/docs/i/985449.

Lagomarsino, Gina, Garbrant, Alice, Adyas, Atikah, Muga, Richard and Otoo, Nathaniel (2012) "Moving towards Universal Health Coverage: Health Insurance Reforms in Nine Developing Countries in Africa and Asia," *The Lancet* 380: 933–943.

Lister, John (2013) *Health Policy Reform: Global Health versus Private Profit*, Farringdon, Oxfordshire, UK: Libri Publishing.

Lister, John and Labonté, Ronald (2009) "Globalization and Health Systems Change," in Ronald Labonté, Ted Schrecker, Corinne Packer, and Vivien Runnels, eds., *Globalization and Health: Pathways, Evidence and Policy*, New York and London: Routledge, pp. 181–212.

Meesen, Bruno, Hercot, David, Noirhomme, Mathieu, Riddle, Valéry, et al. (2011) Removing User Fees in the Health Sector: A Review of Policy Processes in Six Sub-Saharan African Countries," *Health Policy and Planning* 26 (ii): ii16–ii29.

Mills, Anne, Ataguba, John E., Akazili, James, McIntyre, Di (2012) "Equity in Financing and Use of Health Care in Ghana, South Africa, and Tanzania: Implications for Paths to Universal Coverage," *The Lancet* 380: 126–133.

Minh, Hoang Van, Popock, Nicola Suyin, Chaiyakunapruk, Mathorn, et al. (2014) "Progress toward Universal Health Coverage in ASEAN," *Global Health Action* 7: 25856, http://dx.doi.org/10.3402/ghav.725856.

Missoni, Eduardo and Solimano, Giorgio (2010) "Universal Access Plan with Explicit Guarantees: The Chilean Way, in E. Missoni, ed., *Attaining Universal Health Coverage: A Research Initiative to Support Evidence-Based Advocacy and Policy Making*, Milan: Global Health Group at the University of Milan, chapter 7, www.unibocconi.eu/wps/.../Cergas+14+maggio.pdf?

Narayan, Ravi (2011) "Universal Health Care in India: Missing Core Determinants," *The Lancet* 377: 883–885.

OECD (2011) *Divided We Stand: Why Inequality Keeps Rising*, www.oecd.org/els/social/inequality.

Ortiz Hernández, Luis and Pérez Salgado, Diana (2014) Chile and Costa Rica: Different Roads to Universal Health in Latin America, Occasional Paper No. 23, Municipal Services Project, www.municipalservicesproject.org.

Paim, Jairnilson, Travassos, Claudia, Almeida, Celia, Bahia, Ligea, and Macinko, James (2011) "The Brazilian Health System: History, Advances, and Challenges," *The Lancet* 277: 1778–1797.

Pan American Health Organization (2007) *Renewing Primary Health Care in the Americas: A Position Paper of the Pan American Health Organization/World Health Organization*, Washington DC: PAHO/WHO, www.paho.org/English/AD/THS/PrimaryHealthCare.pdf.

Rao, Krishna D., Petrosyan, Varduhi, Araujo, Edson C., McIntyre, Dianne (2014) "Progress towards Universal Health Coverage in BRICS: Translating Economic Growth into Better Health," *Bulletin of the World Health Organization* 92: 429–435, http://dx.doi.org/10.2471/BLT.13.127951.

Ravindran, T. K. Sundari (2012) "Universal Access: Making Health Systems Work for Women," *BMC Public Health* 12 (Suppl 1): 52, www.biomedcentral.com/1471-2458/12/51/54.

Rawaf, S., De Maeseneer, J., and Starfield, B. (2008) "From Alma Ata to Almaty: A New Start for Primary Health Care," *The Lancet* 372: 1367–1375.

Rockefeller Foundation (2010) *Catalyzing Change: The System Reform Costs of Universal Health Coverage*, New York, www.rockefellerfoundation.org.

Rodin, Judith and de Ferranti, David (2012) "Universal Health Coverage: The Third Global Health Transition?" *The Lancet* 380: 861–862.

Rodney, Anna M. and Hill, Peter S. (2014) "Achieving Equity within Universal Health Coverage: A Narrative Review of Progress and Resources for Measuring Success," *International Journal for Equity in Health* 13: 72, www.equityhealthj .com/content/13/1/72.

Rowden, Rick (2013) "The Ghosts of User Fees Past: Exploring Accountability for Victims of a 30-Year Economic Policy Mistake," *Health and Human Rights* 15 (1): 175–185.

Sambo, Luis Gomes and Kirigia, Joses Muthuri (2014) "Investing in Health Systems for Universal Health Coverage in Africa," *BMC International Health and Human Rights* 14: 28, www.biomedcentral.com/1472-698X/14/28.

Savedoff, William D., de Ferranti, David, Smith, Amy L., and Fan, Victoria (2012) "Political and Economic Aspects of the Transition to Universal Health Coverage," *The Lancet* 380: 924–932.

Scheil-Adlung, Xenia (2015) Global Evidence on Inequities in Rural Health Protection: New Data on Rural Deficits in Health Coverage for 174 Countries, ESS Document No. 47, International Labour Office.

Secretary-General (2014) Report of the Secretary-General on the Question of the Realization in All Countries of Economic, Social and Cultural Rights," U.N. Doc. A/HRC/28/35.

Sen, Amartya (2015) "Universal Healthcare: The Affordable Dream," *The Guardian*, January 6, www.theguardian.com/>Business>Health

Sengupta, Amit and Prasad Vandana (2011) "Towards a Truly Universal Indian Health System," *The Lancet* 377: 702–703.

Social Protection Department (2014) Addressing the Global Health Crisis: Universal Health Protection Policies, Paper 13, International Labour Office.

Superintendencia de Salud (2013) Garantías Explícitas en Salud GES/AUGE, Gobierno de Chile, www.supersalud.gob.cl>Inicio>Servicios.

Tarimo, Eleuther (1997) Essential Health Services Packages: Uses, abuse and future directions, *Current Concerns*, ARA Paper number 15, Division of Analysis, Research and Assessment, World Health Organization, WHO/ARA/CC/97.7.

Thomson, Sarah, Osborn, Robin, and Squires, David, eds. (2013) *International Profiles of Health Care Systems, 2013*, New York: The Commonwealth Fund, www.commonwealthfund.org/.../2013/.../internatio...

United Nations (1948) Universal Declaration of Human Rights, adopted and proclaimed by the United Nations General Assembly Resolution 217A (III) on 10 December.

(2015) Sustainable Development Goals, Target 3.8, sustainabledevelopment
.un.org/.../sustainabledevel...

World Bank (1993) *World Development Report* 1993: *Investing in Health*,
New York: Oxford University Press, openknowledge.worldbank.org/
handle/10986/5976.

(2014) Health Statistics, http://data.worldbank.org/indicators/SH.XPD.PCAP.

World Bank Group (2013) Universal Health Coverage Study Series, www
.worldbank.org/...universal-health-coverage-study-seri

WHO Consultative Group on Equity and Universal Health Coverage
(2014) *Making Fair Choices on the Path to Universal Health Coverage*,
Geneva: World Health Organization, www.who.int/choice/documents/
making.../en/

World Health Assembly (2005) Sustainable Health Financing, Universal Coverage
and Social Health Insurance, World Health Assembly Resolution 58.33,
World Health Organization, www.who.int/health_financing/HF%20
Resolu...

(2011) Sustainable Health Financing Structures and Universal Coverage,
Sixty-Fourth World Health Assembly Resolution, Agenda item 31.4,
WHA64.9, A64/VR/10.

World Health Organization (2007) *World Health Report for 2007: Everybody's
Business: Strengthening Health Systems to Improve Outcomes*, Geneva: WHO,
who.int/healthsystems/strategy/everybodys_business.pdf.

(2008a) Essential Health Packages: What Are They for? What Do They Change?
Draft Technical Brief No. 2, WHO Service Delivery Seminar Series.

(2008b) *The World Health Report 2008: Primary Health Care, Now more than
Ever*, Geneva: World Health Organization, www.who.int/whr/2008/en/
imdex.html.

(2010) *World Health Report: Health Systems Financing, the Path to Universal
Coverage*, Geneva: World Health Organization.

(2011) The Abuja Declaration: Ten Years on, www.who.int/healthsystems/
publications/Abuja10.pdf.

(2013) *A Universal Truth: No Health Without a Workforce*, Geneva: WHO, www
.who.int/workforce.

World Health Organization and The World Bank (2013a) WHO/World Bank
Ministerial-level Meeting on Universal Health Coverage, 18-19 February
2013, WHO headquarters, Geneva, Switzerland.

World Health Organization and The World Bank Group (2013b) Monitoring
Progress toward Universal Health Coverage at Country and Global
Levels: A Framework, Joint WHO/World Bank Group Discussion Paper,
www.who.int/healthinfro/universsal_health_co

Wörz, Markus, Foubister, Thomas, and Busse, Reinhard (2006) "Access to Health
Care in the EU Member States," *Euro Observer* 8 (2): 1–4.

Xu, Ke, Evans, David B., Kadama, Patrick, and Nabyonga, Juliet (2006) "Understanding the Impact of Eliminating User Fees: Utilization and Catastrophic Health Expenditures in Uganda," *Social Science & Medicine* 62: 866–876.

Yamin, Alicia Ely (2008) "Beyond Compassion: The Central of Accountability in Applying a Human Rights Framework to Health," *Health and Human Rights* 10 (2): 1–20.

INDEX

Lightning Source UK Ltd.
Milton Keynes UK
UKOW06n0839260616

277076UK00004B/92/P